Light of Samantabhadra

Gorampa Sönam Sengé (1429–89)
with the Sakya and Ngor lineage teachers of the
Sarvadurgatipariśodhana Tantra
(opaque watercolor on cloth, 26" × 31", ca. 1600)

THE KHENPO APPEY COLLECTION OF SAKYA CLASSICS

Light of Samantabhadra

An Explanation of Dharmakīrti's Commentary on Valid Cognition

GORAMPA SÖNAM SENGÉ

Translated by Gavin Kilty

Foreword by
His Holiness the 42nd Sakya Trizin,
Ratna Vajra Rinpoche

Wisdom

Wisdom Publications, Inc.
132 Perry Street
New York, NY 10014 USA
wisdomexperience.org

Library of Congress Cataloging-in-Publication Data
Names: Go-rams-pa Bsod-nams-seng-ge, 1429–1489, author. |
Kilty, Gavin, translator.
Title: Light of Samantabhadra: an explanation of Dharmakirti's commentary on valid cognition / Gorampa Sönam Sengé; translated by Gavin Kilty; foreword by His Holiness the 42nd Sakya Trizin, Ratna Vajra Rinpoche.
Other titles: Rgyas pa'i bstan bcos tshad ma rnam 'grel gyi rnam par bshad pa Kun tu bzang po'i 'od zer. English
Description: Somerville, MA, USA: Wisdom Publications, Inc., [2023] |
Series: The Khenpo Appey collection of Sakya classics |
Includes bibliographical references and index.
Identifiers: LCCN 2022045044 (print) | LCCN 2022045045 (ebook) |
ISBN 9781614297512 (hardcover) | ISBN 9781614297666 (ebook)
Subjects: LCSH: Dharmakīrti, active 7th century. Pramāṇavārttika. |
Buddhist logic.
Classification: LCC BQ3232.E5 G67 2023 (print) | LCC BQ3232.E5 (ebook) |
DDC 181/.043—dc23/eng/20230130
LC record available at https://lccn.loc.gov/2022045044
LC ebook record available at https://lccn.loc.gov/2022045045

ISBN 978-1-61429-751-2 ebook ISBN 978-1-61429-766-6

27 26 25 24 23 5 4 3 2 1

Cover design by Gopa & Ted 2. Interior design by Tony Lulek.

Frontispiece courtesy of Virginia Museum of Fine Arts, Richmond. Berthe and John Ford Collection, Arthur and Margaret Glasgow Fund, 91.514. Photo by David Stover, © Virginia Museum of Fine Arts. Drawing of Dharmakīrti on page 28 by Andy Weber.

Printed on acid-free paper that meets the guidelines for permanence and durability of the Production Guidelines for Book Longevity of the Council on Library Resources.

Printed in the United States of America.

Contents

Foreword by His Holiness the 42nd Sakya Trizin,
Ratna Vajra Rinpoche ix
Preface xi
Translator's Introduction 1

LIGHT OF SAMANTABHADRA
A Commentary on Dharmakīrti's Commentary on Valid Cognition (Pramāṇavārttika)

The Explanation of Chapter 1
Inference for Oneself (Svārthānumāna)

1. Homage and Introduction 31
2. Overview of the Chapters 41

The Three Reasons
3. Perfect Reasoning by Way of Result, Nature, and Nonapprehension 51
4. The Enumeration into Three Types 59

The Indispensable Relationship
5. The Indispensable Relationship 65
6. The Necessity of the Relationship for the Counter Pervasion 71
7. Establishing Pervasion through the Relationship 77
8. Extensive Explanation of Ascertainment by Nature and Result 85

Exclusion and Universals
9. Exclusion of Others and the One Conceptualized as Many 91
10. Verbal Expressions and Conceptualization Engage by Exclusion 95
11. Refuting that They Engage by Affirmation 101
12. Reversal and Isolation 107
13. The Universal of Many Conceptualized as One 113
14. Appearance within a Conceptual Cognition 121
15. Designations 123
16. Engaging by Verbal Expression 131
17. Identifying the Particulars 137
18. Refutations Concerning Exclusions and Isolates 145
19. Establishing the Direct Object as an Exclusion 157
20. Refuting the Universal as an Entity 163
21. Refuting that a Single Result Exists by Way of a Universal 175
22. Refuting Entities to Be of a Single Nature 179

Divisions of Reasoning by Nature
23. Divisions 191
24. Disintegration by Nature 197
25. Negation Reasoning 201
26. Refuting Arguments against the Division into Two 207

Fallacious Reasoning: Refuting the Vedas
27. Analysis of Verbal Expression 215
28. Refuting the Vedas as Being Unproduced by Persons 223
29. The Syllables and Words of the Vedas 237
30. Disintegration and Destruction 249
31. Examination of Vedic Mantras 261
32. There Is No Comprehending the Definitive Meaning of the Vedas 273

The Explanation of Chapter 2
Establishing Valid Cognition (Pramāṇasiddhi)

Validity

33. Becoming Valid 291
34. Explanation of "Became" and Refutation of "Self-Arisen" 299

Establishing by Way of the Forward Sequence

35. Compassion Is the Accomplisher 317
36. Establishing Past and Future Lives 321
37. Training Can Be Developed Limitlessly 367
38. From "Compassion" Comes "Teacher" 373
39. From "Teacher" Comes "Sugata" and "Protector" 377

The Four Truths

40. The Four Truths that Establish "Protector" 383
41. The Origin of Suffering 403
42. The Cessation of Suffering 409
43. The Truth of the Path 417
44. The Antidote to the View of Self 425
45. The Antidote to Craving 445

Establishing by Way of the Reverse Sequence

46. From "Protector" to "Compassion" 461

Notes 465
Glossary 483
Bibliography 497
Index 503
About the Authors 511

THE 42ND SAKYA TRIZIN

Foreword

AMONG THE FIVE MAJOR sciences, *pramāṇa*, or valid cognition, is the key to understanding Buddhist philosophy. The works of the great Indian logicians Dignāga and Dharmakīrti are together known as the "Seven Treatises and the *Sūtra on Valid Cognition*." Because Dignāga's *Compendium of Valid Cognition*, or *Pramāṇasamuccaya*, is the essential source of all later works on pramāṇa, it is referred to as the *Pramāṇa Sūtra*. Dharmakīrti later composed his Seven Treatises as commentaries to Dignāga's writings. Of these treatises, the most important is the *Commentary on Valid Cognition*, or *Pramāṇavārttika*.

I am delighted that the first two chapters of Gorampa Sönam Sengé's *Light of Samantabhadra*, a commentary on the *Pramāṇavārttika*, are now going to be accessible to a new audience of non-Tibetan readers. In the first chapter of the *Pramāṇavārttika*, Dharmakīrti introduces the principles of valid cognition, and in the second chapter, he uses logic to prove the validity of the Buddhist path. Gorampa's writings are based on the teachings of the Five Sakya Founding Masters, interpreting them with exceptional clarity, and thus, in this case, providing us with an excellent way to understand Dharmakīrti's most influential work.

This translation is the first volume of the Khenpo Appey Collection of Sakya Classics, a series of translations of important works focusing on the primary topics of philosophical study in the Sakya tradition. All of the texts in this series were selected by the late Khenchen Appey Rinpoche (1927–2010) as being of particular importance to translate into English. Khenchen Appey Rinpoche was a wise, compassionate, experienced, and humble teacher. He always imparted his knowledge without reservation, according to the level of the audience. Whenever he gave teachings, he always made preparations carefully and circumspectly. Even with difficult content, he was always able to give explanations in a concise, easy-to-understand way.

Aside from being one of the previous century's most eminent Tibetan Buddhist teachers, the Most Venerable Khenchen Appey Rinpoche was also one of my own teachers. It is for this reason that I am encouraged that Wisdom Publications, in association with Khenpo Appey Foundation, is publishing this series that will help to realize Rinpoche's wishes.

I pray that this translation, as well as the whole Khenpo Appey Collection of Sakya Classics series, will be of immeasurable benefit to its readers and all beings, fulfill the wishes of Khenchen Appey Rinpoche, and become a cause not just for the continuation but for the flourishing of the Buddha's teachings.

Ratna Vajra Sakya
The 42nd Sakya Trizin
Patron, Khenpo Appey Foundation
28 June 2022

Preface

I WAS HONORED to accept this commission of translating *Commentary on Valid Cognition* and its commentary. I am a great advocate of reasoning as the path to knowing, and I had studied the root text during my studies at the Institute of Buddhist Studies in Dharamsala in the late 1970s.

A translation project on the *pramāṇa* genre of Buddhist studies is one that requires full attention for a few years. It is a vast area of research and study. The various philosophies and epistemological views that pervaded India and Tibet require detailed unpacking. The piecing together of the historical narrative around epistemological development demands time-consuming research. I feel therefore that my translation may well be inadequate. However, my desire and love for the material has outweighed these other considerations. I apologize therefore for the errors and deficiencies that scholars greater than myself will notice.

I am very thankful to the Khenpo Appey Foundation for sponsoring and asking me to translate this work, as well as to my old friend Christian Bernert, who first approached me.

In Dharamsala I was able to approach the geshes involved in producing the Tibetan editions of the *Science and Philosophy in the Indian Buddhist Classics* series conceived by His Holiness the Dalai Lama. They worked every day in their office at Namgyal Monastery. Whenever I walked in, always unannounced, they were always willing to answer any questions I had on this translation. I refer primarily to Geshé Chisa Drungchen Rinpoché and Geshé Lobsang Khechok. Their combination of learning, humility, and friendliness is one I happily bow to and remain in deep gratitude for.

I also am very thankful to my friend and senior editor at Wisdom Publications, David Kittelstrom. He is a careful, precise editor, with a keen eye. But more than that he offers thoughtful suggestions on content, style, and format. This was especially true for the composition of this introduction.

I am grateful to Alexander Yiannopoulos, who cast a critical eye over the translation, especially for his comments on the meanings of terms in the original Sanskrit.

I often compared this commentary with that composed by the Geluk master Gyaltsab Darma Rinchen and with the annotations of the Sakya scholar Kunga Wangchuk. As they both relied upon the Indian commentaries, Gorampa and Gyaltsab often, though not always, comprehended the stanzas similarly. Therefore it seems that the syntax, and sometimes the grammar, of the root text was glossed and rendered to follow the meaning given by a particular Indian commentary, or by the Tibetan commentator's understanding of the Indian commentary. This was necessary because the root text is so terse. Therefore the translation of the root text as it appears in stanzas between the commentary and in bold type within the commentary is influenced by Gorampa's glosses and explanations.

Given that, I wonder if it is at all possible to produce a translation of the root verses that is not somehow influenced by an Indian or Tibetan commentary. Commentaries explain and clarify, but different commentaries explain differently. This is not a problem if the basic grammatical and syntactical meaning of the root text is consensually agreed upon, because then the student can compare the various glosses by the commentators and make up their mind accordingly. But if the grammar and syntax itself of the root text is not evident to begin with, then any explanation of the root text will be influenced and flavored by the commentary.

For Tibetan commentators there is the added difficulty of the *Pramāṇavārttika* being a translation from the Sanskrit. If the commentator does not know Sanskrit, there will always be a linguistic barrier that prevents them seeing the original text. However, as Sanskrit scholars have said, even in Sanskrit the *Pramāṇavārttika* is difficult to understand. Maybe Dharmakīrti had a point when he said in the colophon that his work would dissolve into his body like a river flowing into the sea.

Although the subject matter of this work is much favored in Buddhist academia, my introduction below does not conform to the standard and format expected by the contemporary academic world. My intended readers are not specialists but ordinary people—Buddhist or non-Buddhist—who are interested in understanding the means and process of knowing, in the sense of encountering something that approaches the definition of truth. If indeed truth will set you free, then the path of knowing, as opposed to the path of gathering information, is one we should all walk.

The root text of this work, composed by the great Indian scholar and practitioner Dharmakīrti well over a thousand years ago, was not accessible to ordinary people of that time, who were mostly illiterate and uneducated. However, there is no reason why that should be the case today. We live in a world where literacy and education are enjoyed by large swaths of the world's population and remain a priority in those places where they are not. I believe it is incumbent on Buddhist translators and scholars to ensure that difficult and complex philosophies found in the Buddhist teachings are accessible to all those who demonstrate an interest. Buddhist philosophy, epistemology, ontology, and so forth are not dry subjects with no soteriological intent. They are intended as provisions to sustain us as we walk the path to freedom and happiness.

Translator's Introduction

The Importance of Knowing

Knowing is essential in Buddhist practice. Its faith is built on knowing, its path is built on knowing, and its practices are built on knowing. But why should that be, and what is "knowing"? Moreover, how can we be sure that what we know is valid and reliable?

Base reality

Buddhist doctrine can be divided up into base reality,[1] path, and result. Base reality is the actuality of our existence—of our being, our mental and physical form, and the external world. It is the natural state of affairs, without exaggeration, deprecation, or deception. Therefore knowledge of this base reality is not a judgment or an evaluation based upon a predetermined and embedded religious or political ideology but an unbiased and nonpartisan knowledge resting on a sound foundation. Buddhism is a religion, and its only reason for existing is to provide its followers with a path to happiness and a freedom from suffering. Therefore, in Buddhism, the pursuit of knowledge is a means to an end that aids and supports us in the achievement of these goals. Otherwise, the pursuit of knowledge would be endless because it is simply not possible to know everything. Therefore the concept of omniscience expressed in some traditions of Buddhism does not literally mean knowing everything that exists. Buddhism is necessarily selective in what it says we need to know.

What is the base reality that is intimately connected with our search for peace and happiness? Answering this involves looking at our state of being, our place in the world, our mind, our sense of who we are, and so on. Is our natural state one of happiness, suffering, something in between, or a blend of both?

Do the world and ourselves actually exist as they appear to us? Will what we perceive as happiness bring us happiness? Is there anything in the world that endures? What is this little life that "is rounded with a sleep"? What is achievement when death comes to us all?

These investigations are soteriological insofar as they are followed with a salvation from suffering in mind and are not the pursuit of knowledge for its own sake. They provide the impetus for a spiritual pursuit, whether based upon an established religion or not. The pursuit of a religious path based only upon fascination, fashion, or some prevailing culture will not be driven by these big questions, and enthusiasm can easily dissipate or be lost in a sterile repetition of ritual or creed.

Therefore a knowledge of base reality is as pragmatic as knowing how to drive before you turn the ignition key, realizing that you are unwell and then going to the doctor, or knowing that the world is threatened with environmental disaster before becoming an activist to try and prevent that. It is the driving force or motivation for a spiritual quest. Therefore, for Buddhist practice, the knowledge of base reality is essential.

In Buddhism, base reality includes the nature of suffering, the types of suffering, and the causes of suffering. It involves asking, for instance, whether we recognize suffering for what it is, and whether suffering has deeper levels we don't recognize. It also involves asking whether the causes of suffering are inside us, external, or a combination of both. Base reality in Buddhism also includes the ultimate nature of existence. Is the way the world appears its final reality, or is there something deeper? Is our experience of life valid in the sense that we can rely upon it? The most important base reality in Buddhism is the mind. What is consciousness? What is the function of mind? What are the types of mind? Is it one with or separate from the physical body? Can it continue without its physical support after death?

Base reality, therefore, as its name implies, forms the basic building block of our world of experience. It is heavily focused on the inner world of mind. To know it is to gain valid and unmistaken knowledge, which will yield conviction and enthusiasm for pursuing a path leading to relief from all unsatisfactory states.

Path

Buddhism speaks of paths leading to destinations. In essence these paths are new and unvisited states of mind, and the way we achieve them is through practice. To travel these paths, therefore, means to transform our minds from harmful and unproductive attitudes and states into those that are beneficial.

Any journey to new places requires a map, or advice from someone who has been there. While it is perfectly adventurous to set out without either and with no concern for where the journey will lead, such a trip is only fun if it is not dangerous and the destination unimportant. The spiritual path is of great importance because it is a journey to happiness—something we all want—and there is limited time to accomplish it. It is also a journey that should be treated with caution because the mind is uncharted territory for us and its exploration is not without risk.

Therefore, a knowledge of the base reality may spur us to travel our path, but before we set out, we need knowledge of the path. In Buddhism, knowledge of the path is gained by study and by listening to teachers with experience. When we talk about a great guru, a true master, and a highly realized lama, it is the experience of the spiritual path they have walked that gives them that title, not their lineage, fame, charisma, or words. Just as we need a GPS or a guide when we drive somewhere new, we need a guide on our spiritual path, and the best guide is our knowledge accumulated from reliance on study and qualified teachers.

The result

Having a sense in advance of the final result of our spiritual endeavors gives us an aim. Knowing how far away it is gives us perspective and helps to regulate practice. In Buddhism the goals can be called *nirvāṇa* or *enlightenment*, and knowing that they can be attained is a great inspiration. The final result of Buddhist practice is produced through the causal process of the path. Therefore, if you know the path and what its potential is, you know the result, and you know that it is attainable.

Faith

Faith essentially means "belief" or "trust." Generally, faith by definition focuses on something not immediately apparent to the senses and has no doubt of its existence. Is faith therefore blind? Being convinced of the existence of something without knowledge, good reason, and evidence is blind faith, but according to Buddhism that is a lower kind of faith. Knowing produces faith because knowing produces certainty. This "knowing" is not always the direct experience of the senses or some kind of extrasensory intuition, but it can be a conceptual cognition and what Buddhism calls a *valid cognition* (*pramāṇa*). The reason why it is valid is a focus of Buddhist epistemology and is a primary topic of this book.

Buddhist faith therefore is produced—or should be produced—by way of knowledge, and that knowledge in turn springs from penetrative analysis of basic reality and the path based upon that reality, as taught by the Buddha. If in our examination of basic reality we discover that we are being deceived, that what we always took for a flawless comprehension of the nature of life, the way it appears, does not really correspond to the way it exists, then we need to change that. We need to correct that wrong cognition and build a life and a way forward based upon that corrected view. This leads to a path based upon that knowledge, a journey with the goal of complete transformation of the mind. Since such an undertaking is dependent upon knowing, what then is this knowing?

What Does It Mean to Know?

On a basic level *knowing* can just mean to be conscious or aware. If we have a mind, we are aware of whatever is presented to that mind. The animate world of living beings is differentiated from the inanimate world of stones and rocks by the presence of an awareness that can be described as a consciousness. Living beings know, while stones do not. There may be an ongoing debate about whether plants and trees have consciousness, but the general Buddhist view is that they do not.

Knowing in this basic sense is not necessarily correct or valid knowing. Someone with a high fever who hallucinates a wind blowing outside is conscious of "wind." There is no wind, but there is a conscious experience of it. However, this is not the kind of knowing described above. The knowing of base reality and so forth is a knowing that can be relied upon and, more importantly, acted upon. It is a knowing not deceived by the object that appears to it or by internal mental and physical factors present at the time. The "wind" is hallucinatory, and the feverish experience of it cannot be relied upon to produce a valid certainty that there is a wind blowing outside, even though the fever-possessed patient may not immediately recognize that.

Therefore *valid* knowing cognizes its object without the distortion that deceives the cognizer. In other words, the object appears to the cognition as it is conventionally and consensually accepted to exist. Such a cognition will be a reliable support for subsequent action. Knowing can take place through the senses, as in the case of seeing an object, or conceptually, as in the case of understanding or comprehending something, but in either case, if that knowing is undeceived about its object, it becomes a knowledge that can be relied upon. To validly know something is to comprehend its reality.

Therefore this kind of knowing is incontrovertible, undeceiving, reliable, authoritative, and trustworthy. The Tibetan term for such reliability (*mi bslu ba*) is used in other contexts to describe a good friend who will not let you down. It is this kind of knowing that is referred to in the opening paragraph above. Validly knowing the reality of our state of being, our minds, the causes of suffering, the causes of happiness, the true nature of existence, of our experience, of self, and so on provides the basis for any kind of spiritual path we follow. The pursuit of such a path will be backed up by this knowledge, which has become a conviction and will stand strong in the face of adversity. On the other hand, spiritual paths that lack such knowledge—motivated only by attraction toward a doctrine, a goal, or a teacher—may have no foundation to sustain them if doubts surface later.

Ways of Knowing

Knowing can take place through the senses. Consciousness is aware of objects such as sounds, forms, tastes, smells, and physical sensations by way of the sensory faculties of the ears, eyes, tongue, nose, and body. Such knowing is experience. In Buddhism this experience is a case of these objects appearing to the sensory consciousness in the way that an object appears to a mirror. The consciousness takes on the aspect of that object in the same way as a mirror takes on the reflection of the object in the form of an image. Our everyday experience is testament to this kind of knowing.[2]

For much of the time sensory experience is valid and understood as valid, and we act upon it with more or less success. The sight of smoke induces the comprehension of fire, and we react accordingly. We see dark clouds approaching, and we reach for the rain gear. However, as noted above, sensory experience can be deceiving. Looking out the window of a moving train, the scenery appears to rush by. Every day the sun appears to rise, move across the sky, and set in the west. Mirages appear as water, colors change when we put on sunglasses, and so on. Most of the time we self-correct and are aware of the deception because of acquired knowledge, contextual clues, and past experience. But not always. Children and animals can be foxed by an image in a mirror. People used to believe the sun moves across the sky. Sensory experience can mislead us. It will need the confirmation of discernment or acquired knowledge, which of course is not direct sensory experience.

Buddhism accepts two ways of validly knowing. The first is the sensory experience described above. The other is conceptual. *Conceptualization*, as used here, is cognition that is not a direct experience by one of the senses. It may have direct, sensory experience as a concomitant cause, but it does not have direct contact with an external object such as a sound or a visible form. Therefore it does not directly rely upon the sensory faculties of the ear, eyes, and so on. It is mental. For example, when we think and analyze, we may conclude or recognize that this is this and that is that. When we look at something or listen to some sound, we discern that it is this or that. Such cognition is *conceptual* because the object or conclusion of such thought is a mental construct. It has been conceived. When I think of chocolate, the mental construct of chocolate that appears within that thought is not actual chocolate. I can't taste it or eat it. It is a conceptualization of chocolate. In the language of Dharmakīrti, the author of this work, it is a universal,[3] one that in this case corresponds to an actual bar of chocolate that I can eat.

But not every mental construct corresponds to a reality or existent that can be verified by a valid cognition. The conception of a self that is separate from and in charge of our body and mind, Buddhists say, is a concept with no corresponding real existence. Buddhism does not generally assert that self does not exist whatsoever; it is not a nihilist doctrine. However, the mental construct of a separate, self-existing I that sometimes appears when we think of ourselves has no counterpart in reality.

With conceptualizing, therefore, the object that appears has been conceived from within. However, Buddhism accepts that conceptual thought—especially inference—can be a valid means of knowing. Direct experience and conceptual cognition make up the two ways of knowing. There is no third way of knowing, and as explained above, knowing is essential in Buddhism. The task therefore is to be able to separate valid cognition from erroneous cognition. Erroneous cognition cannot be a successful support for subsequent action or practice, and it can even be destructive.

Knowing the Unknown

Much of the base reality that needs to be comprehended as a support for faith and practice is not immediately accessible to the direct experience afforded by direct sensory perception (*pratyakṣa*). The deeper nature of self, the deeper nature of happiness and suffering, and the deeper nature of existence in general do not naturally arise to our senses like the full moon rising in the sky. Direct sensory experience, as mentioned above, is akin to a mirror reflecting the image in front of it. If we have sight, we see. If we have hearing, we hear. On its own sensory perception does not seek out or analyze. Those tasks are carried out by mental factors such as the ability to analyze, concentrate, discern, remember, and so on, which occur while the sensory faculty is engaged in reflecting its image. Therefore, to know any deeper realities that lie beyond the realm of the senses, we must rely on conceptual knowledge. Buddhism divides existence into the evident and the hidden. It is these hidden phenomena that are to be accessed, verified, and understood. In so doing, erroneous misconceptions are recognized and discarded. Therefore, in the beginning, valid conceptual knowledge is more important than direct valid experience, even though the latter is often the starting point for the former.

Buddhism, like other religions, posits phenomena that are inaccessible to the senses, but to accept the existence of these hidden phenomena on faith alone is not sufficient. Such blind trust is not valid cognition. The only pathway to validate or repudiate these phenomena involves a penetrative mental process that arrives at ascertainment one way or another. Because this process does not have any final ascertainment of the hidden phenomenon in its immediate purview, it must begin with something accessible and, at least conventionally, accepted. Therefore the process of conceptually knowing something often begins with evident sensory phenomena.

When Buddhism speaks of these hidden phenomena, they often refer to the deeper nature of our immediate world. Therefore, in the Buddhist doctrines of emptiness or ultimate truth and impermanence, it is evident phenomena within our experience that are deemed to be empty and impermanent. When non-Buddhists speak of a primordial nature or substance that pervades all existence, it is evident phenomena that are said to possess this deep nature. Therefore it is said that reasoning begins with evident phenomena.

Analyzing

Sensory perception does not analyze. It does not conceptually dissect the evident phenomenon that appears to it into its constituent parts and examine them. The human ability to analyze and investigate is a process of reasoning. The beauty of reasoning is that it can isolate the more abstract facets of an evident phenomenon for the purpose of evaluation. To use the phenomenon of a pot—which is often used as an illustration in Buddhist epistemological works—a pot is a product, it is transient, it is a cause, it has parts, and so on. These facets, or features, can be isolated out during the process of conceptual investigation. In Buddhism they are known as *isolates* (*vyatireka*, *ldog pa*).

A single phenomenon like a pot can have multiple isolates. In pramāṇa this is known as "the one becoming many."

The purpose of isolating is to learn more about evident phenomena than meets the eye. It is a way into their deeper nature. In reality these isolated features or aspects possess the same nature because, outside of the conceptual arena, they cannot be separated. The pot as a cause and the pot as an effect are aspects of the same pot. As said above, that which appears to conceptual cognition is conceived from within; they were not created by the potter. However, such conceptual separation is valid as long as every aspect has correspondence with the real world of pots. If that is the case, this analytical process can be used to gain valid knowledge of the pot's deeper nature. This is especially true when one aspect of the pot is understood and ascertained to exist but another is not. For example, it is possible to comprehend that the pot is a product. It is reasonable to conclude that anything produced is also transient. Therefore, because it is a product, the pot must be transient. The transience of the pot is inferred through reasoning that relies upon another of its aspects, such as its being a product.

In the conceptual world, not only does one become many, but many become one. The many specific and individual instances of phenomena that qualify as "trees" cannot all appear at once to the direct visual consciousness. However, the innate human ability to conceptualize means that all such phenomena can be conceived under a single universal "tree." As noted above, this kind of universal (*sāmānya, spyi*) is accepted by Dharmakīrti, and much of his first chapter is spent validating it. This "tree" universal is conceived by conceptual cognition and has no substantial reality because it is a mental construct encompassing all instances of actual trees.

Therefore, when someone says "tree" or "trees," a listener who knows the language and the main characteristics of a tree will understand what the other is referring to, and thus communication takes place. This communication happens because a conceptual cognition and verbalization of "tree" eliminates everything that is not a tree, thereby reducing it to an isolate or a universal that subsumes instances or specifics of trees. This "elimination of other," or exclusion (*apoha, gzhan sel*), is a conceptual way of validly knowing because *knowing* means that an object of knowledge conceptually appears in perfect correspondence with the reality. The reality of trees does not include non-trees, and the conceptual knowing eliminates phenomena other than trees. The topic of exclusion is dealt with in Dharmakīrti's first chapter, and is the topic with the largest number of verses. It is treated as a distinct topic in monastic studies, but for Dharmakīrti it is a continuation of the explanation of the indispensable same-nature relationship that exists between reason and predicate. Therefore this topic and others, such as universals, are given their own chapters and headings in the translation, but such division is not always replicated by Gorampa.

Logic

How can we know if our reasoning and analytical process is tainted with error, thereby resulting in an erroneous conclusion? By using logic. The conclusion we seek is not self-evident, and any hidden existence or lack of existence must be revealed through cognition that is in essence inference. Logic leads us to conclusions that are inescapable, where there can be no other possibility, and thus produces conviction. If we are certain that what we see is smoke, and we know smoke is necessarily produced by fire, we will be convinced that fire exists somewhere in that place, even though it is hidden from view.

Therefore logic is all about relationships among phenomena—more specifically between an evident phenomenon and a hidden phenomenon. Dharmakīrti states that this relationship is either one of being the same entity or one of cause and effect. For the first of these, a single phenomenon, as mentioned above, can be conceptually isolated into features that are conceptually distinct even though they are one entity in reality. The heat of the flames of a fire and the luminosity of those flames can be distinguished by the analytical mind. Conceptually, they are distinct features of individual characteristics. But they are features of the same phenomenon and cannot in reality be separated. Where one is, the other will be also. Of course, heat may remain after the flames have died away, but that heat is the heat of the coals and not the heat concomitant with the flames themselves. Therefore, in this type of logic, where there is the one phenomenon, the other will be too, even if it is not directly cognized via sense perception. We do not need to put our hands in a flame to see if it is hot.

Dharmakīrti states that making use of this natural relationship among features sharing the same entity is logic that establishes the existence of hidden phenomena. The example he uses is of the subtle impermanence of sound. He first conceptually isolates the feature of sound as something that has been produced. This feature of sound—that is, it arises from the coming together of certain causes and conditions—is evident to a discerning mind. A phenomenon that is produced must also be subject to destruction. It has a period of duration, after which it will cease to exist.

Dharmakīrti points out that this transient nature is not something that only comes into play when some outer force causes the destruction of that phenomenon, as when a hammer destroys a pot. It is a feature inseparable from a phenomenon at all times of its existence because it came into existence through production. These two features of "being a product" and "transience" are inseparable even though they are distinguished conceptually. Where one is, the other will be. This is a relationship where either feature is "indispensable" as Dharmakīrti calls it. They are mutually inclusive.

Therefore, with the natural existence of this relationship within phenomena, hidden features can be inferred by the presence of other, more evident features of the same entity. In higher Buddhist philosophy the subtle and hidden existence of the "no-self" of phenomena, including persons, can be inferred by the more evident existence of the dependence innate in a phenomenon by way of its dependence upon its causes, its parts, and its apprehension by cognition.

Conversely, the nonexistence of a particular feature will imply the nonexistence of another feature that shares its entity. For example, if I do not possess the full range of cognitive powers to know that something is not present, I cannot be certain of its nonexistence. Lack of appearance does not prove nonexistence. However, if there is a situation in which all conditions for something to necessarily appear are present and complete, and yet that something does not appear, its nonexistence can be inferred. The present Dalai Lama used this latter type of reasoning to refute the existence of Mount Meru, the huge cosmic mountain at the center of our world according to ancient Buddhist and Hindu mythology. According to that cosmology, daytime and nighttime are determined by the sun's passage around Meru. When traveling behind Meru it is nighttime for the part of the world in front of Meru on the other side. This is because Meru blocks the light of the sun and nighttime is the shadow cast by this giant mountain. Therefore Meru must be coarse form of the type visible to the naked eye. If that were so, it must appear to those whose vision is unhindered, but it does not. Therefore it cannot exist. Generally, nonappearance does not prove nonexistence, but in the particular circumstance where logic determines that it should appear, it does prove nonexistence.

The second kind of relationship that occurs within the phenomenal world is that of cause and effect. Cause and effect is a natural law; it is not exclusive to Buddhists. Nothing arises from no cause or from itself. If the effect is present, a cause must have preceded it. The cause can be inferred by the effect, as with smoke and fire. We "know" we have great grandparents even if we have never actually seen them, by the logic of cause and effect. This logic is put to great effect by Dharmakīrti in his second chapter where he uses effects, such as deeds of the Buddha, to infer causes hidden within the mind of the Buddha, and to infer prior causes of the enlightened mind of the Buddha. The same logic is often employed in Buddhist philosophy to infer the existence of a past life or past-life instances of consciousness.

However, some religious philosophies use the presence of an effect to infer the existence of a divine creator. How could the beautiful rose with its unique aroma arise without a divine creator? Does its very presence not indicate the existence of an intelligent design? The world itself is an effect and must have an efficient cause. Creation is the movement of particles, which on their own do not move. The world is sustained, and the world is destroyed. Unintelligent causes can do none of these. There are moral laws governing the universe. These must be divine and have divine causes (see Sharma 1997, 209–10). Even though they subscribe to the logic of a cause being inferred by an effect, Buddhist logicians reject the logic of divine creation. In ancient India logicians from opposing religious philosophies would debate each other, each using logic to assert their contrasting positions. Therefore logic on its own is not enough. Even in Tibet it is said that a skilled debater can prove anything. Logic must be flawless and not tainted with erroneous proofs if it is to produce a valid outcome. Logical thought must be free from distorted deductions. Otherwise, though they may be held with conviction, conclusions reached will be wrong.

In his first chapter Dharmakīrti sets out how the process of logical thought can be pure and free of error. There is a subject or phenomenon about which something must be proved or disproved. These form the subject and predicate of a thesis. Then there is the reason that does just that. For the reason to produce a correct inference, (1) the reason itself must be validly known or proven to be within the subject itself. In the argument "Sound is impermanent because it is a product," it must be known and accepted by the person considering the argument that sound has the feature of being a product. In other words, sound must be a product, and in reality it cannot exist without that feature. Sound as the possessor of features can be conceptually cognized as possessing the feature "being a product." Sound and product, as mentioned above, can be conceptually isolated but are of one entity in reality.

(2) The reason of being a product must be known as being inseparable from being impermanent. Wherever impermanence exists, or in every instance of

impermanence, being a product will be concomitant. (3) Likewise, it must be known that in every instance of non-impermanence, being a product will not be present. If these latter two are established, it can be validly asserted that whatever is a product must be impermanent. It is not enough to just not see it. It must be validly established. Saying that sound is impermanent because it exists is faulty logic because it is not the case that in every instance of non-impermanence existence will be lacking. Some existence is permanent.[4]

These three processes must be gone through and validly established in order to make the process of logical thought pure and free of error. These are the three modes or criteria (*trairūpya*, *tshul gsum*), and Dharmakīrti spends most of his first chapter describing them.

Inference

Buddhist philosophy asserts that there are two ways of validly knowing. One is direct perception, and the other is valid conceptual knowledge. Inference belongs to the latter. Logic that follows the correct path of the three criteria induces valid inference. This is because throughout the process of logical thought, great care is taken to ensure that the process does not fall foul of erroneous conclusions and assertions in establishing convictions within the three criteria. If this is done, a valid conviction must arrive. Sound *is* impermanent. This conviction ascertains the thesis with no room for error, and this is *valid cognition* (*pramāṇa*, *tshad ma*). It is *valid* cognition because it apprehends without being deceived as to the object that appears to it. It can therefore be trusted and relied upon, even though that object does not appear to the perceiver nakedly. If we need convincing, we should use reasoning.

Reasoning is like shining a light on an apparent reality, one that until that moment we took to be true and self-evident. It does not in itself dispel our habit to conceive that untruth, but it does illustrate the contradiction between apparent reality and actual reality. It is a knowledge that supports progress on the path by way of meditation, which is the actual dispeller of the appearance of that falsity. Therefore reasoning must be applied to the mind. Logic is ineffective if not applied.

Such a process of logical thought can also be a kind of meditation because it is in essence a pursuit of hidden and profound existence, vital for progress along the path. As mentioned above, much of what constitutes basic reality is not evident to the senses and must be comprehended by other means. In Buddhist philosophy, the root cause of suffering is the ignorance of the true nature of self and other phenomena. Therefore that ignorance must be made known. This is done by revealing the reality of self and phenomena. However, that reality is covered or veiled by that very ignorance and is therefore difficult to recognize. Logic and its resulting inference is employed in meditation to conceptually cognize that reality. Eventually this conceptual cognition is burned away by the fire of experience, and the practitioner gradually eradicates the causes of suffering. Such a process when completed is nirvāṇa.

All the above is the subject matter of chapter 1 of Dharmakīrti's *Commentary on Valid Cognition.* It is considered by many in the Tibetan tradition to be the most important chapter because it is the basis and source material for the logical medium by which the great classic Buddhist works are comprehended in the monastic curriculum.

The Soteriological Quality of Logic

The above establishes the soteriological function of reasoning. Nevertheless, there were many in Tibet, and many today, who hold that logic is not part of the process of becoming free from suffering and gaining lasting happiness. David Jackson in *The Status of the Pramāṇa Doctrine* describes the debate in twelfth-century Tibet on whether the pramāṇa genre was secular or had soteriological utility. Logic is often regarded as being abstract, divorced from reality, and lacking the embodied passion needed to advance on the spiritual path. Of course, logic pursued solely for self-aggrandizement produces nothing but foolish pride, but when pursued in the search for the truth that will set you free, it is invaluable. The user must be aware to keep the process of logical thought applied to a soteriological goal. This is logic that confronts and challenges one's own established views and positions. No other person is involved in this solitary analytical meditation. Appearances are challenged; especially the appearance that seems to be one and the same as actuality. Even scriptural authority is not submissively accepted but is put under the microscope of logical reasoning to test its validity. In this sense logic can be life-changing, because it can reshape how we view the world. Rather than living under the sway of prevailing views and attitudes, or by various ideologies and emotionally charged prejudices thrust into the public domain, pure logic can become our guide.

Nevertheless, logic does sometimes take the form of a public debate with opponents. Such debates took place in ancient India, with one philosophy pitted against another. These were contests and, as such, followed rules. They were not arguments that driven by emotion and anger, and if one side tried to prevail with irrational or deceptive assertions, they were soon snuffed out with rational argument. Listeners to these debates could be swayed toward one side or the other. Winning, therefore, was important for promoting a particular philosophy, and for Buddhists at least, the authority of scripture was not sufficient to accomplish this.

In Tibet, except during the early transmission of Buddhist teachings, Buddhism had no opponents. Tibet was a Buddhist country. Therefore a system of monastic debate developed in which the questioner tested the knowledge of the respondent using a stylized formula of logical presentation designed to produce contradiction in the other's position. These debate sessions focused on whatever topic was being studied in the monastic classroom at that time. They were designed to sharpen the mind and to ensure that students knew the philosophical content from all sides.

Therefore the expression of logical thought takes place in the private arena of the mind and in the public arena of formalized debate. These two uses of logic are encapsulated in the first and fourth chapters of *Commentary on Valid Cognition*—"Inference for Oneself" and "Inference for Others."

Dharmakīrti

Not much is known about the life of this great Indian logician. According to Tibetan sources such as Butön and Tāranātha (encapsulated in Dungkar 2002, 841), he was a contemporary of the eighth-century Tibetan emperor Trisong Detsen. However, others (Tillemans 2020) state that he could have been born as early as the sixth century because it is recorded that he received his ordination from the sixth-century monk Dharmapāla. Stcherbatsky (1930) places him in the seventh century. Tibetan sources go on to say that he was born in South India in Trimalaya into a brahman family and studied the scriptures well so that, by the age of eighteen, he had become proficient in non-Buddhist tenets systems. He then became so interested in the philosophy of Buddhism that he stopped adhering to non-Buddhist tenets. This caused his parents to eject him from their home, and consequently he traveled north, where he finally arrived at the great Nālandā Monastery and took monastic ordination.

In Nālandā he studied Buddhist tenets under the tutelage of Īśvarasena, who had been a student of the Nālandā master Dignāga (480–540). Dharmakīrti received three separate explanations of Dignāga's *Compendium of Valid Cognition* (*Pramāṇasamuccaya*). Consequently, he realized that Īśvarasena had not fully understood the thinking of Dignāga. This induced him to compose his own commentary to *Compendium of Valid Cognition*, in which he formulated ideas as a reaction to Īśvarasena's own commentary to Dignāga's work (Tillemans 2020). This of course is *Commentary on Valid Cognition*. In total Dharmakīrti is credited with nine compositions on logic and epistemology in the catalogue of Tibetan translation of Indic commentaries and treatises known as the Tengyur.

Tibetan sources go on to say that Dharmakīrti defeated many non-Buddhist philosophers who visited Nālandā in debate. He then traveled to the east and south of India, where he propagated Buddhism and constructed many temples and centers. Although he had many disciples, he was never accompanied by more than five. He passed away in South India.

There are different assertions on what Buddhist tenets Dharmakīrti actually adhered to. Tibetan sources say that he was either a follower of the Sautrāntika tenet system or of the Cittamātra school. The first chapter on logic and inference for oneself has been adopted by Tibetan epistemological thinkers as illustrating the realism of Sautrāntika tenets. There he seems to accept an external reality possessing an intrinsic existence, and therefore ultimately true, while asserting that the inner world of universals and conceptual constructs has no such intrinsic existence, that these are only "false truths."

However, the third chapter, "Perception" (*pratyakṣa*), has been understood to portray Yogācāra idealism, with its denial of phenomena being external to the mind. Therefore, according to Tillemans (2020), he was a nominalist who accepted that a certain class of phenomena was intrinsically real, but his final position, alongside that of Dignāga, was Yogācāra idealism.

Some Tibetan masters state that Dharmakīrti was a follower of Madhyamaka (van der Kuijp 1983, 39). However, the term *Madhyamaka* has been defined differently over the centuries in Tibet.

Tāranātha (1970, 229–30) states that Dharmakīrti also entered the tantric path and took Heruka as his meditational deity.

Tāranātha (1970, 234) and Butön (1999, 154) both cite a verse attributed to Dharmakīrti where he likens himself to Dignāga in his wisdom, to Candragomin in his purity of speech, and to Śūra in his prosody. They cite another verse where Dharmakīrti opines that if his words were to disappear, the teachings of the Buddha would decline, and false doctrines would follow. In the homage of his *Commentary on Valid Cognition*, he candidly states that he doubts that the work will be of much benefit to others because most people "are attracted to the ordinary and do not possess the skill of wisdom" and that they are "resentful and envious." He states that he therefore composed it to familiarize his own mind with its tenets. In the colophon he also laments that his work will disappear when he passes away.

Some commentators have used these citations to pass judgment on his personality, sometimes in a negative light. However, the expression of confidence with unbridled joy is not uncommon among great Buddhist masters, and it may be that the first two citations are merely that. It cannot be inferred that they are a product of pride. Such inference, according to that presented by Dharmakīrti himself, would be based on uncertain reasoning. Moreover, the statement that he wrote it for himself and that his teachings would die with him can be seen an expression of resignation. In his own life he saw that his own teacher, Īśvarasena, had not understood Dignāga's thinking, and when he reviewed a commentary to *Commentary on Valid Cognition* written by his own disciple Devendrabuddhi, he was not satisfied. The high regard in which he has been held for centuries in Indian and Tibetan Buddhist circles illustrates that his thinking was indeed profound and influential. So maybe his comments were just reflecting, sadly, that most people would not comprehend the profundity of this composition.

Dharmakīrti's inspiration, the great master Dignāga, was according to Tibetan sources born near Kāñcī in South India of brahman parents. He was said to be a contemporary and student of the great fifth-century Abhidharma master Vasubandhu. He was ordained as a monk by a follower of the Hīnayāna and became proficient in the tenets of that school. Under Vasubandhu he studied the Hīnayāna and Mahāyāna. For many years he lived in retreat in a cave in eastern India. Once he was invited to Nālandā Monastery to debate with a non-Buddhist philosopher, but after returning to his cave, he remained there for the remainder of his life. He is credited with seven compositions on logic and epistemology in the Tengyur.

Epistemology in India

In his *Commentary on Valid Cognition*, Dharmakīrti attacks, sometimes by name, the philosophies and assertions of the prevailing religions of the day. Alongside Buddhism, these religions were influential and active. With contrasting epistemologies and ontologies, they often criticized each other in compositions or in public debate. Religion was important—life was ruled by it.

Ancient India hosted at least eleven distinct philosophical schools, orthodox and heterodox, and many more subsets besides. Tibetan sources, such as the genre of texts presenting tenet systems, list many of them. There are many well-researched books written on these philosophical schools. Below are the non-Buddhist schools that Dharmakīrti concentrates on.

The Cārvāka were materialists, denying many of the cornerstones of other spiritual traditions. They espoused no design or purpose to the world. They asserted no immortal creator, no abiding soul, and no law of karma. Happiness and suffering for them is random. Consciousness is solely a byproduct of the body and not separate from it, as a mural is essentially part of the wall. Therefore, there can be no past or future existence, just as a mural ceases when the wall is destroyed. Moreover, for the Cārvāka, sense perception alone is valid. For them, seeing is believing.

The Nirgrantha were wandering Jain mendicants who were puritanical in their observance of an ethical code, often going to great lengths to protect all forms of life, even that within the plant kingdom. Like the Buddhists they denied the monism of other Indian philosophical systems, who assert that an eternal and unchanging primordial substance pervades all existence, but they did assert a permanent substance that was subject to change and temporary expression. Tibetan sources state that the Jains posit a self that inhabits the entire body and whose entity is permanent but temporarily transient and that there is a dualism by which phenomena share a common entity but are manifestly distinct. On this point Dharmakīrti was especially harsh on the Jains, saying that if that were true, why don't they run off and drink a camel when looking for curd! (1.182), calling them bewildered by ignorance and incoherent.

Jainism accepted a law of karma and a doctrine of good and evil, asserting that ascetic practice is purificatory and eventually leads to liberation from saṃsāra. They adhered to at least three ways of validly cognizing—direct perception, inference, and scriptural testimony. Jainism still counts millions of adherents today.

The Mīmāṃsā ("critical examination") school was founded by Jaimini, who is estimated to have lived in the fourth century BCE. Followers of this school were orthodox adherents to the Vedas, and the name reflects their contemplation or examination of Vedic texts. For them the Vedas were eternal sounds, not words produced by humans. Higher rebirth could be gained through sacrificial rites, but omniscience was impossible because mental afflictions were intrinsic to the mind and could not be removed. Their prime focus was epistemological, and they paid little attention to deity worship or the idea of a creator and were essentially nontheistic. Including the various subschools, six ways of validly knowing can be ascribed to them: direct perception, inference, scriptural testimony, postulation, negation, and analogy. In his first chapter, Dharmakīrti spends a considerable amount of time refuting the Mīmāṃsā assertions around the Vedas.

The Sāṃkhya ("enumeration") school was mainly nontheistic and enumerated twenty-five realities, of which two are singled out as of prime importance. The first of these is *prakṛti*, which has been translated as "primordial matter," "universal" or "first principle," and so on. It pervades all existence but is hidden. In its natural state, it is in an equilibrium of three qualities (*guṇa*). Nevertheless, it manifests as the world of experience. It is a cause but not an effect and is eternal and unchanging.

The other principle of importance is *puruṣa*, which can be rendered as "self," "person," "soul," and "consciousness." Like the primordial matter, it is absolute, but it is neither cause nor effect. The dualistic relationship between these two is fundamental in the Sāṃkhya pursuit of liberation. Not realizing that the world of experience is the manifestation of the primordial matter is an ignorance that binds sentient beings to suffering. Through the direct teachings of a guru, the Sāṃkhya practitioner understands that experience is the manifestations of *prakṛti* and that self is separate from it. This causes a lessening of attachment to the world. The practitioner develops a meditative concentration that is able to perceive the primordial matter. This brings about a withdrawal of its manifestations. All conventional appearance has subsided, and only the absolute truth of *prakṛti* stands alone. This withdrawal of consciousness is the path to liberation. A person wishing to engage in the world stimulates the all-pervading primordial matter to materialize. Therefore *prakṛti* is deemed to be a prime universal, and its manifestations are particulars of that universal. It is this concept of all existence sharing the same nature that Dharmakīrti attacks in detail in *Commentary on Valid Cognition.*

The Sāṃkhya accepts perception, inference, and scriptural testimony as ways of validly cognizing.

The Vaiśeṣika and Nyāya philosophies are said in Tibetan sources to be very similar with only a few differences. The Nyāya school developed a detailed system of logic. Its name could be translated as "reasoning." They held the Vedas to be infallible. Although it seems they were nontheistic, later Nyāya scholars produced logic for the existence of a divine creator (Sharma 1997, 209–10).

Tibetan sources say that alongside ritual activities such as washing, fasting, and sacrifice, the Nyāya-Vaiśeṣika path to liberation is similar to the Sāṃkhya in that the self is understood to be separate and independent. This is the seeing of reality. Therefore valid knowledge is also essential. The opening statement of the *Nyāya Sūtra* says that only the true knowledge leads to salvation

(Chattopadhyaya 1986, 163). Where Naiyāyikas accept four means of valid knowledge, Vaiśeṣikas, like Buddhists, only accept direct perception and inference (Bhawuk 2011, 172).

It is generally accepted that Dignāga and Dharmakīrti invigorated the science of logic and epistemology in Buddhist studies and practice. Vasubandhu, who may have been a teacher of Dignāga, was also a great master of logic, and his assertions are cited by Dignāga (Stcherbatsky 1930, 29).

The Spread of Pramāṇa[5] Studies to Tibet

It may be that the invitation of the great Indian master Śāntarakṣita to Tibet in the eighth century sparked an interest in Buddhist logical studies among followers of the nascent Buddhist doctrine there. He was a great logician and had already composed a landmark work[6] on Buddhist philosophy before he arrived in Tibet (Sadhukhan 1994, 8). He also aided a Tibetan translator to render a work on logic by Dignāga into Tibetan.[7]

His disciple Kamalaśīla was also an erudite Buddhist master. It was he who participated in a famous debate with a Chinese master at Samyé Monastery. The debate centered on whether liberation from suffering is gained through a gradual path built upon an accumulation of knowledge and merit or whether it was sudden and could be effected by simply knowing the nature of the mind. The former position, presenting the Indian Buddhist monastic tradition, was represented by Kamalaśīla, and the latter was the Chan (Zen) position of the Chinese master. The majority opinion is that Kamalaśīla was the winner, although that debate still continues in some quarters. Whatever the case, Buddhist works from India began to be translated into Tibetan by a succession of brave translators who made the arduous journey to India and studied with Sanskrit scholars to bring back texts translated into Tibetan.

Among those were a number of works on logic and epistemology. Dr. Sanjit Sadhukhan in his *Short History of Buddhist Logic in Tibet* has meticulously listed these translations. Dharmakīrti's *Commentary on Valid Cognition* and its autocommentary on the first chapter were first translated by Ma Lotsāwa Gewai Lodrö (1044–89) with the Indian pandit Subhūtiśrīśānti. Eight commentaries on this work are listed in the Tengyur, translated mainly in the later propagation of the Buddhist doctrine into Tibet that began in the eleventh century. However, there are other commentaries extant in Sanskrit that were not translated into Tibetan. Including the nine works by Dharmakīrti and seven by Dignāga found in the Tengyur, sixty-six works on pramāṇa were translated into Tibetan.

As mentioned above, some in Tibet regarded works on logic as outside the Buddhist doctrine. However, gradually the tradition spread. Ma Lotsāwa, as well as translating *Commentary on Valid Cognition* and two commentaries on it, also propagated the study of logic in central Tibet (Gö Lotsāwa 1976, 70).

Ngok Lotsāwa Loden Sherab (1059–1109), the great scholar of the Kadam lineage, was also influential in the spread of Dharmakīrti's and Dignāga's ideas. He traveled to Kashmir and stayed there for at least seventeen years. There he translated *Commentary on Valid Cognition*, Prajñākaragupta's commentary, and Yamāri's commentary to Prajñākaragupta's work. In all he translated ten works on pramāṇa and often wrote commentaries to his translated works. He founded Sangphu Monastery in 1073, taught throughout central Tibet, and became known as the progenitor of the new pramāṇa lineage.[8]

According to Stcherbatsky (1930, 55), the first Tibetan author to compose an independent work on logic was Chapa Chökyi Sengé (1109–69), a follower of Ngok Lotsāwa. Until recently it was thought that not many of his compositions survived. He was responsible for formulating epistemological and other tenets into a system that allowed and encouraged critical examination by way of debate. This began in Sangphu Monastery and gradually spread to other monasteries, where it still plays a vital role in the monastic curriculum.

The other great luminary in pramāṇa studies was Sakya Paṇḍita Kunga Gyaltsen (1182–1251). He too is considered a founder of a pramāṇa tradition in Tibet. Van der Kuijp (1983, 97) says:

> It can hardly be denied that the principal reasons for the rather sudden emergence of the Sakyapa school of Tibetan Buddhism as an intellectual force capable of challenging the Ngok tradition's virtual monopoly over the more epistemologically oriented domains of Buddhist philosophy were the sheer vision and critical acumen with which Sakya Paṇḍita assailed the whole of the Indo-Tibetan cultural legacy.

He studied pramāṇa with the great Kashmiri master Śākyaśrī, from whom he learned Sanskrit, and also had contact with scholars from the Ngok and Chapa tradition. He retranslated or revised *Commentary on Valid Cognition* with Śākyaśrī, which eventually led to this text eclipsing Dharmakīrti's *Ascertainment of Valid Cognition* (*Pramāṇaviniścaya*) as the main pramāṇa text studied in Tibet. His own compositions include the hugely influential *Treasure of Reasoning* and its autocommentary, which are explications of pramāṇa theory. He composed these works to bring out the essential meanings of Dignāga's *Compendium of Valid Cognition* (van der Kuijp 1983, 100–101). His efforts in the exposition and propagation of pramāṇa led to Sakya Monastery becoming a center for epistemological studies.

After Sakya Paṇḍita the Sakya school became a force for the propagation of pramāṇa studies. Uyuk Rikpa Sengé (d. 1235), a disciple of Sakya Paṇḍita, received teachings on the whole of *Commentary on Valid Cognition* and *Treasure of Reasoning* from his teacher. He composed commentaries on both and taught them at Sakya Monastery. A biography of Uyuk claims that the popularity of pramāṇa studies in all monastic traditions these days can trace its cause back to Sakya Paṇḍita and Uyuk.

Butön Rinchen Drup (1349–1412), the renowned compiler of the Tibetan canon and abbot of Shalu Monastery, composed a commentary on *Ascertainment of Valid Cognition*. Rendawa Shönu Lodrö (1349–1412), a Sakya teacher of Tsongkhapa, composed a work on the system of Dignāga.

The Sakya master Rongtön Śākya Gyaltsen Sheja Kunrik (1362–1449) composed a commentary to Dharmakīrti's *Ascertainment of Valid Cognition*. One of his disciples was Gorampa, the author of this commentary. Another was Śākya Chokden, or Serdok Paṇchen (1428–1507), also a renowned Sakya scholar, although he was sometimes controversial in his views of Sakya Paṇḍita's works. He composed an overview of pramāṇa and a work on its difficult points.

Taktsang Lotsāwa Sherab Rinchen (1405–77) was a prominent Sakya master who criticized Tsongkhapa for categorizing the works of Dharmakīrti and Dignāga, as well pramāṇa studies as a whole, as belonging to the Buddhist praxis of inner transformation, saying that they had no soteriological value in and of themselves. His reasoning seems to be linked to his understanding of the Madhyamaka presentation of ultimate truth. He was not denying the value of pramāṇa studies, and the fact that he felt compelled to launch this criticism indicates how widespread these studies had become.

After the fifteenth century, with the rise and dominance of the Geluk tradition, it seems as if there were fewer great masters who felt compelled to write on pramāṇa within the Sakya tradition. However, Ngawang Chödrak (1572–1641) wrote a large explication of *Treasure of Reasoning*, and Mangtö Ludrub Gyatso (1523–96) wrote two works on pramāṇa and one on *Treasure of Reasoning*. In the twenty-first century, Dzongsar Khenpo Kunga Wangchuk (1921–2008) wrote a commentary on *Commentary on Valid Cognition* that followed Gorampa's commentary often verbatim.

Within the later Geluk tradition that arose with Tsongkhapa (1357–1419), figures such as Gyaltsab Darma Rinchen (1364–1432), Khedrup Gelek Palsang (1385–1438), and the First Dalai Lama, all of whom had devoted themselves to Sakya masters early in their spiritual life, composed major works on the pramāṇa texts of Dharmakīrti and Dignāga. Tsongkhapa first heard teachings on *Commentary on Valid Cognition* from Sengé Ribong, the abbot of Sangphu Monastery. Tsongkhapa wrote very little on pramāṇa, but his appreciation of it is evident from the report in his biography that when he would read *Commentary on Valid Cognition*, tears of faith would come to his eyes (Jackson 1994, 105). In his very short spiritual autobiography, *A Destiny Fulfilled*, he also speaks of the soteriological value of pramāṇa studies, and how chapter 2 of *Commentary on Valid Cognition* gave him complete conviction of the Buddha as a genuine authority for those seeking liberation (Jackson 1994, 102). In the Geluk monastic curriculum, the system of reasoning derived from chapter 1 of *Commentary on Valid Cognition* and from Chapa Chökyi Sengé is used throughout the monastic studies as a way of opening up the broad range of Buddhist philosophical subjects. The text itself was studied and debated in special month-long winter sessions near Sangphu.

In this way, the teachings of Dignāga and Dharmakīrti have been preserved, studied, discussed, and contemplated up to the present day. The Tibetan monastic tradition deserves great praise for such an accomplishment. As mentioned above, the pramāṇa tradition is of great soteriological use in Buddhist practice. It is not just an academic pursuit, and to have preserved this great tradition since its beginnings in the seventh century is something of which the Tibetan people can be justly proud.

The Pramāṇavārttika

The colophon in most versions of the root text tells of three translations of this work into Tibetan. The first was made by Ma Lotsāwa and Subhūtiśrīśānti, the second by Ngok Lotsāwa and Bhavyarāja, and the third by Sakya Paṇḍita and Śākyaśrī.

Commentary on Valid Cognition has four chapters: (1) Inference for Self, (2) Establishing Valid Cognition, (3) Perception, and (4) Inference for Others. In the Tibetan monastic tradition, the first two chapters are considered the most important, because the first chapter constitutes source material for the dialectical medium of study and analysis in the monastic curriculum, and the second lays out the way to establish the Buddha as an authoritative and valid person on whom those who seek liberation can rely. Consequently, only these two chapters of Gorampa's commentary are included here, although his commentary covers all four chapters. Dharmakīrti composed his work to explain the thinking of Dignāga's *Compendium of Valid Cognition*, which he believed had been misunderstood. However, the order of its chapters does not follow those of Dignāga's work, which begins with a chapter on perception. Indeed, chapter 1 seems to be an independent work and not a commentary (Gnoli 1960, xv). This irregularity was noticed by Indian and Tibetan commentators. Gorampa comments on this in detail.

As mentioned, chapter 1 establishes inference as a means of valid knowledge, or valid cognition, and sets out the processes of reasoning that lead to a reliable inference. In doing so, Dharmakīrti attacks non-Buddhist ontological assertions that would be incompatible with the organic relationships between phenomena that are the bases for the logical process. The two relationships of *cause and effect* and *shared entity* are essential starting blocks for the logical thought process, and he therefore spends most of the first chapter establishing them.

The second chapter establishes generally what it means to become a valid authority, meaning one that is reliable, undeceiving, and trustworthy. He sets about establishing the Buddha as the prime exemplar of this valid authority by way of these two natural relationships. This he does by taking the process of spiritual development in the person of the Buddha from the time he first generated compassion until his culmination in the attainment of enlightenment and tracing its logical inevitability in forward and reverse sequence. He bases this process on the homage in Dignāga's *Compendium of Valid Cognition*, which is a praise of the Buddha as being the Compassionate One, the Teacher, the Sugata, and the Protector. These four are in a causal sequence, where each preceding quality becomes an inevitable cause of the following quality. In the reverse sequence, the presence of the succeeding qualities establishes the existence of the preceding qualities as causes.

The logic in this chapter focuses on the sequential development of the Buddha's inner qualities, and therefore the existence of past and future lives is also logically established in this chapter. For the same reason, there is an examination of the four truths, which also have their own sequence. In the section on the cause and antidote to suffering, Dharmakīrti focuses on those ascetics who mortify their bodies in order to gain liberation, going to great lengths to establish that body, in the sense of "that belonging to self," is not the cause of suffering and that breaking off all attachment to it, without applying the antidote of refuting the permanent self, will be an arduous waste of time.

The second chapter branches off into proofs of past and future lives, because the creation of an enlightened being through cause and effect takes several lives to accomplish. In doing so, Dharmakīrti spends some time establishing that consciousness is not created from the physical body.

The *Commentary on Valid Cognition*, or *Pramāṇavārttika*, is extant in Sanskrit (Miyasaka 1972) and was first edited by Rāhula Sāṅkṛtyāyana in 1938 (Gnoli 1960, xxvii). This intrepid scholar and polymath traveled to Tibet four times, bringing back many texts, and also discovered portions of the Sanskrit manuscript of the autocommentary in Sakya Monastery in Tsang province.

The Sanskrit text is difficult to understand, and Gnoli (1960, xxxv) describes the language as compact, precise, and excessively brief. The Tibetan is not easy either. Complete thoughts are not encased in neat four-line stanzas, sometimes a thought finishes midway through a line, and referents are often only implied and can't be determined without a commentary. Tibetan commentators relied upon the commentaries that had been translated into Tibetan. Gorampa refers to the commentaries by Śākyabuddhi, Yamāri, Prajñākaragupta, Śaṃkarānanda, and Devendrabuddhi.

The work is divided into stanzas; the whole text has 1,452 stanzas, of which chapter 1 contains 340 and chapter 2 contains 285.

Gorampa Sönam Sengé

There probably is no better analysis and description of the life and views of Gorampa in Western literature than that found in José Cabezón's introduction to *Freedom from Extremes*, his translation of Gorampa's *Distinguishing the Views*. Therefore I recommend the reader to it.

To summarize what has been written there: the author of this commentary was born in Gowo in 1429 and given the name Sönam Sengé. Later he became so erudite that he was known as Gorampa, "the learned one from Gowo." He was also regarded as an incarnation of the great Sakya scholar Drakpa Gyaltsen (1147–1216). He studied under many Sakya masters, especially at Ngor Ewam Chöden Monastery, where he took ordination from Ngorchen Kunga Sangpo (1382–1456), the well-known founder of the monastery. He twice lived at Dreyul Kyetsal Monastery in Lhasa, where he taught, meditated, and composed. Later he became sixth abbot of Ngor for three years. He founded two monasteries in Tanak, where he established a curriculum of study.

He was very prolific and wrote thirteen volumes of composition. This particular commentary he composed in 1474. He was critical of the prevailing

Jonang and Geluk traditions that had taken root in Tibet, and he criticized Tsongkhapa, especially his Madhyamaka teachings. In doing so, he took up the challenge of defending the Sakya tradition that by then had lost some of its authority.

He died in 1469 and remains a great influence in the Sakya tradition.

LIGHT OF SAMANTABHADRA

A Commentary on Dharmakīrti's
Commentary on Valid Cognition
(Pramāṇavārttika)

༄། །རྒྱས་པའི་བསྟན་བཅོས་ཚད་མ་རྣམ་འགྲེལ་གྱི་རྣམ་
པར་བཤད་པ་ཀུན་ཏུ་བཟང་པོའི་འོད་ཟེར།། །།

GORAMPA SÖNAM SENGÉ
(1429–89)

Dharmakīrti

The Explanation of Chapter 1

Inference for Oneself (Svārthānumāna)

1. Homage and Introduction

I bow with devotion to the bodhisattva and great being Samantabhadra and to the supreme deity Mañjuśrī.

Through the wide skies, the pathway of the gods
that is the mother-like, nonapprehending compassion for all living beings,
the seven horses of the **Teacher** who comprehends
the supreme way and the antidotes to the causes of suffering
pull the sun maṇḍala of the **Sugata**, endowed with three features;
with your virtuous light you are the **Protector** of a multitude of disciples.
To you, who **became** a truly **valid** being, I bow.[9]

Surrounded by an orange glow rivaling that of the brilliant morning sun,
accompanied by beautiful garlands of lightning flashing,
their movement emitting the tinkling sounds of cymbals,
mingling with a light matching that of the crown jewels of a hundred gods,
with your garlands and light you are posed beautifully upon a lotus;
supreme deity, fulfill all hopes in my mind.

The Buddha, the sun-like friend, predicted that Dignāga
would have a mind that worked for the welfare of others,
while Mañjuśrī reassured Dignāga that in the future
he would become the sole eyes of every treatise.[10]

He walked with the gait of one famous in the world
for destroying all opponents in the town of Sarāvatī.
I bow to him, beautified by the net of the practice of the six perfections
and made radiant with the stainless load of the Buddha's teachings.

He who turned the Mount Meru of entity-based reasoning
with the churning rope of the two kinds of perseverance
to produce from the ocean of our and others' tenets
the shining drops of nectar that are the Seven Treatises,
their cooling rays of light proclaiming the virtue
of every part of the profound and vast Dharma,
nourishing the night lotuses that are the Buddha's teachings:
I bow to the moon of orators.
Please open the jasmine flower of my mind.[11]

Resting on a bed of many excellent and virtuous qualities,
the ocean of your mind with its vast and profound knowledge,
its depth beyond fathom and into which flow the four rivers
of grammar and logic from the Manasarovar mind of four pandits,
the abode of a mighty nāga of intellect without fear,
uttering his long-lasting roar of the logic of repudiating and establishing,
Sakyapa,[12] you ocean of qualities, to your billowing waves I bow from
my heart.

To the lineage of lion-like masters, propagators of reason, and others,
with their vast powers of reasoning;
to those supreme scholars who, with the glories of the speech of the
Buddha,
sport within the teachings of Buddha;
to those who hold the victory banner of the Śākya teachings of him
born within the race of the Śākyas;
and to the supreme tutor who provides a glorious feast
of limitless classic works to limitless beings, I bow.

To hear it is music to the ears of those with endeavor and interest,
like the sound of thunder to little birds who wish for the rain.
To contemplate it is like lightning, illuminating many wise beings,
beautiful on the tip of newly grown shoots of grass.

To meditate upon it is like a thunderbolt cracking the rock
of the conceptualizing of apprehender and apprehended.
From the clouds of analysis in the skies of this scriptural tradition,
may I satisfy all beings with the rains of excellent explanation.

Having washed away all the stains of the perverse orator opponents of the perfect Buddha, the Teacher and sole friend, sole source of all temporary and ultimate happiness for all beings, as well as of his teachings, Ācārya Dignāga composed many fragmentary works on valid cognition so that his disciples would be able to follow by way of the path of certainty. Later, he compiled these works and composed his *Compendium of Valid Cognition.* There were many subsequent works explaining this composition, but the one who comprehended it perfectly was the great being and master scholar and practitioner, the glorious Dharmakīrti. As predicted in the *Mañjuśrī Root Tantra*:

A monk with the letter *dha*,
proclaimed in the south,
having defeated the opponents,
this monk will likewise practice mantra.

He composed seven commentarial treatises known as the Seven Treatises. The extensive *Commentary on Valid Cognition* (*Pramāṇavārttika*) presents the extensive refutation of others' positions and the extensive establishment of our own position, as a way to easily understand valid cognition. The intermediate-length *Ascertainment of Valid Cognition* (*Pramāṇaviniścaya*) presents our own tradition extensively and concisely refutes the positions of others. The short *Drops of Reasoning* (*Nyāyabindu*) presents an abridged presentation of our own position. These are known as the three main-body texts.

None of the seven expand on the "Direct Perception" chapter of Dignāga's composition, but two works do expand on the "Inference for Oneself" chapter: *Drops of Proof* (*Hetubindu*), which sets out to determine the general meanings of "property of the subject" and "pervasion," and *Analysis of Relations* (*Saṃbandhaparīkṣā*), which determines the difficult topic of the connection with imputed phenomena. The last two works expand on the "Inference for Others" chapter: the *Principles of Debate* (*Vādanyāya*), which is a presentation of how to question and respond in a debate along with an ascertainment of what it means to be defeated and so on, and *Establishing the Minds of Others*

(*Saṃtānāntarasiddhi*), which teaches that even for the Cittamātra tradition it is not contradictory for the minds of others to be conventionally known from speech. These four works are the branch compositions.

From these seven, this present work will be an explanation of the extensive treatise, *Commentary on Valid Cognition.* There are three main outlines:

1. The translation: The significance of the front matter
2. The composition: The significance of this worthy text
3. The completion: The back matter

The translation: The significance of the front matter

1. The meaning of the title
2. The translator's homage

The meaning of the title

1. Translation
2. Explanation of the title
3. Reason for the title
4. Need for a title

Translation

In Sanskrit, from the four great languages of India, *pramāṇa* means "valid cognition," *vārttika* means "commentary," and *kārikā* means "in verse."

Explanation of the title

Generally, "valid cognition" refers to the topic of valid cognition, or correctly knowing, as well as to the *Compendium of Valid Cognition*, which is the expression of this topic. Here it refers directly to the latter and indirectly to the former. This is because explaining the *Compendium of Valid Cognition* actually facilitates the understanding of what it means to know perfectly. Because it comments extensively on this topic, it is a "commentary." Because it is written in *anuśtubh* meter, it is "in verse."

Reason for the title

"Valid cognition" refers to the topic. "Commentary" denotes the function of the work. "In verse" refers to the style of the text.

Need for a title

There are two reasons for mentioning the title in Sanskrit, two reasons for mentioning it in Tibetan, and two reasons for mentioning it in both languages. These reasons are those found in treatises in general.

The translator's homage

This is "I prostrate to the youthful Ārya Mañjuśrī."

According to the decrees followed by the lotsāwas and paṇḍitas, this is to show that this work belongs to the basket of Abhidharma. *Fundamental Wisdom of the Middle Way* states, "Presentation of the ultimate Abhidharma."[13] This present work determines the view of reality according to the Cittamātra and Sautrāntika schools.

If this work is deemed to be a commentary based on the general topics of all three baskets, then the lotsāwa is simply paying homage to a deity of his choosing. The homage is necessary to ensure the completion of the translation.

The composition: The significance of this worthy text

1. Virtue at the beginning: The supplementary material
2. Virtue in the middle: An explanation of the actual text
3. Virtue at the end: The greatness of this text

Virtue at the beginning: The supplementary material

1. The homage to develop faith
2. The reason for this composition

The homage to develop faith

1. The necessity of the homage
2. A synopsis of the homage
3. A word-by-word explanation

The necessity of the homage

There are three necessities. Realizing that the composer himself is a great being, others will engage in a work composed by him. Because the homage teaches the result that is the three ultimate enlightened bodies as well as enlightened activity, others will engage with a treatise whose topic is the cause of that result. When disciples listen to and teach this work, they will recite these verses of homage, thereby pacifying all hindrances and enabling them to complete their accumulation of merit.

A synopsis of the homage

The homage consists of praise and prostration. The praise consists of the needs of self and the purposes of others and is made to all three enlightened forms.

A word-by-word explanation

> **I prostrate to the one in whom**
> **the web of conceptions has completely disappeared,**
> **who possesses profound and vast forms,**
> **and whose light rays of that**
> **which is good in every aspect**
> **radiate everywhere.**

The homage begins with the line "**I prostrate to** . . ." To whom? To the Buddha, who has perfectly fulfilled the two needs. What are they? The needs of self are fulfilled by **possessing** the three enlightened **forms**: (1) By the power of the antidote applied to the **web of conceptions** of attachment to self and mine, or to apprehender and apprehended, they **completely disappear**—never to return—into an entity that is the enlightened form of natural purity. (2) The enjoyed form, which is **profound** because it dwells only in the realm of Akaniṣṭha and teaches only Mahāyāna Dharma to tenth-level bodhisattvas, who are its sole entourage. (3) The manifested enlightened form, which is **vast** because it teaches all three types of disciples[14] in a form that is suitable for them.

The needs of others is "**good in every aspect.**" This refers to high rebirth and to the permanent goodness of nirvāṇa, which is taught by the **light rays** of the sacred Dharma that are **radiated everywhere**. Alternatively, using the line "Good in every aspect is the incomparable Sage,"[15] the phrase "good in every aspect" would refer to the Buddha. Using the line "With the form that radiates the light rays of the various sacred Dharmas" would mean that the light rays of the Buddha refers to his sacred Dharma. The radiating of that Dharma is applied to the term light rays, and so the line becomes metaphorical.

Some Indian commentators evidently apply the term "good in every aspect" to the bodhisattva Samantabhadra, but the above is correct.

The reason for this composition

Most previous commentators have stated that the first three lines of the homage explain the reason for not composing for others and that the remaining lines explain the reason for composing this work for his own purpose. That is not correct. In his *Ascertainment of Valid Cognition*, Dharmakīrti says:

> The one to whom Ārya Mañjuśrī appeared and cared for possessed a glorious and stainless mind, and these fools of the world do not understand his profound words. Therefore, even if there is just a little contempt toward him who nourishes and devotes himself to the world, it will bring needless suffering. And so, with compassion, I will clarify this work of his.[16]

Thus he states he is composing the work for the sake of others. No one would make the distinction that he composed the *Ascertainment of Valid Cognition* for the sake of others and *Commentary on Valid Cognition* not for the sake of others. Therefore there is a need for others and a need for himself.

Need for others

1. Saying explicitly that it will not be of direct benefit to those who are faulty vessels
2. Saying implicitly that it will indirectly benefit them
3. The word "although" implies that it will be of direct benefit to those who are vessels of great quality

Saying explicitly that it will not be of direct benefit to those who are faulty vessels

> **Most beings are attracted to the ordinary**
> **and do not possess the skill of discernment.**
> **They do not therefore aspire to these excellent teachings.**
> **Moreover, they possess a resentment, the stain of envy.**
> **With these they are wholly endowed, and therefore,**
> **although I do not have the thought that this will benefit others,**

I, Dharmakīrti, **do not have the thought that this** treatise will be of direct **benefit to others**—that is, listeners who are vessels possessed of three faults.[17] **Most** of those **beings** who listen **are attracted to ordinary** non-Buddhist treatises and so forth and **do not possess the skill of discernment** to understand the excellent teachings. **Therefore**, in this way, they possess the fault of not having wisdom. **They do not aspire to these excellent teachings**, and so they possess the fault of having no aspiration. **Moreover, they possess a resentment**, which is **the stain of envy** toward the composers of these excellent teachings, and therefore they possess the fault of prejudice. Thus **they are wholly endowed with these** three faults.

Saying implicitly that it will indirectly benefit them

Indirectly this composition is of benefit to them because when they have trained their minds and eliminated the three faults, it will directly benefit them.

The word "although" implies that it will be of direct benefit to those who are vessels of great quality

This composition will be of direct benefit to those listeners who are vessels of three great qualities. This is because some listeners are not "attracted to ordinary" treatises and are "possessed of the skill of discernment." Therefore they possess the great quality of discernment. They "aspire to these excellent teachings" and so possess the quality of aspiration. Not only that, they do not have "a resentment, which is the stain of envy" toward the composers of these excellent teachings, and therefore they possess the great quality of being unprejudiced. Thus the reason is that they are wholly possessed of these three great qualities of a listener.

The essential meaning is that these lines explicitly state that this work will not be of benefit to those who are vessels possessed of the three faults and that therefore these three faults should be eliminated. The word "although" teaches that it will be of benefit to those who are vessels for the three great qualities.[18]

The above citation from the *Ascertainment of Valid Cognition* illustrates the prejudice and teaches that those vessels possessed of the three faults will be taught indirectly, while directly teaching the motivation of compassion.

The above can be summed up by these lines from *Treasure of Reasoning*:

> With discernment, freedom from prejudice,
> and a mind of compassion for others
> will this be explained.[19]

Those of the past talked of four faults by positing poor discernment as well as no discernment. However, this is not the intention.

Need for himself

> **for a long time, my mind has been acquainted**
> **with this excellent explanation,**
> **and in order to eagerly familiarize myself with it,**
> **I take joy in composing this.**

The **mind** of this composer **has been acquainted for a long time with** the topic of the **excellent explanation**, the *Compendium of Valid Cognition*. Therefore, **in order to eagerly**, or effortlessly, **familiarize myself with** an understanding of its meaning, **I take joy in composing this** *Commentary on Valid Cognition*.

2. Overview of the Chapters

Virtue in the middle: An explanation of the actual text

Some declare that the text is structured around the valid cognitions needed to perceive the three levels of knowable phenomena and around the two kinds of statements of proof needed to teach these to others. The first of these are: inference for oneself, which perceives hidden phenomena; the establishment of valid cognition, which explains the homage of the *Compendium of Valid Cognition* to establish scripture as valid and is for very hidden phenomena; and direct perception, which is for evident phenomena.

This is not correct. If the first three chapters are explained based on their teaching the three object-possessing valid cognizers with regard to knowable phenomena, that would mean that the object-possessors of the three valid cognizers would be incomplete in the *Compendium of Valid Cognition* and *Ascertainment of Valid Cognition.* Also, the second chapter establishes a valid or authoritative being but does not primarily establish scripture as valid. Inference for others expresses inference indirectly by way of direct expression of reasons.[20]

Others say inference for oneself is explained first as a way of explaining the *Sūtra*,[21] followed by an explanation of the homage of *Compendium of Valid Cognition.* Having refuted other positions, direct perception is then explained, followed by inference for others. Some declare that inference for oneself is explained first, followed by an explanation of the homage of the *Valid Cognition Sūtra* and explanation of direct perception, which teaches the divisions of valid cognitions and so on, and lastly an explanation of inference for others. Others claim that out of necessity the "Valid Cognition of Inference for Oneself" chapter from the *Valid Cognition Sūtra* is explained first. Then the right and wrong path are separated out, and the homage verse of the *Valid Cognition*

Sūtra is explained. The four wrong perceptions are refuted, and the "Direct Perception" chapter of the *Valid Cognition Sūtra* is explained. The statements of proof, together with an explanation of "the reality" (*artha*), are explained, and the "Inference for Others" chapter of the *Valid Cognition Sūtra* is explained.

The above claims have identified just a small part of the topics of the final three chapters, but they have not brought out the special chapter arrangement of this work. The claim that inference for oneself is explained first because it is a way of explaining the *Sūtra* is not correct and will be refuted later.

So what is the correct explanation? This is under three headings:

1. The chapter on inference for oneself is explained in order to separate what is meaningful from what is without meaning
2. The chapter on establishment of valid cognition explains the separating of what is correct from what is incorrect
3. The remaining two chapters explain their respective topics [not in this book]

The chapter on inference for oneself is explained in order to separate what is meaningful from what is without meaning

1. First, the connection
2. Secondly, the text of the chapter
3. Finally, the conclusion by way of the title of the chapter

First, the connection

If this treatise is composed as a commentary to *Compendium of Valid Cognition*, why then does it not follow the order of the chapters of that work but instead explains inference for oneself first?

The *Commentary on Valid Cognition* autocommentary[22] of 3,500 lines says:

> The separating of what is meaningful from what is without meaning[23] depends upon inference. Because this is wrongly understood, that will be presented here.

The meaning of this statement is explained under two headings:

1. Refutation of others' positions
2. Presentation of our position

Refutation of others' positions

Some Indian pandits state that "meaningful" means beneficial and "without meaning" means unbeneficial. "Separating" them is the practice of adopting what is meaningful and discarding that which is without meaning. Doing that depends upon inference. Therefore inference is explained first.

Śākyabuddhi[24] refutes this assertion by asking if this act of separating *totally* depends on inference, thereby precluding it not being there, or if instead it is understood to depend on inference *alone,* thereby precluding it from existing elsewhere. In the first case, the act of separating also depends upon direct perception, in which case it would be proper to explain direct perception first. If it were the second position, that would not be correct because the act of separating also depends upon direct perception. If it meant that *only* the act of separating depends upon inference, that cannot be correct because neutral phenomena that lie between those that bring harm and benefit also depend upon inference.[25]

Śākyabuddhi explains his own position, saying that "meaningful" refers to the definition and divisions of valid cognition as explained by Dignāga, because they are logically correct. The definitions and divisions provided by the non-Buddhists are "without meaning" because they are not logically correct. The separating of these two depends on inference alone. He also says that this is stated by Devendrabuddhi in the linking passages of the second chapter, when Devendrabuddhi[26] says, "The Ācārya having presented inference, which is the basis for the explanation of the treatise of the characteristics of valid cognition . . . ."[27]

This needs to be examined. Is inference for oneself included in the definitions of valid cognition explained by Dignāga or not? If it is not included, then valid cognition could not be counted as being of two types—inference and direct perception—and valid cognition would erroneously be solely of direct perception. If it is included, then inference for oneself needs to be explained even before the discussion on inference for oneself because the separating out of inference for oneself depends upon inference. You accept the reason and the pervasion.[28]

Also, the previous assertion is incorrect for the following reason. They think that their assertion is mirrored in the citation from *Ascertainment of Valid Cognition* "Beneficial and unbeneficial refers to achieving and abandoning, and that, without question, needs perfect knowing as a prerequisite."[29] However, these two are not the same. The statement from *Ascertainment of Valid Cognition* refers to the existence or nonexistence of intrinsically existing phenomena in the objects engaged, and their negation in wholly designated valid cognitions. The perfect knowing that precedes that is found in both inference and direct perception and not solely in inference. Furthermore, if these two were referring to the same point, it would be proper to have a chapter on perfect knowing preceding all chapters.

Devendrabuddhi's position is that because it is the basis for the explanation of the treatise on the characteristics of valid cognition, inference for oneself is explained first. In the above statement, "the treatise on the characteristics of valid cognition" evidently refers to only the chapter on direct perception. In his linking passage to chapter 3 (the "Perception" chapter) he says:

> Inference as the basis for the explanation of the ācārya's treatise on the definitions of valid cognition and the explanation of the first half of the verse of homage of the treatise has been taught by the first chapter. Now the definitions of valid cognition are explained. "Because there are two types of knowable phenomena . . . ."[30]

Devendrabuddhi also says that he sees "within the treatise on valid cognition and its definitions are four mistaken conceptions," and that these four begin with the mistaken conception regarding the number of valid cognitions up to the mistaken conceptions concerning the results. The meaning of referring to the third chapter of *Commentary on Valid Cognition* as "the treatise on the characteristics of valid cognition" is that because it teaches the number of valid cognitions and so on, it teaches the actual characteristics of valid cognition. Devendrabuddhi's commentary continues:

> Isn't it the case that in teaching the characteristics of valid cognition, the number and so forth have no significance? That is not so. The number and so forth contain the actual characteristics of valid cognition.

It is not possible to cast toward such an assertion the consequence that it would be proper to explain inference for oneself even before the "Inference for Oneself" chapter. However, the consequence that it would be proper to explain inference for oneself first would apply if the texts were the *Compendium of Valid Cognition* and *Ascertainment of Valid Cognition*.[31] This error can also be leveled against the previous assertions.

The author of the *Ornament to the Commentary on Valid Cognition*[32] distinguishes the order of composition of the treatise from the order in which it was arranged in the volume. The first, the order of composition, followed the order of *Compendium of Valid Cognition*. However, when it came to the arrangement in the printed volume, the "Inference" chapter was made the first chapter because it had an autocommentary. He says that Devendrabuddhi was even mistaken about the order of the chapters, asserting that the true order is the order of composition, because in his *Ornament to the Commentary on Valid Cognition*, in the transitional passage that opens the chapter on inference for others, he says, "Immediately after the inference for oneself, inference for others is explained."

This too is not the intention of the text. The order of the text at the time of its composition is the order at the time it was placed in the volume. And the way it appears there is the actual order. Otherwise, the homage beginning "Web of conceptions . . ." and the pledge to compose should appear at the beginning of the "Establishment of Valid Cognition" chapter. If you think that these are the homage and the pledge to compose of the self-penned commentary and there is no fault here, it was not the practice of Indian scholars for there to be no homage and pledge to compose in treatises and then to place one in a chapter added at a later time.

Presentation of our position

1. The order of the chapters in the *Compendium of Valid Cognition*
2. The order of the chapters in this composition

The order of the chapters in the Compendium of Valid Cognition

In the homage, that which is to be defined—valid cognition—is only mentioned, and then at the beginning of the first chapter on direct perception, it is ascertained as being of two types—direct and inferential. Direct perception and inferential valid cognition are then taught in that order. This is an order of superior coming before inferior because inference ultimately depends upon direct perception, and even knowable phenomena ultimately depend upon intrinsically existent objects.[33]

Of the two types of inference, explaining inference for oneself first is because it is actual inference. When relying upon reasons during the use of inference for oneself, proof statements are not needed. However, proof statements are relied upon when using reasons during the application of inference for others. Therefore inference for others is taught next. *Ascertainment of Valid Cognition* also follows this order because there is no need to do otherwise.

The order of the chapters in this composition

So why do the chapters of [Dharmakīrti's] work not follow those of the *Compendium of Valid Cognition*? Inference for oneself is explained first out of necessity. What is that necessity? Śākyamuni Buddha as a valid being is what is meant by "meaningful," because that is the ultimate point to be established by this treatise. The opposite of that is "without meaning," because that is the ultimate point to be refuted by this treatise.

"Separating" these two involves the following. To have a mistaken conception regarding the entity, which is the assertion that there is no "valid being," is refuted, and the existence of an omniscience, which knows all necessary phenomena, is proven. The mistaken conception regarding the proof, which is that there is no such proof and no process of proof, is refuted, and the four proofs in forward order are explained to establish the existence of a proof, and the reverse order is explained to establish the process of the proof. As all of this depends upon inference arising from entity-based reasoning, inference for oneself is explained before the separating of what is meaningful from what is without meaning, as presented in the second chapter on establishing valid cognition.

Put like this, it is possible to understand the special difference between the *Compendium of Valid Cognition* and *Ascertainment of Valid Cognition* explaining direct perception first because they do not have a chapter on separating what is meaningful from what is without meaning, and this composition explaining inference for oneself first, as being down to the intention of the composer.

Yamāri says something similar:[34]

> It will not be easy to understand the forthcoming explanation on the four truths without the teachings on inferential cognition. Therefore it is proper to explain inference first.

Ravigupta also says:[35]

> In that way, inference is presented to engage with the four truths, and then to teach these truths, the second chapter explains the prostration verse from the homage.

However, their understanding of what is "meaningful" and what is "without meaning" is different, with "meaningful" referring to the sixteen aspects of the four truths such as impermanence and "without meaning" referring to the sixteen aspects such as permanence. Also, on the topic of inference, many "mistaken conceptions" can be seen in our and others' tenets. In order to remove them and "set forth an unmistaken presentation," this will be "well explained" together with the autocommentary.[36] This is the reason for the autocommentary to the chapter on inference for oneself. It is not a reason for making it the first chapter.

What are these mistaken conceptions? In the section on the definition of a perfect reason, there are assertions ranging from one to six ineffective criteria[37] for a perfect reason. In the section on the types of reasoning, there is the assertion that a result will naturally arise from a collection of causes and the inference that present form, for example, arises from taste, thereby asserting that there are more than three types of criteria. In the section on the relationship between the reason and the predicate to be established, there is the assertion that the counter pervasion is proven merely by not seeing the reason in the incongruent class; from seeing smoke without fire coming from a termite hill there arises the assertion that fire and smoke are cause and effect here because of the mere establishment of the concomitant pervasion, even though the counter pervasion has not been established; the assertion that although being produced and being impermanent are substantially separate, they are nevertheless the reason and the predicate to be established in a reasoning by nature; the assertion that if they are of one nature, they cannot be reason and reason possessor; as a branch of that, the assertion that verbal expressions and conceptualization engage their objects by way of the force of the entity; as a branch of that, the assertion that verbal expressions directly express intrinsic existence and the assertion that the universal, as substantially one with or substantially distinct from its manifestations, is the cause of verbal expressions and conceptualization. In the section on the divisions of reasons by nature, there is the assertion that if existence is a reason, then existence is similarly the predicate to be established. In the section on reason by nonapprehension, there is the assertion that merely not being apprehended in the treatises establishes nonexistence. In the section on fallacious reasoning, there is the assertion that the verbal expression can establish the phenomenon expressed; and from the reasoning that it was not produced by a living being and that it is infallible in one area, there is the assertion that the expressions of the Vedas carry the truth.

The refutation of these will occur sequentially in the text.

The Three Reasons

3. Perfect Reasoning by Way of Result, Nature, and Nonapprehension

The text of the chapter

1. A brief presentation of reasoning
2. Extensive explanations

A brief presentation of reasoning

The *Sūtra* states:[38]

> Of inference for oneself, from the two kinds,
> the object is seen from the three-criteria reason.

Thus the basis of inference is reasoning that employs the three criteria. What are these three? How are they ascertained as three? What are their pitfalls?

> 1. **Property of the section and the part pervades.**
> **Such reasoning is definitively and solely of three types**
> **because of an indispensable relationship.**
> **Fallacious reasoning is other.**

Reasoning (1) in which the reason is established as a **property** of the subject under analysis, which is designated as a ***section***,[39] (2) in which the predicate, superimposed as a **part** of this "section," concomitantly **pervades** the reason, and (3) in which the counter pervasion can be implied, is a reason that acts as a basis for inference because it is reasoning in which all three criteria are complete.

Such reasoning, in which all three criteria are complete, **is definitively** enumerated as **solely of three types**—namely, by result, by nature, and by nonapprehension—**because** a reason that is established as the property of the subject and that is ascertained as having **indispensable relationship** with the predicate is definitively enumerated as being solely of three types.

On the term "property of the section," there are two issues to be resolved. One arises from the term *section*, in which there are three phenomena designated as "section" among the subject and its property. The other involves a discussion stemming from the term *property*, in which the consequence is cast that the reason to be applied is not concomitant with the congruent classification. The first of these is dealt with in the autocommentary and the second in the "Inference for Others" chapter. The fact that *Ascertainment of Valid Cognition* addresses these arguments in opposite chapters has to be understood as indicating that both arguments are necessary for the ascertainment of the meaning of "property of the section." **Fallacious reasoning is other** than the above indispensable ascertainment because, in an unestablished reason, the property of the subject is not established and therefore there is no basis for it being considered crucial. In contradictory and uncertain reasons, the indispensability is not ascertained, and they are therefore fallacious.

Extensive explanations

1. Analysis
2. Own position

Analysis

Some scholars divide the text into an extensive explanation of a perfect reason, an extensive explanation of a fallacious reason, followed by an extensive explanation of the relationship. They stipulate that the four verses beginning "Inferring a result by uncollected causes" (verse 1.11) are the extensive explanation of a fallacious reason. This is not correct because it does not accord with the sequence given in the brief explanation. If you think that it was placed before the extensive explanation of the relationship because there are so few words, then it follows that it should also precede the extensive explanation of a perfect reason, because it has fewer words than that section too.

Some scholars group these four verses with the discussion that follows on from them on the enumeration. Others include them as part of the extensive explanation of the relationship and therefore assert that there is no extensive explanation of a fallacious reason. This is also incorrect. The first three lines of the brief explanation have extensive explanations, and it is illogical that the fourth line ("Fallacious reasoning is other") would not also have an extensive explanation. Also, a treatise in which a brief explanation is not followed by an extensive explanation would not be found in the compositions of a true scholar. Furthermore, such an assertion contradicts *Ascertainment of Valid Cognition*, which applies the last two verses of these four solely to the establishment of the relationship.

Some apply the first verse of these four to the discussion following on from the enumeration and the three other verses to the extensive explanation of the relationship. *Ascertainment of Valid Cognition* in the "Inference for Others" chapter only applies the first verse to the enumeration, and this is the basis for their error. However, if that were the case, since *Ascertainment of Valid Cognition* only applies the last two verses to the establishment of the relationship, then the second verse should similarly be applied to the preceding sections.

Own position

Only the commentary of the brahman[40] applies all four verses to the extensive commentary on the topic of fallacious reasoning. The others, including the autocommentary, are not clear on this point. However, in order to be in accord with *Ascertainment of Valid Cognition*, the following can be applied. In its "Inference for Others" chapter, the first verse is cited after the discussion of enumeration, and in the "Inference for Oneself" chapter, the last two verses are cited at the beginning of the establishment of the relationship. The second verse does not appear in *Ascertainment of Valid Cognition.* However, it clearly proceeds in this work from the verse beginning "Comprehending form and so on from taste" (1.9). Moreover, the extensive explanation of fallacious reasoning would definitely have to use the terminology of these verses.

Therefore the extensive explanation has four main topics:

1. Extensive explanation of the three perfect reasons
2. Extensive explanation of the enumeration into three types
3. Extensive explanation of the indispensable relationship
4. Extensive explanation of fallacious reasoning

Extensive explanation of the three perfect reasons

1. The result creates comprehension of the cause
2. The nature creates comprehension of the entity
3. Establishing refutation from nonapprehension

The result creates comprehension of the cause

Are all causal qualities of fire, such as clear blazing, also the cause of the comprehension of smoke?

> 2. **Results indispensable with whatever**
> **have the nature of a cause are reasons.**

Results, such as smoke, which have an **indispensable** relationship **with whatever** phenomena that, in general, **have the nature of** fire as **a cause, are** suitable to be **reasons** for establishing the existence of fire in particular places, because if such an establishment exists, all three criteria are complete. It does not create the comprehension of certain features, like flames, that are other than its indispensable cause,[41] because such perception is mistaken with regard to those features.

The nature creates comprehension of the entity

> **An entity simply of its nature**
> **possesses relationship.**

A product, for example, that is **an entity** of the predicate constitutes perfect reasoning for establishing upon the phenomenon of sound properties, such as impermanence that are **simply of its nature** of being a product and **possess** an intrinsic **relationship** with it. This is because having established that, the three criteria are complete.

Establishing refutation from nonapprehension

1. The ability to refute the definite existence of something whose existence is inaccessible
2. The ability to establish the definite nonexistence of something that should appear

The ability to refute the definite existence of something whose existence is inaccessible

> 3. **Valid cognitions that do not engage**
> **possess the result[42] of no engagement**
> **with a nonexistent.**

Valid cognitions, such as those in scripture, **that do not engage** something such as a pot belonging to a ghost,[43] whose presence is in doubt, **possess the result of** comprehension that there can be **no engagement with a nonexistent**—that is, no designation of the definite existence of that phenomenon in certain places—because the three criteria are complete in establishing that there can be no ascertainment of the existence of that particular phenomenon in certain places.

"Valid cognitions" is plural because it refers to all three types of valid cognition, as in the line "There are those unconnected at the time of the treatises" (1.199).

The ability to establish the definite nonexistence of something that should appear

1. The nature of this type of reasoning
2. Divisions of nonapprehension reasoning
3. Refutations

The nature of this type of reasoning

> **In dependence upon a particular type of reasoning**
> **comes that which is a cause for understanding**
> **the nonexistence of certain phenomena.**

Do all reasons by way of nonapprehension only refute definite existence? **In dependence upon a particular type of reasoning,** known as nonapprehension of that which should appear, the nonapprehension of a pot that should appear is **a** factually concordant **cause for** the **understanding** and expression of the definite **nonexistence of certain phenomena** to be refuted, because the three criteria are complete in establishing the definite nonexistence of a pot that should have appeared.

Divisions of nonapprehension reasoning

> 4. **The establishment of conflict and result**
> **and the nonestablishment of a cause**
> **and an entity that should appear:**
> **the nonapprehension of the reality of nonexistence**
> **is of four types.**

Reasoning by way of **nonapprehension**, which establishes the designation and **the reality of nonexistence, is of four types: the establishment of** a **conflicting** nature, the establishment of a conflicting **result, the nonestablishment of** something that is **a cause** that should appear, **and** the nonestablishment of something that is of **an entity that should appear.**

The first is, for example, fire negating the existence of coldness. The second would be smoke negating the existence of coldness. The third would be the nonexistence of fire negating the existence of smoke, and the fourth would be the nonapprehension of a pot that should appear, negating the existence of that pot.

The text here is teaching the apprehension of a conflicting nature and the nonapprehension of the entity. Therefore it should be understood that this text is implying the apprehension of a conflicting pervader, such as the existence of fire negating the physical sensation of frost, and the nonapprehension of the pervader, such as the negation of the existence of tree negating the existence of an *agaru* tree.[44]

Refutations

> 5. **Any logic of the apprehending of the cause**
> **conflicting with that is flawed**
> **because the cause possesses no conflict.**

If the result of fire is able to negate coldness, is it not equally possible to use the cause of fire as a reason able to negate coldness?

If the direct cause of fire was used as a reason, it could not be ascertained as being a property of the subject. If the mere cause was used as a reason, then **any logic** in which **the apprehending of** firewood, **the cause** of that fire, was used as a reason for **conflicting with that** coldness, would be a **flawed** pervasion **because** it is a logic of firewood, the cause of fire, being able to negate coldness, and firewood, as **the cause** of fire, **possesses no conflict** with coldness.

The above expresses reasoning in which causes are in conflict. This implies the following: apprehension of an entity that conflicts with the cause, such as the closeness of fire, whose heat is experienced, being able to negate goosebumps, the result of cold; and the apprehension of the result that conflicts with the cause, such as smoke being able to negate goosebumps, the result of cold.

Together with the six types described above, this makes eight divisions of nonapprehension reasoning. *Ascertainment of Valid Cognition* adds to that the nonapprehension of the direct result, such as the nonexistence of smoke negating the existence of the direct cause of smoke, and the apprehension of an entity that conflicts with the result, such as the presence of fire negating the existence of the direct cause of coldness. This makes ten divisions.

> 6. **A conflicting result is also asserted as**
> **dependent upon time and place and so on.**
> **Elsewhere it would be erroneous,**
> **like ash to establish no coldness.**

It could be argued, "If the mere cause of fire cannot negate coldness, then does it not follow that the mere result of fire is also not able to negate coldness?"

Concerning a **result** of fire **conflicting** with coldness, its negating of coldness in certain places **is also asserted as dependent upon** circumstances of **time and place and so on**, in which its cause, fire, is nearby, and with smoke getting into the mouth and nose, for example, because this result of fire, in certain places, can negate coldness, and **elsewhere**, not characterized by those circumstances of time and place, **it would be** reasoning that is **erroneous** with regard to the ability to negate coldness. This is **like** using the conflicting result of **ash to establish** that there is **no coldness** in certain places.

Śākyabuddhi, in his commentary, states that the word "also" includes reasoning by result. The brahman, in his commentary, states, "Not only is the conflicting cause not a reason, but a simple conflicting result also is not a reason."

4. The Enumeration into Three Types

Extensive explanation of the enumeration into three types

1. Refuting assertions that there are other divisions of correct reasons
2. Refuting fallacious reasons as being correct reasons

Refuting assertions that there are other divisions of perfect reasons

1. Inferring forthcoming existence from a collection of causes is reasoning by way of nature
2. Inferring form from taste is reasoning by way of result

Inferring forthcoming existence from a collection of causes is reasoning by way of nature

7. **Inferring a result to be produced**
from the collection of causes
is described as being its nature
because of not depending on another.

If perfect reasons are ascertained as being of three types, then where does the inferring of the appropriateness of a result to arise from a collection of causes fit into these three?

Inferring the appropriateness of **a result**, such as a sprout, **to be produced** by using as reasoning the presence of **the collection of** the complete **causes** of a sprout is reasoning by way of nature establishing the appropriateness of a resultant sprout in certain places, because it is a correct reason for establishing that, and the appropriateness of there being a resultant sprout **is described as**

being its nature. This is because the appropriateness of there being a resultant sprout does **not depend on a** cause that is **other** than the causal collection, and it will arise from this collection as its substantial cause.

> 8. **The potential to become the result**
> **of a collection of causes is not definite.**
> **It is related to transformation,**
> **and there is the possibility of interference.**

Why is it not possible to infer the definite arising of the result from the collection of causes?

The complete **collection of causes** of a sprout that will become the continuum of a sprout has, in and of itself, **no definite** pervasion with the establishing of a definite arising of a resultant sprout, because its creation of a resultant sprout **is related to,** or depends upon, the perfect **transformation** of all subsequent **potential to become that result.** This follows because **there is the possibility of interference** in the interim.

Inferring form from taste is reasoning by result

> 9. **Comprehending form and so on from taste,**
> **which depend upon the same collection,**
> **is inferring the property of the cause.**
> **For example, by smoke, the transformation of firewood.**

How is the reasoning that infers the existence of form and so on from the presence of taste, which are not cause and effect, included in the three divisions?

Comprehending from the present **taste** of jaggery as a reason, the existence of **form** and tangibility **and so on** in a certain place, **which depend upon the same collection** of direct causes as the taste of jaggery, relies upon a reasoning by way of result, because by directly **inferring,** or establishing, on certain places that **the property of the cause** of that present taste—that is, a previous taste—has the capability to create present form, it becomes a perfect reason for establishing indirectly form existing simultaneously with it.[45] **For example,** by directly inferring from billowing **smoke** that its cause, fire, has the capability to create the heat arising from the firewood, it is then unmistaken with regard to **the transformation**—that is, heat—**of** the **firewood** that exists simultaneously with it.

10. **Without the engaged capability, taste would not exist,**
and that is the cause of another.
In this way, there is comprehending
of the past and simultaneously existing.

In this way, the present taste of jaggery is a perfect reason for **comprehending**, or establishing, **of** both a **past** taste of jaggery having the ability to create present form, **and** the **simultaneously existing** form of jaggery. This is because **without the engaged capability** of a previous taste of jaggery, the present **taste would not exist, and that** previous taste itself **is the cause**, or cooperative circumstance, **of** form that is **other** than that taste.

Therefore that cognition that comprehends form and so on from the reasoning of the presence of taste is **developed from reasoning by way of result**, which is the cause of that cognition, because it is the result that will be produced from reasoning by way of result.

Refuting fallacious reasons as being correct reasons

1. It is not possible to infer the result from uncollected causes
2. It is not possible to infer the features of the cause from the general result

It is not possible to infer the result from uncollected causes

11. **Inferring a result by uncollected causes**
is reasoning with remainder because of no capability,
like inferring desire from the body.

If the presence of the collected causes is a perfect reason by way of nature, one that establishes the appropriateness of the result to arise, then what kind of reason is that of dispersed causes that establish a result?

The **uncollected**, or dispersed, **causes** of a sprout used as a reason to **infer** the arising of a sprout as **a result** of those causes, on certain bases, is reasoning in which the reason is not seen in the incongruent class. Nevertheless, it **is reasoning with remainder**—that is, it is reasoning of indefinite pervasion. This is **because** these uncollected causes have **no capability** of producing a resultant sprout, and such reasoning is a reason established as a property of the subject.[46] It is **like**, for example, the Mīmāṃsaka[47] school's assertion that the uncollected causes of desire, such as **the body**, the sense faculties, mind, and so on, are presented as a reason to **infer** resulting **desire** and so on in a person.

It is not possible to infer the features of the cause from the general result

> 12. **Merely nonseeing within the incongruent class**
> **and seeing the generality of the result,**
> **understood as reasoning, is an apparent valid cognition,**
> **like the presence of desire and so forth from words.**

If the inferring of form from taste is reasoning by way of result, what kind of reasoning is the inferring of the features of a cause from the reasoning of a general result?

The Mīmāṃsaka and others **understand**, that is, hold, **merely the nonseeing** of the reason **within the incongruent class** to be perfect **reasoning**, in which **seeing**, or presenting as a reason, just **the generality of the result** to infer in certain places the features of the cause, such as grass in the case of fire, **is an apparent valid cognition**—that is, a reasoning of uncertain pervasion. This is because that which is being held as a reason is one that cannot negate existence within the incongruent class. It is **like**, for example, spoken **words**, which constitute a general result of the wish to speak, establishing **the presence of desire and so forth**,[48] which are features of the cause. "And so forth" refers to anger and so on.

The Indispensable Relationship

5. The Indispensable Relationship

Extensive explanation of the indispensable relationship

1. General explanation of the relationship
2. Commentary on the text

General explanation of the relationship

1. The way it is taught in *Ascertainment of Valid Cognition*
2. The way the relationship is taught in this text

The way it is taught in Ascertainment of Valid Cognition

First *inference for oneself* is defined, and it is established that such an inferential cognition is mistaken about its appearing object but is valid in regard to its engaged object. After that, the three criteria are identified. Then the text moves on to the three types of reasoning. First, reasoning by nonapprehension of that which should appear, together with its divisions, is explained. This is followed by reasoning by nonapprehension by way of nonappearance, together with a supplementary discussion. Next comes the definition of reasoning by way of nature, with its divisions, and ascertainment of the pervasion. This is taught by the verses beginning "Because of disintegration without a cause" (178a7/1.193).[49]

Then, reasoning by result is taught and the pervasion ascertained. This is taught by the verses beginning "If it exists without that" (1.34). Then the text teaches that the pervasion relationship of the two types of reasoning by affirmation must be ascertained by the ascertainment of the nature and of the cause and result. This is taught by the verse beginning "Forward and counter pervasion"

(182b5/1.38) and the single verse beginning "From the concomitance and negation" (182b6/1.31).

The single verse beginning "If the phenomenon possessed the cause of a separate entity" (182b7/1.33) is preceded by the connecting phrase "Furthermore." This is an explanation following on from the assertion that being a product may be substantially different from impermanence, but it is not fallible with regard to impermanence because it is not seen in the incongruent class, and it concludes with the line "By the reasoning causing the unknown to be known." That concludes the "Inference for Oneself" chapter.

The ascertainment of the number of types of perfect reasons and so forth is taught in the "Inference for Others" chapter. A brief overview and a detailed explanation of reasoning are features of the *Commentary on Valid Cognition.*

The way the relationship is taught in this text

In this text, in the sequential explanation of the four topics of the brief presentation, first comes the extensive explanation of the three types of reasoning, followed by the enumeration of reasoning by nonapprehension, and then the refutation of types of reasoning other than these. Supplementing that is the enumeration of the three types again, and more refutations of other types of reasoning.

Following on from that is the refutation of the assertion that merely not seeing the reason in the incongruent class establishes the counter pervasion. This leads on to the explanation that if the counter pervasion is not established from merely not seeing, an indispensable relationship is definitely necessary in order to establish the counter pervasion. After that, the teaching in the treatise that mere nonapprehension does not definitively establish nonexistence leads on to an extensive teaching on fallacious reasons.

This description is very coarse because it is evident that throughout this work, from beginning to end, the completion of a previous section induces the next section. The composer says, "Coherent, with methods that accord" (1.214), and so on, and he has applied this to his own composition.

Concerning the indispensable relationship, the explanation that by merely not seeing the reason in the incongruent class the counter pervasion is not established and that therefore "something remains" is taught by the two verses beginning "Mere nonseeing within the incongruent class" (1.13–14). That this is Ācārya Dignāga's position is taught by the following verse beginning "Within the three criteria of the reasoning also" (1.15).

For uncertain relationships other than the above, subsequent verses explain that if the counter pervasion is established by merely not seeing the reason in the incongruent class, this would contradict scriptural citations from our own tradition in six ways. It would contradict reason generally, and furthermore, in other traditions such an assertion is internally contradictory. These are taught, respectively, by the five verses beginning "As an antidote to the error" (1.16–20), by the single verse beginning "From the features of the land" (1.21), and by the verse beginning "A self, consciousness in the earth, and so on" (1.22).

If the relationship is established, the counter pervasion of the two affirming types of reason is established. If there is no relationship, neither the concomitant pervasion nor the counter pervasion of the affirming reasons is established. Therefore the relationships within the two affirming types of reasoning are to be established by way of examples, and through this the pervasion of the negation types of reasoning are also established. These points are taught, respectively, by the single verse beginning "By the entity being in relationship" (1.23), by the two verses beginning "If that is not so, how could the negation of one" (1.24–25), by the three verses beginning "Therefore, in these, the incongruent examples" (1.26–28), and by the two verses beginning "Therefore the nonexistence of the cause" (1.29–30).

This kind of indispensable relationship must be determined by ascertaining the cause and effect and the single nature. This is taught by the three verses beginning "From ascertaining entities of cause and effect" (1.31–33). How is the indispensable relationship ascertained by these two? The ascertaining of cause and effect in reasoning by result is explained in the verses beginning "Smoke is the result of fire" (1.34–38). For reasoning by nature, in the ascertainment of the relationship of sharing the same nature, just what this same-nature relationship constitutes is explained by the verses beginning "With nature also, if not existent" (1.39). The divisions of reasoning by nature that are to be ascertained are taught by the verse beginning "Nature that depends upon" (1.186). The valid cognitions that act as ascertainers are taught by the verses beginning "Because of disintegration without a cause" (1.193).

Therefore the two affirming types of reasoning are ascertained by the force of the two relationships. This is taught by the single verse beginning "Therefore any inferences that take entities" (1.197). Establishing the relationships within the two affirming types of reasoning also establishes the pervasions within the negating types of reasoning—this is expressed from the verse beginning "Because engaging has a prerequisite cognition" (1.198) up to "Spoken by the propounder of reasoning" (1.212).

Enjoy a feast of the unbiased ones!

Commentary on the text

1. Merely not seeing means the counter pervasion is faulty
2. Ascertainment of the relationship is essential for a faultless counter pervasion
3. That ascertainment is of two types
4. Extensive explanation of the nature of these two kinds of ascertainment

Merely not seeing means the counter pervasion is faulty

It could be asked, “Isn’t it the case that the generality of the result is not faulty with regard to the features of the cause because the reason is not to be seen in the incongruent class?

> 13. **Mere nonseeing within the incongruent class**
> **is not the absence of the fault,**
> **because the possibility of fault exists,**
> **like rice in the pot being cooked.**

The **mere nonseeing** of the reason **within the incongruent class is not** the ascertainment representing **the absence of the fault** that wonders if the reason exists in the incongruent class, **because there exists the possibility of the fault** that wonders if the reason exists in the incongruent class. It is **like** using the reason that **rice** left **in the** same cooking **pot** is similar to the cooked rice to establish that the leftover rice must **be cooked.**

The Naiyāyika ask, “If mere nonseeing leaves something remaining, what is the meaning of *remaining*?” In their own assertions they speak of establishing the result from the cause as a “possession of the previous,” establishing the cause from the result constituting “possession of a remainder,” and the kind of general seeing that, for example, a voice is established from the general phenomenon of “life.” However, this is not the meaning of *remaining*.

> 14. **That which demonstrates the counter pervasion**
> **by the mere nonseeing**
> **is said to have something remaining**
> **and is a cause for doubt.**

Here, **that** reasoning stating that a person who speaks is not omniscient because he speaks, thereby **demonstrating**, or establishing, **the counter pervasion by the mere nonseeing** of the reason in the counter pervasion, **is said to have**

something remaining, because the reason is established as a property of the subject, but **is a cause for doubt**, by engaging in the incongruent class with uncertainty.

Ascertainment of the relationship is essential for a faultless counter pervasion

1. The Ācārya states that the relationship must be ascertained
2. Stating that the counter pervasion is established without the relationship leads to extreme consequences
3. The pervasion is established through the force of the relationship

The Ācārya states that the relationship must be ascertained

> 15. **Within the three criteria of the reasoning also**
> **are the ascertainment antidotes to not being established,**
> **to an opposing existence, and to error.**
> **By this, it is stated.**

Ācārya Dignāga asserts that for reasoning to be correct, there must be the ascertainment of a relationship by way of entity, because without such a relationship there can be no comprehension. **By this, it is stated** that **within the three criteria of the reasoning also**, there must be **ascertainment** through the force of valid cognition. This is because these three criteria, which are (1) the reason as a property of the subject, (2) the concomitant pervasion, and (3) the counter pervasion, **are the antidotes**, respectively, (1) **to** the reason as a property of the subject **not being established**, (2) **to an opposing existence**, or conflicting reasoning, which also includes conflicting remainder reasoning, **and** (3) **to error**, meaning nonexclusive uncertain reasoning, and similarly, genuine remainder reasoning and exclusive uncertain reasoning.[50]

In *Compendium of Valid Cognition* he says, "That which is well established in both, will establish."[51] "Both" refers to the subject and the congruent classification. "Well established" means ascertained.

Some say that "By this" means "by him," referring to Dignāga.

6. The Necessity of the Relationship for the Counter Pervasion

Stating that the counter pervasion is established without the relationship leads to extreme consequences

1. Refutation by way of scripture in our own tradition
2. Refutation by way of nonexclusive entity-based reasoning
3. Refutation by way of it being the contradictory reasoning of other traditions

Refutation by way of scripture in our own tradition

1. The consequence that the counter pervasion would not have been taught
2. The consequence that reasoning with remainder would not be fallible
3. The consequence that the reason "possessing life" would create comprehension
4. The consequence that doubt would be reasoning
5. The consequence that by the reason "that which is heard" both are refuted
6. The consequence that the negation of a physical sensation would be correct

The consequence that the counter pervasion would not have been taught

16. **As an antidote to the error the incongruent is stated.**
If not seeing produces the result,

it would still result in comprehension,
although the statement would not be made.

Ācārya Īśvarasena[52] and others have asserted that the mere nonseeing of the reason in the incongruent class establishes the counter pervasion, and they assert that this is Ācārya Dignāga's position also. However, in [Dignāga's] *Entrance to Valid Cognition Reasoning*, it is said that the reasoning establishing the counter pervasion must be **stated** to the opponent within **the incongruent** example, **as an antidote to the error** of being unascertained. It would have to follow, therefore, that such a statement is meaningless, because for you merely **not seeing** the reason in the incongruent class is necessary for, or **produces the result** of, comprehension. **Although the** above necessary **statement would not be made, it would still result in comprehension.** If you agree, then this would contradict *Entrance to Valid Cognition Reasoning* when it states, "Stating both as antidotes at times of nonascertainment and conflict is correct."

17. **Even the words stating nonexistence**
would not establish complete nonexistence.
If the logic of the nonexistence is expressed,
at that time comes understanding of the nonexistence.

"Isn't it that the mere nonseeing of the reason leads to understanding, but in order to ascertain the nonexistence within the incongruent class, the above has to be stated?"

If mere nonseeing does not produce the understanding of nonexistence, then **even the words** of the reasoning, establishing the counter pervasion within the incongruent example, and **stating** that **the nonexistence** of the reason in the incongruent class, **would not establish the complete nonexistence** of the reason in the incongruent class, because that is stating that the reason is merely not seen within the incongruent class, but is not stating any reason proving the nonexistence.

"Isn't the same fault seen in you?"

At that time of producing a spoken syllogism that establishes the counter pervasion within the incongruent example, it will bring about the **understanding of the nonexistence** of the reason in the incongruent class, because it is a faultless statement of proof **expressing the logic of the nonexistence** of the reason within the incongruent class. This is a relationship by way of nature between the reason and the phenomenon to be established.

Explaining the meaning of "the incongruent is stated" (1.16) as referring to a statement of proof by way of incongruence would mean that you would have to accept the words "the reason does not exist in the incongruent class" to mean comprehending that the reason does not exist in the incongruent class. This would thereby contradict scripture everywhere, which refutes that the meaning can be established by words. Also, the way in which it would not become an "antidote to the mistake" is to be understood through speech.

The consequence that reasoning with remainder would not be fallible

> **18. If mere nonseeing were the counter,**
> **how could reasoning with remainder be erroneous?**
> **The counter pervasion would also be reasoning.**

If the **mere nonseeing** of the reason in the incongruent class **were** to establish definitively that it did not exist in **the counter**, or incongruent class, then **how could reasoning with remainder be erroneous?** For example, using fruit with a form similar to ripened fruit as a reason to prove that the remaining fruit is also ripe could not be fallible, because merely not seeing the reason in the incongruent class would be proof enough.

If you agree, then that would contradict Ācārya Dignāga, who said that using similar form and shape and so on to prove that the taste and so on will undoubtedly be similar is not valid reasoning. The above hypothesis, beginning "If the mere nonseeing of the reason in the incongruent class," is to be applied to the following opponents also.

The consequence that the reason "possessing life" would create comprehension

It follows **also** that the Naiyāyika reasoning that the presence of life and so forth used to establish the existence of a self in a living body **would be** perfect **reasoning**, because the reason is a property of the subject and is merely not seen in the incongruent class. This reason is one in which the mere nonseeing of it in both the congruent and the incongruent classes is superimposed as **the counter pervasion**. If you agree with this consequence, this would contradict the Ācārya, who called such reasoning *fallacious reasoning* and compared it to using "that which is heard" as a reason.[53]

The consequence that doubt would be reasoning

Applied to that unestablished, it could not be asserted.

If a reason in which there is doubt as to whether that reason exists in the incongruent class were **applied to** an **unestablished** reason, where there is doubt over whether it exists as a property of the subject, it would follow that **it could not be asserted** and it would not be correct to say that it is faulty in that it does not establish the counter pervasion, because it is the mere nonseeing of the reason in the incongruent class.

If you agree, that would contradict the Ācārya when he says, "The reason existing as a property of the subject is ascertained by both parties in the debate. Regarding the possibilities of its existing or not (and so on) in the congruent classification, one of them is to be stated."[54]

The meaning of this statement is that when the reason as a property of the subject is not established, is in doubt, or does not exist, for both or either of the two debating parties, it is a fault with regard to the subject as the basis of the argument. Likewise, even if the reason is established as a property of the subject as a basis, with regard to the counter pervasion, except for the case of not existing,[55] it has the fault of not being established and so forth in either the concomitant or counter pervasion.

If you respond by saying that the citation does not explain that having doubt with regard to the counter pervasion is at fault because it says "one of them," it is true that it does not say that the counter pervasion not existing is a fault, but it does not say that having doubt toward the counter pervasion is not a fault, because immediately following this citation, it says, "That which is ascertained in both, is established as true, or is refuted but being established in only one or the other or having doubt is not."[56] Elsewhere, he states that such a position is contradictory.

The consequence that by the reason "that which is heard" both are refuted

19. **A feature would become reasoning that precludes,**
    because of not being seen.
    "Would not another valid cognition invalidate that?"
    This is not nonexistence from mere nonseeing.
20. **Similarly, with another it can also be invalidated**
    by another valid cognition.

When establishing sound as impermanent or permanent, taking "that which is heard," an exclusive **feature** of the subject, as a reason, it would follow that the counter pervasion would be established for both impermanence and permanence, **because of** the mere **nonseeing** of that reason in both.[57] If you agree, that reason would **become reasoning that** has the power to **preclude** sound being impermanent and permanent, because whether you present reasoning to prove sound as impermanent or as permanent, both the reason as a property of the subject and the counter pervasion are complete. If you agree, this contradicts the Ācārya when he says, "Either way it is used, 'that which is heard' becomes reasoning that precludes."[58]

You might reply, "Such a reason cannot negate both impermanence and permanence existing in sound, because if both are negated, and if **another valid cognition** negated the possibility of a direct contradiction existing on a single base,[59] such a position **would be invalidated** by the definitive establishment of that valid cognition. Therefore it would be a cognition that is not completely validated."

Then it follows that **this** response **is not** a definitive establishment of **nonexistence** arising **from** the **mere nonseeing** of the reason within the incongruent class, because the reasoning of "that which is heard" negating both impermanence and permanence existing within sound is invalidated by another valid cognition. **Similarly**, it is possible that the definitive establishment of nonexistence by the mere nonseeing of **another** reason in the incongruent class **can also be invalidated by another valid cognition.**

The consequence that the negation of a physical sensation would be correct

> **Because it is unseen,**
> **physical sensation not found in the visible**
> **would not possess any mistake.**

The Vaiśeṣika, a non-Buddhist school, asserts that a neutral **physical sensation**[60] is solely a quality of the air element. They advanced the reasoning that such a sensation is **not** to be **found in the visible** elements of earth, water, and fire because a neutral touch cannot be seen. It would follow, then, that such reasoning is one that does **not possess any mistake** with regard to the counter pervasion **because** the reason **is** merely **unseen** in the incongruent class.

If you agree, it contradicts "The Ācārya says, in the chapter on the earth element, 'If mere nonseeing negates touch in the visible elements, that would be incorrect reasoning.'"[61]

Refutation by way of nonexclusive entity-based reasoning

> 21. **From the features of the land and so on,**
> **separate powers will be evident.**
> **Seeing in one of those is not reason**
> **for the definite existence of the same in others.**

If mere nonseeing were to establish nonexistence, it would follow that one mango looking similar to another mango that possesses a particular taste and power, because they are both mangoes, would possess that same taste and power. The counter pervasion to prove this would be complete because of the mere nonseeing of the reason in the incongruent class. If you agree, then it follows that this is correct perfect reasoning, because the reason existing in the subject and the counter pervasion are complete. You cannot agree with this, because **from the features** such as the quality **of the land** and how they have been cared for **and so on, separate powers** and tastes **will be evident** in the substance of the mangoes. Therefore, **seeing** the existence of a special taste and power **in one of those** mangoes **is not reasoning for the definite existence of the same** taste and power **in other** mangoes.

Refutation by way of it being the contradictory reasoning of other traditions

> 22. **A self, consciousness in the earth, and so on—**
> **how does not merely not apprehending**
> **establish the nonexistence of the reason?**

How does not merely not apprehending the reason in the incongruent class **establish the nonexistence of the reason** in the incongruent class? It does not, because generally, the nonapprehension of something does not conclusively establish its nonexistence. The reason here has to be accepted, because the Vaiśeṣika assert the existence of **a self** in a living body, the Lokāyata school asserts that **consciousness** exists **in the earth**, and as indicated by the term "**and so on**," the Sāṃkhya school asserts that the result exists in the cause even though it is not apprehended.

7. Establishing Pervasion through the Relationship

The pervasion is established through the force of the relationship

1. If the relationship exists, the counter pervasion is established
2. If the relationship does not exist, the concomitant pervasion and counter pervasion are not established
3. How the relationship is illustrated within an example
4. How this establishes the pervasion within reasoning by negation

If the relationship exists, the counter pervasion is established

23. **By the entity being in relationship**
with just that, the entity is lost.
Also, with the cause,
the result is not misleading.

Mere nonseeing does not establish the counter pervasion. Therefore, if the predicate—which is **the** very **entity** of the reason, having an intrinsic **relationship** with **just** the existence of **that** entity held as a reason—is negated, **the** very **entity** of the reason **is lost**. For example, if impermanence, which has an intrinsic relationship with "being a product," is negated, then being a product is also negated.

The word "**also**"[62] leads to the next point. **With** the negation of the phenomena to be established that is **the cause** of that which is held as the reason, the result, which is the reasoning, will be negated, because in the concomitant pervasion and the counter pervasion **the result is not misleading** with regard to the cause. For example, by negating fire, the cause of smoke, the resulting smoke is also negated.

If the relationship does not exist, the concomitant pervasion and counter pervasion are not established

> 24. **If that is not so, how could the negation of one**
> **be the negation of the other?**
> **Does saying that people don't have horses**
> **mean they also don't have cattle?**
>
> 25. **Similar to that, because one thing is nearby,**
> **how does another come to be nearby?**
> **How can saying that some people have cattle**
> **mean that they also have horses?**

If that is not so, and there is no establishment of the relationship between reason and predicate, then **how could the negation of one**, which is the phenomenon to be established, **be the negation of the other,** which is the reason? It could not, because there is no relationship between the reason and the phenomenon to be established.

It is similar if you **say that** some **people don't have horses—does** this **mean they don't also have cattle?** The existence of cattle, which has no relationship to the existence of horses, is not negated. **Similar to that** non-negation, **because one thing is nearby**, or existing, **how does another**, as a phenomenon to be established, **come to be nearby**, or existing? It does not. The reason has no relationship with the phenomenon to be established. For example, **how can saying that some people have cattle mean that they also have horses?** It cannot.

How the relationship is illustrated within an example

1. Even if the incongruent example does not exist, it is understood through reasoning
2. The reasoning on the example is taught to the unaware
3. The way of presenting the two statements of proof to those who understand the reasoning

Even if the incongruent example does not exist, it is understood through reasoning

> 26. **Therefore, in these, the incongruent examples**
> **are not asserted as definite objective bases,**

> **because even if they are not, from the expression**
> **that it does not exist, it will be comprehended.**

In this way, it is through the power of the natural relationship that the concomitant pervasion and the counter pervasion are established. Therefore, for there to be a comprehension of that which is to be proven by the reasoning, that natural relationship must be one of possession of an identical nature or of cause and effect and no other, and both of them are taught with examples. The concomitant pervasion must be taught with a congruent example and the counter pervasion with an incongruent example.

"But for teaching the counter pervasion, does the incongruent example have to be established as an entity?"

The relationship establishes the counter pervasion. **Therefore, in these** two affirming types of reasoning, **incongruent examples are not asserted as definite objective bases**, or established as entities, in the determination of the counter pervasion, **because even if those** incongruent examples **are not** established as entities, **from the expression** of the reasoning **that it**, the reason, **does not exist** in the incongruent class, the counter pervasion **will be comprehended.**

The explanation by most past commentators that although the incongruent example may not be established as an entity, it will be comprehended from the phrase "they are not" does not bring out the connotation of the word "even." Also, the autocommentary between this and the next verse only has the words "in this way" as a connecting phrase. Therefore, they have not understood how the phrase "from the expression that it does not exist" of the preceding verse is to be explained by the following verse.

The reasoning on the example is taught to the unaware

> 27. **Using the examples, its nature**
> **and the entity that is the cause**
> **are taught to the unaware.**
> **For the wise ones, only the reasoning is stated.**

So what is this reasoning? This is the reasoning that teaches, **using the example** of a pot, that impermanence **is the nature** of being a product, **and** using the example of a kitchen hearth, that fire exists as **the entity that is the cause** of that smoke. These relationships of a product having a same-entity relationship with impermanence and fire having a causal relationship with smoke **are**

taught to the unaware debate opponent, because the reasoning for the two kinds of opponents to understand these two types of relationships exist within the examples.

This also means that when the incongruent example is not established as an entity, because the concomitant pervasion is shown to exist on the congruent example, the counter pervasion will be established.

The way of presenting the two statements of proof to those who understand the reasoning

The wise who understand the pervasion relationship in the congruent example taught above will thereby remember the general pervasion. And **for** those wise **ones** who from the beginning have kept in mind and not forgotten the general pervasion, the generation of an inferential cognition does not depend upon a statement of proof expressing the pervasion; for the generation of such a cognition, it is sufficient **to state only the reasoning** that the reason is a property of the subject.

> 28. **Therefore, if the relationship is understood,**
> **then by stating one of the two,**
> **the other is recalled,**
> **and the meaning is grasped.**

But what is to be done for those unaware opponents who understand the pervasion relationship using the example but are unable to recall the general pervasion? The relationship is taught by the examples. **Therefore, if** an opponent **understands the relationship** by way of the example but does not recall the general pervasion, the pervasion must be made to them because they need to recall the general pervasion.

Do both pervasions have to be stated? For such an opponent, **by stating one of the two** pervasions, **the other** unspoken pervasion **will be recalled**, because this will cause them to **grasp its meaning**.

Concerning the above, some say that "wise ones" are those who merely understand that the relationship exists in the example and assert that for them there is no need to state the pervasion. This is not correct. Merely knowing the relationship is within the example is not the meaning of "wise ones" here. Also, the pervasion would have to be made explicit for them to recall the general pervasion.

Some explain the verse preceding the above as follows: Stating that if those phenomena do not exist, those reasons also will not exist will produce an understanding of the counter pervasion. If it is understood from such a statement, how is it to be stated? The way it is stated for those who are not wise is taught by the lines beginning "Using the examples, its nature" (1.27). For those who are wise, it is stated as taught by the line beginning "For the wise ones." They explain the meaning of "only the reasoning is stated" as a valid cognition that ascertains the reason as a property of the subject.

However, this is not correct. It is contradictory to identify the stating of the counter pervasion as the stating of the concomitant pervasion within the example. Also, "mere understanding"—as the opposite of "unaware"—is not synonymous with "wise" as used here. Also, to explain "only the reasoning is stated" as the ascertainment that the reason is a property of the subject would mean that the pervasion, as expressed in the line "by stating one of the two," would also have to be an ascertainment.

Our own position is the thinking of the *Commentary on Valid Cognition* autocommentary and of the root text and autocommentary of Sakya Paṇḍita's *Treasure of Reasoning*. Other Tibetan commentators have not explained these three verses (1.26–28) as presented above.

How this establishes the pervasion within reasoning by negation

> 29. **Therefore the nonexistence of the cause and of nature**
> **are also reasons for establishing certain instances.**
> **Moreover, with the reasoning of being apprehended,**
> **nonapprehension will be established.**

A result and a phenomenon possessing a particular nature are both infallible with regard to the cause and to that nature itself. **Therefore the nonexistence of the cause**, such as fire, **and of nature**, such as "tree," **are also** perfect **reasons for establishing certain instances** of the nonexistence of fire or of an *agaru* tree in certain places, because the three criteria for such an establishment are complete. **Moreover, with the reasoning** that it would **be apprehended** if it existed, the **nonapprehension** of a pot is a reason that **will establish** the definite nonexistence of a pot in certain places where it should appear, because all three criteria for such an establishment are complete.

The autocommentary says, "This kind of reasoning is explained as being the reasoning of a cognition of negation, because such a nonapprehension is in the nature of being a reasoning that negates. The nonapprehension of the cause and of the pervader are the reasonings of both."

> 30. **Nonapprehension, therefore, is explained**
> **as being of three types, but there are many types:**
> **noncognition, cognition of the conflicting, and so on,**
> **by way of the divisions of syllogisms.**

This reasoning by way of **nonapprehension** in terms of the relationship **is therefore explained** and classed **as being of three types.** However, **there are many types:** the **noncognition** of the cause, the pervader, and the nature make three; **cognition of a conflicting** cause, pervader, and nature to make six; and the phrase "**and so on**" indicates the apprehension of a conflicting result and the apprehension of a result that conflicts with the cause, to make eight in total **by way of the divisions of syllogisms.**

That ascertainment is of two types

1. The two types of ascertainment
2. The consequences of those two types not being present

The two types of ascertainment

> 31. **From ascertaining entities of cause and effect**
> **or from ascertaining the same nature**
> **comes the ascertainment of the indispensable relationship,**
> **not from merely nonseeing or seeing.**

If the ascertainment of an indispensable relationship is necessary for a perfect reasoning, by what is that ascertainment made? **Ascertainment** of the indispensable relationship of the two types of affirmation reasoning does **not** come **from merely not seeing** the reason in the absence of the predicate **or** from merely **seeing** it in the presence of the predicate. This is because **the ascertainment of the indispensable relationship comes from** the valid cognition of **the ascertainment of** the reason and the predicate to be **entities of cause and effect or of the same nature.**

The consequences of those two types not being present

> 32. **If other, what ascertainment is there of another**
> **ascertaining the existence of another?**

> **A phenomenon possessing the reason of separate entity**
> **would be like cloth becoming colored.**

In the category of reasoning by way of result, **if** the reason and predicate are **other** than being established—that is, they are not established—as having a causal relationship, then **what ascertainment is there of another** that is smoke **ascertaining the existence of another** that is fire? There would be none because smoke is a separate substance, having no relationship with fire.

In the category of reasoning by way of nature, if the reason and predicate are other than being of one nature, and impermanence, for example, was **a phenomenon that possessed the reason of,** or was a result of, a **separate entity** cause that arose after the cause that created a product, then it follows that the fact of being a product would not mean that it was definitely in the nature of disintegration, because its own disintegration would have to rely upon a separate and distinct cause that arose after its own cause. Reliance does not produce ascertainment. It **would be like cloth,** which relies upon dye **to become colored.** It is not definite that such a cloth will become dyed.

> 33. **If the phenomenon possessed the cause of a separate entity,**
> **it is not the cause because it arose after.**
> **If it were the result,**
> **how could there be an ascertainment?**

Furthermore it would follow that impermanence, as **the phenomenon,** or predicate, to be established, would be substantially separate from being a product because it would be that which **possessed the cause of**—that is, was the result of—a cause that was **a separate entity** that arose after the cause that created a product. If you agree, then is impermanence the cause of a product or the result of a product? If you assert the former, the consequence is that impermanence **is not the cause** of a product **because it arose after** the product. **If it were the result, how could there be an ascertainment** of the pervasion that establishes the existence of impermanence in certain places because of the reasoning of there being a product? It would follow that there could not be any such ascertainment because impermanence is the result of being a product.

8. Extensive Explanation of Ascertainment by Nature and Result

Extensive explanation of the nature of these two kinds of ascertainment

1. Applying the direct relationship to affirming reasonings
2. Applying the counter relationship to negation reasonings

Applying the direct relationship to affirming reasonings

1. Explanation of the ascertainment of the cause and result in reasoning by result
2. Explanation of the ascertainment of the one nature in reasoning by nature
3. Ascertainment of the two types of affirming reasonings by the force of the relationship

Explanation of the ascertainment of the cause and result in reasoning by result

1. Explanation of the valid cognition that ascertains cause and result
2. Refuting that the result is fallible with regard to the cause
3. Summary of how the result is infallible with respect to the cause

Explanation of the valid cognition that ascertains cause and result

34. **Smoke is the result of fire,**
following on as the quality of result.
If it exists without that,
it is beyond having a cause.

"Doesn't it follow that smoke is not correctly cognized as being infallible with regard to fire, because it is not correctly cognized as infallible from merely seeing it in the presence of fire and merely not seeing it in the absence of fire?"

There is no pervasion here. **Smoke is** suitable to be designated as **the result of fire** because **its existence** or nonexistence necessarily **follows** from the directly affecting existence or nonexistence of fire. There is pervasion here because that which necessarily follows on from the existence of a directly affecting cause is **the** general **quality**, or characteristic, **of result.**

Refuting that the result is fallible with regard to the cause

1. Refutation by way of consequence
2. Refutation by way of analysis

Refutation by way of consequence

The Vaiyākaraṇa (Grammarian) school says that results, in terms of concomitant and counter pervasions, are fallible with regard to their causes, because smoke, which is the result of fire, arises from a termite hill even though there is no fire. In that case, it follows that this smoke **is beyond having a cause**—that is, it does not have a cause, because **it exists** and is **without** a cause.

> 35. **It would always exist or not exist**
> **because it would not depend on another.**
> **Entities arising occasionally**
> **do so from circumstance.**

If you agree, it follows that smoke must **always exist or not exist** at all—that is, it could not exist only occasionally—**because it would not depend on other** circumstances. The former consequence pervades because whatever **entities arise occasionally do so from circumstance.**

Refutation by way of analysis

> 36. **If a termite hill is in the nature of fire,**
> **then that hill itself is fire.**
> **However, it is not in the nature of fire.**
> **How could smoke arise from it?**

Is a termite hill in the nature of fire or not? **If** it is, **then** it follows that the smoke is not rising from a termite hill that is without fire, because **the hill itself is fire.** If it is not, then **how could smoke arise from** a termite hill? **However, it** could not because that termite hill **is not in the nature of fire.**

> 37. **Fire, in the nature of being the cause of smoke,**
> **possesses that specific potential.**
> **If smoke arose from that which is not the cause of smoke,**
> **it would exist without cause.**

This pervades[63] because only the existence of **fire,** which is **in the nature of being the cause of smoke, possesses the specific potential** to create that smoke, whereas the nonexistence of fire does not. Furthermore, **it would** follow that this smoke **exists without any cause,** because it is **smoke that arises from that which is not the cause of smoke.**

Summary of how the result is infallible with respect to the cause

> 38. **That entity has that cause and therefore**
> **does not arise from the incompatible.**
> **From the concomitance and negation,**
> **it is seen in the concomitance with that.**
> **This is a summarizing verse.**

That which is the **entity** of smoke **does not arise from** a termite hill, which is **incompatible** with fire, **because it has the cause** of, or is the result of, **that** fire. This is because **it is seen** that smoke arises or not **in** dependence upon **the concomitance or negation** of fire, and that the existence or absence of fire is the concomitant creator or negator of smoke. **This** stanza **is a summarizing verse.**

Explanation of the ascertainment of the one nature in reasoning by way of nature

1. Establishment of the same-nature relationship, which is that to be ascertained
2. An explanation of the divisions of this type of reason, the base of the ascertainment
3. Explanation of non-dependence reasoning, which is the ascertainer

Establishment of the same-nature relationship, which is that to be ascertained

1. Establishing the indispensable same-nature relationship
2. Refuting the argument that the reason and the phenomenon to be established are not separate

Establishing the indispensable same-nature relationship

"The causal relationship is established with reasoning by way of a result, but with reasoning by way of nature, what is it whose absence means no arising?"

This has already been explained by the verse (23) beginning, "By the entity being in relationship . . . ." However, some argue that one part of this assertion is being used as reasoning.[64] Therefore the verses on a presentation of exclusion are taught to refute this argument.

> 39. **With nature also, if not existent, there would be no occurrence**
> **by way of the relationship with the mere existence.**
> **If that was not existing, that entity would be nonexistent**
> **because of being not separate.**

To reiterate: **With** reasoning by way of **nature also**—using, for example, "being a product" to establish sound as impermanent—there is an indispensable relationship of **there being no occurrence if not existent**, because the phenomenon to be established and **the mere existence** of the reason itself have an intrinsic **relationship**. Therefore a product, which has the very **entity** of impermanence, **would be nonexistent if** impermanence **did not exist because** they are one, with **no separate** nature.

Exclusion and Universals

9. Exclusion of Others and the One Conceptualized as Many

Refuting the argument that the reason and predicate are not separate

It will be asked, "However, whatever is a product is necessarily impermanent because these two are not of a separate nature. If that is agreed, then isn't one part of the assertion that product establishes sound as impermanent being used as a reason?"[65]

The response to this is in two parts:

1. Entity exclusion by way of verbal expression and conceptualization
2. Non-entity exclusion by way of verbal expression (1.185)

Exclusion of non-entities by way of verbal expression

1. Establishing an object-possessor engaging by exclusion
2. Establishment of the direct object as an exclusion (1.134)

Establishing an object-possessor engaging by exclusion

1. Both verbal expressions and conceptualization engage by exclusion
2. In particular, how verbal expressions engage (1.92)
3. Both engage with universals (1.134)

Both verbal expressions and conceptualization engage by exclusion

1. Specific explanation
2. General explanation (1.76)

Specific explanation

1. Though one entity, verbal expression and conceptualization divide up and engage by exclusion

2. Though separate, verbal expression and conceptualization gather as one and engage by exclusion (1.68)

Though one entity, verbal expression and conceptualization divide up and engage by exclusion

1. How the reason and that which is endowed with the reason are valid with regard to the excluded object
2. Establishing how verbal expression and conceptualization engage by exclusion (1.43)
3. Refuting arguments based on the analysis of reversal and isolation (1.59)

How the reason and that which is endowed with the reason are valid with regard to the excluded object

40. **Because all entities dwell by nature**
in their own individual entities,
they are the support of being isolated
from entities, both compatible and other.

In reasoning by way of nature, the reason and the predicate are not of a separate nature, but it is not the case that one part of the assertion is being used as a reason, because the reason, the predicate, and the subject have distinct isolates.[66] How is this possible? **All** intrinsically existent **entities**, such as sound, **are the support of** many isolates. These have been **isolated from entities** of **compatible** kind **and** from **other** phenomena of incompatible kind. This is **because** these phenomena **dwell by nature** unmixed with another, without conceptual superimposition, **in their own individual entities.**

41. **Therefore an entity is isolated from varieties.**
By this reason is it separated into classes.
Because of this feature,
it will definitely be cognized.

This reason explains that these many isolates are separated out by a conceptual mind that engages correctly in the process of exclusion. The phrase "all entities" (in verse 40) indicates that each entity can have many isolates. **Therefore an entity** of sound **is isolated from varieties** of phenomena that are not sound but of compatible kind and of incompatible kinds such as permanence and non-product. **By this reason it** can be **separated** out **into** the many **classes**, or isolates, such as sound, product, and impermanence, because they all exist within the entity of sound. Here "classes" is synonymous with "isolated."

Because of this feature of sound of being capable of having many isolates, sound **will definitely be cognized** as being impermanent from the reason of being a product, because sound is one, but from the perspective of exclusion it is being taught that it can exist as the reason, the predicate, and the subject. They are of one entity but distinct isolates.

> 42. **A particular feature understood by a particular dharma**
> **is not understood by something other than that.**
> **Therefore they exist as separate aspects.**

Therefore sound, product, and impermanence, which are in reality the subject, the reason, and the predicate in the logic that proves sound to be impermanent by the reason of it being a product, **exist as separate aspects**, and **a particular feature** of momentariness existing on sound that is **understood by a particular dharma** going by the name of *impermanence* **is not understood by something other than that**, such as that going by the name of *product*. Therefore this should be applied to the other two also.

Having negated the assertion that impermanence is a separate substantial entity that arises after the coming into existence of a product, which is put forward by the Buddhist Vātsīputrīya school and others, it is established that they are of one nature. If that is so, the argument runs that it is incorrect to separate the reason and the predicate. It is in answer to that argument that this presentation on exclusion, in which isolates can be separated, is given. It is not given to establish that product and impermanence as one entity and as separate isolates are not dependent on each other. Therefore the assertion by some scholars that the relationship of same nature means to be of one nature and separate isolates, and that the first verse (1.39) establishes their single nature whereas the verses from "all entities" establish separate isolates, may sound correct; however, they have not understood the intent of the text.

10. Verbal Expressions and Conceptualization Engage by Exclusion

Establishing how verbal expression and conceptualization engage by exclusion

1. Reasoning and inferential cognition engage by way of exclusion
2. Subsequent ascertainment engages by way of exclusion
3. How other verbal expressions validly engage by exclusion
4. How it is not correct that they engage by affirmation
5. Refuting that they engage by affirmation

Reasoning and inferential cognition engage by way of exclusion

1. Presenting the proof for engagement by exclusion
2. The consequences of asserting that it engages by affirmation
3. Summary of the points of engagement by exclusion and affirmation

Presenting the proof for engagement by exclusion

1. Engaging by exclusion is not pursued in order to see intrinsically existent phenomena
2. Engaging by exclusion is pursued in order to exclude superimposition
3. Verses that summarize the above

Engaging by exclusion is not pursued in order to see intrinsically existent phenomena

43. **With a phenomenon whose nature is one with that,**
    which are directly experienced,

> **what other parts not seen would there be**
> **if examined by inferential valid cognitions?**

It might be asked, "If inferential cognitions, in dependence upon verbal expression and reasoning, engage by way of exclusion, how is that established?"

In the statement that engaging is in order to exclude any superimposition upon something previously experienced by a direct perception, the phrase "something previously experienced" refers to the following. **With** regard to **a phenomenon** like sound, whose nature of impermanence is one with that sound, and **which are experienced** by a **direct** and valid aural perception, **what other parts** that are **not seen** by that sensory valid perception **would there be if examined by inferential valid cognitions?** There would be none, because all phenomena of the same substance and duration as that sound are directly and simultaneously cognized by that direct perception.

Engaging by exclusion is pursued in order to exclude superimposition

> 44. **Like regarding mother-of-pearl as silver**
> **because of seeing similar form,**
> **one does not apply other qualities**
> **through reasons of being mistaken.**

"In that case, after a valid direct perception, how does inferential cognition engage?"

After a valid direct perception of sound has experienced impermanent sound, it is necessary to engage an inferential cognition in order to cognize that sound is impermanent. If **one did not apply other qualities** to sound, such as permanence, **through reasons of being mistaken** with regard to its impermanence because of the occurrence of other similar phenomena, then there would be no need to engage an inferential cognition in order to cognize that sound is impermanent after the direct perception. However, because other similar phenomena do appear, then **like** mistakenly **regarding mother-of-pearl as silver because of seeing** its **similar** white **form**, one mistakenly regards sound as permanent. Therefore, to exclude that, after the direct perception, it is necessary to engage an inferential cognition in order to cognize that sound is impermanent.

Verses that summarize the above

> 45. **Therefore, when beholding an entity,**
> **all its qualities are seen.**
> **Not ascertaining because of being mistaken,**
> **one engages in order to establish.**
> **This is a summarizing verse.**

Therefore, because of those reasons, the inferential cognition and reasoning that establishes sound as impermanent engages by way of exclusion. This is because, **by beholding an entity** such as sound by way of a direct perception, **all qualities**, such as impermanence, **are seen**—that is, they are present. Therefore engaging by way of exclusion is not pursued in order to experience them. However, through the fact of **not ascertaining** that sound is impermanent **because of being mistaken, one engages** by exclusion **in order to establish** that. **This** verse **is a summarizing verse.**

The consequences of asserting that it engages by affirmation

> 46. **If an inferential cognition also apprehended an actual entity,**
> **all qualities would be apprehended**
> **because it ascertains one quality.**
> **With exclusion, this fault does not follow.**

If, like a direct perception, **an inferential cognition also apprehended an actual entity** such as sound by way of affirmation, it follows that an inferential cognition that perceives the impermanence of sound would **apprehend all** the **qualities** of the sound, such as its being a product, **because it ascertains** by way of affirmation the **one quality** of sound such as impermanence. If you accept this consequence, then there would be no other engaging valid cognitions.

The response might be "But doesn't the same apply to your position?"

With engagement by **exclusion** as pursued by inferential cognitions, when such an inferential cognition apprehends the one quality of impermanence, **this** ensuing **fault**, that it would apprehend all qualities, **does not follow**, because inferential cognitions engage specifically to exclude superimpositions.

Summary of the points of engagement by exclusion and affirmation

> 47. **Therefore, in this way, it can be declared that**
> **reasoning is an excluding object-possessor.**
> **Otherwise, once the subject has been established,**
> **what other phenomena, not established, could there be?**

Engaging by affirmation would have these faults, whereas engaging by exclusion would not. **Therefore, in this way,** as explained above, **it can be declared that** an inferential cognition that depends upon **reasoning is an excluding object-possessor,**[67] because **otherwise,** if it engaged by way of affirmation, then after a **subject**, such as sound, were experienced by a direct perception, it would be impossible to engage reasoning and inference to establish sound as impermanent, because **once that** sound **has been established** by a direct perception, **what other phenomena could there be**—such as impermanence, which is an entity of that sound—that are **not established** by that direct cognition? There would be none.

Some apply this verse to an immediate inferential cognition,[68] but this contradicts the autocommentary, which states that this is a summarizing verse.

Subsequent ascertainment engages by way of exclusion

> 48. **Even in some experiences where consciousness**
> **is a conceptual consciousness apprehending a universal,**
> **it has exclusion as its mode of operation,**
> **merely not superimposing separate aspects.**

It could be argued, "If you assert that an inferential cognition engages through exclusion by way of excluding superimposition, then it would follow that the **consciousness** that ascertains the color blue, **even in some** faultless **experiences** of blue color by a direct perception, would not be an engagement by exclusion because there is no superimposition to be excluded. You cannot agree with this premise because the ascertaining cognition **is a conceptual consciousness apprehending a universal**, and you assert that this type of consciousness engages by exclusion."

An ascertaining cognition of the color blue **has exclusion as its mode of operation**, because for as long as its operation is active, the person in whose mental continuum this ascertaining cognition exists **does not superimpose**

aspects separate from its particular mode of ascertaining, and it is an ascertainment capable of just that.

> 49. **The ascertainment and the superimposing consciousness**
> **possess the natures of negating and that which is negated.**
> **Therefore this consciousness is known as one**
> **that engages by isolation from superimposition.**

The reason is valid: **This** consciousness ascertaining the color blue is a **consciousness known as one that engages** its object **by** way of **isolation from superimposition** of aspects that are separate from its particular mode of ascertaining, because with regard to a single object **this ascertainment** and **the consciousness that superimposes** mutually **possess the natures of negating and that which is negated.**

How other verbal expressions validly engage by exclusion

> 50. **To exclude any number of superimposed aspects,**
> **ascertaining cognitions and verbal expressions**
> **will have separate modes of operation**
> **solely in that number.**

Ascertaining cognitions and verbal expressions that possess their objects of impermanence and of being a product, both of which exist within the subject sound, **will have separate modes of operation** and are not synonyms,[69] because in order **to exclude** within sound **any number of superimposed aspects** such as non-product and permanence, they will engage **solely in that number** of phenomena to be excluded.

How it is not correct that they engage by affirmation

> 51. **Other than that, if a single verbal expression or cognition**
> **were to pervade a single entity,**
> **others would not be objects, and therefore**
> **they would be synonymous.**

Other than engaging in order to separate from superimpositions, **if a single verbal expression**, such as "a pot is a product," **or** a single ascertaining **cognition**

were to pervade—that is, engage—by way of affirmation a **single** partless **entity** such as a pot, then **other** phenomena not apprehended as objects by the verbal expression and concept "a pot is a product" **would not be objects** apprehended by any other verbal expressions and concepts either, because this verbal expression and concept apprehends all features of a pot.

If you agree, then the phrase "a pot is impermanent" **would therefore be synonymous** with "a pot is a product," because they would be separate object-possessors each with an object not separate from the object of the other phrase.

11. Refuting that They Engage by Affirmation

Refuting that they engage by affirmation

1. Stating the assertion
2. Explaining the refutation
3. Negating faults

Stating the assertion

> 52. **According to those, the cognition apprehends**
> **the features as various separate entities.**
> **The part that brings about the distinct features**
> **has a nature inseparable from the potentials.**

According to those of the Vaiśeṣika school, **the features** of a pot, such as being a product and impermanence, are **various** related substantial **entities**, and they are also substantially **separate** from the substantial entity that is the pot possessing these features. Therefore the conceptual **cognition apprehends** each of the features and the holder of the features individually and will not apprehend anything else. Alternatively, this conceptual mind will apprehend the holder of the features characterized by its individual features but will not apprehend it as being characterized by anything else. Therefore, they say, these verbal expressions and concepts engage by way of affirmation and are not synonymous.

Explaining the refutation

The holder of the features must possess the potentials to bring about the various features. Therefore, the pot, as holder of the features, is **the part**, or cause, **that brings about the distinct features.** Is the **nature** of that pot **inseparable from those potentials** or is it other than those potentials?

> 53. **If the nature is apprehended in its entirety,**
> **which particulars brought about will not be ascertained?**
> **They are connected to the very nature.**
> **If one is known, both are apprehended.**

If it is the former, it would follow that the consciousness that ascertains the pot ascertains all the potentials that the pot possesses, because all those potentials and **the nature** of the pot, with which they share the same substantiality, are ascertained and **apprehended in** their **entirety** or, in other words, by way of affirmation. **If** you agree, then **which particulars brought about** by the pot **will not be ascertained?** It would follow that they are all ascertained.

The response might be, "Is it not the case that when the possessor of the features is ascertained, the *potentials*, which are of the same substance as that possessor, are also ascertained, but the *features*, which are separate from that possessor of the features, are not ascertained?"

If the pot, as the possessor of the features, is ascertained by way of affirmation, it follows that the possessor of the features is also ascertained as being that which brings about the features, because **those** potentials, which are possessed by the possessor of the features and which bring about the features, **are connected to the very nature** of the possessor of the features, meaning that they are substantially one.

If you agree, then it follows that **if** the ascertaining cognition apprehending the pot as the possessor of the features **knows one**—referring to the one feature possessor bringing about the features, then **it apprehends both**—referring to the features being brought about by the possessor of the features. This is because if it is not ascertained that the features are brought about by the feature possessor, then the possessor is not ascertained as being that which brings about the features. For example, if you don't know the servants, you don't know the master.

> 54. **If the potentials of phenomena were separate,**
> **what are they to that? It would not bring them about.**
> **If it did, they would be endless.**

It might be argued: "**If the potentials** that bring about the various **phenomena** of the features **were separate** from the possessor of those features, then the above fault would not occur."

What are those potentials **to that** possessor of the features? It would follow that they have no relationship to it because they are substantially separate from the possessor of the features, and the possessor of the features **would not bring about those** potentials.

You might not accept the reason, stating that it is the case that it does bring about those potentials. However, **if it did**, the possessor of the features **would** have potentials that are **endless** because the potentials that bring about the features would also need to be brought about.[70]

> 55. **If held as that which brings about one,**
> **that is seen and is not other than the unseen.**
> **Therefore, if it apprehends, it apprehends all.**

Therefore it must be asserted that the potentials are one with the possessor of the features. If that is so—if by the ascertainment "a pot is a product," a possessor of features **is held as that which brings about one** feature—then it would follow that this cognition would hold all the potentials that bring about other features not desired to be seen, because **that** pot, as possessor of the features, **is seen** by way of affirmation and that possessor of the features is **not other than** all those potentials that bring about other features. This is because it is of one nature with them.

If you agree, then if an ascertaining cognition that ascertains a pot apprehends the holder of the features by way of apprehending one quality, it follows that it apprehends all features, because **if it apprehends** it as bringing about one feature, **it apprehends** it as bringing about **all** features.

Negating faults

> 56. **If, to negate error, it is asserted**
> **that others are also apprehended,**
> **these exist as precluding object-possessors.**
> **Moreover, that which is other would be similar,**
> 57. **because it engages its object without superimpositions.**
> **Furthermore, whatever other entities there are,**
> **how could they be the objects?**
> **This ascertainment does not ascertain them.**

It could be **asserted**, "If the pot, as holder of the features, is apprehended by way of one of its features such as existing as a product, this means **that** all **other** features **are also apprehended**, but that by itself does not generate ascertainment. Therefore it is possible that there will be **error**, or superimposition, generated in dependence upon other features such as impermanence, and in order **to negate** that, other verbal expressions and valid cognitions are employed. Therefore they are not synonyms."

However, it would follow that **these** subsequent verbal expressions and cognitions do **exist as precluding**, or excluding, **object-possessors** because they are verbal expressions and cognitions that engage in order to exclude superimpositions. **Moreover**, it would follow that the cognition that ascertains the pot as a product, **which is other** than the subsequent verbal expressions and cognitions, **would be similar** in engaging by exclusion, **because** for as long as its operation is active, **it** will be a cognition that **engages its object without superimpositions** outside its own mode of ascertainment. **Furthermore, whatever other** properties **there are**, such as the impermanence of the pot, **how could they be the** conceived **objects**[71] of the cognition ascertaining a pot as a product? It follows that they could not be, because **this** cognition is an **ascertainment** and it **does not ascertain** the impermanence of the pot.

It might be argued, "In that case, the impermanence of the pot and so on are not objects of a direct perception of a pot, because such a cognition does not ascertain these phenomena."

Response: That does not follow, because the ascertainment above is distinguished by reasoning, and that is not found in direct perception.

"Then doesn't it follow that direct perception do not know any of its own objects?"

> 58. **Direct perception apprehends**
> **by negating features as parts.**
> **However, there exist circumstances**
> **for knowing, and that is knowing.**

A **direct perception apprehends** a pot, for example, in which the **features**—being a product, impermanence, and so on—are **negated as** being separate **parts**, and therefore there are ultimately no distinctions in the knowing cognition. **However**, in terms of designation, there is a distinction between what is and what is not known. **There exist** conducive **circumstances for knowing**—

that is, ascertaining—the features of a pot, **and that** absence of error **is** conventionally designated ***knowing***. For the opposite, when these circumstances are not there, that is *not knowing*.

The circumstances conducive to ascertainment include a cognition's clarity, familiarity, appropriateness, interest, and so on. Obstructing circumstances would be things like remoteness from those conducive conditions, cognitive impairment, and so on.

12. Reversal and Isolation

Refuting arguments based on the analysis of reversal and isolation[72]

The Vaiśeṣika school argues: "If verbal expressions and concepts, by engaging isolates or features, are object-possessors that exclude, then if 'cow' as a reversal of 'horse' and the isolate of 'non-horse' upon 'cow' are separate, it would follow that this is an assertion no different from our assertion on universals.[73] If they are not separate, then verbal expressions and the cognitions that take as their objects feature-possessors and the features alone would not engage separately."

The reply to this assertion is in three parts:

1. Reversal and isolation are not different in reality but engage by way of separate verbal expressions
2. As they are not different in reality, the comparison with your assertion of universals is not valid
3. Engaging in the previous argument by way of the reality

Reversal and isolation are not different in reality but engage by way of separate verbal expressions

1. Engaging is merely by way of separate verbal expressions
2. Teaching that there is no fault in the above
3. This process applies to all phenomena of similar class

Engaging is merely by way of separate verbal expressions

59. With regard to those, verbalization and ascertainment
isolated from another or reversed from another
are acts of convention.

With regard to those verbal expressions and conceptualizations that engage by way of isolation or exclusion of the other, reversal and isolation are not different in reality, but "this cow" **isolated from another** such as "horse," and "this cow" **reversed from another** such as "horse"—as separate **verbalizations** expressing feature and the feature-possessor—as well as the **ascertainments** arising from those expressions, do not actually engage separately because the feature-possessor and the feature **are** only separated by **acts of convention**. This is because the feature and feature-possessor that they engage are merely imputed as separate.

Teaching that there is no fault in the above

1. The validity of engaging by way of the sixth (genitive) case
2. The necessity of specific language

The validity of engaging by way of the sixth (genitive) case

> 60. **By these two, one is being spoken of as one,**
> **but with the phenomenon expressed divided,**
> **the grammatical case separates them,**
> **setting them out as distinct entities.**

"If the feature and the possessor of that feature are not really separate, then does it not follow that the sixth case, as used in the phrase 'the cowness *of* a cow,' does not express any separation?"

By these two verbal expressions of the feature and the possessor of that feature, a "cow" is expressed as that which is excluded from being a horse. The reality is that **one is being spoken of as one, but** the expression of **the** sixth **grammatical case**, from among the eight cases, which **separates** out the feature from the possessor of that feature can **set out**, or express, the feature and the possessor of that feature **as distinct entities**, although in reality they are not separate. This is because they are expressions that engage in a single **phenomenon** that is to be **expressed** and that has been **divided** by a distinction created by language.

The necessity of specific language

"If a single isolate is expressed by two verbal expressions, then there is no need of language separating out feature and possessor of feature?"

61. **Other features, eliminated and not eliminated,**
are bases for the particulars of convention,
following the desires of the knower.

On "cow" as a feature-possessor, there are many features, such as not being a horse, not being a buffalo, and so on. The single feature of not being a horse wherein **other features**, such as not being a buffalo, are **eliminated, and** not being a horse, which is **not eliminated, are the bases**, or reasons, **for the particulars of the convention** of that verbalization, which expresses that feature and feature-possessor respectively, because they are features **that follow the desires of the knower**, or listener.

Therefore separating out feature and possessor of feature existing on a single phenomenon has a purpose, which is to comprehend that single phenomenon by way of eliminating or not eliminating other features.

This process applies to all phenomena of similar class

62. **All such verbal expressions**
express a substance and an entity
that in the phenomenon expressed
are not distinct features at all.

"Non-horse" and "non-horseness" are examples of a universal and a possessor of a universal. Likewise, "the whiteness of the cow" and "the white cow" are examples of quality and possessor of a quality. "The cow going" and "the going of the cow" are examples of action and the possessor of an action. **All such verbal expressions express a substance**—a possessor of a particular property—**and an entity**, which is the property itself. **In the** actual **phenomenon expressed, these are not** actual **distinct features at all** because the features are just the verbalizing of the elimination or nonelimination of other features with regard to a single phenomenon.

63. **By wanting to know something,**
whatever is said to aid that,
to give activity to it, and other
are not distinct features other than that.

Moreover, **by wanting to know something** at a particular time, by way of the elimination or nonelimination of other features, **whatever is said** by way of grammatical affixes **to aid that** expression, **to give activity to it**, to give any **other** thoughts about it, or features such as "white" that do not give any specific explanation, those expressions **are not distinct features** in the reality of the phenomenon expressed, which is **other than** the elimination or nonelimination of other features. A single phenomenon is merely being spoken of by way of different expressions.

As they are not different in reality, the comparison with your assertion of universals is not valid

> 64. **Therefore, for exclusion of others as the object,**
> **such possession leveled at those is removed.**
> **If a class and those of that class were distinct,**
> **faults would occur.**

Therefore, for those Buddhists who assert the **exclusion of others as the object** of verbal expression, the assertion regarding the expression of particulars **possessing** types of a separate nature[74] **is removed** from the error **leveled at those** of the Vaiśeṣika tradition, because exclusion and isolation are not separate in reality. There is pervasion to this argument, because **if a class**—that is, a universal—**and those of that class were** substantially **distinct**, and if a universal verbally engaged with its particulars by way of a distinct reality, three **faults would occur.**

What are these three? (1) That verbal expression would not engage with its particulars under its own power because it would engage its particulars having expressed a universal of a separate nature. (2) The features within an instance would exist with no common basis because the verbal expression would not imply such features. (3) The expression would engage with its particulars only nominally because the universal is expressed as a distinct entity. These three faults are taught by Dignāga.[75]

Engaging in the previous argument by way of the reality

1. Explaining that this fault exists in others
2. Explaining that this fault does not exist in us
3. Clarifying how this fault exists in others

Explaining that this fault exists in others

The Vaiśeṣika say that if the possessor of a property and the property itself are not separate, then the specific words that constitute the sixth (genitive) case, the plural forms, and so on would be inappropriate.

> 65. **For those who insist that words**
> **are expressed by the power of the entity,**
> **not reliant primarily upon the wish to express,**
> **it would be correct to argue by way of**
> **the sixth case, word declensions, and so on.**

For those of the Vaiśeṣika and the Vaiyākaraṇa schools **who insist that words** such as the sixth case, plural forms, and so on **are expressed by the power of** being separate **entities** and are **not reliant primarily upon the wish to express, it would be correct for them to argue by way of the sixth case, word declensions**—that is, plural forms—**and so on**—that is, supplementary phrases, such as "the entity of the cow, the cow itself"—are not words that engage because in reality they are not separate.

Explaining that this fault does not exist in us

> 66. **With whatever words, the speakers,**
> **without relying upon an external object,**
> **ascertain the expressions**
> **and express them accordingly.**

However, for me, **whatever words** there are of the sixth case, plural forms, and so on, engage appropriately, even with those phenomena that in reality are not separate, because **the speakers**—those who form the conventions—**without relying upon** a separate **external object, ascertain the expressions** of whatever distinct and non-distinct phenomena, **and** those phenomena are **expressed** with that language **accordingly.**

Clarifying how this fault exists in others

> 67. **With wives, six villages, and so on,**
> **what causes would establish distinctiveness?**

> **Or with "the nature of space, space itself,"**
> **what causes are there for this?**

If you assert that all verbal engagements of singular and plural forms are themselves created by individual and multiple entities, then it would follow that a single woman or a single sand grain would not engage with the plural forms "**wives**," "sand grains," **and so on** because **what causes would** there be to **establish distinctiveness**? There are none. Moreover, the phenomena of **six villages**[76] would not engage with the singular form "a row of houses" because **what** single **cause would** there be in those phenomena to **establish** non-**distinctiveness**?[77] There would be none.

Or, the use of the genitive case in the phrase "**the nature of space**" and supplementary phrases such as "the entity of space, **space itself**" would not engage, because in reality **what** separate **causes** of those verbal expressions **are there for this**? There are none.

The word "or" leads to the next point above.

13. The Universal of Many Conceptualized as One

Though separate, verbal expressions and conceptualization gather as one and engage by exclusion

1. Separate phenomena appearing as one are labeled as universals by class
2. Refuting that such labeling exists in reality
3. Conceptualization apprehending universals are therefore false
4. The indirect cause of that falseness

Separate phenomena appearing as one are labeled as universals by class

The autocommentary says:

> Now, how are those that possess entities, which are reversed into one, known as universals? Is it because they are unconnected to others? Or because others do not exist? How they are universals has been explained previously. Not being mixed, that is one. Those unconnected are similitudes possessing isolates of them and have been explained previously. Furthermore . . . .[78]

As for the meaning of this passage, some say the following. "There are two types of universals: those that exist in reality and those that exist to the cognition. Concerning the first, all pots are similar in being reversed from being non-pots, and a pot is therefore said to be a universal, as it is pervasive of all pots. Concerning the second type, it is simply the fact that all pots, which appear as separate forms, are held as one in a conceptual cognition because similar types are mixed to become one. The former has been explained previously, and now the latter will be explained."

That is not correct. Previously, it was not explained that a pot is a universal because it was pervasive of all pots but because a single pot can be divided up into many isolates. Moreover, both your types of universals are explained in the following section beginning from the line "In dependence upon separate entities" (verse 68).

Others say: That which is reversed from other entities and not connected with those of different types is a universal by way of being isolated from those phenomena. Therefore they say that a universal is labeled solely on synonyms of an intrinsically existent object and that this is explained by the section beginning with the line "Because all entities dwell by nature" (verse 40).

Others assert: He gave the answer that whatever exists on each part reversed from dissimilar types is labeled a universal.

Both these explanations are incorrect. If *universal,* as previously explained, meant that this term was being affixed to intrinsically existent objects, then the reason, the predicate, and the subject as found in the actual reasoning by nature would have to be accepted as intrinsically existent objects. This would completely obviate the need for an extensive explanation of exclusion at this juncture.

Therefore I will explain the above passage by relying upon the core teachings of Sakya Paṇḍita. Those of you who delight in the secret words of logicians, bow your heads and listen.

It might be wondered, "If reversals and isolates are not in themselves separate, then intrinsically existent phenomena and reversals cannot be universals. The reason is that intrinsically existent objects do not intervene with each other and therefore there cannot be a universal of a single substance. Moreover, reversals and isolates are not in themselves separate, and so there cannot be any universal of a separate substance."

In this context there are two types of universal. As the line "dwell by nature in their own individual entities" (1.40) states, intrinsically existent phenomena, which are "not mixed" with each other, "are the support of being isolated from entities, both compatible and other" (1.40). "That is one."[79] Universals "unconnected with"—that is, reversed from—phenomena of similar and dissimilar types, which "are similitudes" of intrinsically existent objects, "possessing isolates of them, have been explained previously."

In brief, the single entity sound, from the point of view of exclusion, divided up into the isolates of sound, product, and impermanence, means that sound is a universal, and that was explained previously. *Treasure of Reasoning* states:

> The exclusion of others deals with separate objects.
> Even one thing, therefore, will have separate isolates.[80]

Also:

> As for the need of such dividing:
> one taken alone is not understood.
> In order to understand, it is divided.[81]

"Furthermore" [in the autocommentary] indicates that distinct from that universal in which one is divided into many, a universal in which many appears as one will now be explained. *Treasure of Reasoning* states:

> Those of the same activity and characteristics
> are determined as one by the force of imprints.[82]

Also:

> As for the need of condensing into one:
> Activities of establishing and refuting on distinct entities
> are comprehended when gathered together as one.[83]

It is clearly stated in the root text, the autocommentary, and *Treasure of Reasoning* that sound, product, and impermanence existing within sound are all universals, and that isolate, universal, and exclusion of others are all identical in meaning. Despite this, the presentation of universals and particulars these days bears no resemblance to that. This and the determining of our own position has been dealt with in my *Madhyamaka Overview.*

> **68. In dependence upon separate entities,**
> **phenomena appear as one.**
> **The nature of such a cognition**
> **obscures other entities.**

Therefore, in response to the above query: the explanation of universals in which the one is divided into many been explained previously. Here, **in dependence**

upon, meaning indirectly produced from, particulars of trees, which are **entities separate** from that which are not trees, comes the conceptual cognition in which the **phenomena** of the particulars of trees **appear as one** tree form. This **cognition** is one in which the particulars of trees appear as one tree form because **the nature**, which is produced by imprints, **obscures other entities**—that is, the intrinsically existent objects of particulars of trees.

> 69. **This obscuring will obscure that separateness,**
> **although they are distinct by nature.**
> **Consequently, by their nature,**
> **the entities appear as not distinct.**

This pervades because **although** tree particulars **are distinct by nature, this obscuring**, or concealing,[84] cognition **obscures that separateness**, and **consequently, the entities** of tree particulars **appear** as one and **as not distinct, by** the **nature** of the isolates separated from non-trees.

> 70. **By the force of thought,**
> **that is proclaimed to be a universal.**

That tree form appearing to a conceptual cognition **is proclaimed to be a universal** with regard to tree particulars **by the force of thought** conceiving entities of external trees. This is because, to the conceptual mind apprehending a tree, that tree form appears as a universal concomitant with its own tree particulars.

Therefore that form appearing to a conceptual cognition is a universal from the perspective of that cognition, and it is the phenomenon directly expressed by verbal expression. Also, common-basis designation and all establishing and refuting directly take place within the perspective of that cognition, even though that does not exist in reality. This distinction is explained to mean that it does not exist as it is conceptualized, and when subsequent conceptualizing thoughts analyze its way of being, it is the objective aspect[85] of a conceptual cognition and therefore is an intrinsically existing phenomenon. However, from the aspect of it being conceptualized as an external object, it is a universal and does not exist as an entity. The autocommentary states:

> Those who explain will analyze this way, but those who designate do not do that. They think of and visualize their object solely as

> being suitable to function, and those things that are being conceptualized are engaged in as one.[86]

The meaning of this passage is summarized in *Treasure of Reasoning*:

> When explaining, it is wise to divide.
> When engaging, attainment is reached
> by falsely gathering as one.[87]

Also, by way of unmistaken understanding, I add my own secret words of logic:

> That aspect, from its own perspective, is a universal.
> In reality the consciousness is intrinsically existent.
> The universal depends on being determined as external.
> The intrinsically existent is attained by clear appearance.

Refuting that such labeling exists in reality

> **In the way it is conceptualized by that,**
> **it does not exist in any ultimate reality.**

That universal **in the way it is conceptualized by that** conceptual cognition **does not exist in any ultimate reality** in those tree particulars.

> 71. **Those particulars do not pervade.**
> **A pervading separate [entity] does not appear.**

This is because **those particulars do not pervade** each other. Therefore there is no single substance universal. Moreover, **a pervading** universal as a **separate** entity **does not appear.**

> **It is not distinct from the consciousness.**
> **How can it pervade separate entities?**

[Question:] "The form that appears to conceptual cognition is asserted as being a universal. Why does it not exist ultimately?"

How can the entity of that aspect, without depending on its false perspective, be a universal that **pervades the separate entities** of trees? It cannot, because **it**

is not distinct from the consciousness of that conceptual cognition and is of a single substance with it.

Conceptualizations apprehending universals are therefore false

> 72. **Therefore this conceptual cognition**
> **that apprehends as one entity is false.**
> **Being mutually separate and possessing**
> **the actuality of the name are the seed of this.**

Therefore this conceptual cognition that apprehends as one entity the actuality of tree particulars **is false** because those particulars are many.

The indirect cause of that falseness

1. Identifying the indirect cause
2. Refuting that it is not a cause

Identifying the indirect cause

What is the cause of the apprehension of a universal? The tree particulars that are **mutually separate and possess the actuality of the name** *tree* **are the seed,** or cause, **of this** apprehending of the tree universal. This is because they constitute an indirect cause.

Refuting that it is not a cause

1. Using two conducive examples to establish that the many become a cause
2. Using two damaging reasons to refute that other causes are universals as entities

Using two conducive examples to establish that the many become a cause

> 73. **Being understood as one,**
> **knowing the object, and so on,**
> **will accomplish a single purpose, although distinct,**
> **by being naturally ascertained,**
> **as with sense organs, for example.**

74. **Some medicines, although distinct,**
are seen to cure fevers and so on
combined or individually,
whereas others do not.

"How can many tree particulars produce the result of a single apprehension of a tree universal?"

Although particulars of trees **are distinct** as substances without a universal as an entity, *trees* **is understood as being one** universal. They **will accomplish a single purpose**, such as making a fire and a home, because accomplishing those things **is naturally ascertained by** dependence. **For example, sense organs,** sense objects, **and so on** do not share a single universal but create a single **knowing of the object**—that is, sense consciousness. **Some medicines,** such as moonseed, hypecoum, and so on, do not possess a single universal, but those two **combined** in a compound **or** used **individually can be seen to** produce the single result that will **cure fevers and so on, whereas others** such as yogurt and turnip **do not.**

Using two damaging reasons to refute that other causes are universals as entities

75. **Having no distinction, this universal would not cure.**
They are distinct because of the different soils and so on,
but it would follow that they have no distinction.
Moreover, being unchanging, it would not be effective.

It might be asked, "Isn't it because moonseed and so forth do possess a single universal that they cure fevers? Therefore your examples are not valid."

In that case, **this** medicine **universal would not cure** fevers because **it would have no distinction** among particulars of medicine. This pervades because those medicine particulars **are distinct because of the different soils** they grow in **and so on, but it would follow that they would have no distinction** in their ability to cure fevers. **Moreover**, a medicine universal **would not be effective** in producing a result because it would have no ability to cure fevers as it would **be unchanging**—that is, permanent.

14. Appearance within a Conceptual Cognition

General explanation

1. Explanation of appearance within an establishing conceptual cognition
2. Establishing other designations within that appearance

Explanation of appearance within an establishing conceptual cognition

> 76. **Within conceptual cognition, having apprehended the nature,**
> **the actuality does not exist but is similar to the actuality.**
> **There is a distinction from those not possessing the result of that,**
> **and [this cognition] was created from the ultimate reality.**

It can be argued, "If a universal is established by a conceptual cognition apprehending the particulars homogenously, then because the intrinsically existent particulars themselves do not appear to the conceptual cognition, that cognition does not apprehend them homogenously. And because the particulars that appear to the conceptual cognition cannot perform a function, that cognition cannot gain its engaged object."

In the homogenous apprehending of particulars that appears to a conceptual cognition, that cognition has three features by which it gains its engaged object. **The conceptual cognition** apprehending a tree universal, which has been generated after the direct cognition **that apprehended the nature** of the tree particulars, has three aspects: The aspect of its *entity* is that although the appearance within that cognition **does not exist as the actuality** of trees, that appearance **is similar to the actuality** of trees. The aspect of the *result* is that this cognition will gain tree particulars that are **distinct from** the actuality of

those not possessing the result of being trees. The aspect of the *cause* is that this cognition **was created from the ultimate reality** of the intrinsically existent tree particulars.

> 77. **Its nature appears as an external object,**
> **as one, and as reversed from others.**
> **That does not exist as the reality**
> **because the parts conceptualized do not exist.**

The way the object appears to that conceptual cognition apprehending a tree, which is endowed with these three features, also has three aspects: **Its nature** is that the form is held with the appearance and concept as one, and therefore it **appears as an external object**, such as a tree. The similar type particulars appear as homogenous and therefore appear **as one, and** they appear **as** if **reversed from other** phenomena that are not trees.

The form of **that** appearance **does not** truly **exist as the reality** it appears to be **because the parts conceptualized do not exist** with the ability to function as they appear.

15. Designations

Establishing other designations within that appearance

1. Establishing universal and common basis designations
2. Property possessor and property are established in accordance with the universal
3. That which is categorized has no existence in reality
4. Though they have no existence in reality, there is a need for such categorization
5. Presentation of proof that such categorization does not exist in reality
6. Refuting that the above contradicts scripture
7. Summary of how verbal expression and conceptual cognition engage

Establishing universal and common basis designations

1. Establishing universals and common bases by mistaken designation
2. Although mistaken, they still gain their intrinsically existing phenomena
3. Although similar in being mistaken, not found elsewhere

Establishing universals and common bases by mistaken designation

78. **Those phenomena that exist for consciousness**
are in this way possessed of a nature of being isolated.
Therefore they are as if not of distinct types,
also appearing excluded from others, and that is a universal.

> 79. **Consciousness and verbal expression,**
> **having the domain of a common basis within that,**
> **will expand mistaken designations.**

Those aspects of the **phenomena** of trees **that exist for**—that is, appear to—the conceptual **consciousness** that apprehends "trees" **are** designated, from a mistaken perspective, as universals and common bases because **in this way** they appear **possessed of a nature of being isolated** from non-trees. **Therefore they** appear as one, and as trees **not of distinct types, and that is a universal.**

Moreover, the form of the agaru tree, as a division of those forms, also **appears excluded from other** tree particulars because the conceptual **consciousness and verbal expression, which have the domain of a common basis within that** appearance, **will expand mistaken designations** of universals and common bases.[88]

Although mistaken, they still gain their intrinsically existing phenomena

> 80. **All of those entities,**
> **depending upon those not pervasive with each other,**
> **are therefore exclusion-of-others object possessors,**
> **connected with those entities.**
> 81. **They are supports for finding entities,**
> **like, for example, an inferential cognition, as was explained.**
> **Though similar in being mistaken,**
> **they are not gained from others,**
> **like the light of a lamp as a jewel.**

Also, **all those** cognition and verbal-expression designations of intrinsically existent **entities are exclusion-of-others object possessors** and **are supports for finding** the intrinsically existent **entities** of the engaged objects. This is because they are designations indirectly **connected with those** intrinsically existent **entities** and are designations **that depend upon**—that is, are indirectly created from—**those** intrinsically existent entities that are **not pervasive with each other.** It is **like, for example, an inferential cognition, as was explained** previously, which, in dependence upon the perfect reasonings by way of result and nature, is infallible with regard to its engaged object.

Although similar in being mistaken, not found elsewhere

Though they are similar in being mistaken with regard to the appearing object, intrinsically existent entities will **not be gained from other** conventional designations, which have no connection to an engaged object, much **like** regarding **the light of a lamp as a jewel** will not locate a jewel.

Property possessor and property are established in accordance with the universal

A third doubt added to those above is, "If a universal is established by a conceptual cognition apprehending intrinsically existent particulars homogenously, then the designations of property possessor and property cannot be established because property possessor and property do not exist within intrinsically existent phenomena."

> 82. **Within that, even many have become a single result,**
> **depending upon that which is other**
> **than those not possessing that result.**
> **Verbal expression and cognition engage correctly**
> **the designation of the single.**
>
> 83. **Similarly, even a single**
> **clearly revealing those phenomena,**
> **distinct from those phenomena**
> **not possessing that resultant nature,**
> **is known as being of various properties.**

Within that form, which appears to a conceptual cognition, **even many** tree particulars **have become a single resultant** type, and it appears as **depending on that which is other than those not possessing that resultant** nature of being trees. Because of this reason, the sound that is a **verbal expression and** the conceptual **cognition engage correctly the designation of the single** class *tree*.

Similarly, even a single agaru tree appearing to a conceptual cognition can be **known as being of various** isolate **properties** because it appears as distinct from those not possessing the resultant nature of a tree and as **distinct from those phenomena not possessing the resultant nature** of being an agaru tree. A conceptual cognition is necessary to divide a single agaru tree into many isolate properties so it can **clearly reveal those** many results produced by the agaru tree as **phenomena** belonging to the agaru tree. This is the meaning of the lines cited above (from Sapaṇ's *Treasure of Reasoning*):

> One taken alone, it is not understood.
> In order to understand, it is divided.

Most previous commentators have divided the above under two individual headings: "Causes for the designation of universal to engage" and "Causes for the designation of feature and feature possessor to engage." This shows they have not understood the presentation of the conducive example, which states that just as the designation of universal engages with the appearance within a conceptual cognition, so designations of property-possessor and property also engage with the appearance within conceptual cognition. The manner in which the designation of universal engages was taught previously.

Moreover, the autocommentary states, "The actuality that appears to the consciousness is given the designation of universal, common basis, and property and property-possessor."[89] But at this juncture he does not talk of the designation of a universal.

That which is categorized has no existence in reality

> 84. **These objects of verbal expressions and the common bases,**
> **though they have no existence**
> **and cannot possibly exist as entities,**
> **are expressed as they are known.**

These objects of verbal expressions, which refer to those with the designation of property-possessor and property, **as well as the common bases, cannot possibly exist as** intrinsically existing **entities. Even though they have no existence** in reality, in the way they appear to a conceptual cognition, **they are expressed as they are known** in the world.

Previous commentators have explained the phrase "These objects of verbal expressions" as referring to universals. They have not understood that the universals were previously taught not to exist ultimately in the verse (70) beginning "In the way it is conceptualized," and it is on the basis of property possessors and properties, as well as common bases not existing ultimately, that "these objects of verbal expressions" are mentioned.

Though they have no existence in reality, there is a need for such categorization

85. **The presentation of property-possessor and property,**
of whatever is separate and not separate,
is not an examination of the object
but the way they are known in the world.

86. **Similarly, it is solely in dependence upon this**
that scholars can present all to be proven,
as well as the proof,
in order to engage in the ultimate reality.

"If they have no existence in reality, why is it necessary to establish such designations?"

The presentation of property-possessor and property as separate upon one object even though they are one, of the common bases **of whatever is separate, and** of the universals of whatever is **not separate** is **the way they are known** and used **in the world**; it **is not an examination of the** reality of the **object. Similarly, it is solely in dependence upon this** way **that scholars can present all to be proven as well as the proof.** The necessity of that **is in order to engage the** insight into the nature of intrinsically existent **ultimate reality.** This should be applied to every mention of obtaining an intrinsically existent and engaged object by way of refutation and establishing, with the appearance falsified as being permanent and being one.

Presentation of proof that such categorization does not exist in reality

87. **Phenomena that are of an ultimate reality**
are, by themselves, not mixed together and not many.
Being a single entity and being many
is a corruption by cognition.

88. **These specifics of "universal" and "feature"**
are objects of cognition. Within that, isolated from others,
particulars of phenomena are conceptualized.

With regard to the intrinsically existent **phenomena of ultimate reality**, the designation of a **being a single entity**, although many, and of **being many**, although single, **is a corruption**—that is, a mistake—**by cognition**, because **by themselves** phenomena of ultimate reality that are many **are not mixed together** as one, **and** the single are **not many. These specific**, or distinct, designations **of "This is a universal" and** "This is a **feature"** engage with **objects** which appear to a conceptual **cognition** but do not directly engage with the intrinsically existent phenomena because they are verbal expressions and cognitions that blend the many to become one, and the one to become divided into many. This pervades because such a process is not possible with intrinsically existent phenomena.

"If that which appears to the cognition is false, how can multiple properties be possible?"

Within that conceptualized form, many **particular** properties **of phenomena** are **conceptualized** in a mistaken perspective, because from a mistaken perspective they appear as phenomena that are **isolated from** many **other** reversals.

Refuting that the above contradicts scripture

89. **In the conceptualization "This is to be proved, this is the proof,"**
the sight of any entity has disappeared.
Here a feature mixed with a universal
is not to be held as an intrinsically existing phenomenon.

90. **That is not apprehended anywhere,**
in the form of a universal, a feature, and so on.
Many particulars cannot exist in that alone.

It might be asked, "Ācārya Dignāga states, 'An inferential cognition apprehends a feature characterized by an exclusion of others,' thereby asserting that it apprehends an intrinsically existing phenomenon mixed with a universal. Does the above not contradict this?"

In the conceptualization that thinks, **"This is to be proved, this is the proof,"** there is no apprehending of an intrinsically existing phenomenon characterized by impermanence, because **the sight**—that is, the appearance—**of any entity** intrinsically existing **has disappeared**. The statement of Dignāga **here** is saying that a valid cognition apprehends a **feature mixed with a universal;** it

should not be understood that **an intrinsically existing phenomenon** mixed with a universal is apprehended by a valid cognition. This statement is teaching that the feature appearing to a conceptual mind mixed with a universal of an exclusion of others is what is apprehended by a valid cognition.

That intrinsically existing phenomenon **is not** directly **apprehended anywhere in the form of a universal,** in the form of a particular **feature,** or in the form of properties and property possessors, as indicated by the phrase **and so on,** because **many particulars cannot exist in that** intrinsically existing phenomenon **alone.**

Summary of how verbal expression and conceptual cognition engage

> 91. **Completely reversed from all that,**
> **verbal expression and conceptual cognition**
> **do not comprehend in accord with existence**
> **because they engage as universals.**
> **This is a summarizing verse.**

Verbal expression and conceptual cognition, completely reversed from all that are not the entities of that intrinsically existing phenomenon, **do not** directly **comprehend in accord with existence because they** directly **engage as universals.**

At this point, **this is a summarizing verse.**

16. Engaging by Verbal Expression

In particular, how verbal expressions engage

1. Refuting the position of others regarding the referent of a convention
2. Establishing our own position on the referent of a convention (1.110)
3. Refuting the arguments of others (1.113)
4. Summary of what is established and refuted (1.132)

Refuting the position of others regarding the referent of a convention

1. Refuting that an intrinsically existing phenomenon is the referent of a convention
2. Refuting that the entity of a universal is the direct referent of a convention
3. Refuting that those that possess the universal constitute the referent of a convention

Refuting that an intrinsically existing phenomenon is the referent of a convention

In response to the above verse (1.91) whose second line begins "Verbal expression and conceptual cognition," the Vaiyākaraṇa school says, "It is not correct to say that an intrinsically existing phenomenon is not the actual object of a verbal expression because the phrase 'Bring me a pot' engages with the bringing of a vessel whose function is to carry water."

92. **Verbal expressions reveal those assigned as conventions.**
The convention is not applied to that phenomenon.

> **At that time, there is no intrinsically existing phenomenon.**
> **Therefore that was made for designation.**

An intrinsically existing phenomenon is not the direct object expressed in a verbal expression because that phenomenon is not the direct object of a convention. This pervades because **verbal expressions reveal those** phenomena for which these verbal expressions have been **assigned as conventions.** The logic is that it is **not** possible for **the convention** to be directly **applied to that** intrinsically existing **phenomenon** because **at the time** of using the designation, the **intrinsically existing phenomenon** present at the time of making the convention **is not there.** This pervades because **that** convention **was made for** comprehension of that phenomenon when using **designation.**[90]

Refuting that the entity of a universal is the direct referent of a convention

> 93. **By all means, the person will know**
> **that which has the ability to function,**
> **and to accomplish that task, thinks that it engages,**
> **applying that which expresses those phenomena.**
> 94. **Regarding that, the class is not suitable to perform the function.**

The Vaiśeṣika assert that the direct referent of a convention, without resorting to falsity, is a universal that is substantially separate from the particulars or, in the case of the Sāṃkhya, of one entity with the particulars, and because that is present at the time of designation also, the above fault does not occur.

Regarding that assertion that **the class** alone is the phenomenon being expressed, the class *cow* cannot be the direct object of the convention *cow* without resorting to falsity[91] because it **is not suitable to perform the function** of being a cow. This pervades because when initiating the convention, **the person** seeking a cow **will by all means know that which has the ability to function** as a cow **and to accomplish that task,** that person **thinks** "**it engages** with that which performs that particular function" and **applies** the convention **that expresses those phenomena.**

Refuting that those that possess the universal constitute the referent of a convention

1. Expressing the assertion
2. Refuting the assertion

Expressing the assertion

> **Those capable, which possess that.**

[Objection:] "Convention is applied to **those** particulars **capable of** performing a function, **which possess that** class. Therefore the fault posited above is not applicable."

Refuting the assertion

1. Those possessing the class are similar to a single specific
2. There is no need to conceptualize a separate universal
3. Even though there is no separate universal, identification is valid

Those possessing the class are similar to a single specific

> **Why can't that be directly applied?**
> **If "because they are limitless,"**
> **then they are similarly.**

The opponents are posed a question: "**Why can't that** convention **be directly applied** to the particulars—that is, without the intervention of a universal?"

If they answer, "The convention cannot be applied to them **because they are limitless,**" we reply that the convention cannot be applied to those particulars possessed of that class because **they similarly are** limitless. The fact of being a class does not make the particulars fewer.

There is no need to conceptualize a separate universal

> 95. **Those that perform homogenously**
> **reversed from those that do not,**
> **what can it not do?**
> **It is simple. A separate type is not necessary.**

Those phenomena **that perform** the functions of providing milk, ploughing, and so on **homogenously reversed from** all **those that do not** perform those functions, into a form falsely appearing as an external phenomenon is an exclusion of others. **What can** a verbal expression of **such** an exclusion of others **not do?**

In reply they say, "When talking about possessing a class, Dignāga posits a fault saying, 'Because those in possession have no power.' It is similar here because my 'possessed of a class' and your 'possessed of an isolate,' apart from having different names, are the same."

That this fault does not apply here will be explained later. However, **it is simple** to find the fault in the above. For a verbal expression and a cognition to collectively engage the particulars, an actual **separate type is not necessary**; a verbal expression and a cognition will collectively engage the particulars by way of a homogenous reverse of what they are not even though there is no separate class.

> 96. **Also, by eliminating everything else,**
> **there will be engagement,**
> **and thus they make the verbal expression.**
> **If such did not preclude from those,**
> **how could this be?**

The reason for this is as follows. Is the verbal expression *cow* a preclusion of what it is not? If it is not, **how could there be** a phenomenon to which it applies? There could not be, because **if such** an expression **did not preclude** the desired phenomena **from those** undesired, this would be the result. This pervades because the speaker **also** thinks that **by eliminating everything else** from the sought phenomena, the listener **will engage** with the desired phenomena and thus **make the verbal expression.** The word "also" indicates not only that the listener eliminates what is not but also that they must engage. Alternatively, the commentaries gloss it as meaning "solely."

> 97. **If preclusion exists,**
> **the necessity of verbal expressions**
> **is simply that, is it not?**
> **At that time, what does your separate universal do?**

It could be argued, "**If preclusion** within this verbal expression *cow* **exists** and is not lacking, then does not the verbal expression become unnecessary?"

Positing a separate class as the engaged object of a verbal expression is not correct because **the necessity of verbal expressions** is to engage in that which is sought-after by preclusion of another, and **is simply that, is it not?** It is, and so that is what occurs. **At that time, what does your separate universal do?** It is completely unnecessary.

17. Identifying the Particulars

Even though there is no separate universal, identification is valid

1. The cause of identification
2. Refutation of other causes of identification
3. Dismissing arguments on the cause of identification

The cause of identification[92]

It can be argued, "If there is no single universal, a cognition that identifies the many particulars cannot be generated."

> 98. **Even though the particulars are distinct,**
> **having seen phenomena**
> **of such and such functions,**
> **when seeing others,**
> 99. **the object-possessing verbal expressions**
> **separate out that other than those**
> **to bring them together and identify them.**

Even though the particulars of *pot* **are** substantially **distinct**, without a single universal, it is perfectly valid to develop a cognition of identification. This is because **having** previously **seen phenomena**, such as a clay pot, **of such and such** similar **functions**, such as the carrying of water, then later, **when seeing others** also, such as gold pots and so on, **the object-possessing verbal expressions**—that is, inner expressions—of exclusion, which **separates out** resultant activities that are **other than those** of carrying water and of holding the nature of being a pot, are able **to bring together** the past and the present by saying, "These are those seen in the past," thereby **identifying them** as one.

Refutation of other causes of identification

1. A single universal is not the cause of an identifying cognition
2. The particulars accompanied by a universal are not the cause of an identifying cognition
3. Many particulars existing in dependence upon a universal is not the cause of an identifying cognition
4. A universal dependent on some of the particulars is not the cause of an identifying cognition

A single universal is not the cause of an identifying cognition

Although according to others it is,
such a cognition is not from a universal alone.
100. **If so, it would be a consciousness constantly of just that.**
It would follow that the particulars are not known.

Although according to the assertion of **others**, a cognition of identification comes from a universal, **such a cognition is not** generated **from a universal** that **alone** is the sole apprehended object held by such a cognition, without any dependence upon the particulars. **If so**, serious consequences would follow. What are they? The apprehension of the universal **would be a consciousness constantly of just that** universal because it would be a cognition developed from holding only the universal as its apprehended object. If you agree, then **it would follow that the particulars could not be known** because only the universal would be known.

At that time, there could never be
a connection of possessing that.
101. **There could be no certainty on possessing.**
How could you apply the designation?

Moreover, if you agree, then **there could never be a connection** between the particulars and **that** universal **possessed** by them, because **at that time** there would be no cognition of the particulars. Furthermore, **how could you apply the designation** "That instance has a universal"? You could not, because **there**

could be no certainty on the connection of those particulars **possessing** a universal. You must accept the premise.

The particulars accompanied by a universal are not the cause of an identifying cognition

> **"Particulars accompanied by the single entity**
> **were the cause of the consciousness."**
> 102. **Does that single entity not eliminate the separateness of those?**
> **Because they are separate, we do not accept that in those**
> **is found the cause for a consciousness of a single entity.**

It can be argued, "If the **particulars accompanied by the single entity** of a universal **were the** objective **cause of the consciousness** that holds a universal, then would the fault of the cognition of the universal not knowing the particulars not occur?"

Does that single entity of a universal **not eliminate the separateness of those** particulars? Even if it did not, **because they are separate**—that is, using the reason of them being separate—**we do not accept that in those** particulars **is found the cause for a consciousness of a single entity** universal. However, you posit separate particulars as creating a cognition of a universal.

Many particulars existing in dependence upon a universal is not the cause of an identifying cognition

> 103. **"Although many exist in dependence on a single,**
> **being non-distinct, they will generate the cognition."**
> **Even if they are not individual,**
> **it is the single that generates the cognition.**
> 104. **Because of having no power,**
> **the cognition does not apprehend.**

It can be argued, "**Although** the many, divorced from a universal, will not generate the cognition of the universal, **many** particulars **exist in dependence on a single** universal, and therefore becoming **non-distinct, they will generate the cognition** that apprehends the universal."

Those particulars have no power to generate the cognition that apprehends the universal because **even if those** particulars **are not individual, it is the**

single universal **that generates the cognition** apprehending the universal. If you agree, then it follows that **the cognition** of the universal **does not apprehend** the particulars as its appearing object **because** the particulars **have no power** to create the cognition of the universal.

The response might be, "There is no real certainty about your first consequence. The individual phenomena of blue and so forth can generate a visual consciousness, and so it does not follow that a collection of phenomena, such as those that are blue, has no power to create such a consciousness. Likewise, a single universal has the ability to generate the cognition apprehending the universal, and therefore it does not follow that the particulars do not possess the ability to create the cognition apprehending the universal."

> **Because individually the ability is seen,**
> **for a visual consciousness of blue and so forth,**
> 105. **even as a collection they have that ability.**
> **The particulars in no way have such an ability.**

These two are not similar. It can be established that **blue and so forth, even as a collection, have the ability** to create **a visual consciousness of blue, because** it can be **seen** that these phenomena **individually** also have **the ability** to generate a visual consciousness. **The particulars**, without depending upon a universal, individually and collectively, **in no way have such an ability** to create the cognition of the universal, because with no entity of a universal, it is not possible to create a cognition apprehending that universal. This reason you must accept.

A universal dependent on some of the particulars is not the cause of an identifying cognition

> **"Depending on some or other of those,**
> **it has the potential, but on its own it cannot."**
> 106. **They assist with that single.**
> **How could they not assist in that single cognition?**
> **This would be the result of those,**
> **and whatever assists is a creator.**

"Isn't it the case that a universal that **depends on some or other of those** particulars **has the potential** to create the cognition of the universal **but** a universal

on its own cannot create such a cognition? Therefore it is not that the particulars have no power to create the cognition of the universal."

How could those particulars **not assist in that single cognition** of the universal? It follows that they could, because they assist in the creation of that single universal. Furthermore, it would follow that **this** universal is **the result of those** particulars, because it is assisted by the particulars. You have to accept both of these reasons. Also, there is pervasion because **whatever assists**[93] **is a creator.**

Dismissing arguments on the cause of identification

> 107. **"Not appearing as distinct, it cannot be asserted**
> **that the cognition comes from the distinct."**
> **They do appear as distinct,**
> **because they are apprehended thinking,**
> **"Those particulars are similar."**

It could be argued, "**It cannot be asserted that the cognition** of the universal is generated **from the distinct** particulars because those particulars are **not distinct, appearing** solely as one."

Those particulars of that cognition apprehending a universal **do appear as distinct because they are apprehended thinking, "Those particulars are similar."**

> 108. **"If they are similar, how are they held**
> **by a cognition as distinct?"**
> **From those similar in the same resultant type.**

It might be argued, "Those particulars, **how are they held by a cognition as distinct?** They are not, because **if they are held as similar** by a universal apprehending cognition, which they are, they must be held as a single universal. There is pervasion here, because if a universal and its many particulars are apprehended, the particulars are apprehended with the thought 'They are similar,' and that is the apprehending of both the universal, which is the cause of holding the particulars as similar, as well as the particulars themselves."

The cognition that holds the particulars as similar is not generated from the universal and the particulars. It is generated solely **from those** many particulars that are **similar in** producing **the same resultant type.**

> **"In the results of those,**
> **the cognitions are also distinct."**
> 109. **As causes of comprehending them as one,**
> **the cognitions are not distinct.**

"It is not correct that the many can generate the one result because **the** sensory **cognitions** that are **the results of those** phenomena, such as golden pots, **are also distinct.**"

The visual **cognitions** apprehending pots are distinct in reality, but from the perspective of exclusion they **are not distinct. As causes of comprehending them as one** cognition apprehending pots, they are similar.

> **Being entities that are causes of a single,**
> **the particulars also are not distinct.**

The pot **particulars also** are distinct in reality, but from the perspective of exclusion they **are not distinct** types, because they are similar in **being entities that are causes of a single**-type direct perception apprehending pots.

"Isn't this one result the actual phenomenon of a universal?"

> 110. **Lacking that which is not the cause,**
> **an entity other than,**
> **and concomitant with, those particulars**
> **is nowhere to be seen and has been refuted.**

That one result arising from the many particulars is just an exclusion appearing as **lacking that which is not the cause** of those particulars, but it is not an entity of a universal, because if there were **an entity** of a universal that was **other than, and concomitant with, those particulars**, it would be seen, but it **is nowhere to be seen and has been refuted** in my *Madhyamaka Overview*.

Establishing our own position on the referent of a convention

> **A convention has the significance of comprehending that.**

Because it is not correct that intrinsically existing phenomena, a universal as an actual entity, and those that possess the universal are the phenomenon being expressed, the **convention** *tree* **has the significance**—that is, it produces the result—**of comprehending that** tree exclusion. This is because that convention has a resultant awareness of the apprehension of *tree* with regard to the representation within the conceptual cognition of tree. Śākyabuddhi says, "The reversal comes from the seeing of the intrinsically existent object, and the aspect that appears to the conceptual cognition is reversed from other aspects. This exclusion, solely by being in the entity that is not imputed, is the object of the verbal expression because it is that alone that appears to the consciousness of the verbal expression. At that time, it is established as a designation and exclusion object-possessor."[94]

It can be argued, "It follows that the verbal expression *tree* does not achieve its intrinsically existent object of a tree when used as designation because the convention is not directly applied to the intrinsically existent object of a tree but is applied to a tree exclusion of other."

> 112. **That which generates the cognition**
> **does not perform that function.**
> **Being an attribute for eliminating,**
> **and depending upon distinct entities,**
> **we assert that it is nondeceptive regarding the phenomenon.**[95]

That verbal expression *tree*, **which generates the** conceptual **cognition** apprehending tree endowed with three features, is not a direct application of a convention to the intrinsically existent object of a tree. But when being used as a designation, **we assert that it is nondeceptive regarding the phenomenon** of tree because it **is an attribute**—that is, a cause—**for eliminating** non-tree, **which does not perform that function** of being a tree, **and** because **it depends** indirectly **upon the entity** of trees **distinct** from non-trees.

> 111. **Not performing the function of that,**
> **having the appearance**
> **of something similar to that**
> **which performs that function,**
> **it is the seed of just an entity**
> **distinct from other entities.**

What are the three features? The valid conceptual cognition apprehending tree is endowed with three features: (1) In terms of its aspect, which does **not perform the function of that** tree, its nature is that it **has the appearance of**

something similar to that which performs that function of a tree. (2) **It is the seed of**—that is, it possesses the cause of—producing **just an entity** that **is distinct from other entities** of non-trees. (3) That which appears to this cognition does not exist as the phenomenon of tree.

> 113. **Why? It is an object-possessor by way of exclusion,**
> **with an entity dependent upon performing.**

Why is this? The verbal expression *tree* **is an object-possessor by way of exclusion** because it is an object-possessor that conceives an external tree and possesses an **entity** of a conceptual cognition that is indirectly **dependent upon** that which **performs** the function of tree.

18. Refutations Concerning Exclusions and Isolates

Refuting the arguments of others

1. Refuting the consequence of there being mutual comprehension
2. Refuting the position that without something to preclude there can be no exclusion
3. Refutations on the examination of whether an isolate exists as an entity
4. Refuting the argument of there being no common basis

Refuting the consequence of there being mutual comprehension

1. Stating the consequences put forward by others
2. Refuting the above with corresponding reasoning
3. Generating certainty with an entity-based answer
4. Establishing that all verbal expressions ascertain

Stating the consequences put forward by others

If the meaning of tree is apprehended
by the isolation of non-tree,
114. **there will mutual dependence on the part of both,**
and one will be apprehended.
If none, neither is apprehended.
Therefore determining a convention is not possible.
This others have stated.

If a conceptual cognition does not apprehend tree and non-tree by way of affirmation but **apprehends** solely by exclusion, then it follows that there will be a **mutually dependent** comprehension of **both** tree and non-tree by the conceptual cognition, and in order to **apprehend one**, the other must have been apprehended previously. This is because that conceptual cognition must apprehend **the meaning of tree by the isolation**, or exclusion, **of non-tree**, and non-tree also must be ascertained by the exclusion of tree. There is pervasion because without the apprehension of tree and non-tree, they cannot be excluded.

If you accept this, then **if there is no** previous apprehension of tree and non-tree by this conceptual cognition, it follows that it **will apprehend neither** tree nor non-tree, because the comprehension of tree and non-tree is mutually dependent. **Therefore it is not possible** for a verbal expression **to be determined a convention** with regard to an exclusion that dispels non-tree, for such a convention is made solely with regard to the entity of a universal, by way of affirmation. **This** Kumārila and **others have stated.**

Refuting the above with corresponding reasoning

> 115. **With the above, for determining a convention,**
> **is there a preclusion of non-tree or not?**
> **If there is preclusion, there is no apprehension of tree.**
> **How could it be understood?**

With the above presentation of the fault that by exclusion there has to be comprehension of tree and non-tree by mutual dependence, we then ask, "**For determining the convention** *tree*, **is there a preclusion of non-tree or not?**" **If** you say **there is preclusion**, then **how could** the person who applies the convention *tree* **understand** non-tree at the time of that convention? It follows that they could not understand it because at that time **there is no apprehension of tree**. There is pervasion. The reason is established because, in order to comprehend the present tree, one is seeking for and establishing the convention *tree*.

> 116. **From the convention, those will not be excluded,**
> **and those who designate**
> **will not engage by elimination,**
> **as with, for example, a particular of tree.**

If you agree, it follows **from the convention** that this particular person **will not exclude those** non-trees as being the referent of this expression, because at the time of the application of the convention, non-tree is not known. You must accept the reason and the pervasion. In that case, if you agree, then later, **those who designate** *tree* **will not engage by** the **elimination** of non-tree, because the verbal expression *tree* does not eliminate non-tree. **For example**, the agaru tree, as **a particular of tree**, is not excluded from the referents of the convention *tree*, and therefore from that convention there is no engaging by way of eliminating that particular.

> 117. **"There is no establishment by negation of the other.**
> **In front there is something,**
> **on which is revealed a single.**
> **Convention is applied, 'This is a tree.'**
> **At the time of designating,**
> 118. **it will be understood.**
> **Therefore this fault does not exist."**

You might think: "When applying the convention, **there is no establishment by** way of the prior **negation of the other** non-tree, but it is by affirmation alone that **in front there is something**, such as an agaru tree, **on which is revealed a single** universal with its own separate entity. The **convention is applied** to that universal, and we say, **'This is a tree,'** and that is applied to all specific trees. From that verbal expression, later, **at the time of engaging in designation, that** universal, or the particulars that possess that universal, **will be understood. Therefore this fault** of mutual dependence, or the possibility of engaging with non-tree that you posit, **does not exist."**

> **This also is a tree or this alone?**
> **Thus our previous consequence is not refuted.**

To this also we ask, with regard to this phenomenon possessed of branches and leaves, is the convention applied in the sense of "**This also is a tree**"—that is, by way of preclusion of nonexistence—**or** in the sense of "**This alone** is a tree"—that is, by way of preclusion of existence elsewhere?[96] If it is the former, then when using the designation, the verbal expression *tree* will not engage by way of elimination of non-tree because at the time of applying the convention, the convention of *tree* does not eliminate non-tree.

If it is the latter position, then the convention of *tree* is applied by elimination of non-tree. However, in that case, it would not eliminate non-tree because it does not know "non-tree." This is so because it does not know "tree." **Thus our previous consequence is not refuted.**

Generating certainty with an entity-based answer

You may argue, "By seeing whether the particulars of tree and non-tree possess the entity of a universal of tree or not, then at the time of the convention, we apply the convention 'this alone is a tree.' Therefore, at the time of the designation, we do not make the mistake of engaging in non-tree, and because the convention is applied to the universal, it is also applied to all particulars. Therefore this applies to everything else. Those who propound the system of exclusion cannot say the same, because for them there is no universal as an entity, and at the time of designation, the phenomenon present at the time of the convention is no longer there. Therefore there can be no knowing of the phenomenon at that time."

119. **A consciousness that comprehends a single,**
which is a comprehender maintaining a single,
naturally separates causes and non-causes.

We answer that for us too, **a consciousness that comprehends** the homogenous results of trees and so forth as **a single** class, **which is a comprehender maintaining a single** phenomenon, firstly sees distinctly by the power of direct perception the particulars of tree and non-tree. After that a conceptual cognition comprehends them as belonging to homogenous classes. This is a cognition, without reliance upon a convention, that **naturally separates** those that are **the causes** of this cognition, such as the agaru trees, from those that are **not the causes** of that comprehension of a single class, such as stones. This cognition is produced before the convention of *tree* is formed.

120. **The entities that exist to that cognition**
appear as the very cause of that cognition,
lacking the nature of those that are not the cause,
as if they were of one entity,
naturally knowing the distinction.

121. **Convention is applied to the distinction,**
and from that, comprehension will occur.

> **The cognition is mistaken,**
> **comprehending as a single entity.**

The aspect of **the entities that exist**—that is, appear—**to that cognition, appear** as external trees that are **the very cause of that cognition** and appear as **lacking the nature of those that are not the cause** of that cognition—that is, non-trees. Because those external trees appear and are determined **as if they were of one entity, it naturally knows** by categorization agaru trees and so on **as being distinct** from non-trees. After that, the **convention** "this is a tree" **is applied to** the exclusion that appears to the conceptual cognition, in which there is **the distinction** from non-tree. **From that** verbal expression applied in this way, at the time of designation also, the exclusion that appears to the conceptual cognition will arise, and **comprehension will occur. The cognition** at that time **is mistaken** in the sense that what appears to it seems to be external, **and** so it **comprehends** by holding the previous and present **as a single entity.** Therefore, although there is no universal and the phenomenon that was there at the time of applying the convention is no longer present, there is no fault as posited in the consequence above that at the time of using designation, the phenomenon cannot be known.[97]

Establishing that all verbal expressions ascertain

> 122. **To reverse objects of cognition**
> **and to engage them in other objects,**
> **verbal expression is employed,**
> **because that ascertains the object.**

Verbal expression is employed in order to reverse objects of doubt **of** the **cognition** of the listener **and to engage them in other** conclusive **objects.** This is applied for **that** listener to **ascertain** their sought-after **object.**

Refuting the position that without something to preclude there can be no exclusion

An argument runs, "Even if the verbal expressions *tree* and so forth engage by way of exclusion, expressions such as *knowable* cannot engage by way of exclusion because *unknowable*, which is what is to be excluded, does not exist. This is because if it could become an object of cognition, it would become knowable, and if it could not become an object of cognition, it could not be excluded."

> **123. Otherwise applying would make no sense.**
> **Therefore, with the words *knowable* and so on**
> **established as designation, there will be preclusion.**

With the words "All phenomena are **knowable**" **and so on established**—that is, understood—**as designation,** in conjunction with other words, **there will be preclusion** of the object of doubt on the part of the listener because it is speech in which a phenomenon is applied to verbal expression, and the listener is able to preclude any object of doubt. **Otherwise**, if that were not so, **applying** a phenomenon to verbal expression **would make no sense.**

Refutations on the examination of whether an isolate exists as an entity

1. The way in which an isolate is expressed
2. Presenting scripture to establish the above
3. Refuting argument on the meaning of that scripture
4. An isolate has no real existence
5. Refuting the assertion that subsequent expressions and reason make no sense

The way in which an isolate is expressed

An argument runs, "If the isolate that you assert exists as an entity, then the fault you levied against a universal existing as an entity can be applied here also. If it does not exist as an entity, there cannot be any purpose in expressing it."

> **124. Whatever is distinct from whatever is negated,**
> **because of homogenous forms distinct from those,**
> **is given as possessing the appearing aspect.**

Forms of trees such as the agaru tree, **which are distinct from those** non-trees, appear as **homogenous, because of** which this universal **possesses the appearing aspect** of trees apprehended as external trees. To that, the expression *tree* **is given.** This has a purpose because **whatever is** a tree is **distinct from whatever** is not a tree, and therefore the querying person **negates that** non-tree and engages with tree.

Presenting scripture to establish the above

> **125. "Isolating from the other,**
> **some part of that entity**
> **will be understood."**
> **This has been taught.**

The aspect formed in the conceptual cognition apprehending tree is held as an external tree, and that is an isolate of tree. Therefore that is the direct referent of the expression "That is a tree." **This is taught** in the *Compendium of Valid Cognition*, where it says, **"Isolating from the other, some part of that entity will be understood."**[98] Also, "Verbal expression expresses only those entities characterized by being isolated from other phenomena."[99] And further, "Verbal expression excludes other expressions and meanings and expresses its own meaning."[100]

The meaning of the first citation is: from the expression *tree*, the "part" that is the entity of a tree, which is an aspect of the conceptual cognition of tree, will be understood. How is the aspect of that cognition established as being a part that is the entity of a tree? By isolating from the other, or non-tree.

The meaning of the second citation is: the verbal expression *tree* expresses the entity of tree that appears to a conceptual cognition characterized by exclusion. This point is the one expressed by the line "Those phenomena that exist for consciousness" (verse 78).

The meaning of the third citation will be given at the appropriate point in the text.

Refuting argument on the meaning of that scripture

> **"In this, there is no actual entity at all."**
> **126. From the verbal expression it will be comprehended,**
> **and comprehended by isolating the other.**
> **There is no comprehension of that**
> **characterized by something other.**

The argument to the first citation runs, "**In this** aspect that appears to the conceptual cognition, **there is no actual entity** of tree **at all** because it is simply the substance of consciousness."

The argument to the second citation says, "If it expresses an entity that has been characterized by being an isolate, then it is similar to the assertion that states that the object of a verbal expression is something that possesses a universal."

The meaning of "an entity characterized by being an isolate" is that **from the verbal expression** of "tree" and so forth, **that** representation of a tree appearing to a conceptual cognition **will be comprehended, and** it will be **comprehended by** way of **isolating** from **the other**, or non-tree. This is because that representation of tree is held as being a tree.

From verbal expression **there is no comprehension of that** representation of a tree **characterized by something** that is a separate universal isolated from non-tree. This is because some **other** separate universal does not exist to characterize that representation.

The argument against the third citation is: "With regard to the verbal expression *tree*, there must be both an exclusion of non-tree and a separate establishment of tree, because the verbal expression *tree* excludes non-tree."

127. **Verbal expression does not create the two.**
One does not exist with the other.

The **verbal expression** *tree* **does not create the two** factually separate actions of establishing tree and excluding non-tree because the very establishing of tree is the exclusion of non-tree. This is because tree and non-tree are explicitly contradictory in that **one does not exist with** the nature of **the other.**

An isolate has no real existence

It has no entity.
Seeing it as possessing an entity
is the contrivance of the cognition.
128. **Therefore it has no ultimate existence.**

This isolate that is the direct object of a verbal expression **has no ultimate existence**, because although **this** isolate **has no entity, seeing it as possessing an** external **entity is** simply **the contrivance of the cognition.**

As something other,
that isolation from the entity
could not be the entity,

because it must be said that
they are distinct from this.

If that which is isolated from non-tree existed **as something other** than a non-reality of tree, is it a reality of an agaru tree or a reality other than an agaru tree? If it were the former, then it **could not be the entity** of a palāśa tree because **that isolation from the entity** of non-tree is the reality of an agaru tree. If it were the latter, the agaru tree would not exist as a reality of tree, because that isolation from the reality of non-tree exists as a reality other than that of the agaru tree. You cannot assert both positions **because it must be said that these** agaru and palāśa trees **are distinct from this** non-tree.[101]

Refuting the assertion that subsequent expressions and reason makes no sense

This argument runs, "If a representation within a conceptual cognition is expressed in words, then the expression 'a tree is impermanent' spoken after the expression *tree*, as well as the reasoning to establish that, become meaningless, because a representation within a conceptual cognition is the intrinsically existing phenomenon of consciousness, and therefore when that representation is expressed, impermanence and so forth would also be expressed."

129. **If one is to remove something mixed in,**
it is only the expression and the reasoning
that performs the deed of removing.
There is in that no entity expressed
that will be removed.

With regard to the representation of tree within the conceptual cognition apprehending tree, **if one is to remove something**, such as permanence, that in the perspective of the cognition appears **mixed in** with it, **it is only the expression** "a tree is impermanent" **and the** establishing **reasoning that performs the deed of removing** the above. The expression *tree* will not perform the action of removing, because **in that** representation **there is no entity expressed**, existing as an intrinsically existing phenomenon, **that will be removed** by the expression *tree*.

130. **With the expression of that,**
all would be comprehended
because of the capability of the entity.
Therefore many results with same basis.

This holds because if an intrinsically existing phenomenon were being explicitly expressed, then **with the expression of that** intrinsically existing phenomenon, **all** existents within that phenomenon **would be comprehended.** This would be so **because of the capability of** such **an entity** being substantially one with impermanence and so forth.

Therefore the expression *tree* and the expression "a tree is impermanent" have **many results**—that is, purposes—and possess **the same basis**, or object-possessor, because they are expressions of the many parts excluded within a tree.

Śākyabuddhi says:

> It can be argued, "The aspect of that appearance is not distinct from the consciousness, and so, when you verbally express that entity, which is similar to the consciousness, isn't it the case that by the force of that entity, you will gain the comprehension of everything?"
>
> This is not the case. By being non-distinct from the consciousness, it is an intrinsically existing phenomenon, and that is a self-cognition similar to the consciousness. At that time it is not being expressed like an external intrinsically existing phenomenon. That aspect is conceived as being an external phenomenon and appears as the universal of that external. It is this that appears to the cognition produced from verbal expression, and it is the referent of the verbal expression. Being of one nature with the consciousness does not make it the referent of the expression. This is expressed in the lines:
>
> > Phenomena are conceptually cognized,
> > and therefore self-cognition is not conceptual.[102]

Refuting the argument of there being no common basis

It is argued, "If a verbal expression engages with its object as an exclusion, then it is impossible for an utpala flower, for example, to have a common basis with blue."

> 131. **If a single preclusion is revealed upon a single,**
> **at that time another remains excluded.**
> **That appears as single which pervades that.**

At such a time, it is made into cognition,
132. **and there will be a common basis.**

There may be no common basis in reality, but in the perspective of an exclusion such a common basis exists. **At the time** that the expression *blue* is uttered, if **a single** isolate **precluding** non-blue is **revealed upon a single** flower, **another**—that is, an isolate of utpala—is not **excluded** and **remains** unestablished. Likewise, when the word *utpala* is uttered in that situation, **that** blue and that utpala **appear as** a **single** object-possessor **pervading that** flower. **At such a time, it is made into** a conceptual **cognition, and there will be a common basis** of blue and utpala.

Summary of what is established and refuted

When preclusion is uttered by verbal expression,
the entity is reached.
It is said that it exists on that.
133. **A single entity by a verbal expression is not.**
It would appear to a cognition,
but it does not and is ascertained
as having no real existence.

When, with respect to a pot, the **preclusion** of non-pot **is uttered** by the **verbal expression**, it is possible that **the entity** of that pot **is reached**, or gained, because **it is said that** preclusion of non-pot **exists on that** pot. If, with respect to a pot, **a single-entity** universal is being uttered **by a verbal expression**, the entity of that pot **is not** gained, because if such a real universal existed on the pot, **it would appear to a** valid **cognition, but it does not** appear. This pervades because whatever is suitable to appear but is not seen **is ascertained as**—that is, pervaded by—**having no real existence**.

Both engage with universals

134. **Therefore for verbal expressions and cognitions also,**
which are subjects possessing exclusions,
it is impossible to engage with an entity.

The difference between expressing an exclusion and expressing a real universal has been explained. **Therefore verbal expressions and** conceptual **cognitions also, which are subjects possessing** objects of **exclusions**, are explained as being subjects possessing, as their objects, universals not existing as actual entities. This is because they are subjects possessing universals as objects, and **it is impossible** for them **to engage with** universals as **entities.**

19. Establishing the Direct Object as an Exclusion

Establishment of the direct object as an exclusion

1. Analysis
2. Actual topic

Analysis

Some commentators, when analyzing the validity and faults of the two modes of engagement, do so by analyzing reasons for the following: (1) If conceptual cognitions and verbal expressions engage by way of exclusion, it is possible to gain the referent object and a common basis. (2) If engagement were by way of a separate universal, neither would be possible. (3) A single verbal expression engages with many objects. (4) Arguments for the nonexistence of a single universal are refuted.

They say that the first of these is taught by the lines beginning "With the expression of that" (verse 1.130), the second point by the lines beginning "A single entity by a verbal expression is not" (1.133), the third by the lines beginning "In order to illustrate the results" (1.137), and the fourth by the lines beginning "If aside from the isolate" (1.163).

These explanations are not correct. "With the expression of that" comes at the end of the verse above and not at the beginning of the following verse. Also, the section beginning with the lines "Because the nature of an entity is singular" (1.134d) refutes the universal and the particulars being one substance or separate substances but does not solely teach the impossibility of there being a common basis in a separate universal.

Some say that the text beginning from "Verbal expressions reveal those assigned as conventions" (1.92) is the extensive explanation of the way verbal expressions engage. That is then divided into the headings (1) subjects possessing entities and (2) subjects possessing objects of nonexistence. Also, in the explanations on the difference between a universal and exclusion, there are discussions on whether the referent is gained from the expression, whether a common basis can exist upon a universal, and whether something is a reason for a universal.

The first of these, they say, is taught by the lines beginning "When preclusion is uttered by verbal expression" (1.132b), the second by the lines beginning "A single entity by a verbal expression is not" (1.133), and the third by the lines beginning "With the expression of that" (1.130). This is also incorrect. The text from the lines beginning "Therefore for verbal expressions and cognitions also" (1.134a) is a summary combining both verbal expressions and conceptual cognition and is not teaching the engagement by verbal expression alone. The lines beginning "Because the nature of an entity is singular" (1.134d) refute the universal and particulars being one or different substantially, and primarily establish the universal as having no reality. The lines up to "it is impossible to engage with an entity" (1.134c) are explaining the modes of engagement by verbal expressions and conceptual cognitions as object-possessors. Therefore it is important that each topic is clearly delineated.

Some say that the lines following "Because the nature of an entity is singular" (1.134d) is a refutation of the argument against the text that precedes it, which teaches that a universal has no reality. This is incorrect because the first six lines teach the reasoning that establishes that a universal has no reality, and the refutation of the argument comes after that.

Actual topic

1. Examination and refutation of a universal as an actual entity
2. Refuting the argument that the same fault could be applied to the exclusion universal
3. Though there is no universal as an actual entity, a single verbal expression is still valid
4. Refuting the arguments of those who posit a universal as an actual entity

Examination and refutation of a universal as an actual entity

The argument states that the lines "A single entity by a verbal expression is not. It would appear to a cognition, but it does not" (1.133) and "It is impossible to engage with an entity" (1.134c) are not correct because a universal as an entity does exist, and that is the actual thing being expressed by a verbal expression.

> **Because the nature of an entity is singular,**
> 135. **how does it appear distinctly to the cognition?**
> **A single does not occupy the same realm of activity**
> **both concomitant and nonconcomitant.**

In that case we ask, "Are the universal and the particulars substantially one or separate?" If the former, **how does** the nature—that is, the aspect—**appear distinctly to the cognition?** It cannot, **because the nature of an entity is singular.** This pervades because you accept that verbal expression and conceptual cognition engage by way of affirmation.

Furthermore, it would follow that a black and white cow[103] would both be concomitant with and nonconcomitant with a black dewlapped cow because it is of the same substantial entity as the universal of a cow and is also a black and white cow. You cannot agree with the premise because **a single** black and white cow **does not occupy the same realm of activity** that is **both concomitant and nonconcomitant** with a black dewlapped cow.

The Vaiśeṣika school says, "Universals and particulars are substantially distinct."

> **If distinct, there could be no cause**
> 136. **for a nonseparate designation.**

In that case, it would follow that on the utpala flower, as a property-possessor with its property blue, **there could be no cause for** producing **a nonseparate**—that is, common-basis—**designation** because the utpala and blue are substantially **distinct.**

Refuting the argument that the same fault could be applied to the exclusion universal

The reply to the above: "The same fault deduced from the above analysis could be applied to your position."

> **In all those, isolation exists,**
> **and such consequential faults do not exist.**

Such consequential faults of there being no universal and the impossibility of a common basis **do not exist** with regard to the particulars because, from the perspective of exclusion, that which is **isolated** from the incongruous class **exists in all those** particulars.

Though there is no universal as an actual entity, a single verbal expression is still valid

1. A single expression engages by similar results
2. Refuting engagement by way of a universal as an actual entity
3. Determining how a single result is produced
4. Illustrating by example the way a single expression engages

A single expression engages by similar results

"If there is no universal as an actual entity and a universal by exclusion is a superimposition, then it would not be possible for a single verbal expression to engage several particulars."

> 137. **In order to illustrate the results,**
> **the elders created a single-expression convention**
> **for the distinct with same-type results,**
> **because of the isolation from that**
> **which does not contain those results.**

In order to illustrate the results of the existence of a cow, such as the activities of ploughing and milking, **the elders created a convention by way of a single expression** *cow* **for distinct** cows that have no universal as an actual entity but that produce **results of the same type.** This is not done because there is a universal as an actual entity but **because** there is mere exclusion by way of the similarity found in **the isolation from that which does not contain the results** of the cow.

"Why is the convention created with a single expression and not with individual and distinct expressions for the many particulars?"

> 138. **Illustrating the distinct**
> **would be complex, impossible,**
> **and with no results.**

The many and distinct particulars of *cow* are not given conventions by way of individual expressions because **illustrating** them by **distinct** expressions **would be complex and impossible**. Even if it were possible, there would be **no results.**

Refuting engagement by way of a universal as an actual entity

Not with entities,
but all abide in their individual natures.
139. **Whatever the nature of multicolored**
is not found in grey.

The verbal expression *cow* **does not** engage **with a** single **entity**, or universal, because **all** particulars of entities **abide in their individual natures**, unmixed with others. Therefore there can be no single universal as an actual entity. **Whatever nature a multicolored** cow has **is not found in** a single-colored **grey** cow, for example.

Determining how a single result is produced
"Why is it said that particulars of cows produce a single result?"

Isolation from that which does not have
the result is found in both,
140. **and although in reality they are not distinct,**
distinct verbal expressions are not correct.
Therefore, if you want the result of that,
it is that distinct from that without those results.

From the perspective of exclusion, it is acceptable to speak of a multicolored cow and a single-colored grey cow possessing the same results, because the **isolation from that which does not have the result** of those cows **is found in both** of them. Therefore **it is not correct** that for all cow particulars there is **verbal expression** of type—that is, *cow*—engaging or not engaging **distinctly** with them, because **in** the **reality** of being reversed from not producing the results of cows, **they are not distinct.**

Therefore, if you want a designation to express the single **result** of the particulars of cows, it can only be the exclusion that is **distinct from that without the results** of the particulars, because there is no cow universal as an actual entity.

Illustrating by example the way a single expression engages

141. **For example, the eye and so forth**
are the cause of
a single consciousness of form.
Therefore it can reveal
the undifferentiated result.

142. **At times all can be comprehended simultaneously.**
Therefore, even if that nature is held
as not distinct from a universal,
it is taught by that arising from the linguistic convention.

The way a single expression engages with the many that produce results of the same class, even though universals are not actual entities, can be illustrated with **an example. The eye and so forth**—that is, the visual appearance and mental engagement—**are the cause of a single consciousness** apprehending **form.** Because of this, the single expression "causes of the visual consciousness" is used.

"What is the purpose of this?"

Even if you hold the nature of eyes and so forth **to be not distinct from** the entity of **a universal, it is taught that** the single entity **arising from the linguistic convention** "causes of the visual consciousness" has a purpose, because at that time **it can reveal**, in general, the causes of a visual consciousness, which is the **undifferentiated**—that is, common—**result** of the three conditions. The purpose of this is that **all** three conditions **can at** certain **times be comprehended simultaneously**. This is explained in *Treasure of Reasoning* by the lines:

> Activities of establishing and refuting on the distinct
> are comprehended gathered together as one.[104]

20. Refuting the Universal as an Entity

Refuting the arguments of those who posit a universal as an actual entity

1. Refuting the assertion that a single verbal expression engages by way of a universal as an actual entity
2. Refuting the assertion that a single result exists by way of a universal as an actual entity

Refuting the assertion that a single verbal expression engages by way of a universal as an actual entity

1. The assertion
2. The refutation

The assertion

> 143. **"Isn't it because there exists a single**
> **that there is a single sound for the many?"**

"**Isn't it** the case that a verbal expression engages with the many not because there is a similar result but **because there exists a single** universal as an actual entity, **a single sound** or verbal expression *cow*, that engages with **the many** particulars that are cows?"

The refutation

1. The reason for this single existence abiding is not established
2. There is no pervasion that sound engages
3. Although similar in being distinct, there are differences

The reason for this single existence abiding is not established

1. Refuting the posited abiding of this single existence
2. Damaging the single existence itself

Refuting the posited abiding of this single existence

1. Refuting together two posited possibilities
2. Refuting both possibilities individually

Refuting together two posited possibilities

> **Abiding dependently or because of the particulars?**
> **Neither of them is correct for that.**

This single universal within the many particulars, **does it abide** in the manner of a single universal **depending** upon many particulars, **or** is it **because** the many **particulars** illustrate the single universal? If these are examined, **neither of them is correct** with regard to **that** universal, as will be explained.

Refuting both possibilities individually

1. Refutation of the universal existing by way of dependence
2. Refutation of the universal existing by way of the particulars

Refutation of the universal existing by way of dependence

> 144. **With no effect on permanence, there is no support.**
> **With jujube and so on, they would fall.**
> **Creation of that place is enabled by the pot and so forth.**
> **That would be impossible with the above.**

If the first of the two above possibilities were correct, it would follow that the particulars **would not be the support** for a permanent and completely separate universal **because** they could have **no effect on** that **permanent** universal. You might reply, "There is no pervasion. A pot, for example, has no effect on the jujube inside it but is its support."[105]

We reply that just as that the pot has no causal effect on **the jujube**, water, **and so on** that depend upon that pot, they are similarly not supported [for their existence] by that pot. This is because without that pot **they** are things that **would fall** to other places. Their place and their material holder[106] are similar.

Therefore the **creation of** the material holder abiding in **that place is enabled by the pot and so forth.**

"Isn't it the same with particulars and the universal?"

It would be impossible for the particulars to create the abiding of the material holder of that universal in that same place because **the above** universal is a permanent phenomenon.

"Isn't it possible that the universal of those particulars is not something newly produced by the particulars but that they are the support maintaining the existence of something already existing?"

> 145. **Even without them it would still be in place.**
> **Moreover, it is not correct that they maintain,**
> **because analyzing as distinct or not distinct,**
> **it is not correct.**

The particulars have not maintained the existence of that universal because it follows that **even without** the particulars **it would still be in place. Moreover, it cannot be correct that** the particulars **maintain** the existence of the universal, **because** by **analyzing** that existence created by the particulars **as** either **distinct or not distinct** from the particulars, **it is** seen **not** to be **correct** that it is maintained by the particulars. This is because, if they *were* distinct, the particulars would not have maintained the existence of the universal because it would follow that they would exist as substantially separate from the universal. And if they *were not* distinct, it would follow that the particulars would not have maintained the existence of the universal because they would be substantially one with the universal.

Refutation of the universal existing by way of the particulars

1. The example of that which illustrates and that which is illustrated is not established
2. Even if it is established, it is not established that it possesses the class

The example of that which illustrates and that which is illustrated is not established[107]

> 146. **For there to be the possibility of a generation of**
> **a consciousness of that entity,**
> **it is produced in the presence of another.**

This is what is illustrated.
That agent is asserted as being the cause.

According to the latter of the two positions posited above, that which illustrates and that which is illustrated must be cause and effect. This is because **for there to be the possibility of a generation of a consciousness** focusing upon **an entity** of that which is illustrated, the apprehending of that **is produced in** dependence upon **the presence of another**—that which illustrates. **This** generation of what is apprehended **is what is illustrated. That agent**—that is that which illustrates, creating the apprehending of that which is illustrated—**is asserted as being the cause** of that which is illustrated.

147. **If it were possible for this to exist prior,**
it could not depend upon that.
Because those cannot become that,
how can it arise from those
that contain the universal?

This reasoning is valid because, for example, **if it were possible for** the generation of the consciousness apprehending **this** pot and so on, which is to be illustrated, **to exist prior**, without a dependence upon that which illustrates, it would follow that this **could not** directly **depend upon that** which illustrates, which directly generates the consciousness apprehending that which is to be illustrated.

How can that universal, which is to be illustrated, **arise from those** particulars, which **contain the universal?** It cannot, **because those** particulars, by the power of direct effect, **cannot become**, or possess the ability to generate, the apprehending consciousness of the universal.

It might be replied, "There is no pervasion here, because the particulars that are established as the illustrators of the universal are not creative entities[108] that have the capacity to generate the consciousness apprehending that universal, but it is that sense faculty that is the creative entity apprehending the universal, and therefore in this way the particulars are established as the illustrators of the universal."

148. **The sense faculty is not the creative entity**
from the particulars, as is eye medicine.
At times when present or not present,
there is no distinction in comprehension.

We reply that **the sense faculty is not the creative entity** producing the apprehending of that universal **from the particulars** in the same way that **eye medicine** has a direct effect on the visual sense faculty, because **at times when** those particulars are either **present or not present, there is no distinction in** clear and non-clear **comprehension** of the universal by the sense faculty.

Even if it is established, it is not established that it possesses the class

> 149. **If you assert that by**
> **being the illustrators of the class,**
> **they would possess the class,**
> **a beacon and so on would possess cows and so on.**

Even **if you assert that** merely **by** the particulars **being the illustrators of the class, they would possess the class,** or maintain it, then it would follow that illuminators, such as **a beacon and so on**—referring to the sense faculty and the mind—**would possess,** or maintain the existence of, universals such as **cows and so on** because they are causes that illuminate the cognition of those universals.

Damaging the single existence itself

1. The consequence that as a separate phenomenon there can be no cognition of the universal
2. The consequence reasoning is also established with regard to the other
3. Refuting other rejoinders

The consequence that as a separate phenomenon there can be no cognition of the universal

> 150. **If the class exists as other than**
> **the particulars or as the same,**
> **how could there be a cognition**
> **within particulars not previously existing?**
> 151. **That seen in one**
> **could not possibly be seen in another.**

If the class exists as one, either as substantially **other than the particulars,** as asserted by the Vaiśeṣika school, **or as** substantially **the same,** as asserted by the

Sāṃkhya school, then **how could there be a cognition** of the universal, by way of the abiding a cow universal, **within** newly arisen cow **particulars not previously existing?** It would not be possible because **that** universal which is **seen in one**—that is, in previous particulars—**could not possibly be seen in another,** in new particulars not seen before.

The consequence reasoning is also established with regard to the other

> **If it is not other, it does not pervade.**
> **Even if other, it would not depend.**
> 152. **It will not pervade and is not to be found in those,**
> **it does not have one part in the latter,**
> **it does not abandon its earlier support.**
> **Alas, what a cause of great loss!**

If it is stated that the reason is not proven, we reply that the universal **does not** ultimately **pervade** the later particulars, because **if it is not other** than the previous particulars, as the Sāṃkhya assert, then it must be one with them. **Even if** the universal is **other** than the particulars, as the Vaiśeṣika assert, it follows that they would not exist in the later and separate particulars because **it would not depend** upon the later and separate particulars. The universal existing in the earlier particulars **will not pervade** the later; the universal **is not to be found in those** later and already created particulars, and the universal **does not have** one part existing in the former and **one part in the latter**. The first reason is established because that universal **does not abandon its earlier support**—that is, the earlier particulars.

Therefore, the universal supposedly abiding in the earlier particulars and also in the later particulars is, **alas, a cause of great loss!**

Refuting other rejoinders

1. Refuting that there is a universal while particulars do not exist
2. Refuting that there is a universal while particulars do exist

Refuting that there is a universal while particulars do not exist

> 153. **That which abides does**
> **not move from its own place.**
> **If from that, it was created in another place,**
> **that would be correct.**

The Vaiśeṣika teacher Kaṇāda asserts that the universal is one, unmoving, partless, and suitable to appear as pervading all particulars. His disciple Pethara disputes the reason "because it is not a support," asserting that until an instance exists, it has no universal but that the universal from the earlier particulars will pervade the later. In that case, we reply that there cannot be a universal in the later particulars because **that** universal **which abides** in the other earlier particulars **does not move** to another **from its own place**, that is, the earlier particulars. Also, **if** that universal moved **from that** earlier instance and **was created in another place**—that is, a new instance—then **it would be correct** to say that the universal existed in the later particulars, but that is not possible.

"Isn't it the case that although the universal does not move from the earlier instance, it nevertheless pervades the later?"

> 154. **Wherever there abides an entity,**
> **it will have no connection with such a place.**
> **Pervading the subjects of those?**
> **How is that not embarrassing?**

Wherever—that is, in whatever place—**there abides an entity** of a newly arisen instance, the universal **will have no connection with such a place**, but to say that universal **pervades the subjects of those** later places—that is, the particulars that exist there—**how is that not embarrassing?** It is illogical.

Refuting that there is a universal while particulars do exist

> 155. **If class exists in all,**
> **in one it would be illustrated by those particulars**
> **and would be indivisible.**
> **Therefore it would be seen everywhere.**

Beluka[109] also disputes the reasoning "because it is not a support," saying that **if class exists in all** objects, then isn't it the case that the newly produced particulars must have a universal?

It follows that such a universal **would be seen everywhere**, where there are and are not particulars, because **in the one** place where there are particulars **it would be illustrated by those particulars, and** it **would be indivisible** in all places.

They reply, "It exists in all places, but it is not seen in some places because seeing the universal depends upon it being illustrated by the particulars."

> **It does not depend upon the particulars.**
> 156. **If the illustrator were not comprehended,**
> **the illustrated would also not be comprehended.**
> **Why have you reversed your position**
> **on those that possess it?**

We reply that seeing that universal **does not depend upon the particulars,** because this would mean that, by way of dependence, **if the illustrator**—that is, the particulars—**were not comprehended, then** that which is **illustrated**—that is, the universal—**would also not be** truly **comprehended**, because that is your assertion. If you agree, then **why have you reversed your position on** the mode of comprehending the universal and **those** particulars **that possess it?** Previously, your position was that the particulars were comprehended by apprehending the universal, and here your position is that the universal is comprehended in dependence upon the particulars.

There is no pervasion that sound engages

1. Presenting the proof of no pervasion
2. Refuting the statements of others

Presenting the proof of no pervasion

> 157. **Though there is no undifferentiated phenomenon,**
> ***cooks* and so forth can be expressed.**

There is no pervasion that when a single verbal expression and conceptual cognition engages with the many, there is a single entity of a universal as its cause, because **although there is no undifferentiated phenomenon**—that is, no single universal—many individuals **can be expressed** by a single verbal expression **such as *cooks*** or *servers*.

Refuting the statements of others

1. Refuting that the cause of the expression comes from the work of cooking
2. Refuting that the cause of the expression is the universal of cooks

Refuting that the cause of the expression comes from the work of cooking

"Isn't the case that the single work of cooking and so on performed by those beings is the cause for the single verbal expression and conceptual cognition?"

> **Because they are distinct,**
> **work would not be a reason.**
> **This class of work would not be the cause**
> **because of a connection to the work.**
> 158. **That is the reason for the expression**
> **being applied to another.**
> **The work also is not being sustained.**

Then it would follow that the individual acts of **work** performed by those individual beings **would not be a reason** for a single verbal expression and conceptual cognition **because they are** many and **distinct**.

They reply, "The intrinsically existent phenomena of the tasks are many, but they are of one class, and so they are the cause of a single verbal expression and conceptual cognition."

It would follow that **this class of work would not be the cause** of a single verbal expression and conceptual cognition *cooks* with regard to these many individuals **because** it has no direct connection to the individuals but only **a** direct **connection to the work. That is the reason for the** single **expression** "cooking" **being applied to** aspects of the work, which are **other** than the workers. Moreover, it would follow that during the times these beings are not cooking, the expression *cooks* could not be applied to them because **the** cooking **work also is** not in operation and **not being sustained.**

It could be argued, "The class *work* is connected to work, and work is connected to substantiality. Therefore the class *work* is indirectly connected to substantiality. In that case, it is the cause for the single verbal expression and conceptual cognition *cooks* to engage with substantially existing beings."

> **Because the connection does not exist,**
> **it is not correct that the universal**
> **is the cause for the verbal expression.**
> 159. **Not being established, it is not correct**
> **because of absurd consequences.**

In that case, it would follow that during the times of no work, the class *work* would have no connection with the work because the work has ceased and does not exist. If you agree, then it follows that **it cannot be correct that the universal *work* is the cause for the** single **verbal expression** and conceptual cognition with regard to the people during the time there is no work, **because the connection** to those people by way of the work **does not exist**, even indirectly. This pervades because the connection **not being established** means that **it is not correct** for the universal to be the cause of engagement via a single verbal expression. If it were correct, **the absurd consequence** would follow that even a horse could be the cause of a single verbal expression and conceptual cognition engaging a cow.

"Isn't it the case that the work done previously and the work to be continued in the future are the causes for the single verbal expression and conceptual cognition?"

> **They are not causes of the consciousness and expression**
> **because they have gained a non-cause.**
> **The potential is also not the cause**
> **because there is no concomitance.**

It follows that the previous and future work **are not causes of the consciousness and** the **expression** of the present **because they** do not exist in the present. If you say this does not pervade, then it follows that the single verbal expression and conceptual cognition **have gained a non-cause**—that is, are without causes—because not existing does not have to mean that it is not a cause of that.

"Isn't it the case that the potential of the work is the cause of the single verbal expression and conceptual cognition *cooks* being applied to the individuals who are cooking?"

The potential of individual tasks **is also not the cause** of the single verbal expression and conceptual cognition applied to the many **because there is no concomitance** among the separate substances.

Refuting that the cause of the expression is the universal of cooks

> 160. **If there were a universal of cooks and so on,**
> **it would be existing in the very beginning,**
> **and later, no connection because of no difference.**
> **Would it not be clear, as is existence and so on?**

"Isn't it the case that because there is a single **universal of cooks and so on**, there is the single verbal expression and conceptual cognition *cooks* applied to a group of cooks?"

If that were so, then it follows that **in the very beginning**, as soon as these persons were born, unconnected to the act of cooking, the single verbal expression and conceptual cognition *cooks* would be applied, because at that time the universal of cooks **would be existing**. You have to accept the reason because your own texts state, "The various universals that possess the features of meeting and abiding within phenomena do so right at the creation of these phenomena."[110]

If, in transgression of that text, there is no connection to a universal at the very beginning, then it would follow that **later** on, that substantially existing person would also have **no connection** to the universal **because** it is **no different** in the sense of being permanent.

"The universal is connected to a substantial existence from the beginning, but it is not clear. Therefore, at the beginning, the single verbal expression and conceptual cognition do not engage with it."

It follows that the universal **would be clear** from the beginning because the universal is something that should appear, **in the same way** that **existence**, substantiality, **and so on**, are clear from the beginning.

> 161. **If made clear dependent upon the effect of the action,**
> **there is no dependence because of no change.**
> **Even if perfected by circumstance,**
> **it would be impermanent from what action?**

If you reply, "The universal is not clear in the beginning but is **made clear in dependence upon the effect of the action** of cooking," then it must follow that the substantially existing person **has no dependence** upon the act of illustrating the universal **because** it does **not change. Even if** you don't accept the reasoning because you assert that this substantially existing person is **perfected by circumstance, it would be impermanent** as it is changed by circumstance. In that case, **from what action** could it illustrate the permanent universal in dependence upon the work? It could not because it would be impermanent.

Although similar in being distinct, there are differences

> 162. **Even if they are similar,**
> **there being the proximity of a class,**
> **with some engaged, others not,**
> **is the reason for expressions and consciousnesses.**

It might be thought, "A group of cooks, pots, and wool are equally distinct with no actually existing universal, and so it cannot be correct for a single verbal expression and conceptual cognition to engage or not engage with cooks."

Even if they are similar in **being** distinct, but because of **the proximity** and non-proximity **of a class** exclusion, **some** beings can be **engaged** with the single verbal expression and conceptual cognition *cooks* and **others**, such as pots and wool, are **not** engaged in that way, because that exclusion **is the reason for** universal **expressions and consciousnesses** to engage.

21. Refuting that a Single Result Exists by Way of a Universal

Refuting the assertion that a single result exists by way of a universal as an actual entity

1. The assertion of Kapila[111]
2. The extensive refutation

The assertion of Kapila

> 163. **"If aside from the isolate,**
> **there were nothing other that pervaded entities,**
> **the result of a single would not be that of another**
> **because it would be totally distinct."**

Kapila says that **if there were nothing other that pervaded entities**, such as the one nature of all entities, **aside from**—that is, except for—**the isolate** of exclusion, then the sprout, as **the result of a single** seed, **would not be** the result **of others**, such as water and fertilizer, **because it**, the seed, **would be totally distinct** from the water and fertilizer. Therefore the many, being of a single nature, give rise to a single result.

The extensive refutation

1. Refuting by reason the Sāṃkhya position
2. This reasoning also refutes the Immodest Ones[112]

Refuting by reason the Sāṃkhya position

1. A single nature is not the object engaged
2. The object to be engaged is solely an intrinsically existing phenomenon
3. Examining the two modes of engaging by way of universals

A single nature is not the object engaged

1. Refuting that a single nature could create
2. Refuting entities to be of a single nature
3. Refuting that the nature and its manifestations are one

Refuting that a single nature could create

1. If a single nature could create, the conditions would become meaningless
2. If the many could create, the universal would be meaningless
3. Although the many create, they are different

If a single nature could create, the conditions would become meaningless

164. If the many create the single result
because of the existence of a single nature,
conditions that cooperate would be meaningless
because it would exist in the single entity.

If the many, such as water and fertilizer, **create the single result** of a sprout **because of the existence of a single nature**, such as the prime universal,[113] then these **conditions** of water and fertilizer and so on **that cooperate** in the production of the sprout **would be meaningless, because** the ability to produce the sprout **would exist in the single entity** of the seed, because it—that is, the universal—would exist there.

165. Not moving from an entity that is not distinct,
the attributes lack the certainty.

To reiterate this point, it would follow that the seed would constantly have the power to produce a sprout because it is of the nature of—that is, **not moving from**—the prime universal, **an entity that is not distinct** from the power to directly produce the sprout. **The attributes**—that is, the cooperating conditions—would definitely not be necessary to produce the sprout because they would **lack the certainty** of dwelling with the prime universal that is in the nature of the seed.

If the many could create, the universal would be meaningless

> **If one is missing, there are no results.**
> **Therefore they arise from the particulars.**
> 166. **Those that have the power to create**
> **exist as ultimates and are not concomitant.**
> **Results will not arise from that which is concomitant.**

If you agree with the previous consequence that the cooperating conditions would be meaningless, then we say that **those** results—that is, sprouts—**will arise from the particulars** of the conditions, because when the conditions come together, even though there is no prime universal, they will arise, and **if** even **one** of those conditions **is missing, those results will not** arise. **The results**—that is, the sprouts—**will not arise from that** prime universal being **concomitant** with the particulars, because **those that have the power to create** something such as a result **exist as ultimates, and** those ultimate existences **are not** mutually **concomitant.**

This verse negates the assertion that there exists a common basis for entities and a universal as well as the assertion that whatever has the power to create does not have to have ultimate existence.

Although the many create, they are different

They might argue, "If water, fertilizer, and so on, which are distinct from the seed that produces the sprout, will indeed produce a sprout, then every seed of barley and so on will produce sprouts of rice, because they are no different in being distinct."

> 167. **Therefore, although distinct entities,**
> **some are causes while others are not.**
> **Such is the nature.**

There are absurd consequences to the position of a single nature being able to create. **Therefore** take a seed of barley and a seed of rice. **Although** similar in having **distinct entities, some** seeds, such as those of rice, **are causes** of rice seedlings, **while other** seeds, such as those of barley, **are not** causes of rice seedlings. This is because **such is the nature** of phenomena.

22. Refuting Entities to Be of a Single Nature

Refuting entities to be of a single nature

1. Presenting the consequence and refuting the response
2. Refuting similarity to the exclusion universal
3. Refuting that intrinsically existent phenomena are not creating forces
4. There is no fault in the assertion that the many create
5. There are faults in the assertion that the one creates

Presenting the consequence and refuting the response

> **If not distinct, creation and destruction**
> **would occur simultaneously.**
> 168. **In reply, "That is not so. They are distinct from that."**
> **When one is destroyed, if it still remains,**
> **the entity is not one with that.**
> **Therefore there would be no cognition**
> **of feature and universal.**

If all entities were one and **not distinct**, then the **creation and destruction** of various entities of the past and future **would occur simultaneously** because they would all be of the same substance. **If in reply** you state, "It is not that they are completely non-distinct. Coming from that prime universal, **they are distinct** for the time being, and **so it is not** the case that they are created and destroyed at the same time, because for the time being they are impermanent but their nature is permanent."

It follows that **the entity** of the prime universal **is not one with** the entity of the features because **when one** feature **is destroyed**, the prime universal **still remains** undestroyed. If you agree, then in reality the universal and its features must be separate. **Therefore there would be no** factual verbal expression and conceptual **cognition** engaging "This is the **universal** of this feature" or "This is a **feature** of this universal," because they would be unrelated to each other and substantially separate.

Refuting similarity to the exclusion universal

The argument runs, "The fault posited in the argument above on the destruction of the universal at the time when the instance is destroyed could also be applied to the exclusion universal, because if the exclusion universal is destroyed when one instance is destroyed, then the remaining particulars would be devoid of a universal. If the exclusion universal is not destroyed at that time, then the universal and the features would substantially separate."

> 169. **Because this isolate has no nature,**
> **whether it remains or not is not examined.**
> **The cognition of a universal is a corruption,**
> **and therefore there is no negation.**

Here, with regard to an exclusion universal, the isolation from everything that something is not, present in all particulars from the perspective of exclusion, is an *exclusion*. Also, the representation within a conceptual cognition, as the creator of the exclusion, is known as an *exclusion*. On the basis of the first, when an instance is destroyed, **it is not** appropriate to **examine** what kind of phenomenon is this isolate exclusion that in reality **remains or not, because this isolate** exclusion **has no nature.**

On the basis of the second, with regard to **a cognition of a universal**, which conceptualizes the many as one, when an instance is destroyed, **there is no negation** of that cognition by way of examining what kind of phenomenon that in reality remains or not, **because** the appearance within such a cognition of being an external instance **is a corruption**—that is, it is a mistaken consciousness. It is not substantially one with the external instance but substantially one with the consciousness. This is the same point as expressed in the lines:

It is not distinct from the consciousness.
How can it pervade separate entities? (1.71)

Tibetans have designated exclusion in three ways: the intrinsically existing phenomenon itself, the nonaffirming negation that is the isolation from all that which is not the intrinsically existing phenomenon, and the representation within the conceptual cognition as the actual object expressed by a verbal expression. On the basis of the first, they add the reasoning that the particulars would be simultaneously created and destroyed. The first two lines of the above verse are on the basis of the second, and the latter two lines are on the basis of the third type of exclusion. They say that with regard to the universal superimposed by the conceptual cognition of the universal, when the instance is destroyed, there is no negation of it by way of examining whether it remains in reality, because it is a corruption and, therefore, the universal superimposed by that conceptual cognition is not a reality.

Such an explanation is turning the sayings of old men into valid statements and does not approach the intention of the text. This is because for the first there is no need for any addition. Secondly, asserting that the isolate exclusion is pervaded by being a nonaffirming negation has already been refuted in my *Madhyamaka Overview*. Thirdly, if the universal superimposed by the conceptual cognition is being referred to here, it is no different from the point expressed by the line "because this isolate has no nature" from the first half of the verse.

Refuting that intrinsically existent phenomena are not creating forces

170. "Different from that,
the entity of the producer,
how can they produce?"
The attributes themselves are producers.
"They also possess an inseparable."
171. That does not produce, as has been stated.

The argument is, "**How can** water, fertilizer, and so on **produce** a sprout? **They** cannot, because they are **different from** a seed, which is in **the entity of the producer** of a sprout."

There is no pervasion to this argument because it has already been stated that **the attributes themselves**, such as water, fertilizer, and so on, which are separate entities, **are producers** of the sprout.

In response, "**These** attributes **also possess an inseparable** entity—that is, the prime universal—and therefore the sprout is produced by a single producer and not by the features."

That single entity **does not produce** that sprout, because the consequence **has** already **been stated** that such an entity would render the cooperating causes useless.

> **Even when appearing, they function separately,**
> **not depending on others. They exist in reality,**
> **isolated from others,**
> 172. **explained as causes and results**
> **and as intrinsically existent.**
> **Making use of them brings results.**
> **Therefore they are engaged by all beings.**

Therefore the seed and so on **function separately**—that is, are of separate entities—because **even when appearing** to an unmistaken cognition, they are of their own distinct natures, appearing individually, **and do not depend on anything else**. The word "even" implies the inclusion of individual production and cessation.

Therefore **these** attributes, such as the seed and so on, **exist in reality.** They **are isolated from others**. They are **explained as being causes** that create **and results** that are created **and** they exist **as intrinsically existent. They are** objects to be **engaged by all beings** who seek to actually do something, because **making use of them brings results**. The prime universal does not behave like that, and therefore it is not the producer of results.

There is no fault in the assertion that the many create

> 173. **Similar to the no difference in not being distinct,**
> **everything will not produce everything.**
> **Although no difference in being distinct,**
> **everything will not produce everything.**
> 174. **Though distinct, by nature**
> **some will be the creator.**

Although there is **no difference in** their **being distinct, everything**—seeds of barley and so on—**will not produce everything**—sprouts of rice and other crops—because **although** there is no difference in being **distinct, by** the **nature** of the entities, only **some** seeds of rice **will be the creator** of some sprouts of rice and will not be the creator of sprouts of barley. This is **similar to** your Sāṃkhya assertion that although all entities have **no difference in not being distinct** by nature, all causes will not produce all results.

There are faults in the assertion that the one creates

> **Even if not distinct, it would be contradictory**
> **producing and not producing a single thing.**
> 175. **"Because of existing as distinct,**
> **it will not perform the task."**
> **The cooperating causes would not create.**
> **What does "producing sequentially" mean?**
> **Is it the entity itself or something else?**

Even if all entities were one in the sense of being **not distinct, it would be contradictory** for a seed of barley and a seed of rice to have two separate aspects, with one **producing and** one **not producing a single** sprout of rice, because they would be of the same substance.

The response, "Isn't it the case that it is not contradictory to assert that a seed of barley **will not perform the task** of creating a sprout of rice, **because** a seed of barley temporally **exists as distinct** from a seed of rice?"

In that case, it follows that **the cooperating causes would not create** a sprout of rice because of this reasoning.

The response: "But the prime, single universal engages sequentially in the form of various causes and is a sequential producer of various results."

What does that phrase **"producing sequentially" mean**? Does **it** refer to **the** single **entity** of the prime universal **itself** producing sequentially **or** to **something else**? The first is not correct, because if something permanent were to produce a result, it would have to produce it at the time of the cause. If it refers to something other than the universal, then the universal becomes meaningless.

Refuting that the nature and its manifestations are one

> 176. **The entities that possess those**
> **would become completely distinct or not distinct.**

Also, as entities possessing similarities and differences,
the aspects would be mutually distinct.

It follows that **the entities** of the universal **that possesses those** particulars **becomes completely distinct** as many, because in reality it is one with the particulars. Alternatively, it follows that the many particulars **are** one and **not distinct**, because in reality they are one with the single universal. **Also**—a term indicating that the previous point prompts the latter—it follows that **the aspects** of the universal and its features **would be** of **mutually distinct** natures because they **are entities possessing similarities and differences.**

177. **"It is the case that they are distinct."**
By their very entities there are features
and universals of this and that.
If they are distinct in this way,
they would be distinct.

178. **Even if that were so, just like pots and so on,**
these asserted as universal and features
would also not have mutual universal
and feature possession.

They assert, "**It is the case that** the universal and its features are, respectively, of the nature of potential and particulars, and so in that sense **they are distinct.**"

It follows that the universal and its features are distinct by nature because, **by their very entities** of being potential and instance, we establish that "**This is a feature** of that **and** this is **a universal of that.**" **If**, according to you, **they are distinct** by way of being potential and instance, then **they would be distinct. Even if that were so**, it would **also** follow that with **these asserted as universal and features**, there **would not** be **universal and feature possession**—that is, the connection of a feature possessed by a universal and a universal possessed by a feature—because they are separate entities with no relation to each other, **just like pots**, woolen cloth, **and so on** do not have **mutual** possession.

The object to be engaged is solely an intrinsically existing phenomenon

179. **Aspiring**[114] **to that entity, the person**
seeking the result to be established

will engage, and as the basis of that,
distinct and non-distinct are examined,
and it will be one whose nature is distinct.

The person who seeks the result such as *cow* that is **to be established examines the distinct and non-distinct** intrinsically existent phenomena **as the basis of that** which fulfills the function of a cow, and from these two it is correct that this person engages with **one whose nature is** a **distinct** and intrinsically existing phenomenon, because **aspiring to**, or setting as their focus, **that** whose **entity** is the intrinsically existing phenomenon of a cow, they **will engage** that object.

Examining the two modes of engaging by way of universals

These similar isolates exist.
There is no pervading of entities.
Consequences of engaging and so on would follow.

Even when engaging with the intrinsically existent cow, it is correct to engage by way of exclusion and not by way of an actual-entity universal. This is because, from the perspective of exclusion, universals of **similar isolates exist** with regard to the particulars, but **there is no** single and actual universal that **pervades** equally across the **entities** of the particulars. If there were, certain **consequences of engaging and so on would follow**, such as the person seeking to engage with *cow* engaging with pots and woolen cloth and, as indicated by the phrase "and so on," the consequence that creation and destruction would occur at the same time.

This reasoning also refutes the Immodest Ones

1. Refutation by the previous reasonings
2. Refutation by other reasonings

Refutation by the previous reasonings

1. Refutation by the reasoning of being independently separate
2. Refutation by the reasoning of the search for engagement

Refutation by the reasoning of being independently separate

181. **By this the Immodest Ones, bewildered by darkness,
propounding incoherence, are also refuted
because that is completely impossible.**

This reasoning that refutes the Sāṃkhya assertion that all entities are of one nature also refutes other wrong views. This is because it **also refutes the Immodest Ones**—the Jains—who, **bewildered by** the **darkness** of ignorance, **propound incoherent** tenets that state that curd and camels are of one nature but temporarily separate.

How is that? Curd and camels are not of one nature **because that is completely impossible**—they are definitely separate.

Refutation by the reasoning of the search for engagement

182. **If all are of the nature of each other,
and the features have been eliminated,
when urged to drink curd,
why does he not run off to a camel?**

If all curd and camels **are of the nature of each other**, then **when** someone is looking for curd, having been **urged** by another **to drink curd**, it would be right for them to run off to drink curd, and so **why does he not run off to** drink a **camel?** You accept the pervasion because **the** individual **features** of curd and camels **have been eliminated.**

183. **"But there are some that are preeminent,
and because of those, the feature is engaged."
It follows that without being both it is other
because it is that and not found in others.**

In response: "**But there are some** features **that are** more **preeminent** than camels, such as the white color and the milky appearance, **and because of those,** it is **the feature** of curd that is **engaged.**"

Then **it follows that** curd, **without being both** curd and camel, **is other** than a camel **because that** white color and milky appearance **is** curd and is **not found in others** such as a camel.

Refutation by other reasonings

184. **If all were the nature of everything,**
there would be no separate cognition and expression.
Propounding distinct but combined
does not exist and is therefore not possible.

If all instances of curd and camels **were the nature of everything**, then **it would not be** possible to engage curd and camels with **separate cognition and** verbal **expression** because they are of the same nature. You accept the pervasion because you assert that the cognition and verbal expression of curd engages by way of its entity. If you agree, then for you who **propound** temporarily **distinct but combined** into a single nature, it **would not be possible** for temporary distinction combined into a single nature to occur, because that ascertainment of entities as distinct **would not exist.**

Up to here, all mention of universals in the refutation of other traditions refers to universals as actual entities.

Exclusion of non-entities by way of verbal expression

185. **Because non-entities have no nature,**
it is not expressing the nature.
The expression is established
as expressing the preclusion.

Entities possess their own nature, and so it is possible to wonder if conceptual cognition and verbal expression engage them in reality. However, the verbal expression of non-entities **is not expressing** any actual **nature** of a non-entity **because non-entities have no nature. Therefore the expression** "non-entities" **is established as expressing the preclusion**, or exclusion, of those of incongruent class because it is a verbal expression and cannot engage its object through the force of the actual entity. This is expressed in *Treasure of Reasoning*:

> Entities produced from causes
> do not depend upon non-entities.
> Non-entities are not created by causes
> and are established in cognition,
> having negated entities.[115]

Therefore entities are pervaded by a nature existing as a truth, but the object-possessing conceptual cognitions and verbal expressions engage by way of exclusion, whereas all non-entities are exclusions. This is the essential point concerning exclusions.

Divisions of Reasoning by Nature

23. Divisions[116]

An explanation of the divisions of this type of reason, the base of the ascertainment

1. Division into dependence and non-dependence upon a feature
2. Eliminating arguments against the non-dependence reasoning

Division into dependence and non-dependence upon a feature

What are the types of this reasoning by nature, in which there is intrinsic relationship to the predicate, which is the phenomenon to be established and which was explained previously?

> **186. Nature that depends upon**
> **a specific feature, or alternately alone,**
> **is expressed to determine the thesis,**
> **like a result for disintegration, and existence itself.**

Reasoning by **nature, which is expressed in order to determine the thesis** to be established, such as sound being impermanent, is of two types: for the self-isolate of the reason to appear to the cognition it either **depends upon** another **specific feature** of that reason appearing as the object of that cognition, **or alternatively alone** without such dependence.

The first would be **like** presenting **a** produced **result**, such as something arising from effort, or a living being as a reason, to establish that sound is **disintegration, and** the second would be like presenting **existence itself** and entities as reasons.

Eliminating arguments against the non-dependence reasoning

1. The argument
2. The response

The argument

> 187. **"If the entity of existence is a reason,**
> **why is existence not that to be established?**
> **With features having no concomitance,**
> **it is weakened as the reason**
> **and as the phenomenon to be established."**

The Sāṃkhya say, "**If the entity of existence**[117] **is** suitable to be used as **a reason** for establishing impermanence and so forth, then **why is that existence not** also used as the phenomenon **to be established** when proving the existence of the prime universal? They are similar and therefore can prove that the prime universal exists. You might reply that to establish mere existence upon the subject, which has already been established as existing by valid cognition, would be pointless. Moreover, establishing existence in terms of the features of existence, such as permanence and oneness, can establish the universal, but these features cannot be applied to any examples. Therefore aren't you making the error of using the reason as the phenomenon to be established?[118]

"But the same error occurs if you use existence as the reason, because if you were to use mere existence as the reason, there would be no point. Using features of existence, such as the existence of sound, would have no concomitance. Therefore **with** the **features** of existence **having no concomitance, the reason and the phenomenon to be established are** equally **weakened.**"

The response

1. With existence as that to be established, its definition is incomplete
2. With existence as the reason, the definition is complete
3. There will be no genuine establishment with existence as the phenomenon to be established
4. Existence as the reason induces understanding

With existence as that to be established, its definition is incomplete

If existence is proposed as something to be established, is this the mere existence present in the subject of the thesis that has already been validly established? Or is it the existence characterized by the permanence and oneness present in the prime universal?

> 188. **With that to be established**
> **merely characterized by existing**
> **in the general subject, there is nothing to establish,**
> **and as such there is nothing to refute.**

> 189. **If the features are held as that to be established,**
> **that reasoning is one that is not concomitant.**
> **If existence is that to be established,**
> **its features would be the phenomenon to be established.**

If it is the former, then **that to be established, merely characterized by existing in the general subject** determined equally by both the proposer and the responder in the debate on the existence of the prime universal, is not a valid phenomenon to be established, because **there is nothing** for the proposer of the debate **to establish, and** with **such** a phenomenon to be established, **there is nothing** for the defender **to refute.**

If it is the latter, and it is existence possessed of **the features** of permanence and so on present upon the prime universal that **is held as that to be established**, then it follows that such features cannot be established by reasoning to exist on certain places, because **that reasoning is one that is not concomitant** with the examples containing the phenomenon to be established.

There is no point in holding mere existence as that to be established, and therefore, **if existence is held as that to be established, that** existence **would** have to **be** characterized by **features** of permanence, oneness, and so on. Those features cannot be established as existing for any subject, and therefore it cannot be correct to hold existence present upon the prime universal as **the phenomenon to be established.**

With existence as the reason, the definition is complete

"But isn't this the same as using existence as a reason?"

> 190. **Without holding a feature of that,**
> **if that entity by itself is presented**
> **as that which establishes,**

> **that alone pervades that to be established,**
> **and there is no loss of concomitance.**

Without holding a feature of that existence, such as the existence of sound, as a reason and **if** instead **that entity by itself is presented as that which establishes** sound as impermanent, **that** entity **alone** is suitable to be valid proof, because it is established as a property of the subject and because that which **pervades** the congruent example is pervaded by impermanence, which is the phenomenon **to be established.** In this way, **there is no loss of concomitance.**

There will be no genuine establishment with existence as the phenomenon to be established

> 191. **For that not established there is no phenomenon of existence.**
> **Those that depend upon both possess errors.**
> **Phenomena of nonexistence are contradictory.**
> **How can existence be that which is to be established?**

How can existence, as an entity, **be that which is to be established** upon the universal by way of a reason? It cannot, because to establish existence upon the universal, no phenomenon, whether one of existence or of nonexistence, can be used as a reason. With **a phenomenon of existence**, such as the ability to function, there can be no establishment of it as the property of the subject, which is an intrinsically existing universal, because the intrinsically existing universal itself is **not established** as existing.[119]

Knowable phenomena entities **that depend upon both** existence and nonexistence are not valid reasons for establishing an intrinsically existing universal as an existence as an entity because they **possess errors** in the pervasion that establishes that.

Phenomena of nonexistence, such as the inability to do something, induce the same consequence because they **are contradictory** to existing as an entity.

Existence as the reason induces understanding

> 192. **Establishment of the nature is the understanding.**
> **The pervading of that is the ascertainment.**
> **The ascertainment of the nature is to be understood.**

They respond, "Then using existence as a reason is not appropriate, because if an entity of existence is established, there is nothing left to know. If entities of existence and nonexistence are both established, the pervasion will be faulty. If an entity of nonexistence is used, the pervasion will be contradictory."

The **establishment**, or ascertainment, **of** that which has **the nature** of existence being pervaded by the phenomenon to be established **is the understanding**. The **nature** such as impermanence, for example, **ascertained as pervading that** existence **is** the entity **to be understood** and **ascertained** by the cognition. However, entities of existence and so on not ascertained in this way are not phenomena to be established because a reason whose pervasion is not ascertained cannot establish that which is to be established.

> **If this is reversed, that is reversed,**
> 193. **similar to impermanence**
> **and being produced, for example.**
> **Or, not produced by not being destroyed.**

Therefore, if the reason and the phenomenon to be established are ascertained as pervaded and pervader, it can be ascertained that **if this** phenomenon to be established **is reversed, that** reason **is reversed. For example**, it is **similar to** the fact that when **impermanence** is ascertained as pervading that which has been **produced**, by way of the verbal expression of the concomitant pervasion, it is indirectly ascertained that permanence is pervaded by not being produced. **Or**, when it is ascertained, by way of the verbal expression of the reversal, that **not being produced** is pervaded by **not being destroyed**, it is indirectly ascertained that being produced is pervaded by impermanence.

Regarding this part of the text, using "being produced" as a suitable reason to establish sound as impermanent as an example of using existence to establish sound as impermanent is expressed by the phrase "similar to." Therefore it is clearly a continuation of the previous text. *Ascertainment of Valid Cognition* states, "Like a result for disintegration, and existence itself. . . ." Immediately after this the text states, "Because of disintegration without having no cause, if it will be destroyed," and so on. The fact that the above intervening text is not there also proves this point.[120]

Using *existence* as the reason here is on the basis of "existence" (*yod pa*) and "entity" (*dngos po*) being a translation of the same Indian term (*bhāva*). (Elsewhere in this chapter, *dngos po* is more often a translation of the Sanskrit *vastu.*)

In Tibet, the great classic texts use the term *existence* for both the existence as an exclusion and for existence in reality. Therefore the "existence" used to establish impermanence should be understood as referring to entities.

24. Disintegration by Nature[121]

Explanation of non-dependence reasoning, which is the ascertainer

1. Showing the reason upon the congruent example
2. Applying that reasoning elsewhere

Showing the reason upon the congruent example

1. Presenting the reason
2. Establishing the reason upon the subject
3. Summary

Presenting the reason

"In perfect reasoning by way of nature, if the phenomenon to be established is determined to be related to the reason by being intrinsically of one nature with it, how is impermanence, as the phenomenon to be established, intrinsically related to being a produced existence, as explained previously?"

> **Because of disintegration without a cause,**
> **there is relationship by way of own nature.**

First, it is to be established as existing within a congruent example. The disintegration of a pot is **by way of** its **own nature**—that is, by way of an intrinsic **relationship**. This is **because** its **disintegration** is created from the pot's own direct cause, **without** depending upon **a cause** other than its own direct cause.

Establishing the reason upon the subject

1. Establishing by consequence
2. Establishing by syllogism

Establishing by consequence

It could be argued, "But that reason is not established."

194. **Entities entailing a dependence**
would be seen as never changing.
Though there are many causes,
for some it will not be possible.

Then it must follow that it is possible for **entities**, such as a pot, **to be seen as never changing**, never to be destroyed, because their own destruction **entails a dependence** upon causes other than their own causes.

"Isn't it the case that the causes for the destruction of a pot, such as a hammer, are many, and so it will definitely be destroyed?"

Even though there are many such **causes**, it follows that it **will not be possible for some** pots to be destroyed because it is possible that they will not come into contact with causes for their own destruction, such as hammers.

195. **Therefore there is no bringing of that result.**
Those propounding that destruction has a cause
state wrongly that everything
is a cause for the destruction.

Even if they do come into contact with later causes for destruction, it is not certain that a mere cause will generate a result. **Therefore those who propound** that the **destruction** of a pot **has a** later **cause state wrongly that everything** they think of **as causes for the destruction** of a pot, such as a hammer, will create the destruction of a pot. There is no certainty that they will create that destruction because they are merely indirect causes of the destruction of a pot. There is pervasion because there is no certainty that a mere cause **will bring about the result.**

Establishing by syllogism

196. **Also, because that cause has no ability,**
this will come about by way of its own entity.

> **Those that are other than that**
> **will also be by way of their own entity.**

Also, the destruction of a pot does not depend upon a cause other than the pot's own cause **because that cause**, which is later than the pot's own cause, **has no ability** to generate the entity of disintegration and the non-entity of the state of destruction.[122]

The word "also" has been explained by those of the past as referring to the inability also of generating the non-entity of having been destroyed, but it is clear that it is used to include the previous reasoning.

Summary

This pot that we see here **will** be destroyed **by way of its own entity** because it was created as an entity of disintegration without dependence upon any cause other than its own.

Applying that reasoning elsewhere

Produced existence **other than those** such as a visible pot that will be destroyed by way of their own entity **will also be** destroyed **by way of their own entity**, because they are no different in being created as entities of destruction without dependence upon any cause other than their own.

Ascertainment of the two types of affirming reasonings by the force of the relationship

> 197. **Therefore any inferences that take entities**
> **as their objects are of two types.**
> **From the result and nature is the relationship**
> **to the phenomena to be established.**

Two types of relationship are ascertained. **Therefore any inferential** perfect reasonings **that take as their objects entities**, or affirmations, for their phenomena to be established **are** categorized into **two types** of reasoning—by way of result and by way of nature—because it is only **from** those two that **the relationship to** their **phenomena to be established** is ascertained because they exist as **the result and nature** of their phenomena to be established.

25. Negation Reasoning

Applying the counter relationship to negation reasonings[123]

1. How the first nonapprehension negates that to be negated
2. How the second nonapprehension negates that to be negated
3. Refuting arguments against the division into two

How the first nonapprehension negates that to be negated

1. Negating definite existence is a valid cognition
2. It is not a valid cognition for establishing definite nonexistence

Negating definite existence is a valid cognition

Thus the relationship of result and one nature found in the two affirming reasonings is established, but in a negation reason, what is the relationship between the reason and the phenomenon to be established?

Concerning the reasoning of nonapprehension by way of nonappearance, this is the negation of a resulting designation by negating the cause of that designation. Therefore the reverse of a relationship by way of result determines the relationship between reason and predicate.

198. Because engaging has a prerequisite cognition,
if the nature is not apprehended,
there will be no engaging.
Therefore it is explained
that nonapprehension is valid.

In this way, **if the nature** of that existent **is not apprehended** by a valid cognition, **there will be no engaging** in the designation of its definite existence, **because engaging** in the designation of its definite existence **has a prerequisite cognition** that apprehends that phenomenon. **Therefore**, because of this, **it is explained that** the **nonapprehension** by a valid cognition of an inaccessible phenomenon **is a valid** proof for the negation of any designation of the definite existence of that inaccessible phenomenon in certain places. This is because it is possible that the three criteria are present in the negation of the designation of the definite existence of that inaccessible phenomenon in certain places.

Previous commentators have stated that "In negating definite existence, both are similar" and thus have applied the above to both types of reasoning by nonapprehension. But this contradicts the *Ascertainment of Valid Cognition*, which states that the above is only applicable to the reasoning of nonapprehension by way of nonappearance.

It is not a valid cognition for establishing definite nonexistence

> 199. **There are those unconnected to the treatises**
> **and objects that are beyond the senses.**
> **Those who have no reasons do not apprehend them,**
> **but how does that establish their nonexistence?**
>
> 200. **Because it is not one that possesses the fruit**
> **of existing or not existing,**
> **it does not become a valid cognition.**

There are some things that have **no connection to** the content expressed in **the treatises**, and there are **objects beyond the senses** that exist but cannot be viewed by direct perception, and there are **no reasons** to establish them. The valid cognition by persons with no access to these inaccessible phenomena **does not apprehend them, but how does that establish their** definite **nonexistence?**

It does not, because they exist, though they are not pervaded by being apprehended by the valid cognition of that person.

Therefore the valid cognition in the mind of someone who has no access to the existence of a *piśāca* spirit **does not become a valid cognition** for the assertion of its existence or nonexistence, **because it is not one that possesses the fruit of** an ascertaining consciousness that determines whether the piśāca spirit is **existing or not existing.**

The *Autocommentary* states, "... because valid cognitions possess the fruits of ascertainment."[124]

Devendrabuddhi states, "Those with the nature of distinct features, such as aspects of impermanence, are all apprehended, but because it is mistaken, their nature is obstructed, and it is not an ascertainment. From that nonascertainment, it is like seeing without apprehending, and so it is not a valid cognition toward them."[125]

He also says, "It does not exist in other aspects because a valid cognition is the fruit of engaging."[126]

Śākyabuddhi says, "Also, if a direct valid cognition apprehends all aspects, then all those that ascertain the aspects by way of their engaged object are known as valid cognitions."[127]

Kamalaśīla states, "Even an undeceiving cognition toward an undetermined object is not a valid cognition because there would be absurd consequences."[128]

He also says, "In this way, even if direct perception is generated without distinction, if its complete aspects generate a conceptual cognition within, it is asserted as being a direct perception. Whatever does not generate this is held as an apprehending, but it is not apprehended."[129]

Also, "About that which does not generate certainty because it does not engage by striving for all aspects, it is correct to say that this is not a valid cognition."[130]

Some earlier commentators have said that these citations refute the assertion that direct perceptions ascertain and the statement that by not generating ascertainment they are not valid cognitions. This is not correct. If it were, it would follow that there could be no valid cognition in the realm of a buddha's enlightenment because in that realm there is nothing that generates ascertainment. If you disagree, then it would mean the exalted knowledge in the mind of a buddha would not be pervaded by being direct perception.[131]

Therefore the meaning of these citations is that a wholly designated valid cognition is pervaded by inducing ascertainment by the force of itself or another. This is dealt with in detail in my *Madhyamaka Overview*.

How the second nonapprehension negates that to be negated

1. If there is a feature, definite nonexistence is established
2. The types of reasoning that prove nonexistence

If there is a feature, definite nonexistence is established

> **Some reasons of a special characteristic become valid.**
> 201. **When its nature is not known**
> **from that which causes knowing,**
> **that type of reasoning is expressed.**

You might wonder, "Is it not possible to know definite nonexistence through reasoning by nonapprehension?"

Some nonapprehension **reasons of a special characteristic**—that is, a feature of something that should appear—**become valid**, perfect reasons for knowing a nonexistence because nonapprehension of that which should appear is pervaded by definite nonexistence.

But doesn't this contradict the assertion that nonapprehension does not prove nonexistence? It does not, because **that** particular **type of reasoning is expressed when** there is something that exists but **its nature**—that is, its entity—is not known by seeing it and it **is not known from** any reasoning **that causes knowing.** Such nonapprehension toward such an inaccessible phenomenon does not establish nonexistence.

The types of reasoning that prove nonexistence

1. Proving nonexistence by negating five kinds of relationship
2. Proving nonexistence by apprehending five kinds of contradiction

Proving nonexistence by negating five kinds of relationship

1. Proving by negating cause and pervader
2. Proving by negating the entity that should appear

Proving by negating cause and pervader

"In a reason by way of nonapprehension, if the reason and the predicate exist in a reversed relationship, how is the relationship established in a reasoning of nonapprehension by way of nonappearance?"

In the reasoning of the nonapprehension of cause and pervader, from the concomitant pervasion and counter pervasion of the same-nature relationship and cause-and-effect relationship, it is the counter pervasion that is directly established. It is said that all the reasonings of nonapprehension by way of nonappearance will ultimately establish the phenomenon to be negated as not existing by way of a valid cognition not apprehending that phenomenon to be negated. Therefore, "Finally same-nature relationship is directly established."[132]

> **If the cause is not known,**
> **it is established that the result does not exist.**
> 202. **That possessing the reason of being the nature of the phenomenon**
> **is also the entity not being apprehended.**
> **By certain reasons nonexistence will be known.**

To explain these in order: **If the cause**—fire, for example—**is not known,** not apprehended, **that establishes** in certain places **that the result**, smoke, **does not exist** because the three criteria are complete. **Also, the entity** of tree **not being apprehended** used as a reason for the nonexistence in a particular place of an agaru tree, **possessing the reason of being the nature of the phenomenon** of a tree, is a perfect reason because the three criteria for establishing that are complete.

By certain reasons, by way of the nonapprehension of cause and pervader, the **nonexistence** of the result and the pervaded **will be known** in certain places where, if they did exist, they would be seen, but elsewhere that is not the case, because reasoning by way of nonapprehension of cause and pervader where they should not appear does not necessarily establish that the result and the pervaded are nonexistent.

Proving by negating the entity that should appear

> 203. **If there is no possible cause for not seeing**
> **something that should appear,**
> **and such an entity is not apprehended,**
> **it can be known it does not exist.**

If there is **something that should appear**, such as a pot, for **which there is no possible cause for not seeing** it, such as some obstruction, then from the reasoning that **if the entity** of a pot, which should appear, exists it should be apprehended but it **is not apprehended, it can be known** that in certain places the entity of the pot that should appear **does not exist.**

Proving nonexistence by apprehending five kinds of contradiction

> 204. **If there is a contradictory entity,**
> **it negates the existence.**
> **Therefore, by apprehending a contradictory entity,**
> **it can be ascertained that it does not exist.**

Using as a reason **apprehending a contradictory entity** whereby a phenomenon cannot coexist with the sensation of, say, coldness, **it can be ascertained that** in certain places coldness **does not exist.** This is because **if there is a contradictory entity** that cannot coexist with coldness, **it negates the existence** of that coldness.

26. Refuting Arguments against the Division into Two

Refuting arguments against the division into two

1. Establishing no contradiction by way of three referents
2. Refuting that the referents of verbal expressions are intrinsically existent phenomena
3. Negating the referent of the verbal expression is wrong
4. The object investigated is purely an intrinsically existing phenomenon
5. Abandoning doubts of contradiction with scripture

Establishing no contradiction by way of three referents

Some say that reasoning by way of nonapprehending negates a certainty of existence. But if it establishes a certainty of nonexistence, then the reasoning presented by Dignāga stating that the prime universal is not an existent because it cannot be apprehended is not reasoning by way of nonapprehension because it cannot establish definite nonexistence or negate definite existence. This is because if this universal exists, it cannot be negated, and it is not correct to use the words "not an existent." If it does not exist, then the subject of the reasoning does not exist, and so the reason cannot be found within the subject, and the expression *universal* does not engage with anything.

205. **Phenomena referents of verbal expressions,**
completely created by conceptualization
arising from imprints from time without beginning,
are of three types: relying upon existence,
nonexistence, and both.

The **phenomena** that are the **referents of verbal expressions,**[133] which have been **completely created**—that is, superimposed—**by conceptualization arising from** past **imprints from time without beginning, are of three types:** phenomena that **rely upon existence,** non-phenomena that rely upon **nonexistence, and** knowable phenomena that rely upon **both.**

> 206. **The nonapprehension of that is a reasoning**
> **to establish that this does not hold an entity.**
> **That is not nonexistent because the expression is applied.**

Therefore there is no fault in using the expression "not an existent" in the reasoning of the Ācārya, and no fault in the subject of the reasoning not existing, because from these three referents of verbal expressions, it is the non-phenomenon referent of the universal that is being used, and **to establish that this does not hold** the **entity** of a universal, **the nonapprehension of that** referent holding the entity of a universal **is a reasoning** establishing just that. Moreover, **that** referent for the verbal expression of the universal **is not nonexistent because** that which **the expression** ***universal*** **is applied** to exists.[134]

Refuting that the referents of verbal expressions are intrinsically existent phenomena

> 207. **Unequivocally engaging with the ultimate**
> **means that with expressions for phenomena**
> **seen with distinct particulars,**
> **there will be no engaging**
> **because the causes do not exist.**

It might be argued, "If there is an existing referent to the expression of the universal, this contradicts the assertion that the universal has no intrinsic existence, because all expressions **unequivocally engage with the ultimate**—that is, intrinsically existing phenomena—and therefore referents of verbal expressions and intrinsically existing phenomena are one and the same."

Then it follows that **with phenomena** such as pots having **distinct particulars seen** by distinct viewers, such as being permanent and impermanent, **expressions** such as *permanent* and *impermanent* **will not engage** with the pots **because the causes** for such engagement—that is, being both permanent and impermanent—**do not exist.**

> 208. **Nor with the past and the unproduced,**
> **and certain words could not be lies.**
> **These are asserted as object-possessors**
> **of phenomena of cognition.**

Nor could words of the present engage **with the past and the** yet **unproduced** because right now they do not exist as intrinsically existing phenomena. It also follows that **certain words could not be lies** because they engage as spoken expressions with intrinsically existing phenomena. Because such faults appear, **those** expressions **are asserted as object-possessors of phenomena** that appear to a conceptual **cognition** because they are expressions and do not directly engage with intrinsically existing phenomena.

Negating that the referent of the verbal expression is wrong

It can be argued, "Then the reasoning presented by the Ācārya does not negate the universal itself as an intrinsically existing phenomenon but negates the referent for the verbal expression of the universal as an existent."

> 209. **Denying the verbal expression's referent,**
> **the joining together cannot constitute the thesis,**
> **because the basis of the subject is negated.**
> **A stand-alone phenomenon is established.**

Concerning the assertion that **denies** and thereby establishes through reasoning the nonexistence of **the referent for the verbal expression** of the universal, it would follow that **the joining together** of the subject of the reasoning, which is the referent of the verbal expression of the universal, with the predicate, which is nonexistence, **cannot constitute the thesis** of the reason establishing the nonexistence of the universal, **because the basis of the subject**—the referent for the verbal expression of the universal—**is negated** by that reasoning.

If you agree, saying that the simple nonexistence of the predicate is the thesis, then the simple nonexistence of **a stand-alone phenomenon** to be established, not characterized by the universal, does not become the thesis in the eyes of the opponent in debate who does not assert the existence of a universal because such an opponent has already **established** that.

The object investigated is purely an intrinsically existing phenomenon

The reply: "We are not denying the referent of the verbal expression of the universal by saying that it does not exist but are asserting that it is the object engaged by the expression *universal*."

210. **Those not denying the verbal expression's referent**
should examine the entity
by way of the particulars of existing or not existing,
because there is a dependence in which results arise from this.

211. **Why strive to examine that**
which cannot perform a function?
What is the point of a lustful person
examining whether a eunuch is beautiful?

For **those** who accept that there is **no denying the referent of the verbal expression** of the universal, when examining the universal **by way of the particulars of existing or not existing** as an **entity** that performs a function, they **should examine the** universal as an intrinsically existing phenomenon, **because** generally **there is a dependence in which results arise from this** intrinsically existing phenomenon. **Why strive to examine** the referent for the verbal expression of the universal? There is no point, because **that** referent for the verbal expression of the universal **cannot perform any function.** For example, **what is the point of a lustful person examining whether a eunuch is beautiful?**

Abandoning doubts of contradiction with scripture

You might argue, "If you take the referent of the verbal expression as the subject of the thesis, then this contradicts with the *Compendium of Valid Cognition* when it says, 'That which is conceptualized is not apprehended,' thereby taking the intrinsically existent universal as the subject and using as a reason the fact that it is not apprehended."

212. **Being the object of a conceptualizing consciousness,**
the referent of the expression is conceptualized.
Not established in dependence upon an entity,
this phenomenon was spoken by the propounder of reasoning.

The referent of the verbal **expression** of the universal **is conceptualized** because it is **the** direct **object of a conceptualizing consciousness.** That referent of the verbal expression is **not established**—that is, not apprehended—**in dependence upon** the **entity** of the universal, and it is **this** nonapprehension that is the **phenomenon** of the reasoning, **spoken by the propounder of reasoning** Dignāga, to establish that the referent for the verbal expression of the universal does not exist in dependence upon the entity of the universal because that is the meaning of *nonapprehension*.

Fallacious Reasoning: Refuting the Vedas

27. Analysis of Verbal Expression

Extensive explanation of fallacious reasoning[135]

1. Analysis
2. Actual explanation

Analysis

According to Uyukpa,[136] the text from here onward "has no connection with the context of the treatise." Therefore he designates it as simply supplementary material and not as an extensive explanation of fallacious reasoning. Because of this, most Tibetan commentators since then have followed this classification. This text being supplementary material in no way contradicts its being an extensive explanation of fallacious reasoning. This is because the four extensive explanations naturally follow each other, as explained above.[137] Moreover, if you examine the main topics and their location in the text from hereon, it becomes very clear because the bulk of the following text is an explanation of fallacious reasoning applied to the tenets of the outsiders. Also, *Ascertainment of Valid Cognition* does not include fallacious reasoning in its brief explanation and so does not discuss it at this point. However, in *Commentary on Valid Cognition* this topic is part of the brief explanation, and so it appears here.

Also, the line "because of an indispensable relationship" (in 1.1) expresses this point because in the brief explanation, the lines "because of an indispensable relationship. Fallacious reasoning is other" are stated on the basis of fallacious reasoning being distinct from the definitive indispensable relationship.

Other explanations do not agree where the topic of fallacious reasoning is discussed. This was discussed previously as noted above. Some assertions ignore this large section of text and identify fallacious reasoning as being explained only in four intermediate verses, and others say there is no extensive discussion of fallacious reasoning at all; these are just laughable.

Actual explanation

Some say that doubts over inaccessible phenomena are not negated by reversing the two types of valid cognition but that reversing by scripture will do so because scripture pervades all things.[138] Refuting this assertion is under five headings:

1. Mere verbal expression cannot ascertain and is fallacious reasoning
2. Words do not establish and are fallacious reasoning
3. The expressions of the Vedas establishing the truth are also fallacious reasoning (1.224)
4. Therefore mere scripture is mistaken with regard to its subject matter (1.336)
5. Bringing out internal contradiction and belittling the propounder (1.340)

Mere verbal expression cannot ascertain and is fallacious reasoning

1. There is no establishment because there is no relationship
2. Refuting that this contradicts scripture

There is no establishment because there is no relationship

> 213. **Because verbal expressions do not have a coexisting**
> **and indispensable relationship with entities,**
> **they are not established from them.**
> **They could reveal the thoughts of the speaker.**

From the presenting of **verbal expressions** as reasons, intrinsically existing, external entities, as that expressed by those expressions, **are not established, because** if they **do not coexist with** their external **entities**, expressed by those expressions, then there is **no indispensable relationship** between them. Therefore **those** verbal expressions **could** possibly **reveal**—that is, establish—**the thoughts**, or motivation, in the mind **of the speaker**, because the three criteria for establishing that are complete.

Refuting that this contradicts scripture

1. The words of the scripture that are the basis for the suspicion of contradiction
2. Explaining the citation and establishing that there is no contradiction

The words of the scripture that are the basis for the suspicion of contradiction

It might be argued that if verbal expressions are not valid with regard to their external entity, then it contradicts the words from *Compendium of Valid Cognition*, which say that they are inferentially valid:

> **Trustworthy words, from the generality of**
> **the nondeceptive, are inferentially valid.**[139]

Response: Here [Dignāga] is not speaking about definitive inferential cognitions. When those of insight engage with very hidden phenomena, they cannot engage with valid cognitions arising from reasoning based on entities and therefore must use scripture. The above statement from *Compendium of Valid Cognition* was made based on analyzing which is valid and concluding that "in scripture such and such is valid."

Explaining the citation and establishing that there is no contradiction

1. Illustration of "trustworthy words"
2. Characteristics of "nondeceptive"
3. Explaining "inferentially valid from the generality"

Illustration of "trustworthy words"

> 214. **Coherent, with methods that accord,**
> **and expressing a purpose for living beings,**
> **it is on the basis of examining whether they are such words**
> **and not on the basis of anything other.**

The phrase "trustworthy words" in the citation from *Compendium of Valid Cognition* was not spoken on the basis of it just being scripture. It was spoken on the basis of scripture possessing three features: it is not without **coherence**, meaning that in teaching the points of what is to be developed and what is to be discarded, all previous and subsequent words are connected; it is not without the inability to satisfy needs, meaning that it teaches **methods that accord** with the fulfillment of those needs; and that it is not without purpose, in that it **expresses a purpose** that is needed **for living beings**. Thus **it is on the basis of having examined whether** the scripture **are words** endowed with these three features **and not on the basis of anything other** than those three criteria.

Characteristics of "nondeceptive"

> 215. **Entities seen and unseen,**
> **not harmed by the aspects**
> **of direct perception and inferential cognition—**
> **this is "nondeceptive."**

In the revealing of evident **entities,** which are **seen, and** hidden entities, which are **unseen,** both **not harmed by the aspects of direct perception and inferential cognition** from entity-based reasoning—**this is** the meaning of **"nondeceptive"** in the citation above. This is because the reason "not being harmed by the two valid cognitions when revealing these phenomena" must be used to establish that the scripture is nondeceiving with regard to very hidden phenomena.

On this point, some posit both hidden and very hidden phenomena in the phrase "not seen" and then add their own commentary on "not harmed." Others include both evident phenomena and hidden phenomena in "seen" and explain "not seen" as referring, from among the two types of valid cognition, to "that which is not harmed by a valid cognition that depends upon scripture." These positions do not approach the meaning expressed here because the ascertainment "Valid cognitions that harm are of two types," "from the generality . . . ," and "this is nondeceptive" do not bring out these positions.

Explaining "inferentially valid from the generality"

> 216. **From the generality of trustworthy words,**
> **even though its object is hidden,**
> **this cognition is said to be an inferential cognition**
> **because there is no opportunity.**

The text of the Ācārya is not saying that trustworthy words themselves are valid cognitions, but **from the generality of trustworthy words** complete with the three features that have been ascertained by entity-based valid cognitions nondeceptive with regard to evident and hidden phenomena comes **a cognition** that apprehends very hidden phenomena in dependence upon that scripture, **and even though** the **object** of this cognition **is** very **hidden, it is said to be an inferential cognition.** This is **because** it is a valid cognition that apprehends very hidden phenomena, it is in the mind of an ordinary being, and in the mind of an ordinary being **there is no opportunity** for entity-based valid cognitions to engage with very hidden phenomena.

> 217. **With practices to be developed, phenomena to be discarded,**
> **together with the method, thoroughly ascertained,**
> **nondeceptive with regard to the prime topic,**
> **it is therefore inferentially valid toward others.**

Why is it possible to make inferences from the above generality? Trustworthy words possess the ability to be nondeceptively and **inferentially valid toward other**—that is, very hidden—phenomena because they are **nondeceptive with regard to the prime topic**, the hidden phenomena of the four truths. This is because their **practices to be developed**, whose essence is the truth of cessation, their **phenomena to be discarded**, whose essence is the truth of suffering, **together with the method** of the path and the cause of suffering **are thoroughly ascertained**, exactly as they were taught, by entity-based reasoning.

Previous commentators have inserted "also" as a connector, explaining this verse as being a section of the previous. They make the phrase "thoroughly ascertained" causal and add the words "by teaching."[140] This is coarse interpretation of a subtle point because the former verse is an identification of this type of inferential valid cognition and this verse teaches how it becomes inferentially valid from the generality. Moreover, if the ascertaining of the four truths has to be a cause for teaching the four truths, this would contradict the assertion that there is no ascertaining consciousness at the level of the Buddha.

Words do not establish and are fallacious reasoning

1. Assertion
2. Refutation

Assertion

> 218. **By relying upon a superior being,**[141]
> **things as they are can be known by others.**

"**By relying upon a superior being** who possesses the excellent qualities of seeing things as they are and is free of faults, the words spoken by such a person

can be known by others who are logically minded as portraying **things** exactly as they are."

Refutation

1. There are no superior beings in other traditions
2. Establishing superior beings in our tradition

There are no superior beings in other traditions

> **If it is possible to know a superior being,**
> **this position can be asserted.**
> 219. **Valid cognitions of others having faults or no faults**
> **or saying that this is like this or not**
> **are difficult to develop.**
> **Therefore it is difficult to know.**
> **This, others can know.**

If it is possible to know that someone is **a superior being** in that way, then it is correct to **assert this position** that their words carry the truth. However, for ordinary beings **it is difficult to know** exactly if other beings are superior because **it is difficult to develop valid cognitions of others having faults or no faults or to say that this** person **has or has not this** fault. **This, others**—that is, Buddhists—**can know.**

Establishing superior beings in our tradition

1. The complete abandonment of faults is possible
2. Faults abandoned cannot return
3. Refuting arguments on the causes of faults

The complete abandonment of faults is possible

> 220. **Because all correspondence of being weakened**
> **and becoming prominent is with the opposing force,**
> **from acquaintance it will become integrated,**
> **and some will put an end to afflictions.**

"Then a person with a complete cessation of faults is not possible?"

The opposing force to desire and so forth has the antidote of the knowledge of no-self. This is **because** there is **a correspondence** in which the knowledge of no-self is increased and desire and so forth **is weakened.** If the knowledge of no-self is weakened, desire and so forth **become prominent.** Therefore **some** beings **will put an end to** all their **afflictions**, because **from acquaintance** with the knowledge of no-self over a long time, their minds **will become integrated** with that knowledge.

Faults abandoned cannot return

It might be argued, "Faults may cease once, but they will return, in the same way that a previous mind of faults can later become a mind without faults."

> 221. **Absence of harm, perfect reality,**
> **and the very entity will not be reversed by error.**
> **Even if there is effort, the mind adheres to that side.**

Through acquaintance with the path, when all harms of saṃsāra have gone, there is an **absence of harm.** And because there is a consciousness apprehending intrinsically existing phenomena of impermanence and so on, the **perfect reality** become the nature of the path, **and** furthermore **the very entity** of the mind becomes the antidote to the faults. These **will not be reversed by** faults such as **error**—that is, the harm of saṃsāra—or the imperfect, which is not the nature of the path, because it will not be possible to see the path as a fault and afflictions as excellent qualities. Therefore there will be no need for effort in abandoning these. **Even if there is effort, the mind adheres to that side**—that is, it only makes effort in the path of the knowledge of no-self.

Refuting arguments on the causes of faults

It could be argued, "By the increase and decrease of the knowledge of no-self, the cause of the faults such as desire will correspondingly increase and decrease. In that case, the cause of faults is the apprehending of a self. This contradicts the statement that delusion[142] is the cause of faults."

> 222. **All the types of faults are produced**
> **from the view of the transitory collection,**
> **and that is ignorance.**
> **There is attachment to that and that,**
> **and from these arise anger and so on.**

223. **This is why it was said that**
delusion is the cause of faults.
Elsewhere, if the view of the transitory collection
is abandoned, they are abandoned.

There is no contradiction. **All the types of faults** of saṃsāra **are produced from the view of the transitory collection, and such** a view **is ignorance. This is why it was said that delusion is the cause of the faults**; through ignorance **attachment to that** self arises, **and** from that comes attachment to **that** which is mine, **and from these** arise all faults, **anger and so on.**

Sūtras **elsewhere** state that **the view of the transitory collection** is the prime cause, because **if** that view **is abandoned**, all faults **are abandoned.**

28. Refuting the Vedas as Being Unproduced by Persons

The expressions of the Vedas establishing the truth are also fallacious reasoning

1. Refuting that not being produced by a person is established by reason
2. Refuting that being nondeceptive in one part is established by reason (1.330)

Refuting that not being produced by a person is established by reason

1. The assertion
2. Refutation

The assertion

> 224. **Causes of words of error are faults**
> **arising from a person.**
> **Therefore that not produced by a person**
> **has the reality of truth, some assert.**

"The Vedas **have the reality of truth** because they teach something **that** was **not produced by a person**. This pervades because **the causes of words** possessing the reality **of error are faults** such as desire, and they **arise from a person. Thus some** of the Mīmāṃsā school **assert.**"[143]

Refutation

1. Refuting the pervasion of the root reason
2. Refutation by examining the root reason (1.239)
3. Refuting the thesis of the main reason (1.317)

Refuting the pervasion of the root reason

1. Refuting by presenting parallel reasoning
2. Refuting because of contradiction with their own assertions

Refuting by presenting parallel reasoning

> 225. **The causes of words of truth are qualities**
> **arising from a person.**
> **Therefore why would that not produced by a person**
> **not have the reality of error? Thus others assert.**

Why would they, the Vedas, **not have the reality of error?** It follows that they do, because they teach topics and are **not produced by a person.** This pervades because **the causes of words of truth are** the **qualities** of compassion and wisdom, and their existence **arises from a person. Thus others**—that is, Buddhists—**assert.**

Refuting because of contradiction with their own assertions

1. Presenting the consequence
2. Refuting responses

Presenting the consequence

> 226. **The cause of understanding meaning**
> **is linguistic convention, which depends upon people.**
> **Thus, even if the words were not produced by a person,**
> **the possibility of error remains.**

Even if the words of the Vedas **were not produced by a person,** it still follows that **the possibility of** them being revealed as in **error remains,** because **linguistic convention,** which is **the cause of understanding meaning, depends upon people.**

Refuting responses

1. Their response
2. The refutation

Their response

227. If the relationship is not made by a person . . .

"Your logic is unfounded. **The relationship** between the expressions of the Vedas and their meanings **is not** a convention **made by a person** but is established naturally."

The refutation

1. Refutation by way of an absurd consequence
2. Refutation by analysis

Refutation by way of an absurd consequence

> **. . . there would be an understanding**
> **without knowledge of a linguistic convention.**
> **If that is clarified by linguistic convention,**
> **that other than that which is conceived**
> **would have no capacity.**

It would follow that from the sounds of the Vedas **there would be an understanding** of the phenomenon expressed **without** the **knowledge** that applies **a linguistic convention** to any particular phenomenon. The meaning of the expressions would be understood from the sounds by way of the naturally arising relationship between the sounds and the meanings, without depending upon a linguistic convention.

In response, "A person **will clarify that** naturally arising relationship **by** way of **linguistic convention.**"

The naturally arising relationship, which is **other than that which is conceived** by that person by way of linguistic convention, **would have no capacity** for creating understanding, because when the convention is applied, there is understanding, and when it is not, no understanding is possible, even though there is naturally arising relationship.

Refutation by analysis

1. Refutation by analyzing the subject matter
2. Refutation by analyzing the relationship
3. Refutation by analyzing the verbal expressions

Refutation by analyzing the subject matter

> 228. **If the words ascertain one meaning,**
> **other meanings could not be understood.**
> **If connected with many meanings,**
> **that which is contradictory would be illustrated.**

If the Vedas have a naturally arising relationship with phenomena, is it a naturally arising relationship with one phenomenon only or with many? **If** it is the former, then it follows that many **other meanings could not be understood** from **the words** of the Vedas because these words are **ascertained** as expressing **one meaning** only. If it is the latter, then it follows that words from the Vedas such as "**If** you desire higher realms, give burnt offerings to the fire" **would illustrate** other things **contradictory** to one's desires, such as eating dog meat, because they are naturally **connected with many meanings**—that is, all meanings.[144]

> 229. **Positing not being produced by a person**
> **would be meaningless. If the distinct are connected,**
> **reasoning would be expressed to establish that.**

If you agree, then **positing** the fact of **not being produced by a person** in order to prove that the Vedas are not in error with regard to gaining only that which is desired **would be meaningless** because they reveal that which is contrary to that which is desired.

Furthermore, **if the** sounds and the meaning **are distinct** but **connected**, it **would be** proper to **express reasoning to establish that.** However, the sounds and the meaning expressed are not connected because they are not connected either by being of the same nature or causally. The reason is valid because these two—the sounds and the meaning expressed—are substantially separate, and you assert that the expressions of the Vedas is permanent.

> 230. **Not being composed by a person,**
> **there is no meaning in any way.**
> **If you accept that it was composed,**
> **that is actually like washing an elephant.**

Moreover, **there is no** understanding any **meaning** in the Vedas because they **were not composed by a person.** To this it might be argued, "**Accepting that it was composed** by a person indicates that the meaning will be understood."

This assertion of yours **is actually like washing an elephant**: in order to remove the dirt of error, you assert that the Vedas were not produced by a person, but then they become smeared by the wetness of not being able to reveal any meaning, and to remove that, you assert that they were composed by a person and then become smeared by the dirt of error.[145]

Refutation by analyzing the relationship

1. Refutation by examining permanence and impermanence
2. Refutation by examining whether one or distinct

Refutation by examining permanence and impermanence

1. Reasoning refuting permanence
2. Refutation of an uncertain example and what it exemplifies

Reasoning refuting permanence

> **231. Because they are impermanent,**
> **bearers of the relationship are not permanent.**
> **Therefore that of meaning and sounds**
> **is produced by the cognition of a person.**

Is the relationship between the sounds and their expressed phenomena one of impermanence or permanence? If it is the former, that would contradict it existing by way of its own entity. If the latter is asserted, things such as pots, which are expressed by the sounds of the Vedas and which are the **bearers of the relationship, are not** of a **permanent** substance in their relationship with the sounds of the Vedas, **because they are impermanent. Therefore** it follows **that** the relationship in which the **meaning** expressed **and** the **sounds** that express appear as mixed **is produced**—that is, conceived—**by the cognition of a person** because it exists as a designation and in reality is neither permanent nor impermanent.

> **232. If concomitance with meanings were formed,**
> **it could not be correct that the sounds**

would reverse their nature.
In conceptualized relationships, this fault is not there.

Furthermore, it follows that the sounds of the Vedas will not produce understanding of any new meaning because they have no relationship with any new meaning. If you disagree, we respond that **if concomitant** relationships **with** new **meanings were formed**, it would follow that **it could not be correct that** the **sounds** of the Vedas could hold a relationship that later **reversed their** previous **nature** of having no relationship with future meanings, because they are permanent.

In reply they might say, "Is that not the same for you?"

With the assertion that between sounds and phenomena there is just a **conceptualized relationship, this fault** of placing it in an ultimately existing relationship **is not there**, because it is a relationship posited by conceptual cognition.

Refutation of an uncertain example and what it exemplifies

233. **"Even if the support is destroyed, there is no destruction**
because it is permanent, as is similar with class."
With permanence, what potential of dependence is there?
Why do you assert dependence?

It could be argued, "You say that if the support—that is, the object expressed—is impermanent, then that which depends upon that support, the relationship, must also be impermanent. But **even if the support**, which is the object expressed, **is destroyed**, the relationship **is not destroyed because it is permanent.** If the particulars are destroyed, the **class**, which depends upon them, is not destroyed. It is **similar to** that."

The example and what it exemplifies are both wrong. **Why do you assert** that the separate entities of class and relationship **depend** upon the particulars and the expressed phenomena? This cannot be correct because it would follow that **with** regard to the **permanent** phenomena of class and relationship, **what** effective **potential** can be had by way **of dependence**? There can be none.

234. **If the cooperative causes for producing consciousness**
are brought together, that can be created.

Therefore correct consciousnesses are born from pots and so forth
235. **and asserted to be that which is illuminated.**

In reply, they say, "The phenomena as supports do not newly create but they illuminate what is already existent[146] and because of that they are supports."

Generally, that which is illuminated and that which illuminates are pervaded by being product and producer. **If the cooperative causes**, such as the illuminating sunlight, needed **to produce** a visual **consciousness** apprehending a pot, for example, **are brought together**, then the pot **can create that** apprehension of the pot. **Therefore correct consciousnesses are born from pots and so forth** that have been illuminated by the light of the sun, **and** by being produced in that way, these pots are **asserted to be that which is illuminated.**

Those are not characterized
because they are unchanging.
Asserting that those will illuminate that,
what can the illuminator do?

The same is not established with class and so on. **Those** such as class and relationship **are not characterized** by being phenomena to be illuminated, phenomena to be expressed, and so on, **because they are unchanging.** If you agree, it follows that it is not correct to **assert that those** phenomena to be illuminated and phenomena to be expressed **will illuminate that** class and relationship, because **what can the illuminator do** to produce the apprehending of the phenomena of class and relationship? It can do nothing.

Refutation by examining whether one or distinct

236. **Even if the relationship were an entity,**
it would be distinct, and the cognition would be different.
Not being distinct from that, it would be itself.
There can be no meaning other than these.

Even if the relationship between sounds and the meaning **were an entity,** is that relationship substantially distinct from or identical to the sounds and meaning? If it is the former, then to a nonmistaken **cognition**, the relationship between these two would appear as a substance **different** from the sounds and the meaning, because **it would** appear as substantially **distinct** from these two.

If it is the latter, the relationship between sounds and the meaning **would be** the sounds and the meaning **themselves,** because **it would not be distinct from the** substantially existing sounds and the meaning. If you agree, it could not serve as the relationship between sounds and the meaning.

"What if the relationship is neither identical to nor distinct from verbal expression and phenomena expressed?"

Then it would follow that the relationship between the sounds and the phenomenon expressed could not be an existing phenomenon because it is neither substantially one with nor distinct from the sounds and the meaning. This pervades because **there can be no meaning other than these**—that is, one that is neither substantially one nor substantially distinct.

> 237. **Because they are entities of distinct natures,**
> **the relationship is produced by conceptualization.**
> **Substantially existing, how can it depend upon another**
> **or be the relationship of another?**

Therefore **the relationship** in which sounds and the meaning appear as mixed **is produced by conceptualization**—that is, it is superimposed—**because** the relationship in which these two appear as mixed exists as a conceptual designation, and these two **are entities of distinct natures.**

Furthermore, **how can** the relationship between sounds and the meaning **depend upon another**—that is, the sounds and the meaning themselves—**or** how can it **be the relationship of another**—that is, the sounds and the meaning? It cannot, because, in order, they exist as naturally arisen phenomena and as **substantially existing** phenomena.

Applying this verse also to the text on the refutation of being substantially other is to not comprehend the layout of the text or the application of the phrase "substantially existing."

Refutation by analyzing the verbal expressions

> 238. **The syllables do not have meaning,**
> **while words and so forth are conceived**
> **and have no entity.**
> **As such, how can this real relationship engage?**

If the relationship between verbal expressions of the Vedas and phenomena expressed exists in reality, does it exist in reality with the syllables or with the words? If the former, it follows that there can be no real relationship between the phenomena expressed by **the syllables** and the verbal expressions themselves because the syllables by themselves **do not** reveal the **meaning** of phenomena. If the latter, **how can words**, speech, **and so forth engage in a real relationship** with the phenomena expressed? They cannot, because they **are conceived** by conceptual cognition **and have no entity.**

The intrinsically existing phenomena of the moments of sound that appear to the aural consciousness cannot individually reveal the phenomena to be expressed, and a collection of them is not possible, and so these cannot be actual expressions. However, a conceptual cognition holds as one the previous and following parts of the sounds, which then appear. These are posited as words, speech, expressions, and so on. Therefore, in that sense, they do not exist in reality.[147]

Concerning syllables, the name *syllables* is imputed on the intrinsically existing parts of the sounds. A collection of these parts is held as one by a conceptual cognition, and up to the duration of a blink of the eye,[148] is posited as being an actual syllable. Of these two, the first, syllables, has been explained as being incapable of revealing expressed phenomena, and the second is a non-entity, in the same way as speech and words are non-entities above.

Refutation by examining the root reason

1. Refuting the reason to be a property of the subject, as well as the proof
2. Refuting the pervasion together with the proof (1.284)
3. Refuting features of the reason being a property of the subject (1.292)

Refuting the reason to be a property of the subject, as well as the proof

1. Refutation by examining the proof
2. Refutation by examining illustrations

Refutation by examining the proof

1. Refuting the reason of not remembering the author
2. Refuting the reason of the recitation being without beginning

Refuting the reason of not remembering the author

239. Because of not remembering the authors
they also assert they were not created by a person.

Even to such they say that!
Therefore there is a pervasion of darkness.

Followers of Jaimini [the Mīmāṃsaka] say **they also assert** that the Vedas **were not created by a person because they cannot remember the authors! Even to such** an assertion **they say** it is like **that! Therefore** their world is **pervaded by darkness** because that reasoning has no establishment and no pervasion whatsoever. The Buddhists remember Nirbhartsanā, Vāmanadeva, Viṣvamitra,[149] and so forth as authors [of the Vedas]. The reason also evokes the "old well"[150] approach and so on, and therefore the pervasion is uncertain.

Refuting the reason of the recitation being without beginning

1. Presenting the reason
2. Refutation

Presenting the reason

240. **If this person had not heard it from others,**
they could not express the arrangement of words and syllables.
Thus, some assert, even for others.

Some Mīmāṃsakas **assert** that **even for** Hiraṇyagarbha[151] and so on, who are **other** than reciters of the Vedas, and who are asserted to be creators, there must have been reciters who went before them, because they too are reciters. Similarly, **if this** current and last **person** to recite the Vedas **had not heard it from others, they could not express the arrangement of words and syllables** of the Vedas. Therefore there will have been preceding reciters. In this way, the Vedas are established as having no original creator.

Refutation

1. On examination, creators without beginning is not proven
2. Even if it were proven, this does not prove they are without creators
3. Even if it is proved that they are without creators, this does not prove they speak the truth

On examination, creators without beginning is not proven

> 241. **With other propagated texts also,**
> **without instructions, where can we see**
> **other persons reciting them?**
> **Why can this not be similarly inferred?**

Why can it not be similarly inferred with other texts, such as the *Kumārasambhava*,[152] **propagated** by composers that they **also** have no creator? It follows that this can be inferred because **without** the presence of earlier **instructions, where can we see other persons reciting them?** They would not be able to recite them.

> 242. **Established as being from a particular type,**
> **there is similarity, as with fire from wood.**
> **Furthermore, for the cause that is not seen,**
> **it is validly known that they arose from it.**

Furthermore, for Vedic texts whose **cause**, their authors, **is not** directly **seen, it** can **be validly known that they arose from those** persons—that is, they were created by persons—because their spoken words are similar to the worldly spoken words created by persons. This pervades because when it has been validly **established** that a type of result is born **from a particular type** of cause, then **similarly** other results of that type are born from that cause. **It is like** the fact that certain types of **fire** are produced **from wood**, so therefore other fires of a similar type are created from wood.

> 243. **Because similar results are seen,**
> **they do not reveal that feature.**
> **The proliferation of reasons**
> **are all mistaken.**

Therefore **those** expressions of the Vedas **do not reveal that feature** of not being created by a person, **because it is** validly **seen** that they are spoken words **similar** to the spoken words that **result** from persons. In that case, **the proliferation of reasons**, such as their authors being without an originator, presented in order to establish the words of the Vedas were not created by a person, **are all** of **mistaken** pervasion, as has been established.

Even if it were proven, this does not prove they are without creators

244. **Even if they are completely without beginning,**
they are not dependent upon no person.
Others would also not depend upon a human
and be non-creations of a person.

Even if the fact that a reciter of the Vedas must have been preceded by a previous reciter does prove that the Vedas **are completely without beginning, they are not dependent upon no person**, because if that proved **non-creation by a person**, then phenomena **other** than the Vedas, such as children playing with stones and earth, **would also not depend upon a human** because they are beginningless.

245. **Also, the practices of barbarians and so on**
and the words that propound nonexistence,
if without a beginning, would be similar
because they possess a previous cause that created them.

Also, it would follow that **the practices of barbarians** to take their mothers as their brides **and so on**, the worldly practice of holding ceremonies at the birth of a child, and **the words** of the Lokāyata school **that propound** the **nonexistence** of past and future lives **would be similar** to the Vedas, uncreated by persons, because they are **without a beginning.** The reason stands **because** since time without beginning, they must have **possessed a previous cause that created them.**

Even if it is proved that they are without creators, this does not prove they speak the truth

246. **Even if proved as not created by persons,**
what qualities are there? It is similar to those.
Because differences in forming the meanings are seen,
there will be doubts.

Even if that is asserted, and **proved**, that the Vedas **are not created by persons, what qualities are there** to prove that they possess truth? There are none. **It is similar** to proving that **those** perverted practices are not created by persons.

Even if it is proven that the Vedas are not created by persons because they are without beginning, it follows that **there will be doubts** generated with regard to the phenomena they express, **because** many **differences in forming the meanings are seen** among the teachers who explain them.

29. The Syllables and Words of the Vedas

Refutation by examining illustrations

1. Refuting that the syllables were not created by persons
2. Refuting that the speech was not created by persons
3. Refuting that the sounds and the potential are permanent

Refuting that the syllables were not created by persons

> 247. **Because the syllables are no different from others,**
> **what effect could that affirmation have?**

If you establish that the Vedas were not created by a person, are you establishing that it is the syllables or the speech that was not created by a person? If you **affirm** that **the syllables** were not created by a person, **what effect could that have?** It could have none, **because** they **are no different from other** worldly syllables. You must accept the reasoning because the cognition that recognizes them as being the same is one cognition and engages them with the same recognition.

Refuting that the speech was not created by persons

1. Speech is not distinct from syllables
2. The sequence of the syllables is not speech

Speech is not distinct from syllables

1. Refutation by the reasoning of the nonapprehension of that which should appear
2. Refutation by reasoning that examines the aspects

Refutation by the reasoning of the nonapprehension of that which should appear

> **Speech is not distinct from syllables**
> **because such is not apprehended.**

In reality, **speech is not distinct from syllables because such is not apprehended.** If you agree, then they would be created by persons.

Refutation by reasoning that examines the aspects

1. Refutation by examining whether it has parts
2. Refutation by examining whether it is permanent or impermanent
3. Refutation by examining whether there is pervasion

Refutation by examining whether it has parts

1. Refuting that it has parts
2. Refuting that it does not have parts

Refuting that it has parts

1. Refuting that individually the parts express no meaning
2. Refuting that individually the parts express meaning

Refuting that individually the parts express no meaning

> **248. With the nature of many components,**
> **those distinct parts have no meaning.**
> **They do not possess an entity**
> **but are imputed to possess an entity,**
> **like Lion and so on.**

If speech exists as distinct from syllables, does that speech have many components or is it partless? If it is of **the nature of many components**, or parts, does each component have the ability to reveal the meaning expressed by the whole speech? If you reply that **those distinct parts** on their own **have no** ability to reveal the **meaning** of the speech as a whole, we say that while these parts when not combined **do not possess** the ability to reveal the **entity** to be expressed, it follows that when they are combined **they are imputed** by a conceptual cognition **to possess** the ability to reveal the **entity** to be expressed, because individually they are unable to reveal the meaning but combined they are able. It is **similar to** a brahman boy who is not a lion but is named **Lion** (Siṃha) **and so on**. If you accept this, then it follows that speech was created by persons.

Refuting that individually the parts express meaning

249. **"Doesn't each part contain the meaning?"**
Imputation on the many would be wrong,
because by comprehending one component,
the meaning of the speech would be comprehended.

If you say, "**Doesn't each part** of speech **contain the meaning** expressed by the whole speech?" then it follows that for speech to convey understanding, the necessary **imputation on the many** parts **would be wrong, because by comprehending one component** or part of speech, **the** whole **meaning of the speech would be comprehended.**

250. **Even if all are comprehended at the same time,**
features over time would not be correct.

It can be argued, "As **all** parts of the speech **are** heard **at the same time**, by comprehending one part, won't all meanings be **comprehended**?"

Then it **would not be correct** that understanding the meanings from the speech depends upon the many sequential **features**, determined by listening **over time** to the parts of the speech, because by hearing one part of speech, all parts of the speech would be heard at the same time.

Refuting that it does not have parts

Even if it were one, it would not be distinct,
and understanding sequential would not be possible.

Even if you assert "Then speech **is one**, without parts," it follows that **it would not be possible to understand**—that is, listen—**sequentially** because speech is **not** of **distinct** parts.

Refutation by examining whether it is permanent or impermanent

> 251. **If impermanent, it is produced from effort,**
> **so why is it not created by persons?**
> **If permanent, it would be apprehended permanently,**
> **with no concealing obstruction.**

The speech that is distinct from syllables, is it impermanent or permanent? **If it is impermanent**, then it will be **produced from effort** because it is impermanent and there are no other causes apart from effort. If you agree, then **why is** the speech **not created by persons?** It has to be, because it was produced through effort.

Even **if it is permanent**, then the speech of the Vedas **would be apprehended**—that is, heard—**permanently** because it would be a permanence that could be heard, **with no concealing obstructions** to hinder the hearing.

> 252. **"If some cooperating causes are missing,**
> **it will not be heard."**
> **Evidently it depends upon another,**
> **but here too as ascertained, this is contradictory.**

It could be argued in response, "**If some** of the **cooperating causes** for hearing the speech **are missing, it will not be heard**, and so it will not be heard permanently."

In order to create an aural consciousness, that sound **depends upon other** conditions. This **is evident**—that is, I too accept that. **But here too,**[153] **as ascertained** before, because it is affected by conditions, **this contradicts** its being permanent.

Refutation by examining whether there is pervasion

1. Refuting that it does not pervade
2. Refuting that it does pervade

Refuting that it does not pervade

> 253. **If it does not pervade,**
> **it would not apprehend all.**

Does the partless speech of the Vedas pervade all objects? **If it does not pervade** these objects, then the speech of the Vedas **would not apprehend all** other objects, only a single object, because it would exist only on one object.

Refuting that it does pervade

1. Presenting the consequence
2. Refuting responses

Presenting the consequence

> **If it does pervade,**
> **everyone would apprehend at the same time.**

If you say that this speech **pervades** all objects, then it follows that **everyone** able to hear sounds **would apprehend** all sounds **at the same time** because all these sounds capable of being heard would pervade all objects.

Refuting responses

1. Refuting that being a compounded entity makes a difference
2. Refuting that being well compounded makes a difference

Refuting that being a compounded entity makes a difference

> 254. **Even if that which is compounded is apprehended,**
> **by what is unchanging compounded?**
> **If the sense power is well compounded,**
> **that will still hear all.**

Even if you say, "Not all sounds will be apprehended simultaneously because only sound **that is compounded** by the circumstance of being capable of being heard **will be apprehended** by an equally compounded sense power."

By what circumstance does the sound become **compounded**? It cannot become as such because it **is unchanging**. Furthermore, **if the sense power is well compounded** into being capable of hearing sounds, **that** person **will still hear all** sounds at the same time because the sound heard by that person and all other sounds are identical in the sense of being partless.

Refuting that being well compounded makes a difference

255. **"From the feature of being well compounded,**
there will be distinctions,
and one phenomenon is ascertained."
How would that hear a confusion of sounds?

It could be argued, "**From the feature of** the **well-compounded** sense power capable of hearing one sound only, the sense power engages with **distinctions.** Therefore it **is ascertained** that the aural consciousness only apprehends that sound and does not hear all sounds."

How would that aural consciousness **hear** the noise of **a confusion of** many **sounds**, such as poetry and music? It could not, because it is ascertained as apprehending only one sound.

256. **"In that, there is the hearing of disparate sounds,**
but there are no verbal expressions."
Speaking of something separate from sound
is simply belief.

In reply, "**In** the hearing of **that** clamor there **is** just **the** simultaneous **hearing of** many **disparate sounds** that are not verbal expressions. **There is no** simultaneous hearing of many **verbal expressions** of speech."

Speaking of something possessing the entity of verbal expression that is **separate from** mere disparate **sound is simply** something you **believe** because you want to. It is a statement without reasoning.

257. **If other sounds remained,**
how would the verbal expressions be heard?
Alternatively, because the ability is ascertained,
how would the distinct sounds be comprehended?

Furthermore, **if** a person began to recite the Vedas amid that clamor, and **other sounds remained** unrecited, **how would the verbal expressions be heard?** They would not, because only disparate sounds would be heard.

Alternatively, how would the aural consciousness **comprehend the** many **distinct** and disparate **sounds**? It would not, because **the ability** to hear the disparate sounds individually **is ascertained.** If that were not ascertained, there would similarly be no ascertainment in hearing the verbal expressions individually.

> 258. **Mere sound is not asserted to be verbal expression**
> **because it has this and that fault.**
> **If made evident by the mere sounds,**
> **how does that not exist in the verbal expression?**

The Mīmāṃsaka **do not assert mere sound to be verbal expression because it has this and that fault** of having former and later parts, and those former and later parts cannot possibly become a whole. Therefore they say that it is the partless words and speech made manifest by the sequence of mere sounds that is the verbal expression.

How could a sequence **not exist within the verbal expression** of spoken words? It must exist because it is something that is **made evident by the** sequence of **mere sounds.**

The sequence of the syllables is not speech

1. The presented sequence is not uncreated speech
2. The manifest sequence also is not uncreated speech
3. A sequence separate from the syllables is negated by the above
4. Therefore the sequence was created by persons

The presented sequence is not uncreated speech

> 259. **"The sequence of syllables is the speech."**
> **Not being distinct from the syllables, it is not.**
> **Also, they are not established,**
> **because that would contradict other sequences.**

It is argued, "There is no speech distinct from the syllables, and so **the sequence of syllables is the speech**, and it is that that we establish as being uncreated."

The sequence of syllables **is not** something uncreated by persons because it is a single phenomenon **not distinct from the syllables.** You accept the reasoning. **Also,** a sequence of **those** syllables of the Vedas is unequivocally **not established** as being uncreated by persons, **because** if that sequence were not created by others, **that would contradict** that sequence of syllables being used in **other sequences** elsewhere, and that sequence is definitely used elsewhere.

260. **Because they pervade and are permanent,**
there would be no sequence of place and time.
The faults of being impermanent and not pervading
have been described before.

It follows that the syllables of the Vedas would have **no sequence of place**, in which a former place is left and another engaged, and **no sequence of time**, in which some things exist previously and some exist later, **because they pervade** all things **and are permanently** spoken.

They might reply, "They are impermanent and do not pervade all things." It is not correct to say that the syllables of the Vedas are **impermanent and do not pervade** all things because **the faults** of such assertions **have been described before**—that is, "If impermanent, they are produced from effort" (1.251) and with the verse beginning "If it does not pervade" (1.253).

The manifest sequence also is not uncreated speech

1. If it were permanent, it could not be made manifest
2. If it generates an entity, it is not a manifestor
3. Merely not obscuring is not manifesting
4. Generating aural cognition is not manifesting

If it were permanent, it could not be made manifest

261. **The manifest sequence is not the speech**
because permanence being manifest has been refuted.

"The **sequence** of the already-existent and permanent syllables made **manifest** by the action of the tongue and palate **is speech**, and that is established as not being created."

The syllables are **not** made manifest by the actions of the tongue and palate **because** the syllables are **permanent**, and making permanence **manifest** by circumstance **has** already **been refuted**.

If it generates an entity, it is not a manifestor

From the process of actions, they exist as results.
262. **Something in existence is known,**

and therefore the cause of a cognition of another
is asserted as the manifestor.

Syllables are **the result** of actions of the tongue and palate, and by these actions they do not become something that is merely manifested, because it is **from the** power of the **process of** these **actions** that the entities of syllables **exist**, or arise. This pervades because from the cause of that to be made manifest, **something** already **in existence is** manifested and is evidently **known** to the consciousness. **Therefore** such actions that are **the cause of a cognition** to apprehend **another**—that is, that which is made manifest—**are asserted as** being **the manifestor**, and so it is not possible for a manifestor to generate the actual entity of that which is made manifest.

As with a lamp, for example.
Otherwise, how does it differ from the creator?
263. **From the process of collective actions**
they are definitively apprehended and are the results,
because within a manifestor that is not possible.

For example, the light of **a lamp** will make manifest for cognition an already existing pot. **Otherwise**, if the manifestor created the entity of that which is to be manifested, then **how does this** manifestor **differ from the creator**—that is, substantial cause—of that to be manifested? There is no difference, because it is the creator of the entity of that to be made manifest. By this process, the syllables **are the** main **results** of the actions of the tongue and palate but are not something made manifest, because **from the process of collective actions** of the tongue and palate, the entities of the syllables **are definitively apprehended.** This pervades **because within a manifestor** as a cause it **is not possible** to have a creator of the actual entity.

Here, the syllables created from the actions of the tongue and palate are "syllables" imputed on the parts of syllables.[154] There are many such instances.

Merely not obscuring is not manifesting

264. **If you say absence of concealment**
of the entity is manifesting,
how would the power of these collective actions
make it possible for nonexistence?

If you say that just the actions of the tongue and palate making **absent the concealment of the entity** of that sound **is manifesting, how would the power of these collective actions make it possible** to create the mere absence of concealment? It would not because mere absence **does not exist** as an entity.

> 265. **Other things would also become manifested**
> **because it would be no different from sound.**
> **If you accept that this is so, all causes would be useless.**

Clay pots and **things other** than sound **would also become** entities to be **manifested** by the clay, potter, and so on **because** sound is to be made manifest by tongue, palate, and so on, and the way **sound** arises from tongue, palate, and so on **is no different from** the way a clay pot arises from clay and so on.

If you accept that this is so, then it would follow that **all** the **causes** such as clay and so on **would be useless** in producing the entities of clay pots and so on because they are mere manifestors of clay pots and so on.

> 266. **If recognition, application to existence, and so on**
> **are asserted as proof, there are no examples,**
> **because entities disintegrate moment by moment.**
> 267. **This also uproots other bad reasons.**

If you assert that the actions of the tongue and palate and so on are the manifestors of already existing permanent sounds, how do you establish that sound is permanent? **If you assert** that **recognition** of preceding and succeeding moments as one and that verbal expression is **applied** to objects **existing** from the past **and so on as proof,** these are not perfect reasonings to establish sound as permanent because **there are no** congruent **examples** for this reason to establish sound as permanent. This is **because entities disintegrate moment by moment.**

This reasoning that shows there are no congruent examples for the above reason establishing sound as permanent has other purposes: **this also uproots other bad reasons** used to prove the permanence of sound.

Generating aural cognition is not manifesting

It might be argued, "Manifest syllables means the aural cognition clearly hearing those syllables, and a sequence of that is the speech of the Vedas."

> **Cognition not possessing the support of a person**
> **is damaged simultaneously by this assertion**
> **and by direct valid perception, inferential perception,**
> **and common knowledge.**

Then it follows that this aural **cognition does not possess the support of a person** because it is the speech of the Vedas uncreated by a person. If you agree, then we say that cognition not possessing the support of a person is not possible. This is because the assertion of cognition not depending on a person **is damaged simultaneously**—that is, individually and without relying upon each other—**by** the fact that the Mīmāṃsaka themselves **assert** that cognition is a quality of a person. It is also established **by direct valid perception** that cognition depends upon a person, by **common knowledge** in the world that cognition depends upon a person, and by an **inferential cognition** supported by the reason of concomitant and counter pervasion of cognition and person.

A sequence separate from the syllables is negated by the above

> 268. **A sequence distinct from the syllables**
> **has been clearly examined.**

A sequence existing separately from the syllables is refuted by the above. **A sequence distinct from the syllables** is not speech uncreated by a person because it **has been clearly examined** and refuted by the previous reasoning of nonapprehension of what should appear.

Therefore the sequence was created by persons

> **If it were conceived by superimposition,**
> **how could it not possess the support of a person?**

Therefore the sequence was created by persons. **How could** the sequence of syllables **not possess the support of a person**? It does, because although it is not existing as one with or separate from the syllables, it is **conceived by superimposition.**

30. Disintegration and Destruction[155]

Refuting that the sounds and the potential are permanent

1. By existing, sound is established as impermanent
2. Therefore the previous reasoning is established
3. By this, the capability is refuted as being permanent

By existing, sound is established as impermanent

1. Presenting the main reason, with the establishment of the pervasion
2. Refuting arguments on the establishment of the pervasion

Presenting the main reason, with the establishment of the pervasion

> 269. **Disintegration has a relationship**
> **with mere existence, and therefore**
> **sound is impermanent.**

Sound, because it exists, **is impermanent** in that it is momentary. If you say this does not pervade, **disintegration has an** intrinsic **relationship with mere existence** as an entity because it is integral to the very cause of the entity itself, without depending upon another later cause that is other than the cause of the entity. In the arguments, it is entities that is being presented here, as explained previously.[156]

Refuting arguments on the establishment of the pervasion

Followers of the Vedas and others do not assert these entities to be disintegration by nature. Instead, they assert that the nonexistence of wood, pots, and so on after their destruction when they no longer exist is the disintegration of those entities, and that this disintegration must depend upon causes such as fire, a hammer, and so on. Non-dependent disintegration does not exist, they say. Refutation of that is in two parts:

1. Negating that the establishment of the pervasion does not exist in the reason
2. Negating that the root reason is not ascertained

Negating that the establishment of the pervasion does not exist in the reason

1. Refuting that destruction arises from causes
2. Negating consequences

Refuting that destruction arises from causes

1. Refuting that destruction is a separately created entity
2. Refuting that destruction is created innately
3. Refuting that destruction is created as a third party

Refuting that destruction is a separately created entity

> **If fire creates a separate entity,**
> **because it would not have disintegrated,**
> 270. **the wood would still be seen.**

If fire creates the destruction of wood, does it create something that is **a separate entity** from the wood or the same substance as the wood? If it is the former, **the wood** already burned by the fire **would** later **be seen, because** after it has been burned by the fire **it would not have disintegrated**—that is, it would not have been destroyed. This is because when burned by the fire, it would simply be the destruction created by the fire, and that would be a separate entity from the wood.

> **"That itself is this disintegration."**
> **How can another be the disintegration of another?**
> **Even if that were so, why does wood not appear?**

It could be argued, "There is no fault, because **that** separate nature of destruction **itself is the disintegration**—that is, the destruction—**of this** wood."

How can that destruction created by fire **be the disintegration of another**, the wood? It cannot, because it is another entity separate from the wood. Furthermore, **even if that** separate nature of destruction **were** the destruction of the wood, **why does wood not appear** at that time?

> 271. **"It does not, because it is held by that."**
> **This is not so because it is not concealed by that.**
> **Because it is born, disintegration would possess disintegration.**
> **Even if so, that wood would be seen.**

As a response to this question: "The wood **does not** appear **because** that separate entity of destruction **has taken hold of**—that is, possesses—the wood."

In that case, the separate entity of destruction is merely the concealer of the wood because it is a separate entity from the wood, and by possessing it, the wood is not seen. If you agree, we say that **it is not** known that the separate entity destruction is the concealer of the wood, **because that** entity **does not conceal** wood; it is impossible.

Also, that entity would be in the nature of **disintegration** in that the destruction that is produced from fire **would possess disintegration because it is born** from its own cause. In that case, **even with such** an assertion, it follows that **that wood would** again **be seen** after the wood is burned by fire, because after the wood is burned by fire, the destruction of the wood would be destroyed.

> 272. **"If the executioner is killed,**
> **the criminal does not return.**
> **It is the same with this."**
> **The executioner is not the executed.**

It could be argued, "**If the executioner** of a criminal **is killed, the** executed **criminal does not return. It is the same with this** destruction of the wood. The wood will not return."

The logic of the wood returning when the destruction of the wood is destroyed, and the logic of the criminal returning when the executioner of that criminal has been killed are not similar. The destroyed wood and the killed criminal are similar, but **the executioner** of the criminal **is not the executed** criminal.

Refuting that destruction is created innately

> 273. **If disintegration is not another,**
> **wood itself would be disintegration.**
> **It is not the cause because it is absent.**
> **There is no aspect other than that.**

If you say, "The **disintegration** caused by fire **is not an** entity **other** than the wood," then in that case **wood itself would be disintegration**, because the disintegration of the wood also is not a separate entity from the wood. If you agree, then it follows that fire **is not the cause** of the disintegration of the wood, **because** even **with the absence of** fire, the disintegration of wood is born from the cause of the wood.

Refuting that destruction is created as a third party

If you say that the disintegration created by fire is not substantially one with nor substantially separate from the wood, we reply that **there is no aspect** of disintegration **other than that** of being substantially one with or substantially separate from the wood, because wood substantially exists.

Negating consequences

1. Negating the consequence that destruction and the entity coexist
2. Negating the consequence that entities have no disintegration
3. Negating the consequence that the same fault occurs with conceptualization
4. This process refutes other reasonings

Negating the consequence that destruction and the entity coexist

> 274. **"If disintegration is something without a cause,**
> **then because it exists permanently,**
> **the entity and disintegration will coexist."**
> **How could a nonexistence be permanent?**

It could be argued, "**Disintegration**, or destruction, is substantially permanent because it **is something without a cause.** If so, and you agree, **then** it follows that **the entity** of wood **and** its **disintegration**—that is, the destruction of the wood—**will coexist because** that destruction of wood **exists permanently.**"

The nonaffirming negation that is the destruction of the wood is without cause, but **how could** it possibly **be** substantially **permanent**? It could not, because it does **not exist** as an entity.

Negating the consequence that entities have no disintegration

> 275. **The consequence that entities have no disintegration**
> **is not appropriate to this nonexistence,**
> **because it is not asserted that entities**
> **will disintegrate by way of disintegration.**

"If disintegration does not exist as an entity, then it follows that it could not destroy anything, and therefore nothing would ever disintegrate."

It is not appropriate to cast **the consequence that entities have no disintegration** as damage to the assertion that a separate-entity destruction **does not exist** as an entity. Why? **Because it is not asserted that entities will disintegrate by way of** a separate **disintegration.** This is because entities being produced momentarily from their own causes is what is asserted as disintegration.

"If separate disintegration does not exist as an entity, then in the statement 'disintegration of entities has no cause,' how should 'no cause' be understood?"

> 276. **An entity disintegrating does not depend on another.**
> **Therefore, to understand this,**
> **mind superimposes a distinction,**
> **and at that time, it is explained there is no cause.**

An entity naturally **disintegrating does not depend on** a cause **other** than the cause of the entity. **Therefore** the way **to understand this** non-dependence is that the conceptual **mind superimposes a distinction** between an entity and its disintegration even though they are not distinct, **and** it is **explained** that **at that time** of disintegration, **there is no** separate **cause.** However, explaining destruction that has already occurred as being without cause is an explanation of there being no cause at all. There is this difference.

Negating the consequence that the same fault occurs with conceptualization

> 277. **"If the nonexistence comes into being from itself,**
> **then your thinking is similar."**

There is no such change at all.
It simply becomes nonexistent.

It could be argued, "**If** the destruction that is the **nonexistence** of the entity of the wood does not depend upon any cause other than the cause of the wood, and thus **comes into being from** the existence of the wood **itself, then your thinking** on whether this disintegration is one with or distinct from the wood **is similar**, because if it is other, the wood would never disintegrate, and if it were one, there would be no production at all."

With the destruction of the wood, **there is no such change at all** in terms of being one with or separate from that entity of wood, because **it is simply** the wood **becoming nonexistent** upon its destruction.

278. **This conception occurs with existence.**
The affirmation is in relation to entities.
Saying that it is a nonexistence
is also saying it is a non-entity.

This conception on being one with or distinct from the entities only **occurs with existence** as an entity because **the affirmation**—that is, the action—of being one with or distinct from is solely **in relation to entities.**

Therefore the destruction of the wood **is said to be a nonexistence**, and that is **saying that it is also** a mere negation and **non-entity**. It is not the affirmation of another existent, and so it not one with or distinct from entities.

279. **If there were the slightest action,**
it would depend upon another.
It does not perform the slightest action,
so how would it depend upon another?

Therefore, how **would** the nonaffirming negation that is the destruction of the wood **depend upon** some cause **other** than the cause of the wood? It would not, because the entity of a cause **does not perform the slightest action** upon it. This holds because **if there were the slightest action** by some cause, then the destruction **would depend upon another**—that is, a cause—and if there were not any action, it would not be dependent.

This process refutes other reasonings

> 280. **This dispels erroneous consequences**
> **that if it were without a cause,**
> **disintegration would exist before production.**
> **Also, it would exist and be a disintegration.**

This teaching on destruction being a non-entity has other purposes because it **dispels consequences** presented to show **errors** in the assertion that destruction is without cause. What are these "errors"? One would be that **disintegration**, destruction, **would exist before** the **production** of the entity—that is, from the very beginning—**because it is without a cause. Also**, if that is asserted, then destruction **would exist and** must **be a disintegration** separate from entities such as sprouts because it exists from the beginning.

How are these dispelled? If destruction is without a cause, these three errors of existing from the beginning and so on do not follow because it does not exist as an entity.

The Mīmāṃsaka position is that once the wood has been destroyed, the entity of wood no longer exists, but the destruction itself exists as an entity, and the term *disintegration* is used here to refer to that. The Buddhist position is that this term refers to the wood being created from its own cause as a momentary phenomenon. Therefore it is important not to confuse these two usages. Also, the explanation of being without cause means that *destruction* is completely without a cause, while *disintegration* does not rely upon a cause other than the cause of the wood.

Negating that the root reason is not ascertained

> 281. **"For example, some that are created**
> **are asserted as obstructing.**
> **Likewise, existents are of the nature of disintegration,**
> **existents not created are not."**

It could be argued, "Existence is not necessarily pervaded by disintegration. **For example, some that are created** such as pots are alike in existing but **are asserted as obstructing**, while some such as cognition are produced without the ability to obstruct. **Likewise**, existents are of two types: **existents** that are created **are of the nature of disintegration**, while **existents** that are **not created** do **not** disintegrate."

> 282. **From causes ascertained**
> **come results ascertained.**
> **Because there are no distinct causes,**
> **there is no distinct nature of impermanence.**

Results such as pots and cognitions are individually **ascertained** as being obstructing and nonobstructing because they are similarly produced **from causes** individually **ascertained** to create that which obstructs and that which does not obstruct. Existence does **not** arise with **distinct natures of** permanence and **impermanence because there are no distinct causes** that create permanence and impermanence.

Therefore the previous reasoning is established

> 283. **Therefore the relationship between those**
> **is negated as being permanent.**
> **That with the capability of sound**
> **can also be dispelled**
> **by the faults taught previously.**

The reasoning that teaches that existence is pervaded by being impermanent also **negates** the **relationship between** sounds and meaning **being** an entity and **permanent** because it teaches that whatever is an entity is necessarily impermanent.

By this, the capability is refuted as being permanent

The capability of sound being permanent **can also be dispelled by the faults** found in the assertion of the relationship as permanent, as **taught previously**: "Because they are impermanent, bearers of the relationship are not permanent" (1.231). This is because that line and the following could be translated, "Because bearers of the capability are impermanent, there is no permanence in the capability."

Refuting the pervasion together with the proof

1. The reasoning proving that the Vedas were not created is faulty
2. Teaching faults that render the reasoning contradictory
3. Refuting the "flawless" proof

The reasoning proving that the Vedas were not created is faulty

> 284. **Not being created by a person does not establish**
> **a knowledge of things as they are.**
> **With firelight and so on, other forms are seen**
> **without the errors of the faults of a person.**

Saying that they **were not created by a person**, who would be motivated by desire and so on, **does not establish** that the Vedas will create **a knowledge of things** exactly **as they are**, because it is not pervasive that being uncreated by a person results in pure knowledge of things exactly as they are. If you do not agree: something not created by a person, and which is **without the errors of** being motivated by **the faults of a person** such as attachment, is not necessarily something that exclusively creates an unmistaken consciousness, because **it can be seen** by example how **firelight**, moonlight, **and so on** can become causes of **other** mistaken **forms** and not causes of unmistaken consciousness. Respectively, these would be, for example, at night seeing a blue utpala flower as yellow and seeing yellow as white.

Teaching faults that render the reasoning contradictory

> 285. **If they are asserted as uncreated,**
> **they will not become a cause for knowing.**
> **With permanence, actual capability**
> **can never be produced.**

They, the Vedas, **will not become a cause for knowing** the meanings expressed because **they are asserted as** being an **uncreated** permanent existent. This pervades because **actual capability can never be produced with permanence.**

"But isn't the conceptual cognition of space born from permanent space?"

> 286. **Certain cognitions with a superimposed domain**
> **are created from imprints of conceptualization**
> **but do not occupy the domain of an entity.**

Certain cognitions apprehending space that arise causally from the **imprints of** previous **conceptualization** and that occupy **a superimposed domain,**

are created from those previous imprints **but do not occupy the domain of an** apprehended **entity** of space, because if they did, it would be created permanently.

Refuting the "flawless" proof

1. Expressing the assertion
2. Refuting the assertion

Expressing the assertion

> 287. **"Because it is seen that created speech is untrue,**
> **words uncreated will possess truths**
> **because the reverse pervades and is contrary."**

It could be argued, "In the reasoning of not being created by persons, used to prove that the Vedas possess truths, there may be no concomitant pervasion, but there is a counter pervasion, and so it is correct reasoning. With the **words** of the Vedas **uncreated** by persons, if the pervader of being created by persons is reversed, then the pervaded, the possessing of untruths, is also reversed, and so the words are established as **possessing truths**. This is **because the reverse** of the reasoning of not being created by persons is that which is created by persons, and that **pervades** the possessing of untruths, which **is contrary** to possessing truths, the predicate of the thesis to be established. This is so **because it is seen that** all **untrue speech** was **created** by persons."[157]

Refuting the assertion

1. There is no proof and so there is no counter pervasion
2. The ascertainment of the three criteria must be within the reason
3. If the counter pervasion exists, the concomitant pervasion is established

There is no proof and so there is no counter pervasion

> 288. **For its nonexistence, no reason is shown,**
> **so there is a doubt over its existence.**
> **Even in contradictory entities,**
> **pervasion can be seen.**

There is a doubt that the reason of not being created by persons could **exist** in the incongruent class of possessing untruths, because to establish **its nonexistence, no reason is shown.**

In reply, "That is not so, because possessing untruth cannot exist in two contradictory phenomena—that is, created by persons and uncreated by persons; it is one thing."

If that is seen in one of those phenomenon, that does not prove that it definitely does not exist in five other contradictory phenomena, because **even in** the **contradictory entities** of being produced by effort and not produced by effort, it **can be seen** that they are all **pervaded** by being impermanent.

In reply, "Mere nonapprehension within the incongruent class establishes definitive nonexistence."

> 289. **Nonexistence in all**
> **is not proven by nonapprehension,**
> **as has been explained previously.**
> **If nonexistence is not established,**
> **there is doubt concerning the counter.**

Merely not apprehending **all** entities that should or should not appear does not definitely establish nonexistence. The **nonexistence** of something **is not proven by** its **nonapprehension, as has been explained previously**. Therefore, with regard to the reason of not being created by persons, **there is doubt concerning the counter** of the incongruent class—that is, the counter pervasion is not established. This is because **nonexistence is not established** in the incongruent class—that is, it is not ascertained.

The ascertainment of the three criteria must be within the reason

> 290. **If the concomitant pervasion, the counter pervasion,**
> **and existing in the subject of the thesis**
> **are established by cognition possessing**
> **the result of ascertainment, that is proof.**

If there is doubt over the counter pervasion, it cannot be a correct proof. This is because **if** the three criteria, which are **the concomitant pervasion, the counter pervasion, and** the reason **existing** as a property of **the subject of the thesis,**

are established by valid **cognition possessing the result of ascertaining** these three—that is, it is the cause—then **that** alone **is** a perfect **proof.**

If the counter pervasion exists, the concomitant pervasion is established

> 291. **The expression of the counter**
> **of the phenomenon to be established**
> **is the congruent classification of this.**
> **Therefore all the reasons possess concomitance.**

It would follow that **all the reasons**, such as not being created by persons, that are presented to prove that the Vedas carry the truth **possess concomitance** with the congruent class, because the reason of not being created by persons used to prove that the Vedas carry the truth is ascertained as being the reverse of the incongruent class. This pervades because **the expression of the counter** to the incongruent class—that is, possessing untruths—**of the phenomenon to be established**—that is, possessing truths—would be concomitant with **the congruent classification of this** reason of being uncreated by persons—that is, possessing truths.

31. Examination of Vedic Mantras[158]

Refuting features of the reason being a property of the subject

1. Granting the results of peace and so on depends upon convention
2. Refuting that the results are granted solely by the power of the syllables
3. Refuting the argument over the parts of the syllables
4. Establishing the special features of mantra performance

Granting the results of peace and so on depends upon convention

Previously, the Vedas themselves—their syllables, words, and speech—were generally negated as being uncreated by persons. Here in particular, the mantras of the Vedas are negated as being uncreated by persons.

> 292. **If there are those who make use of convention,**
> **results of the mantras will be forthcoming.**

If the Vedic mantras are uncreated by persons, they will not accomplish special results, because **if there are those** special people **who make use of convention**—that is, apply them—in order to produce the **results of the mantras**, results **will be forthcoming**, but otherwise not.

Refuting that the results are granted solely by the power of the syllables

1. The consequence that if the order were reversed, the mantras would grant results
2. The consequence that they would grant results constantly
3. The consequence that they would grant results to all

The consequence that if the order were reversed, the mantras would grant results

> **If it were power of the entity,**
> **then even with another it would occur**
> **because there is no difference.**

If results were produced from the **power of the entity** that is the permanent sound of mantras not depending upon being given meaning, **then even with** the complete count of syllables recited in **another** order, the special results of the mantras **would** still **occur, because there is no difference** between the mantra in its right order and the entity of the sound of the mantra. This is because there is no difference between the order and the syllables of the mantra in the sense of being unitarily permanent, as you assert. Therefore you must accept this reasoning.

It could be argued, "Reversing the order would not produce the results because the formation of the syllables is the mantra."

> 293. **The formation also would be a separate entity,**
> **as has been dispelled previously.**

It is not from the formation of the syllables alone that results of mantras will be accomplished because **the formation** of the syllables **also would be a separate entity** from the syllables themselves, and that **has been dispelled previously** with the verse beginning "The sequence of syllables is the speech" (1.259). Also, a formation that is not a separate entity from the syllables would also be subject to the same fault.

The consequence that they would grant results constantly

> **They would permanently produce their outcome.**
> **If dependent, they would have no power.**

It would follow that **these** mantras **would be permanently producing their** desired **outcome** because they are permanent phenomena that produce their desired results.

In reply, "They would not be permanently producing their results because they produce their results **in dependence** upon the rituals."

Rituals and so forth **would have no power** to have any effect upon the mantras because these mantras would be permanent.

The consequence that they would grant results to all

1. Direct expression of the damaging consequence
2. Refuting the features of the agent as being determinative
3. The assertion of an agent is contradictory
4. Refuting the response that our position is similarly faulty

Direct expression of the damaging consequence

> 294. **If the power of the entity were so,**
> **they would produce results for all.**

It follows that the mantras **would produce results for all**, whether brahmans or outcastes, because **the power of the entity** of the permanent sound of the mantras, which does not depend upon persons, would produce **such** results. This pervades because with the power of the entity, there are no persons who are close or distant.

Refuting the features of the agent as being determinative

It could be argued, "There is no such fault, because the differences between a brahman and an outcaste, in terms of their high or low caste, are established by way of their own entities, and thus there is a difference in whether the results of the mantra will be accomplished or not."

> **Because they would not be formed,**
> **it does not depend upon the differences in agents.**
> 295. **Distinct entities are brought together by distinct actions.**
> **The power is not determined**
> **by the features of agents.**
> **They arise merely from conventions.**

The mantras producing their results **does not depend upon the differences** of caste **in agents** such as brahmans and outcastes **because** the mantras **would not be formed** from circumstances. This pervades because **entities are brought together** by circumstance and are **distinct** results created **by the actions** of distinct causes, not in any other way. **The power** of a mantra **is not** separately

determined by the features of agents of high or low castes, such as brahmans and outcastes, established by way of their own entities. This is because these differences **arise merely from** the **conventions** of the world and are not established by way of their own entities.

The assertion of an agent is contradictory

> 296. **If there is nothing that can be affected,**
> **what could they do as the agent?**
> **Clearly manifesting and being the user**
> **were refuted earlier.**

What could a brahman **do as the** ritual **agent** to make any difference to a mantra? He could not make any difference because the mantra **has nothing that can be affected** by circumstance.

In reply, "The brahman does not make any new difference to the mantra, but he **clearly manifests** it **and is the user** of the mantra."

The mantra, because it is permanent, is not something to be manifested, and permanence being made manifest by circumstance was **refuted previously**.

> 297. **"The cognition from those is the manifestation,**
> **and that connects to the results."**
> **If the speaker is the cause of being made manifest,**
> **the listener would also be connected to the results.**

It could be argued, "The production of **the** aural consciousness **cognition** that hears the sound of the mantra **from those**—that is, brahmans—**is** the meaning of the mantra made **manifest, and that** cognition is what **connects to the results** of the mantra."

Then it follows that **the listener**, who is separate from the reciter of the mantra, **would also be connected to**—that is, would gain—**the results** of the mantra being recited, because they would generate the aural cognition that hears the sound of the mantra, and because the mantra being **made manifest** by **the speaker** and being heard, you assert as the actual **cause** of gaining the results of the mantra recitation.

> 298. **The action of creating sound**
> **that is not actually manifest,**

or of those that are mentally recited,
would have no purpose because
sounds are the domain of the ear.

Furthermore, **the action of creating sound** that is inaudible to an aural consciousness, such as sounds that are whispered and are produced from minimal actions of the tongue and palate **or those that are mentally recited, would have no** power to achieve the **purpose** of the mantra recitation because the mantra sound **is not actually manifest.** The reason stands **because** actual manifest **sounds** are pervaded by being **the domain of the ear.**

299. **"Because it is created indirectly from that,**
the cognition is also the manifesting."
Possessing an object is not established
because it follows on from a conceptual cognition.

It could be argued, "**The** conceptual **cognition** to which appears aspects of the mantra that are recited mentally or are whispered at that time **is also the** mantra sound **manifesting because it is created indirectly from that** mantra sound. Therefore mental recitation would not be without purpose."

The conceptual mind to which appears the aspect of the mantra recited mentally or in whispers at that time **possessing an** apprehended **object** that is the intrinsically existent mantra sound **is not established because it** is a conceptual cognition that **follows on from a** previous **conceptual cognition.**

Refuting the response that our position is similarly faulty

It will be argued, "But according to your assertion, the results of the mantra are achieved in dependence upon convention, so how does mental recitation not become meaningless?"

300. **The natures of the intrinsically existent and the universal**
are asserted to be one nature,
and those who create the convention will express them.
For entities, this is not noncontradictory.

Whispered and mentally recited mantras are not contradictory to the production of the results of mantras because they are consecrated by way of the mental application of the user of the mantra. This is so because a universal of the mantra is apprehended as being an intrinsically existing entity and is then recited. There is pervasion because **the natures of the intrinsically existing** mantra **and the** mantra **universal are asserted**—that is, held—**to be one nature, and those who create the convention will express** the mantra.

In the assertion that the results are attained from **the entities** themselves, **it is not noncontradictory** that the results will arise from mental recitation, because within mental recitation there are no intrinsically existent phenomena.

Refuting the argument over the parts of the syllables

1. The argument
2. The response

The argument

> 301. **"If there were no sequence,**
> **then there would be no distinct results.**
> **from hearing 'taste' and 'ocean.'"**

"**If there were no sequence** of syllables separate from the syllables, then **from hearing** the words **'taste' and 'ocean,'** which in Sanskrit are *rasa* and *sara*, **there would be no distinct resultant** understanding of *taste* and *ocean*, respectively, because the sequence makes no difference and neither do the syllables. The first reason you accept, and the second is established because the syllables are singly permanent."

The response

1. The cause-and-effect sequences are created by persons
2. Therefore any other sequence will produce a different result
3. Establishing that the sequence of syllables is created by persons

The cause-and-effect sequences are created by persons

> **They possess the support of a person.**
> 302. **The syllables are produced**
> **from the volitional consciousness,**
> **and by consciousness the sound is produced.**

It is not the case that by the reason of *rasa* and *sara* having no separate sequences, there will be no separate results. This is because the sequences have the separation of **possessing the support of a person.** There are three sequences: those of volition, of aural consciousness, and of memory. For those of volition there are distinct sequences: with the *rasa* sequence, **the volitional consciousness** of *ra* **produces the syllable** *ra* **and** the volitional **consciousness** of *rasa* **produces the sound** *sa*. With *sara*, the process is the reverse.

> **Possessed of that feature, it is ascertained by the ear.**
> 303. **The consciousness created by that consciousness**
> **hears not too quickly, and in dependence upon remembering,**
> **the memory of that entity comes later.**

The resultant aural consciousness sequences exist separately because with *rasa*, after the aural consciousness hears *ra*, the sound *sa* that **possesses the feature of that** *ra* **is ascertained by the ear**—that is, it is heard. With *sara* the process is reversed.

The resultant memory consciousness sequences are separate. This is because with *rasa*, **the consciousness** apprehending *ra*, which was **created by the consciousness** that heard *ra* **hears** *sa* but **not too quickly**, so that the former and latter are heard and ascertained individually. **Later, in dependence upon remembering** the former, *ra*, **the memory of the** latter **entity**, *sa*, is created. With *sara* the process is reversed.

> 304. **The syllables are of those of cause,**
> **apprehension, and mind,**
> **spoken of as cause-and-effect sequences,**
> **and are created by persons.**

Therefore the cause-and-effect sequences of **the syllables** *rasa* and *sara* are created by persons because, as described, there **are** the three sequences **of causal** volition, an **apprehending** aural consciousness, **and** a **mind** remembering. They are **spoken of as** the **cause-and-effect sequences** of the syllables, **and** they **are created by persons.**

Therefore any other sequence will produce a different result

> 305. **Therefore the entities of the syllables**
> **are separate within words.**
> **Coming from the formative actions of agents, they are distinct**
> **and are results distinguished by bringing together.**

The syllables are created from volition as separate phenomena. **Therefore the entities of the syllables within** the **word** *rasa* **and** the **word** *sara* **are** substantially **separate**, not of the same nature. This is because **they are** created as substantially **distinct** phenomena **coming from the formative actions of** the **agents** with distinct volitions. Therefore these two syllables will create **resultant** understandings with distinct features of "taste" and "ocean" because they are **distinguished by** the sequences that **bring** *ra* and *sa* **together** and *sa* and *ra* together.

Establishing that the sequence of syllables is created by persons

> 306. **The sequence of those syllables, furthermore,**
> **occurs from dissemination by persons,**
> **established as not contradictory to their wishes.**
> **Sequences abiding would be contradictory.**

The sequence of those syllables, furthermore, occurs from dissemination by persons because they are sequences that are **established as not contradictory to**—that is, established by the force of—**the wishes** of those persons. This pervades because if the **sequences abided** in reality, unmade by persons, they **would contradict** those wishes.

> 307. **Because persons and syllables**
> **are established as cause and result,**
> **all sequences of syllables are from persons,**
> **like the logic of fire and wood.**

Therefore **all the sequences of syllables** of the Vedas, because they are sequences of syllables, arise **from persons.** This pervades **because persons and syllables are** validly **established as cause and result**. It is **like**, for example, **the logic** that says if **fire and wood** are established as being cause and effect, then a phenomenon possessing the features of fire will be the result of wood, its own cause.

Establishing the special features of mantra performance

1. Establishing special persons by their power and knowledge
2. Disputing the proof that there are no special persons
3. If it is established that there are no special features, that goes against your assertion

Establishing special persons by their power and knowledge

> 308. **The person who, by knowledge and power,**
> **possesses the means to create the sequences**
> **of that known as mantra is superior**
> **because that does not exist in others.**

The person possessing the means, or capacity, **to create** under their own power **the sequences** of the syllables **of that** which is **known as mantra is superior** to ordinary beings **by way of knowledge** of composition and ritual **and** by the **power** to bring about effects according to their desire. This is **because** their knowledge and power **do not exist in other** ordinary beings.

You might respond, "This reason does not hold up because it can be seen that ordinary beings who understand the *Garuḍa Tantra* can apply mantras to dispel poison and so on."

> 309. **Those who know tantra and perform mantras**
> **rely upon the power of the main person**
> **and engage with the methods explained.**
> 310. **If you wish for results to arise from mantras,**
> **they must be spoken as formed and created by persons.**

For **those who know tantra and** who **perform** secret **mantras**, their application of mantra **relies upon the power of the main person**—the creator of the tantra. It is not a nonreliant activity because it is performed by **engaging with the methods**—that is, the pledges, essential instructions, and so on—**explained** by the creator of the tantra. Therefore, **if you wish for results to arise from mantras, they must be spoken as** mantras **formed** from circumstance in general **and created by persons** in particular because mantras uncreated by persons will not produce results.

Disputing the proof that there are no special persons

> **The proof that persons have no ability is repudiated by this.**
> 311. **Cognition, senses, speaking, being a person, and so on**
> **expressed as proof is fallacious validity.**
> **It is reason with remainder,**
> **without an understanding of the reality.**

This explanation that performing mantras endowed with knowledge and power exists has another purpose: to **repudiate** all the Mīmāṃsaka expressions of **proof that persons have no ability** to see things beyond the senses. They say, "If you assert someone is a special person, then from the reason of that person having cognition and so on, it can be proven that they are not special."

We reply that having **cognition,** having **senses, speaking, being a person, and so on expressed as proof** that a person is not special **is fallacious validity,** or reason, from which a perfect proof bringing about a correct **understanding of the reality does not exist.** Because **it is** a **reason with remainder** with doubt concerning the pervasion, the pervasion is not established.

If it is established that there are no special features, that goes against your assertion

1. The consequence that it must be false because the definitive meaning is something conceptualized by persons
2. There is no difference in understanding the definitive meaning in those possessed of desire
3. If the words are valid, that contradicts your assertion

The consequence that it must be false because the definitive meaning is something conceptualized by persons

> 312. **The sounds do not say,**
> **"I say this is the meaning and this is not the meaning."**
> **This meaning is conceptualized by persons,**
> **and they too are possessed of desire.**

You say there are no special persons, but Jaimini is a special person, and that would contradict his own words "I understand the meaning of the Vedas."

The sounds of the Vedas **do not say, "I say this is the meaning and this is not the meaning."** This is because they are inanimate. Therefore the statements that say "**This** and this alone is the **meaning** of this expression in the Vedas and nothing else" have to be **conceptualized by** the Mīmāṃsaka **persons** themselves, **and** it **also** follows that these Mīmāṃsakas cannot know whether the Vedas are valid or not because **they are possessed of desire** and so on.

There is no difference in understanding the definitive meaning in those possessed of desire

> 313. **Only they know the reality and others do not?**
> **Who made this distinction?**
> **Why do you not accept those**
> **who similarly have the forms of persons?**

Who made the distinction that **only** Jaimini **knows the reality** of the Vedas **and others do not?** They are both similar in being persons. **Why** in your tradition **do you not accept** that there are those persons who possess the knowledge of the meanings of the Vedas? It follows that you should assert this because you are a person and yet you understand their meanings. Likewise, **those who similarly have the forms of persons** will also possess knowledge of the meanings of the Vedas.

If the words are valid, that contradicts your assertion

> 314. **"The words of those, by way of valid cognition,**
> **will infallibly know the meanings."**
> **For those phenomena that are very hidden,**
> **valid cognition is not possible.**

It will be argued, "**The words of those** persons, **by** the type of **valid cognition** known as that induced by the force of the entity, **will infallibly** establish the very hidden meanings of the Vedas, and in dependence upon those words I can **know the meanings** of my Vedic scriptures."

Valid cognitions induced by the force of the entity in the minds of ordinary beings cannot infallibly establish the very hidden meanings of words, because **it is not possible for them** to encompass **those phenomena that are very hidden.**

> 315. **Because those words are created by those**
> **who have infallibly established by valid cognition,**
> **and those words conclude the scripture is valid,**
> **it is meaningless to establish them as uncreated by persons.**

Furthermore, as to valid cognition by way of scripture, **it is meaningless to establish** the scripture as being **uncreated by persons** to prove that the scripture itself is valid, **because those words are created by those** persons **who have infallibly established by** way of a **valid cognition** induced by the force of the entity, and they are the very **words** that enable you to **conclude, "That scripture is valid."**

> 316. **If it were possible to know very hidden phenomena**
> **without scripture, it would be asserted**
> **that there are some who comprehend**
> **phenomena beyond the range of the senses.**

Also, **it would be asserted**—that is, it follows that it would have to be asserted—**that there are some** special persons **who comprehend** the very hidden **phenomena beyond the range of the senses,** because **it would be possible to know very hidden phenomena without scripture** by valid cognition induced by the force of the entity.

32. There Is No Comprehending the Definitive Meaning of the Vedas

Refuting the thesis of the main reason

1. Teaching that there is no comprehending the definitive meaning of the Vedas
2. Therefore there is no valid cognition establishing the definitive meaning
3. Refuting other responses that assert there is proof
4. Refuting the existence of a definitive meaning by way of its own entity

Teaching that there is no comprehending the definitive meaning of the Vedas

317. **A nature of desire and so on,**
not knowing the meanings of the Vedas from others,
and not knowing the Vedas themselves,
from what do you know the meaning of the Vedas?

Jaimini says, "This and nothing else is **the meaning of the Vedas.**" **From what do you know** this? It follows that you cannot know it because your **nature** is that **of desire and so on**, and so without depending upon the teachings of others, you cannot know it. Furthermore, because they too are possessed of desire, you will **not know the meanings of the Vedas from** the teachings of **others.** Also, **you do not know** the meanings of the Vedas even by depending on what **the Vedas themselves** teach.[159]

Therefore there is no valid cognition establishing the definitive meaning

318. Therefore, from hearing "Desiring a high rebirth,
make offerings to the fire," by what valid cognition
does it not mean "Eat dog meat"?

Therefore, if you agree with the above, then **from hearing**—that is, from the sounds—"If you **desire a high rebirth, make offerings to the fire," by what valid cognition** can you establish that **it does not mean** "If you want a higher rebirth, **eat dog meat**" and instead means "Pour oil into the fire purified by the mantra"? You cannot establish this because there is no unequivocal knowing of that particular meaning.

Refuting other responses that assert there is proof

1. Refuting that it is established by common knowledge
2. Refuting that it is the Vedas themselves that speak

Refuting that it is established by common knowledge

1. Common knowledge cannot establish very hidden phenomena
2. Teaching that it contradicts common knowledge
3. If it were established by common knowledge, that would contradict your own statements
4. Common knowledge is a cause for doubt

Common knowledge cannot establish very hidden phenomena

319. "They are commonly known in the words of the world."
By what are they able to distinguish the meaning
of the expressions engaging in various meanings?
How can they see phenomena beyond the senses?

It is argued, "The individual meanings of the individual expressions of the Vedas are **commonly known in the words of the world**, and from that I can ascertain the meanings of the individual expressions of my Vedic scriptures."

By what reason that enables seeing the meaning of the Vedas **are these** worldly persons **able to distinguish** that such and such alone and none other is **the meaning of the expressions** of the Vedas, which **engage in various**

meanings? Such a person cannot distinguish these things—**how can they see** those **phenomena** of the Vedas, which are **beyond the senses**?

Teaching that it contradicts common knowledge

> 320. **Expressing phenomena not commonly known,**
> **we see expressions like "higher rebirth" and "goddess."**
> **Toward other, similar expressions,**
> **there will be such thoughts.**

Common worldly knowledge cannot establish the meanings of the expressions of the Vedas because it is evident that the Vedas **express phenomena not commonly known** in the world. This is because **we see expressions like "higher rebirth" and "goddess,"** which in the world are known, respectively, as the abode of the gods and the females who live there. But in the Vedas they are understood to refer, respectively, to a special joy experienced by humans and to the stick for starting the fire.[160]

You may reply, "From the explanation of 'Desiring a higher rebirth, make offerings to the fire,' it can be established to mean 'Pour oil into the fire purified by the mantra.'"

It follows that a person cannot know the unequivocal meaning of explanations of "Make offerings to the fire," and **other, similar expressions** because they do not know this from their own mental ability, from the teachings of others, or from the expressions of the Vedas themselves. If you agree, then **there will be such thoughts** that it could mean, "If you want a higher rebirth, eat dog meat," as the consequence has stated above.

If it were established by common knowledge, that would contradict your own statements

> 321. **That commonly known are the words of humans,**
> **which you do not assert as authoritative.**
> **Now from these the meanings will be understood?**
> **What is this rejection and acceptance?**

That commonly known are the words of humans and the words of persons **you do not assert as authoritative. Now** you assert that **from these words the**

meanings of the Vedas **will be understood? What is this rejection and acceptance** of these words? It is contradictory.

322. **"What is the reason for conception**
of something beyond common knowledge?"
Because worldly knowledge is not authoritative,
what is the reason for holding that?

It could be asked, "**What is the reason** that **something beyond the common knowledge** of the world, such as the meaning of 'make offerings to the fire,' **can be conceived** to mean 'Eat dog meat'?"

According to your assertion, these things can be commonly known, but **worldly knowledge is not authoritative,** and so, similarly, **what is the reason for holding** the meaning of **that** expression to be "Pour oil into the fire purified by mantra"? There is none.

Common knowledge is a cause for doubt

323. **Common knowledge creates doubt**
when ascertaining the meanings of an expression
because it is seen that it engages
in various meanings.

The **common knowledge** of the world **creates doubt** as to whether something is this or that **when ascertaining the** sole **meaning of an expression** from the Vedas. This is **because it is seen that** common knowledge **engages in various meanings** of the expressions in the Vedas.

324. **Those not finding certainty**
will have doubts about those very expressions
having the possibility of various meanings
because there is no impossibility of other meanings.

Therefore, **those** beings who do **not find** any **certainty** that determines an unequivocal meaning to **those very expressions** of the Vedas, which **have the possibility to reveal various meanings, will have doubts about** the exact meaning **because** they cannot be certain **there is no impossibility of** there being any **other meanings** than the one that is desired.

Refuting that it is the Vedas themselves that speak

1. Establishing that the Vedas are cleverly created by persons
2. If they were not created by persons, there could be no definitive meaning

Establishing that the Vedas are cleverly created by persons

> 325. **Some say, "'This is the path,'**
> **the tree stump has said."**
> **Others speak of itself.**
> **Examine the specifics.**

It is argued, "The Vedas themselves revealed the definitive meanings to Jaimini, and he taught it to others."

It is Jaimini himself who speaks of the definitive meanings of the Vedas. This is because he does so by referencing the Vedas. Also, **examine the specifics** of what he said and did not say, for they are similar. For example, **some** deceiving people might **say, "'This is the path,' the tree stump has said." Other** people, without referencing a tree stump, **speak of** the path by way of **itself** and just say, "This is the path." In terms of what these two speakers actually say, there is no difference.

If they were not created by persons, there could be no definitive meaning

> 326. **Capable of engaging with all,**
> **from what are they ascertained**
> **as manifestations of a single meaning?**
> **Only ascertained from what is wished to express,**
> **by what is that beyond the senses known?**

From what are the expressions of the Vedas **ascertained as** being expressions in which there is **manifestation of a single**, naturally existing **meaning?** It follows that they are not because they are **capable of engaging with all** meanings.

Furthermore, the words of the Vedas are **only ascertained** as being expressions of individual meanings by way of **what is wished to express. What** valid cognition can **know** the naturally existing relationship they have with the phenomena expressed? There isn't one, because the naturally existing relationship with the phenomena expressed **is beyond the senses**—that is, it is not an object of a valid cognition.

> 327. **The wish to express is the cause of ascertainment.**
> **Linguistic convention is the manifestation of that.**
> **Without persons, that would not exist.**
> **How can that have a single meaning?**

How can the sounds of the Vedas **have** ascertainment as expressions of just a **single meaning**? It follows that they cannot, if they were not created by persons. This pervades because **the wish to express is the cause of** the sounds that **ascertain** individual meanings, in the form of expressions. Moreover, **linguistic convention is the manifestation of that** wish to express, and **without** it being created by **persons**, such convention **would not exist.**

Refuting the existence of a definitive meaning by way of its own entity

> 328. **If they are naturally ascertained,**
> **any other would not be fitting.**
> **Furthermore, any linguistic convention**
> **would also be pointless.**

It would follow that it **would not be fitting** to wish to assert the sounds of the Vedas as having **other** meanings because **they are naturally ascertained** as the expression of one meaning only. **Furthermore**, this reasoning establishes that **any linguistic convention** engaging in the process of creating understanding from the expressions of the Vedas **would also be pointless.**

It could be argued in reply, "But if the naturally existing relationship were made manifest from linguistic convention, then it would not be pointless."

> **From linguistic convention, how will there be any ascertainment**
> **that makes manifest the naturally existing features?**
> 329. **That engaging independently with whatever is desired—**
> **what ascertainment will there be of that?**
> **Therefore linguistic convention, by being capable,**
> **will not make manifest solely that which is desired.**

From linguistic convention, how will there be any ascertainment that makes manifest or links **the features** of the **naturally existing** relationship between the sounds and the meaning? There cannot be any because linguistic convention engages only by way of desire. **Therefore linguistic convention will not**

make manifest the **sole** meaning **desired, by** way of those sounds **being capable** of naturally engaging, because **what** naturally existing **ascertainment of** the phenomena expressed **will there be**? There can be none, because linguistic convention **engages independently with whatever** meaning **is desired.**[161]

These have been intermediate verses.

These two verses are **intermediate verses.**

Refuting that being nondeceptive in one part is established by reason

1. The assertion
2. The refutation

The assertion

330. **Because they are one part of the Vedas,**
others are similarly true.
For example, "Fire reverses cold."
Thus the others have said.

Words of the Vedas **other** than those that state "Fire reverses cold" **are similarly** possessed of the **truth because they are one part of the Vedas**, just as the words **"Fire reverses cold"** are true, **for example. Thus the others**—that is, the elders of the Mīmāṃsaka—**have said.**

The refutation

1. Showing that this is reasoning with remainder
2. Showing the damage done to the thesis itself
3. Refutation by way of consequence

Showing that this is reasoning with remainder

331. **Having a similar taste because of a similar nature,**
and being also cooked by being from the same pot,
are mistaken by possessing a remainder.
The knower of reasoning has refuted these.

The knower of reasoning Dignāga **has refuted** reasonings such as "It is part of the Vedas" as being perfect reasonings because they **are mistaken by possessing a remainder** of doubt about the pervasion. This is using the reasoning, for example, of having **a similar nature** or shape to prove that the remaining fruit **have a similar taste** to the fruit already eaten, and of being similar by being **from the same pot** to prove that the remaining rice must **also be cooked.**

Showing the damage done to the thesis itself

> 332. **They propound agents from permanent persons,**
> **entities that are permanent,**
> **that beyond the senses being apprehended by the senses,**
> **entities not equated with causes,**
> **duration, and disintegration.**
>
> 333. **Furthermore, they propound contradictions**
> **in those areas dispelled by the two valid cognitions**
> **or by inferential cognition based on scripture.**
>
> 334. **Without in any way dispelling the contradictions,**
> **they do not reveal the meaning of the treatises.**
> **Claiming them to be possessed of truth**
> **is like the lustful woman foolishly claiming victory.**

The Mīmāṃsaka **are like a lustful woman foolishly claiming victory** over her master.[162] This is because **they do not in any way dispel the contradictions** to the three kinds of valid cognition for engaging in a treatise. Also, **without revealing** the three features, such as connection and so on, that act as supplementary conditions for engaging with a treatise, they use the reason of the Vedas being nondeceptive in one part **to claim that** every part **is possessed of truth.**

How do the above contradict the three valid cognitions, and how are they not dispelled? The Vedas talk of things that are in contradiction to the three valid cognitions because **they propound agents** produced **from permanent persons; entities,** such as sound, **being permanent**; a universal that is **beyond** the objects of **the senses being apprehended by the senses;** and **entities not equated with causes** being produced by permanent causes, not equated with **duration** whose duration is made by a separate entity, and not equated with **disintegration** but destroyed by later causes other than the phenomenon's own cause.

Furthermore, they assert that cognition is a very hidden phenomenon and that sound is permanent, for example, which are **in those areas** that can be **dispelled by the two kinds of valid cognition** induced by the force of the entity,[163] **or** they assert that wrongdoing as the result of mental affliction can be cleansed by washing, which **contradicts inferential cognition based on scripture.**

The Vedas do not dispel at all the contradictions to the three kinds of valid cognition because they give no answers to refute them.

Refutation by way of consequence

> 335. **If that establishes validity,**
> **then what is not valid in this?**
> **In the many words spoken by people,**
> **there would be no one thing not true.**

If seeing that one part of what is spoken is true **establishes** that all remaining words **are** similarly **valid**, or true, **then in the many words spoken by people, what** is there that **is not valid**, or true, **in this?** There can be nothing, because in those words **there would be no one thing** that is **not true** because of the possibility of one part being true.

Therefore mere scripture is mistaken with regard to its subject matter

1. The scripture on its own has no connection with the meaning
2. Consequently there can be no ascertainment of the meaning

The scripture on its own has no connection with the meaning

> 336. **Because they abide with the speaker,**
> **they are not the nature or result of the entities.**
> **Anything other than these**
> **will not be unmistaken.**

These sounds have **no** same-**nature** relationship with **the entities** that are the content they are to determine, **nor are they the result of** them, because there is no content that they determine, **because they abide with the speaker**—that is, they are produced from just the wish to express. Therefore the content to be determined is not established from the verbal expression because it cannot be established that the verbal expression has either of the two types of relationship with the content to be determined. This pervades, because there is a same-nature relationship, and a cause-effect relationship, and **anything other than these will not be unmistaken** with regard to the thesis to be established.

> 337. **"The verbal expressions that engage**
> **are created by beholding the phenomena to be expressed."**
> **With mutually exclusive phenomena**
> **how could they possibly engage?**

It could be argued, "It is not established that the verbal expression is not the result of the content to be expressed because **the verbal expressions that engage** the phenomena **are created** as an indirect result of the content to be expressed. A direct cognition that **beholds the phenomena to be expressed** is produced, and from that, a wish to express it is created. From that, the words are created, and so they are indirectly created by the phenomena to be expressed."

How could those verbal expressions **possibly engage with** a single pot by way of expressing it as both permanent and impermanent, which are **mutually exclusive phenomena**? They could not, because the pot does not exist as an entity that is both permanent and impermanent.

Consequently there can be no ascertainment of the meaning

> 338. **Scripture and entities cannot be established**
> **in an indispensable relationship for any comprehender.**
> **Therefore, from that, what meanings can be ascertained?**

There is not a relationship between the words and the meaning. **Therefore, from that** scripture used as a reason, **what meanings can be ascertained** by valid cognition? There cannot be any, because the **scripture and** its **entities** expressed **cannot be established in an indispensable relationship** as the object of any valid cognition **of someone** wishing to **comprehend** these meanings from the scripture.

> 339. **Therefore, even reversing that,**
> **nonexistence of an entity will not be established.**
> **Therefore a resulting, definitive nonexistence**
> **is not gained by not apprehending.**

Therefore, using the reason that the scripture is a valid authority, **even reversing that** scripture **to establish the nonexistence of an entity** whose existence is in doubt **will not** occur, because the scripture is not a valid authority. **Therefore a resulting definitive nonexistence** of a phenomenon whose existence had been in doubt **is not gained by** an ordinary valid cognition **not apprehending** it, because if the phenomenon whose existence is in doubt did exist, there would be no certainty that an ordinary valid cognition would apprehend it.[164]

Bringing out internal contradiction and belittling the propounder

> 340. **The Vedas being a valid authority,**
> **propounding that some can perform actions,**
> **asserting washing as Dharma,**
> **arrogantly proclaiming their caste,**
> **engaging in torture to destroy wrongdoing:**
> **these are the five signs of the confused intellect of the foolish.**

Those **foolish** Naiyāyika possess five signs **of a confused intellect**. They assert **the Vedas as a valid authority** even though those teach a variety of inner contradictions. They **propound that some** permanent beings **can perform actions**. They **assert washing** the body **as Dharma** that will purify the mind of accumulated wrongdoing. They **arrogantly proclaim their** brahman **caste** even though they are without the qualities of wisdom, ethics, and so on. **They engage in torture** of their bodies by way of the five fires **to destroy wrongdoing. These are the five signs.**

The conclusion by way of the title of the chapter

> **The first chapter on inference for oneself from the *Commentary on Valid Cognition*.**

This has been the chapter on inference for oneself, the first chapter, of *Light of Samantabhadra: An Explanation of the Extensive Treatise That Is a Commentary on Valid Cognition.*

Virtue! Virtue! Virtue!

The Explanation of Chapter 2

Establishing Valid Cognition (Pramāṇasiddhi)

I prostrate to him who became valid,
resolved to work for the benefit of others,
the Teacher, the Sugata, and the Protector.[165]

The chapter on establishment of valid cognition explains the separating of what is meaningful from what is not meaningful

1. The connection taught by way of the relationship
2. The explanation of the text of the chapter
3. The conclusion taught by way of the title of the chapter

The connection taught by way of the relationship

Both Devendrabuddhi and Śākyabuddhi identify the "treatise on the characteristics of valid cognition" of the Ācārya as being the [first] chapter on direct perception from the *Valid Cognition Sūtra.*[166] They assert that the commentary on that chapter is the "Direct Perception" (third) chapter of *Commentary on Valid Cognition*, the main cause for direct perception is inference for oneself, which has been explained, and now comes the explanation of the homage at the beginning of Dignāga's direct perception chapter. This is their assertion, and it seems that this is the significance of "The separating of what is meaningful from what is without meaning . . . ."[167]

Those Tibetans who say that Devendrabuddhi's thinking was that "the treatise on the characteristics of valid cognition" refers to the *Valid Cognition Sūtra* as a whole are simply bubbles of nonsense rising from the lake of a coarse intellect. The two "Ornament" (*Alaṃkāra*) commentaries[168] say that "separating what is meaningful from what is without meaning" refers to making discriminations within the four truths and that this is establishing validity. Before that, inference for oneself is explained.

The manner in which the order of the chapters approaches the thinking of the root text, a detailed examination of separating what is meaningful from what is without meaning, and our final assertion can all be understood from the previous explanation.[169]

The explanation of the text of the chapter

1. Examination
2. The actual meaning

Examination

Some in the past have divided the homage of *Compendium of Valid Cognition* into a forward and reverse order, and with regard to the former, they first explain "valid," then "became," then "resolved to work for the benefit of others," and so on. This does not relate to the text of the homage, because "became valid" is the thesis to be established, and the other four qualities are the proof in both forward and reverse order, but there is no explanation of "valid" and "became" in reverse order.

You might think, "Doesn't the line 'Therefore validity itself . . .' teach the reverse order?" In that case, the line "Because of that, validity . . ." in the section on the forward order would also teach the reverse order. Therefore these passages are summaries of the outcomes of two ways of explanation and do not teach the reverse order.

Validity

33. Becoming Valid

The actual meaning

1. Explanation of "became valid," the thesis to be established
2. The excellent proof of the above (after 2.28)
3. The purpose of praising by way of being valid (2.283)

Explanation of "became valid," the thesis to be established

1. Teaching how the Bhagavan is a valid person
2. Explanation of the word "became" (2.7)

Teaching how the Bhagavan is a valid person

1. The teaching of "validity" from the *Compendium of Valid Cognition*
2. Refuting any contradiction with other texts of our tradition
3. Applying that to the actual topic

The teaching of "validity" from the Compendium of Valid Cognition

1. Definition and meaning
2. Refuting that there are three general faults of the definition
3. Ascertainment upon illustrations of the definition

Definition and meaning

In the homage of *Compendium of Valid Cognition*, praise is offered to the Bhagavan by calling him "valid." What is the nature of this validity? By what criteria is the Bhagavan established as valid?

1. **Validity is a nondeceptive consciousness**
existing through having the capacity
to perform a function; it is undeceiving.

Here, the nature of **validity is a nondeceptive consciousness.** This nondeceptiveness has three features: What objects is it undeceiving toward? **It is undeceiving** toward objects that are to be engaged or isolated. What agent is undeceiving? A valid consciousness that embraces its phenomenon exactly as it exists is an undeceiving cognition. How is the action undeceiving? When engaged in an intrinsically existing phenomenon, it is nondeceptive toward it as **existing through having the capacity to perform a function.** By isolating a non-intrinsically existing phenomenon, it is undeceiving toward it as being unable to perform a function. This is the exclusive Sakya way of explaining "nondeceptive."

Refuting that there are three general faults of the definition

1. Refuting nonpervasion
2. Refuting excessive pervasion
3. Refuting impossibility

Refuting nonpervasion

It could be argued, "The 'nondeceptive' part of the definition of valid cognition suffers from nonpervasion because valid cognition of that which arises from sound is not undeceiving."

Even that arising from sound is nondeceiving
because it reveals the actual intention.

"Arising from sound" refers either to knowing the motivating thought from the verbal expression or to knowing the phenomenon expressed. If it refers to the first, then **even that arising from sound is nondeceiving because it reveals,** as the engaged object, **the actual intention** in the form of the expression of the speaker.

2. **The phenomenon as object of the action of the speaker,**
will be clear to the cognition.
To that, the sound will be valid.
It does not possess the cause of the phenomenon.

The form of a **phenomenon**, such as a pot, is the mental **object of the action of the speaker**—that is, the wish to express, which will clearly reveal the object. This **is clear to**, or arises to, **the cognition**. **To** establish **that** wish, **the sound** "pot" at a time free of the five circumstances[170] **will be valid**—that is, suitable to be a correct reason—because all three criteria will be complete. Therefore the cognition arising in dependence on that sound will be undeceiving with regard to its engaged object.

If the phrase "arising from sound" refers to the knowing of the phenomenon to be expressed, then the knowing of that phenomenon, determined by that expression, is not a valid cognition by way of being produced from the phenomenon expressed, as determined by that expression, because **it does not possess the cause**. In other words, it is not the result **of the phenomenon** expressed, as determined by that expression.

Refuting excessive pervasion

It could be argued, "The 'nondeceptive' part of the definition of valid cognition suffers from excessive pervasion because conventional cognition[171] is also undeceiving."

> 3. **Because it apprehends the apprehended,**
> **the conventional is not asserted as such.**

A **conventional** consciousness, such as the concept of a pot universal induced by the direct perception of a pot, **is not asserted** as undeceiving toward the pot **because it apprehends** by way of a pot that was already **apprehended** by the direct perception of the pot that induced the concept.

Refuting impossibility

The Vaibhāṣika school says "The 'consciousness' part of the definition of valid cognition suffers from the fault of impossibility: a consciousness could not possibly exist on the material sense power, which is an illustration of that definition."[172]

> **Cognition is valid cognition.**
> **For engaging those things to be developed**
> **and those to be discarded,**
> **consciousness is paramount.**

A cognition that knows its comprehended object **is a valid cognition**, but material sense faculties and so forth are not valid cognitions. This is because a valid cognition has results that are either interrupted or uninterrupted.[173] The first of these is the practice of **engaging** and not engaging by way of knowing individually **those things to be developed and those to be discarded. For** that, that **consciousness is paramount**, whereas material sense faculties and so forth are not.

> 4. **With aspects of their objects distinct,**
> **there will be cognitions that distinctly know,**
> **because if that exists, this will exist.**

If that consciousness holding the aspect of its comprehended object **exists, this** knowing of the second and uninterrupted result **will exist**, but without it, even with the presence of material sense faculties and so on, it will not be there. The latter reasoning stands because cognitions existing **distinctly with aspects of their objects** means that **distinct** designations **known** by that **cognition** can be established.

Ascertainment upon illustrations of the definition

It could be asked, "How can 'consciousness' and 'nondeceptive,' as parts of the definition, be ascertained on illustrations of valid cognitions?"

> **From itself, it knows its own nature.**

From knowing **itself**, a wholly designated valid cognition[174] **knows its own nature** of being a consciousness. This is because a direct self-knowing consciousness, which experiences itself, is able to induce certainty with regard to itself being a consciousness. This teaches that all wholly designated valid cognitions are self-ascertaining with regard to the "consciousness" part of the definition. Moreover, it also indirectly teaches a direct self-knowing consciousness to be self-ascertaining with regard to the "nondeceptive" aspect of the definition, because the inducing of certainty in the engaged object by the self-knowing consciousness's own power and the inducing of certainty in its nondeceptive aspect by its own power are essentially the same point.

It could be argued, "But because it is not distinct from consciousness, isn't a valid cognition also able to induce certainty by the power of its own nondeceptiveness?"

5. **From designation, it is a valid cognition.**

It is **from** a subsequent ascertaining consciousness, which is an ascertainment as a cognitive **designation**,[175] that the innate characteristic[176] of a wholly designated **valid cognition** is determined as nondeceptive. This is because if a subsequent ascertaining consciousness nondeceptively ascertains its engaged object, that creates the designation of being a valid cognition.

"Is this ascertaining consciousness induced by its own power or by the power of another?" The answer to this can be known from the following lines:

> Two object knowers, two self-knowers,
> and inferential cognition ascertain from self.
> Initial cognition, unengaged cognition,
> and cognition with cause of error are ascertained from others.[177]

Most Tibetans say that the first line (2.4d) is exclusively referring to those ascertained from self and the second line (2.5a) refers only to those ascertained from others. This clearly indicates that they are not differentiating on what basis ascertainment from self and ascertainment from others are established, and they do not know how to establish valid cognitions of ascertainment from self and others exclusively on the basis of wholly designated valid cognitions. The explanation here is the unique commentarial tradition of Jamyang Sakya Paṇḍita, and in this explanation it is important to distinguish between the "consciousness" aspect being an innate characteristic and not a designation, and the valid cognition itself also being an innate characteristic and not a designation. This is explained in my *Madhyamaka Overview*.

It could be argued, "If consciousness is ascertained from itself and the nondeceptive aspect is ascertained from designation, then do not treatises on valid cognition become meaningless?"

Treatises dispel the confusion.

Treatises on valid cognition are not meaningless, because if you do not know the characteristics of a wholly designated valid cognition, you cannot know how to establish the Buddha as valid. Therefore they possess the purpose of **dispelling the confusion** over valid cognition and the characteristics of valid cognition, creating correct understanding.

Refuting any contradiction with other texts of our tradition

It could be asked, "Does this definition not contradict the words 'revealing unknown phenomena' from a passage in the works of Dignāga?"

> **Revealing unknown phenomena also.**[178]

It does not contradict because "**revealing unknown phenomena**" is synonymous with the former definition, and therefore it **also** teaches the definition of a valid cognition.[179] Devendrabuddhi says that it is a separate definition. The *Ornament* commentaries say it refers to a separate definition and separate definiendum. Both these positions are refuted by *Treasury of Reasoning.* Some say the former definition is the position of Dharmakīrti and the latter the position of Dignāga. This is refuted in my *Madhyamaka Overview.*

It could be argued, "Then this does not pervade a valid cognition cognizing a negation."

In reply, Indian and Tibetan masters have said that there is no fault here because the above is referring to the engaged object as the phenomenon that is the basis of the negation, the phenomenon that is the object to be negated, or to the apprehended object aspect of a conceptual cognition. However, Sakya Paṇḍita states, "It is valid because it examines whether it has intrinsic existence." This will be explained more fully below.

> **"After the perception of the nature,**
> 6. **a consciousness of the universal is gained,**
> **which is the revealing of unknown phenomena."**
> **Knowing characteristics not known is the intent,**
> **and these characteristics are analyzed.**

It can be argued, "**After the** direct **perception of the nature** of an intrinsic existent such as the color blue, the **consciousness** holding **the universal** of the color blue **is gained.** It follows that this must be the gaining of a valid cognition because it is the '**revealing of unknown phenomena**' insomuch as it is the knowing of a universal that was not known by the direct perception."

Although it is a consciousness that newly knows the universal of blue, this does not become the "revealing of unknown phenomena," because a consciousness newly **knowing** the existence or nonexistence of **characteristics** that were **not known** previously is the definition of a valid cognition. **That is the intent,** or meaning, of that particular definition. Why is this? A wholly designated valid cognition must know whether **these characteristics** exist or not because the ascertaining consciousness induced by that valid cognition **analyzes** whether the characteristics exist.

Applying that to the actual topic

7. **Possessing that, the Bhagavan is valid.**

The Bhagavan is a **valid** person because he is a person **possessing**, as his nature, **that** nondeceptiveness with regard to the needs of disciples. Most Tibetan masters explain this line to mean "possessing" both definitions.[180] This is to not understand that the former verse (verse 5) is identifying the meaning of *valid* in the homage of *Compendium of Valid Cognition* and the subsequent verse is eliminating any contradiction with other texts.

34. Explanation of "Became" and Refutation of "Self-Arisen"

Explanation of the word "became"

1. "Became" is stated in order to refute a self-arisen Buddha
2. Establishing that this validity relies upon a method
3. Extensive refutation of "self-arisen"

"Became" is stated in order to refute a self-arisen Buddha

It could be asked, "Isn't it sufficient to state 'valid' in the praise? What need is there to state 'became'?"

> **To refute not being created,**
> **the word "became" was stated.**

In the homage of *Compendium of Valid Cognition*, **the word "became" was stated** for a purpose. It is there **to refute** a self-arising validity **not created** from its own causes.

Establishing that this validity relies upon a method

> **Therefore it is correct to say that his validity**
> **derives from accomplishment.**

Therefore it is correct to say that the Bhagavan's **validity derives from** having persevered in the faultless causes of that **accomplishment**, because he is a valid person and because self-arisen validity has been refuted.

Extensive refutation of "self-arisen"

1. Refuting permanent self-arisen valid cognition
2. Refuting impermanent self-arisen validity
3. Refuting the assertion of something being self-arisen
4. Refuting the functioning ability of that which is self-arisen

Refuting permanent self-arisen valid cognition

It could be argued, "It is not correct to state 'became' in order to refute permanent validity because the permanence of Īśvara[181] existing by way of his own entity possesses validity."

> 8. **Permanent valid cognition does not exist.**
> **Knowing existing entities is valid cognition.**
> **A knowable, by being impermanent,**
> **means that this will be unstable.**

Īśvara **does not exist** with **permanent valid cognition** because only **the knowing** of **existing entities is valid cognition**, and **a knowable** phenomenon, **by being impermanent, means that this** object-holding consciousness **will be unstable.**

In reply, it could be argued, "Even if valid cognition is impermanent, the person that possesses such valid cognition is permanent, and valid cognition is generated from that."

> 9. **It is not correct that those created gradually**
> **are created from permanence,**
> **because there would be no dependence.**
> **Nothing would be affected in any way.**

It is not correct to say **that those** valid cognitions **created gradually** over time **are created from** a **permanent** individual. This is **because** such a permanent individual creating such a valid cognition **would not depend** upon circumstances. Such a permanence **would not be affected in any way** by circumstance.

Refuting impermanent self-arisen validity

> **Even if impermanent, there is no valid cognition.**

Even if you state, "An **impermanent** Īśvara existing by way of his own entity and existing at all times possesses validity," no factual designation of the definite existence of such an Īśvara is possible because **there is no valid cognition** that establishes the existence of Īśvara.

Refuting the assertion of something being self-arisen

1. The assertion
2. The refutation

The assertion

> 10. **Remaining and engaging, of various shapes,**
> **performing functions, and so on.**

The assertion is, "It is not established that there is no valid cognition to prove the existence of Īśvara; the environment, animate forms, and resources of the world are preceded by the mind of a supreme being because they **remain and engage,**[182] like an axe. They possess **various shapes**, like a palace, and they **perform functions**, like a battle axe. '**And so on**' refers to number and size. These are proof, and that supreme being is none other than Īśvara."

The refutation

1. Refutation by analysis of the thesis
2. Refutation by analysis of the proof

Refutation by analysis of the thesis

> **This is establishing what has been accepted.**
> **Alternatively, there is no illustration.**

Remaining and engaging is not perfect logic to establish that the environment and animate forms of this world are preceded by the mind of a supreme being, because if it only establishes that they are preceded by the mind of a being, then it is **establishing what has been accepted**—that is, a tenet already established by the Buddhists, as exemplified by "The various worlds are created by karma."[183] **Alternatively**, even if it establishes that they were created by Īśvara, **there** could be **no illustration of** that.[184]

Refutation by analysis of the proof

1. Teaching that the proof is generally at fault
2. Refutation by examining shape in particular
3. How this refutes other reasonings
4. Supplementary topics on this reasoning

Teaching that the proof is generally at fault

Also, there is doubt.

Also, there is doubt over the pervasion in the logic of remaining and engaging and so on establishing that the environment and animate forms of the world were created by Īśvara, because that logic does not establish that such creation was by Īśvara.

Refutation by examining shape in particular

1. Refutation by examining the phenomena of shape
2. Refutation by examining the name "shape"

Refutation by examining the phenomena of shape

1. Using particular shapes is unestablished fallacious reasoning
2. Merely being similar in having shape is uncertain fallacious reasoning
3. Applying that logic elsewhere is flawed refutation

Using particular shapes is unestablished fallacious reasoning

11. **Whatever shape and so on is established,**
following on from the existence
or nonexistence of consecration,
any inference from that would be correct.

If something with a particular shape is created by a person, then **whatever shape and so on**—the shape of a shrine, for example—that **follows on from the existence or nonexistence of** a person to **consecrate** it—that is, create it—that shape does not establish that the environment and animate forms are created by a living being. If such a shape were **established** as the "property of the subject" upon the environment and animate forms, then **any inference** of the environment and animate forms being created by a person coming

from that reasoning **would be correct.** However, such a shape is not logically established as the property of the subject upon the environment and animate forms.[185]

Merely being similar in having shape is uncertain fallacious reasoning

> 12. **Well created as distinct entities,**
> **but not being distinct by way of similar verbal expression,**
> **is not correct to use as inference,**
> **like, for example, fire from a whitish substance.**

You might assert that the above phenomena are not distinct in their mere possession of shape. Shapes that are **well created** by persons, such as shapes of **entities** like shrines and so on, and that are **distinct** from those not created by persons **are not distinct** in possessing shape, as they are **similar** in being engaged by the **verbal expression** "shape." However, **it is not correct to use this to infer** that environment and animate forms are created by a person, because a mountain, for instance, is not created by persons. It would be **like, for example,** establishing the existence of **fire from** the presence of **a whitish substance**: the pervasion would be uncertain.[186]

> 13. **If that were not so, then just as the pots and so on**
> **created by a potter are formed with clay,**
> **even a termite nest would be created by him.**

If it were not so that being similar merely because of possessing shape does not establish that they were created by persons, **then** it follows that **even a termite nest would be created** by a potter, because in being **formed with clay** it is similar to the **pots and so on created** with clay **by a potter.**

Applying that logic elsewhere is flawed refutation

> 14. **Because it is concomitant with the thesis,**
> **the resultant generality is the proof,**
> **but being distinct because of having a relationship,**
> **thus positing the fault of being distinct,**
> **is asserted as that of similar effect.**

It might be argued, "Analyzing a specific when the reason presented was mere shape and then presenting a fault is flawed refutation by way of similar effect, because you are positing a fault by analyzing a specific, whereas the reason presented was a generality."

This is not flawed refutation because the generality of shape is not a suitable reason here. In a situation where a generality is a suitable reason, to posit a fault by way of a specific is flawed refutation by similar effect. For example, you can say that in the reason "being a product" establishing that sound is impermanent, both sound and a pot, **having a relationship** of being products, are **distinct because** the product aspect of a pot is not found in sound, and the product aspect of sound is not found in the example [pot], **thus positing the fault of being distinct**. This **is asserted as** flawed refutation by way **of similar effect** because **the resultant generality** of being a product—that is, the mere product aspect—**is** a suitable **proof** and yet a specific of the reason of being a product is being used and a fault is presented.[187]

The mere aspect of being a product is suitable proof for establishing sound as impermanent because it exists as a property of the subject that is sound, and **because it is concomitant** solely **with** impermanence, the predicate of **the thesis.**

Some earlier masters stated that "flawed refutation by similar effect"[188] is an arbitrary appellation.[189] This is not correct, because it would follow that terms such as "similar connecting" and "similar non-connecting" would also be arbitrary appellations. Some divide this term to form "actual flawed refutation by effect" and "that which is similar to a flawed refutation by effect." That is mistaken because it is wrong to divide the words up in this way.

So what does the term mean? *Compendium of Valid Cognition* states:

> From another part of the effect,
> the thesis is seen to be unestablished.
> This is called being similar by effect,
> and according to the thinking of the speaker,
> there are three types.[190]

This is explained in the *Autocommentary to Treasure of Reasoning*:

> "Similar by effect" refers to the following. When the reasoning "sound is impermanent because it is a product, like a pot" is pre-

sented, for example, the opponent replies by stating that the product aspect of sound will not establish sound as being impermanent because the product aspect of a pot is not found in sound. This is of three types, according to the intent of the speaker. Saying that the effect of the pot is not found in sound is false nonestablishment. Saying that the effect of sound is not found in the impermanence of a pot, and so on, is false contradiction. Saying that the effect of sound has no significance with either permanence or impermanence is false fault-finding of the exclusive example, because only a concordant phenomenon is used as an example. The reason for this is that the inferential cognition engages with a generality and not a specific. Here, the phenomena have been ascertained as distinct, and so the inferential cognition will not engage.[191]

Refutation by examining the name "shape"

15. **Seeing that a verbal universal**
establishes particular types
is incorrect as valid proof.
Like speech and so on having horns,
for example, because of *go*.

If the verbal universal "possessed of shape" engages equally with things possessing a shape, then **seeing that the verbal universal** "possessed of shape" **establishing particular types** of shape, such as shrines and so forth, pertains equally **is incorrect as a valid proof** to establish that the environment and animate forms of this world were created by a living being, because such a universal encompasses natural phenomena like mountains. **For example**, to state that **speech**, regions, **and so on have horns because** the [Sanskrit] word ***go*** engages them is uncertain reasoning. As it is written:

Speech, regions, light rays,
cattle, sense faculty of the eye, diamonds,
higher realms, water, and nine:
the wise examine *go.*[192]

> 16. **Because of depending upon wishing to express,**
> **there is nothing verbal expressions do not exist upon.**
> **By their existence the phenomenon would be established,**
> **and everything would be accomplished by all.**

Furthermore, it follows that **all** beings **would accomplish everything** because **there is nothing that verbal expressions do not exist** as being capable of engaging with. You accept the pervasion and **by the existence** of that verbal expression **the** expressed **phenomenon would be established.** The logic is correct **because** merely by **depending upon wishing to express** these verbal expressions, the phenomenon would be engaged.

How this refutes other reasonings

> 17. **By this, the assertions of Kapila and so on**
> **of being without mind and so forth**
> **because of impermanence and so on,**
> **and of having mind because if the bark is peeled it dies,**
> **can also be analyzed.**

This explanation that verbal expression alone cannot be used to infer the existence of a phenomenon can be **analyzed** to **also** reveal the faults of **Kapila**—that is, the Sāṃkhya—**and so on**—that is, the Jaina. The Sāṃkhya assert that the intellect and happiness[193] are **without mind** and, as indicated by the phrase "**and so forth**," are not internal **because they are impermanent** and, as implied by the phrase "**and so on**," are creations. The Jaina **assert** that trees **have mind because if their bark is peeled away, they die.** The mere expressions of the reasons are established, but there is no pervasion. The actual reason of the former—that there is creation and destruction—is not accepted by the Sāṃkhya. With regard to trees, a death that puts an end to life is not accepted by Buddhists. If you use the expression "dying" as a reason, then phenomena such as lamps show it to be uncertain reasoning.[194]

Supplementary topics on this reasoning

1. The entity of the reasoning is the main establishment
2. Not the verbal expression but the entity itself is the main establishment

The entity of the reasoning is the main establishment

18. **If the nature of the entity is not established,**
there will be this effect. However, if established,
the features are not established, but this does no harm.
Like that which depends upon space, being on sound, for example.

If the nature of the entity—that is, its reality, which is to be used as a reason—**is not established** as existing upon the basis (subject) of the argument, then **there will be this effect** of the reason not being the property of the subject. **However, if** being a product, for example, is used as a reason and is **established** as existing upon the basis of the argument, **the features** of being a product, such as the product aspects of sound and pot, **are not established** as existing upon the basis of the argument, **but these** unestablished features **do no harm** to the reasoning.

For example, when presenting the reason of being a product in order to establish sound as impermanent, the aspect of a product, **which depends upon**—that is, which is combined to be identical with—the quality of **space**[195] and which an opponent has posited as being an aspect of a product, is not established as existing **on sound**, the subject of the debate, but that does not harm the reason being a property of the subject.

Not the verbal expression but the entity itself is the main establishment

19. **Sounds may not be established,**
but if the entity is established,
it will be established, as Buddhists present
the proof of solidity and so forth
to the Aulūkya, for example.

Some **sounds**—that is, verbal expressions—of the reason **may not be established** by the two proponents in a debate as appearing with the same meaning within the subject of the debate. **However, if the entity**—that is, the meaning—of the reason **is established** by the two proponents as appearing with the same meaning within the subject, the reason **will be established** as being a property of the subject.

For example, to the Aulūkya[196]—that is, the Vaiśeṣika, who assert that subtle particles are permanent—**Buddhists present the proof**: a subtle particle is impermanent **because it has solidity and so forth**. The "and so forth" refers to possessing the quality of obstruction. For the Vaiśeṣika, the term *solidity* cannot be established upon a subtle particle of the four elements, but the meaning, which is "tangibility," can be.

The Vaiśeṣika posit two types of substance. Self, mentality, directions, time, and space are substances that "pervade everywhere." The four elements—earth and so forth—are substances that do not pervade everywhere. The measure of substances that do not pervade everywhere is one of the qualities of substance. They label such a subset *solidity*. For subtle particles, however, they do not accept that appellation. Therefore that verbal expression does not serve as proof, but since the meaning, which is "tangibility," is accepted by both proponents, it serves as a perfect proof of the impermanence of subtle particles.

> 20. **If that is erroneous and so on,**
> **then even if the verbal expression is not erroneous,**
> **know the proof to be faulty, because from the entity**
> **is the entity established.**

Therefore, **if that** meaning of the reason **is erroneous and so on**—that is, the reason is unestablished and contradictory—**then even if the verbal expression is not erroneous, know the proof to be faulty, because** it is **from the entity**, or meaning, of the reason that **the entity**, or meaning, of the thesis must **be established**.

> 20[b]. **"Because of moving and of having limbs,**
> **it has horns and is an elephant."**
> **With such proofs, meanings are expressed**
> **by way of common knowledge,**
> **but those intended to be expressed are not.**[197]

Examples of the verbal expression of the reason being correct but the meaning being incorrect are: a cow **has horns because it moves** (*jagat*), and the calf of an elephant **is an elephant because it has limbs** (*karin*).[198] When **these proofs** are presented, the **meanings expressed** by the terms "move" and "having limbs" are **common knowledge** in the world as referring only to cows and elephants. Therefore the understanding of having horns is exclusively applied to being a cow. However, the phenomena **intended to be expressed** by the terms "moving" and "having limbs" **are not** confined to cows and elephants, because they can be applied to humans also.

Refuting the functioning ability of that which is self-arisen

1. For one phenomenon to be both cause and non-cause is contradictory
2. There being no removing, it cannot be a cause
3. There being no concomitance, it cannot be a cause
4. Refuting the assertion that the former reasoning is uncertain

For one phenomenon to be both cause and non-cause is contradictory

21. Just as that entity is a cause,
at what times is it a non-cause?
That asserted as a cause by whatever
is not asserted as a non-cause.

If you assert that the unitary and permanent Īśvara creates all living beings, then **just as the entity** of Īśvara **is** at times the **cause** of effects, then **at what times is it a non-cause**? But there can be no time when it changes, because it is permanent existing as a cause of effects. You must accept the reasoning.

Furthermore, at the time when **this** Īśvara is **asserted as a cause by whatever** circumstance, you **do not assert** him **as a non-cause**, but it follows that you would have to assert this, because even at the time of being a cause, there has been no change of state from being a non-cause to becoming a different entity.

22. From their connection with weapons, medicines, and so forth
come the wounds and healing to Caitra.
In that case, why not conceive of a tree stump as a cause?
23. There being no difference in nature,
it is not feasible to create.

If you say there is no pervasion, then to heal a wound on the body of Caitra,[199] **why** can you **not conceive of a tree stump**, which has no connection with the healing, **as a cause** for that healing? It follows that it would be correct to conceive in this way, because even though something does not change to a different entity from its being a non-cause, it still exists as a cause. You cannot agree because **the wounds to Caitra**'s body **come from their connection with**

weapons and so forth, and **the healing** of the wound **comes from the connection with medicines** and so forth.

You reply that the first reasoning is not established, but it follows that **it is not feasible** for Īśvara **to create** an entity different from the time of being a non-cause, because **there being no difference** between the former and latter **natures** is what being permanent means.

There being no removing, it cannot be a cause

> **Because there is no negating of permanence,**
> **it is difficult to understand even the capability.**

It is difficult to understand, by way of valid cognition, how Īśvara has **even the capability** to produce a result, **because** by removing Īśvara **there is no negating** of the result, as he is **permanent.**[200]

There being no concomitance, it cannot be a cause

> 24. **Whenever they exist, it will appear.**
> **If you conceive of that other than those**
> **as being the cause of that,**
> **the causes would be an infinite regress.**

It can be seen that **whenever** potters, clay, and so on **exist**, a pot **will appear**, whereas Īśvara, who is completely **other than those**, is not the cause of a pot. **If you conceive of** him **as being the cause of that** pot, then **the causes** would be confused with each other in terms of all results, and they **would be an infinite regress.**

Refuting the assertion that the former reasoning is uncertain

1. Refuting that the reason is uncertain because of outer circumstances
2. Refuting that the reason is uncertain because of inner circumstances

Refuting that the reason is uncertain because of outer circumstances

You might argue, "There is no consequence, as posited above, that it cannot be a cause because it does not change from its state of non-cause to one of a different entity. This is because earth and so forth are permanent, and therefore, although it does not become a different entity from its state of not producing a shoot, it is still the cause of the shoot."

> 25. **To produce a sprout, earth and so on**
> **completely change in nature to become causes.**
> **If well carried out, we can see the features.**

For **earth**, seeds, **and so on to produce a sprout,** they **completely change** to a different **nature** from the state of nonproducing to a different entity and **become causes.** If they do not change, they do not become causes, because **we can see the** good **features** of the sprout when ploughing and so on **is well carried out.**

Refuting that the reason is uncertain because of inner circumstances

> 26. **"As the sense faculty and object combined**
> **do not become different and are causes for consciousness,**
> **so this is likewise." It is not so,**
> **because here too they exist differently.**

> 27. **If individually, they have no capability,**
> **and they do not become different natures,**
> **then even together they would have no ability.**
> **Therefore they are established as being different.**

You might argue, "Just as **the sense faculty and** an **object** it is engaged with when **combined do not become different** from the time when they were not together **and are causes for** producing a sense **consciousness, likewise, this** Īśvara, while not becoming different from his state of being a non-cause, **is** a cause. Therefore the argument is not ascertained."

Here too, it is not the case that the three conditions [of object, sense faculty, and consciousness] together are not different entities from their time of not being together, **because they do exist differently** from when they are not together. **If** they did not, it would follow that **even** when they had come **together, they would have no ability** to produce a sense consciousness, because **they have not become different natures** from those conditions when they were **individually, without any capability** to produce a sense consciousness.

Therefore the three conditions together **are established as being different** from the time when they were not together.

> 28. **Therefore individually they have no capability,**
> **but combined it is possible they are qualities.**
> **These are causes. Īśvara and others are not**
> **because there is no change.**

Therefore those three conditions **are causes** for sense consciousnesses and so on because **individually they have no ability** to produce sense consciousnesses and so on **but combined it is possible they are qualities** having the ability to produce sense consciousnesses. **Īśvara and others are not because there is no change** in their entity.

The excellent proof of the above

1. Examination
2. The meaning of the text

Examination

Masters of the past unanimously explained the necessity of including the word "became" by way of preclusion and affirmation.[201] For preclusion they say that the refutation of the arguments is found in the verse beginning "Permanent valid cognition does not exist" (2.8). The argument against the latter is found in the verse beginning "A valid cognition knows hidden phenomena" (2.29), and that the answers to this argument are in the four verses beginning "Those with doubts" (2.30). This is not the thinking of the treatise's author, because the line "Therefore it is correct to say that his validity derives from accomplishment" (2.7d) also expresses the preclusion, and it is not the case that the affirmation is explained separately.

Even if it is, in the verse on the arguments (2.29), three arguments are raised,[202] and the four following verses (2.30–33) only answer the first argument. Therefore it would follow that the other two arguments are not answered. You might think that the forward and reverse proofs are the responses to the two latter arguments. In that case, it would be correct to designate the three arguments as the opposing all the following text, whereas to designate them as the opposing only the four subsequent verses is to cover one's head with a cloth and not notice who is carrying the tail.

In short, the two latter arguments are arguments against the necessity of the word "became," but the four verses are not answers to that argument. The four verses are responses to the first argument, but that argument is not one against the term "became," and therefore there is no connection between the two. So what is the explanation? This part of the text concludes the explanation of the thesis "valid" and "became," and now the line "A valid cognition knows hidden existence" (2.29) is an argument against valid cognition. The arguments against the necessity of "became" are that there is no accomplishing of that, and even if accomplishment were possible, there can be no striving for that. The three arguments are taught in one verse (2.29).

The response to the first argument is not actually expressed in the homage of *Compendium of Valid Cognition*, but Ācārya Dharmakīrti has supplied these four verses. Having established by reasoning the existence of a valid cognition that is fully cognizant of what is needed, it is possible at that time to establish an omniscience of knowable existence. This is expressed by the verse beginning "One who knows the realities of what is to be developed and discarded" (2.32). Therefore holding the bodhisattva's path of seeing as an illustration of an omniscience that knows completely what is necessary to know is not accepted in this tradition.

The response to the second argument is given by the four forward proofs. It can be proven by reasoning that, in the beginning, he "resolved to work for the benefit of others" by nurturing the objects and aspects of compassion over many lives until his mind became an entity of compassion. If that is established, he is established as the "Teacher" who applied himself to the path in order to destroy suffering, as taught by the lines "The Compassionate One, in order to destroy suffering, applied himself to methods" (2.132). If that is established, the "Sugata" endowed with the three features[203] of the state of abandonment is established as taught by the lines beginning "By that cause, trained in the methods" (2.138). If that is established, a perfect understanding that is clear with regard to the truth of the path is established. If that is established, he is the "Protector" that teaches to others the path that he has seen, as expressed by the line "The Protector speaks the path he has seen" (2.145c). Therefore "Great compassion is the accomplisher" (2.34).

The response to the third argument is given by the four reverse proofs. First, it is established through reasoning that he is the Protector, who teaches without error the aspects of the four truths to others. If that is established, it is established that he manifestly possesses the three features of insight. If that is established, it is established that being the Teacher who applied himself to the path must have come before that. If that is established, it can be established that the great compassion that wishes to dispel the suffering of others must have preceded that. Therefore, the Teacher, who strove in the two methods of accomplishment, is established by "Protector because he taught the four truths" (2.146d).

Therefore the forward proof is a reasoning by nature wherein the suitability of the result to arise is established by the reason of the collection of causes being complete in number. The reverse reasoning is by way of result, in which previous causes are established. Therefore, there are two separate purposes: one establishing the mere existence of validity and the other being that the "Teacher" strives in the accomplishing of that validity. This explanation will be of benefit to fortunate disciples.

Establishing by Way of the Forward Sequence

35. Compassion Is the Accomplisher

The meaning of the text

1. The misconception that there is no accomplisher[204]
2. Refuting the wrong conception and explaining accomplisher

The misconception that there is no accomplisher

> 29. **A valid cognition knows hidden phenomena.**
> **There is no accomplishing of that,**
> **and therefore endeavor in such does not exist.**
> **Thus some have said.**

Some Jaiminīya [Mīmāṃsaka] **have said** that it is incorrect to posit that the Bhagavan Buddha is a valid being and that such a state depends upon accomplishment, because generally **a** being of **valid cognition** is one who **knows** all **hidden phenomena,** but they say such a person does not exist. Moreover, **there is no** cause that **accomplishes such** a state, **and therefore endeavor in such** a cause **does not exist.**

Refuting the wrong conception and explaining accomplisher

1. Refuting that there is no valid cognition and establishing its validity
2. Refuting that there can be no accomplisher
3. Refuting that there is no endeavor and establishing that endeavor (2.146)

Refuting that there is no valid cognition and establishing its validity

1. It is correct to search for one possessed of complete knowledge of what is necessary
2. It is correct to analyze whether that teacher knows or not
3. Possessing full cognizance of what is needed is validity
4. Presenting the proof of that validity

It is correct to search for one possessed of complete knowledge of what is necessary

> 30. **Those with doubts, wondering whether those who teach**
> **without knowing are mistaken,**
> **will seek out those possessed of the knowledge**
> **in order to strive in what they teach.**

Regardless of whether they know all hidden phenomena, one who knows well the methods to gain liberation is a valid being for those who seek liberation. This is because if this teacher were to **teach** the means to attain liberation **without knowing** it, **those** discerning beings **with doubts, wondering whether** this teacher **is mistaken**, thinking that he might teach the wrong methods, **will seek out those** spiritual friends **possessed of the knowledge** of the methods to attain liberation. They would do so **in order to strive in** the methods to attain liberation **taught by them**.

It is correct to analyze whether that teacher knows or not

> 31. **Therefore it is the wisdom to be accomplished**
> **that should be looked for.**
> **Knowing how many insects there are**
> **is of no use whatsoever for me.**

Therefore those who seek liberation **should look for** the presence of **the wisdom to be accomplished**, to be striven for. It is worthless to examine whether this teacher **knows** or does not know **how many insects there are** and so on, because that **is of no use whatsoever for me** who strives for freedom.

Possessing full cognizance of what is needed is validity

32. **One who knows the realities of**
what is to be developed and discarded,
together with methods and causes,
is asserted to be valid;
one who knows all things is not.

Therefore the **one who knows** unerringly **the reality of that which is to be developed**, the truth of cessation, **together with the method**, the truth of the path, **and** who knows the reality of what is to be **discarded**, the truth of suffering, together with its **causes**, the truth of the origin of suffering, **is asserted to be** a **valid** being, because such a being knows completely all the means of gaining liberation, whereas **one who** only **knows all** hidden phenomena **is not** a valid being. This is not asserted in the beginning because it cannot be established by reasoning but not because it is not possible:

This does not refute the omniscience
of knowing all things.
Because I cannot know these things,
I leave them with contentment.[205]

Presenting the proof of that validity

33. **They are those who see the reality of what is desired,**
whether they can see far away or not.
If seeing far makes for a valid being,
come and devote yourselves to vultures!

Whether such teachers **can see far away or not, those who see the reality of what is desired**—that is, the four truths—are valid beings. **If** being able to **see far**, without knowing the phenomena that are desired, **makes for a valid being**, then get rid of those wise beings who know that which is desired by others but who cannot see far, and **come and devote yourselves to vultures** and ḍākinīs as your teachers!

Refuting that there can be no accomplisher

1. Establishing by reason that compassion is the accomplisher
2. How "Teacher" arises from that compassion (2.132)
3. How "Sugata" arises from "Teacher" (2.139c)
4. How "Protector" arises from "Sugata" (2.145c)
5. Therefore there is accomplishment (2.146c)

Establishing by reason that compassion is the accomplisher

1. The nature of the accomplisher
2. The cause of the accomplisher
3. Refuting arguments against that

The nature of the accomplisher

> 34. **Great compassion is the accomplisher,**
> **and that comes from training.**

The line "There is no accomplishing of that" (2.29) is not correct. There is the establishment of such a valid being because **great compassion**, with its aspect of wishing to liberate living beings from suffering, equanimous to all beings, regardless of receiving something in return, **is that accomplisher.**

36. Establishing Past and Future Lives

The cause of the accomplisher

That great compassion has a cause: it **comes from training** in the objects and aspects of compassion over many lives.

Refuting arguments against that

1. Refuting the argument that such training is not possible
2. Refuting the argument that even though repeated practice is possible, it does not go beyond its own nature (2.120)

Refuting the argument that such training is not possible

1. Presenting the argument
2. Refutation

Presenting the argument

> **"Because cognition depends upon the body,**
> **there is no accomplishment through training."**

Those who hold nihilistic views say that compassion **is not accomplished through training** over many lives **because** there are no past and future lives. **Cognition and conception depend upon the body**, and so when the body is destroyed, the continuum of cognition ceases. The way in which cognition depends upon the body is that cognition is in the nature of the body in the same way alcohol possesses the power to create drunkenness. Or, like a lamp and its light, cognition is a creation of the body, or like the sweetness of sugar, it is a quality of the body.

Refutation

1. Brief refutation
2. Extensive refutation

Brief refutation

This is not so. Dependence is refuted.
35. **When birth is taken, breath, sense faculties, and cognition**
are not produced solely from the body
without dependence upon similar types.

This is not so. The argument that compassion is not developed through training because cognition directly depends upon the body does not follow, because such **dependence is refuted** by reasoning. How? **When** an ordinary being **takes birth,** their **breath, sense faculties, and cognition are not produced solely from the body, without dependence upon** previous **similar types** of instances.

36. **There would be absurd consequences.**
Seeing the ability to connect, what other would there be?
By what will it not connect?

If they were produced in such a way, **there would be absurd consequences,** such as the creation of mind and so on in stones and rocks and so on. **Seeing** that the consciousness of this life has **the ability to connect** from the past to the future, **what other** reasons **would there be? By what** reason do you assert that an ordinary being at death **will not connect** to the future? The reasoning is similar.

Past scholars state that the first line of the verse (2.34d) constitutes the brief refutation and deal with the extensive refutation under headings such as "The consequences of there being no former lives" and "Establishing by reason the existence of future lives." They do not distinguish between primarily establishing the existence of future lives in this section on establishing the training in the objects and aspects of compassion, and the later explanation primarily establishing the existence of future lives in the section on establishing the appropriated aggregates, which, as the possessors of saṃsāra, illustrate the truth of suffering. They have not understood how to assign the verses beginning "There would be no place where heat and moisture" (2.37) to the extensive explanation of the consequences or how to assign the verses beginning "For the final mind" (2.45) to the extensive explanation of connecting to a new birth.

Extensive refutation

1. Extensive explanation of the reasoning behind the absurd consequences
2. Extensive explanation: connecting to a new birth is not a contradiction

Extensive explanation of the reasoning behind the absurd consequences

1. The absurd consequences of mind created from a body composed of the elements
2. The absurd consequences of mind created from a body with sense faculties
3. The absurd consequences of mind created from a permanent body

The absurd consequences of mind created from a body composed of the elements

It could be argued, "It is not the case that this would mean the absurd consequence of mind being created from stones, rocks, and so on because some elements are seeds of the mind and others are not."

37. **There would be no place where heat and moisture**
    would not produce living beings.
    Therefore all would be in the nature of seeds.
38. **In that case, if sense faculties and so on could arise**
    without depending upon their own type,
    then just as one could, all could,
    because there would be no difference.

It follows that **all** elements **would be in the nature of** being **seeds** of mind and so on, because when all other conditions are met, **there would be no place where heat and moisture would not produce living beings.** All instances of the earth element would be in the nature of being seeds of mind and so on. **In that case, if sense faculties and so on could arise without depending upon their own** previous similar-**type** causes, **then just as one** element **could** become sense faculties and so on, it follows that **all could, because there would be no difference** in the reasoning.

The absurd consequences of mind created from a body with sense faculties

1. When reversed they are established as cause and effect
2. Refuting that this contradicts scripture
3. If proved by reasoning, it contradicts the assertion

When reversed they are established as cause and effect

> 39. **If each sense faculty is damaged,**
> **there is no damage to mental cognition.**
> **When this changes, those also change,**
> **as can be seen.**

If you assert that the body is the direct support of mental cognition, you must assert that the body possessed of sense faculties is the direct support of mental cognition. If that were so, we reply that mind is not a consciousness directly depending upon the sense faculties of the eyes and so on, because **if each of the sense faculties is damaged** by some adverse circumstance, **there is no** direct **damage to mental cognition.** It is **those** sense faculties of the eyes and so on that depend upon mind, because **when this** mind **changes** owing to grief and so on, the sense faculties **also change, as can be seen.**

> 40. **Therefore those dependent upon cognition itself,**
> **which is the support for the existence of cognition,**
> **are the causes of sense faculties.**

The sense faculties depend upon mind. **Therefore**, for someone possessed of a body, subsequent sense faculties are created from a previous mental cognition, because **those** karmas, **which depend upon** previous mental **cognition itself, the support for the existence of** subsequent **cognition, are the causes of** subsequent **sense faculties.**

> 41. **If such throwing causes exist,**
> **in the future too, similar will arise.**

Therefore, **if** karmas, which depend upon previous cognition, **are throwing causes**[206] of **such** subsequent sense faculties, then **in the future too**, at the time of death, sense faculties will **similarly arise** from mental cognition. The *Treasure of Reasoning* states:

By the reason of the collection of causes being complete
and there being no hindrance, no future limit will be reached.[207]

Refuting that this contradicts scripture

It may be argued, "This contradicts the scripture that states 'Body and mind follow each other.'"

Because that consciousness affects,
the mind is said to depend upon the body.

Such a citation is not saying that mental cognition directly depends upon the body. The body affects the bodily consciousness. **The consciousness of that** body **affects** that cognition. Therefore **the mind is said to depend** indirectly **upon the body.**

If proved by reasoning, it contradicts the assertion

42. **"Without sense faculties, that cognition is not there."**
Without that, they are also not there.
With such, they are causes of each other
and therefore are results of each other.

It could be argued, "The sense faculties are the direct support of the mental cognition because, **without the sense faculties, that cognition is not** produced."

In that case it follows that the mental cognition also is the direct support of the sense faculties because, **without that** cognition, the sense faculties **are also not** produced. **With such** an assertion, it follows that after death **they become results of each other** because at death **they are causes of each other.**

The absurd consequences of mind created from a permanent body

1. Presenting reasoning for the absurd consequences
2. Refuting faults and negation by way of contradictory assertion

Presenting reasoning for the absurd consequences

43. **There is no succession from that without succession.**
Not being affected, it could have no dependence.

If cognition successively arises from a body,
by that, succession is illustrated.

According to the Lokāyata materialists, mental cognition is produced from a permanent body. It would then follow that mind is **not** produced **in succession from** the body because the body is permanent and **without succession.**

Refuting faults and negation by way of contradictory assertion

It might be argued that there is no pervasion because a permanent body in dependence upon conditions will successively create mind. We reply that it follows that the body **could not have any dependence** upon conditions because it could **not be affected** by conditions.

In reply, it might be argued, "There is no such fault. **Cognition is created successively** even **from a** permanent **body** that depends upon successive cognition."

It follows then that **by this** the body too **illustrates succession**—that is, has previous and subsequent moments—because it creates mind successively in dependence upon successive cognition.

44. **Preceding instants would be causes**
of each instant not yet produced.
Because of being causes,
they would be seen at all times.

If you agree, it would follow that **preceding instants** of the body and mind of a person **would be causes of each** subsequent **instant not yet produced,** because that body and mind possess a continuum of succession. If you agree, it follows that the previous body and mind being a cause of subsequent body and mind would be **seen at all times,** even at the time of death, **because** previous body and mind **is a cause** of subsequent body and mind. If you agree, that would establish the existence of future lives.

Extensive explanation: connecting to a new birth is not a contradiction

1. Using the mind at the time of death is uncertain reasoning
2. The example is invalid
3. Refuting the proof that it is not an invalid example

Using the mind at the time of death is uncertain reasoning

The Lokāyata materialists say, "The final mind of an ordinary being at death does not connect to a subsequent cognition because it is the mind at death, like the mind of an arhat at death."

> 45. **For the final mind connecting to another mind,**
> **what is there that is contradictory?**
> **The mind of an arhat at death,**
> **from what is it asserted**
> **that there is no connecting?**

Being **the final mind at death** is not perfect reasoning to establish that the mind at the death of an ordinary person does not connect to a future cognition, because **what is there that is contradictory** to valid cognition with regard to that mind **connecting to another mind?** There is no contradiction at all.

The example is invalid

The mind of an arhat at death is not a perfect example to establish that the mind at the death of an ordinary person does not connect to a future cognition. **From what** valid cognition **is it asserted that there is no connecting?** There is no valid cognition to establish that.

Refuting the proof that it is not an invalid example

1. Refuting that it is established by Buddhist scripture
2. Refuting that it is established by the Lokāyata's own reasoning

Refuting that it is established by Buddhist scripture

It can be argued, "As it is well known in your Buddhist tenets, it can be used as an example."

> 46. **Why would you follow a tenet**
> **not established by valid cognition?**

It follows that it would not be correct for the materialist Lokāyata to assert that the mind of an arhat at death does not connect to future minds, as stated in Buddhist tenets, because they do not assert that this tenet is a valid tenet, and so **why would they follow a tenet** that teaches something **not established by valid cognition?** It would not be correct.

Both Śākyabuddhi and Devendrabuddhi explain the tenet asserting that the mind of the arhat at death does not create a subsequent mind as a definitive assertion, and the teaching that it does create a subsequent mind as a provisional one. Ravigupta asserts the opposite. However, in order to prove an internal contradiction in their own beliefs, we are just asking what reasons the Lokāyata have for stating that the mind of the arhat at death does not connect to a subsequent mind. It is not saying that our own position is that it does connect.

Refuting that it is established by the Lokāyata's own reasoning

1. The assertion and the question
2. Extensive explanation of the refuting logic
3. Negating arguments that it is erroneous (2.114)
4. Conclusion: Establishing by refutation (2.119)

The assertion and the question

> **If it is devoid of a cause,**
> **why do you not mention it here?**

"The mind of the arhat at death does not create a subsequent mind because **it is devoid of a cause** of that mind—that is, a body."

In this section on your establishing that the final mind of an ordinary being at death does not create a subsequent mind, **why do you not mention this** lack of cause, the body, as a reason? It would be correct to mention it because it would be correct to state it as the establisher of the example and because the reasoning is similar. If you agree, then what can "mind at death," as a reason of uncertain pervasion, do? It is meaningless.

Extensive explanation of the refuting logic

1. Refuting that the body is the direct cause of the mind
2. Refuting that body and mind are material causes and effects (2.60)
3. Refuting body and mind as support and supported but not producers (2.63)
4. Refuting by other reasons that mind and body are cause and effect (2.73)
5. Refuting that mind is in the nature of the body (2.79)
6. Refuting by examination that body can create mind (2.84)

Refuting that the body is the direct cause of the mind

1. Refuting by examining whether it is a direct cause
2. Though a mere cause, it is not an indispensable cause
3. The absurd consequences of it being a direct cause

Refuting by examining whether it is a direct cause

It is argued, "I state that the above reason establishing that a subsequent cognition is not created exists on both the subject of the argument and the example."

> 47. **Because it would apprehend just like cognition,**
> **mental consciousness does not come from**
> **that possessed of sense faculties.**
> **Because of distinct abilities to produce consciousness,**
> **it is not also created from all.**

If the cognition is created from the body, it is either created from a body possessed of sense faculties or not possessed of sense faculties. First, **mental consciousness is not** directly produced **from** a body **possessed of sense faculties.** If it were, then **just like cognition** by way of the eyes, **it would** clearly **apprehend** visual form, because it would be an other-apprehending[208] cognition directly produced from the eye's visual sense faculty.

Applying this reasoning to the other sense faculties and having refuted that the mental consciousness is created from each of them, it is then argued that it is created from all five together. We respond: a single mental consciousness **is not also created from all** five sense faculties together, **because** they possess **distinct abilities to produce** their own empowered results, such as the visual **consciousness.**

> 48. **Because of having no mind,**
> **it is not produced from another.**
> **Because of having one cause, they exist together,**
> **like the sense faculties, or material form and taste, for example.**
> **By way of phenomena, the mind will change.**

If you assert that cognition is directly produced from a body without sense faculties, we reply that conceptual cognition is **not** directly **produced from another**—that is, a body without sense faculties—**because** it [the body] would **have no mind.**

It is argued, "If body and mind were not support and supported, that would contradict the fact that they coexist."

The body and conceptual cognition of someone do not exist together because of being a support and that which is supported. **They exist together because** they are created from **one cause**, even though they are not support and that which is supported. It is **like, for example, the** five **sense faculties** of some beings existing together, **or material form and taste** existing together in dependence upon a single collection.

It is argued, "When the body develops an illness, the mind changes. Therefore the mind is directly dependent upon the body."

Then it follows that the blood of another person stabbed by a knife would be the support of mind, because **the mind** can **be changed by way of** such external **phenomena.**

Though a mere cause, it is not an indispensable cause[209]

> 49. **Because of always following on from that,**
> **something existing, which affects, is a cause.**
> **Therefore it is the seventh case,**
> **and "because of being produced" was taught.**

What is the meaning of *cause* as in "devoid of a cause" stated above (2.46c)? If it refers to the body being a cause that affects the features of mind, then it does not follow that the lack of such a cause means the nonexistence of a mind. With regard to results, **something** that by **existing** previously **affects** the result's entity **is a** material **cause.**[210] Therefore, if it were negated, the result too would be negated, **because always**—that is, certainly—that result **follows on from** a prior **existence** affecting that result's entity.

The cause is prior to the result, and **therefore**, when the Buddha said, "If this exists, this will occur," and "**Because** this is **produced**, this will be produced," he was **teaching** by **the seventh** (locative) **case** "if this exists" and by the fifth (ablative) case "because this is produced" that the cause is prior. The phrases "this will occur" and "this will be produced" teach that the results are subsequent. He explained this so that it would be understood that the cause is prior and the result is subsequent. Such a material cause and that possessed of a material cause do not apply to body and mind.

50. **Clearly, at certain times,**
it affects the continuum of the mind.
By this it would not be negated,
like fire and so forth with pots.

Clearly, at certain times, the body can indirectly **affect** instants of the **continuum of the mind.** Just **this** affecting of instants of the mind does **not** mean that if the body were negated, the continuum of the mind **would be negated,** because the body does not exist as a material cause of the mind. For example, **fire and so forth** affects features, such as the hardness, of **pots** and other materials, but the negation of fire does not negate the continuity of pots.

The absurd consequences of it being a direct cause

1. Presenting the logic of the absurd consequences
2. Refuting the response that there are no conducive conditions
3. Refuting the response that there are unconducive conditions

Presenting the logic of the absurd consequences

51. **If the body remained,**
the mind would not be negated.

If the meaning of *cause* is that the body is a direct cause of mind, then a dead body **would not negate the** existence of **mind,** because **the body,** a direct cause of mind, would **remain**—that is, would still exist.

Refuting the response that there are no conducive conditions

It could be argued, "A dead body has no mind because breath, a conducive condition for mind, is not there."

If present, that is present and is under its control.
Therefore from that comes breath and not that.
52. **Without effort, breathing in and out**
would be produced from what?

Breath is produced **from** mind, whereas the continuity of mind is **not** produced from **that** breath, because **if** the mind, which affects the breath, is **present,** breath **is present, and** breath **is under the control** of the mind. **Without**

the **effort** of the mind, **from what would breathing in and out be produced?** It would not be produced.

> **From those that are strong and weak,**
> **it would be strong or weak.**
> 53. **In the assertions there would be similar consequences.**

Moreover, it would follow that **from those** breaths that are **strong or weak**, mind would **be strong or weak** accordingly, because mind would be something produced from the material cause of breathing. Furthermore, **within the assertions** that that body is the direct cause of mind and that breath as the condition for mind is not present in a dead body, **similar consequences** could be posited that a dead body would have breath because body as the direct cause of breath is present.

It could be argued, "From the assertions in your tradition also that previous mind is the cause of subsequent mind, it could similarly be asserted that mind is present in a dead body."

> **If mind is a cause, it is not similar,**
> **because another throwing cause that places**
> **is asserted as the cause.**

The consequence that mind must exist in a dead body because **if mind** exists as the **cause** of mind, the causes are complete, **is not a similar** consequence, **because another throwing cause**—the karma from a previous life—**placing** the mind with the body **is asserted as the cause** for the mind dwelling in the body.

Refuting the response that there are unconducive conditions

1. The assertion and the refutation
2. Refuting faults by way of an example
3. Summary of the reasoning

The assertion and the refutation

> 54. **"As with a wick and so on,**
> **faults creating unconducive conditions**
> **means that body will not be the cause."**
> **When by death the fault is weakened,**
> **life would return.**

It could be argued, "**A wick and so on** is the cause of a lamp, but if there are unconducive conditions, such as it being wet, it will not create a flame. Likewise, body is the direct cause of mind, but if there has been a **fault** of illness **creating unconducive conditions**, then a dead **body will not be the cause** of mind. Therefore the consequence that mind must exist in a dead body is incorrect."

When by death, caused by poison and so on, **that fault** of poison **is weakened**, or reversed, it follows that **life would return** because there would no longer be any conditions unconducive for life, and the direct cause of life, the body, would be complete.

Refuting faults by way of an example

> 55. **"Even though the fire is gone,**
> **the changes to the wood are not reversed.**
> **Similarly, there is no reversing."**

It will be argued, "There is no pervasion. After wood has been burned, **even though the fire is gone, the changes to the wood**, such as it turning to ash, **cannot be reversed** into wood again. **Similarly**, at death the causes that transformed the mind, such as poison, can be reversed, but **there is no reversing** of that mind."

> 56. **This is not so, because medical treatment exists.**
> **Some changes created are sometimes not restorable,**
> **while some are restorable, such as fire with wood and gold.**

> 57. **The first, no matter how small, are not reversible.**
> **Those whose changes can be reversed**
> **will appear again, like gold restored to solidity.**

It follows that the changes wrought to body and mind by poison and so on are **not** irremediable like burnt wood, **because medical treatment exists**—there is a remedy. This pervades because there are two types of causes that create changes. There are those that **create changes to some** entities, **such as wood** transformed by **fire**, that **sometimes are not restorable** by transformative conditions. Then there are **some** entities, such as **gold** transformed by fire, that **are restorable** by transformative conditions. **The first**, the unrestorable changes, **no matter how small** they are, **are not reversible**. The second, **those** entities **whose**

changes can be reversed, are entities that **will appear again, like** molten **gold restored to solidity.**

"But this contradicts the medical texts that describe incurable illnesses."

> 58. **Those spoken of as not even slightly curable,**
> **refer to the difficulty of finding a cure or to the end of life.**
> **If referring only to the faults,**
> **nothing would not be cured.**

Those illnesses **spoken of** in the medical texts **as not even slightly curable** are not presentations focused solely on the fault of the illnesses but **refer to the difficulty of finding** doctors and medicine to **cure** the illness, **or** to the fact that it is **the end of life** for the sick person. Otherwise, **if** they were **referring only to the faults** of the illnesses, it would follow that there would be **no** illnesses **that cannot be cured** because any illness is capable of being cured by medicine.[211]

Summary of the reasoning

> 59. **At death, when the poison and so on are reversed,**
> **or that which is bitten cut away,**
> **it would be devoid of the causes of change.**
> **What prevents a return to life?**

After **death, when the poison**, the infectious disease, **and so on** within the body **have been reversed, or** the part of the flesh **bitten** by the snake has been **cut away, what prevents** that which has died **returning to life? It** would return because there **would be** a body **devoid of the** unconducive **causes of** the **changes** to the mind.

Refuting that body and mind are material causes and effects

1. A material cause will be negated
2. If it is not negated, it is not a material cause
3. Applying that to context
4. Refuting that this contradicts coexistence

A material cause will be negated

> 60. **Without the material cause changing,**
> **there cannot be the creation of that**
> **possessed of that material cause.**
> **For example, without clay changing, there are no pots.**

Generally, **without a material cause changing, it cannot create** a result **possessed of that material cause. For example, without clay changing, there** can be **no pots** and so on arising from that material cause that is clay.

If it is not negated, it is not a material cause

> 61. **An entity without changing,**
> **producing the form of an entity,**
> **cannot be a material cause of that,**
> **like ox and wood bison and so on,**
> 62. **and like body and mind.**

If there is a causal **entity** that **produces the form of a** resultant **entity without changing,** that cause **cannot be a material cause of that** result. **For example, an ox,** without changing, can produce a **gayal**[212] **and so on.** Therefore that ox is not the material cause of a gayal.

Applying that to context

Mind and body, like an ox and a gayal, are not material cause and that possessed of material cause because one does not necessarily follow the other.

Refuting that this contradicts coexistence

It could be argued, "If body and mind are not material cause and that possessed of material cause, that contradicts that they can coexist."

> **It is a result created from its cause,**
> **with a coexisting condition, existing together,**
> **like, for example, fire and molten copper.**

The body and mind of someone do not coexist by way of being material cause and that possessed of material cause, because that [body] is **a result created**

from its material **cause with** mind as the **coexisting condition** for producing a subsequent body. Therefore they **exist together. For example,** when copper has been heated by fire, **fire and the molten copper** exist together because they arise from one cause.

Refuting body and mind as support and supported but not producers

1. Presenting the consequence
2. Refuting responses

Presenting the consequence

> 63. **It does not exist as a support for existing and not existing.**

It follows that the body is not the direct cause of cognition because it does **not exist as a support** for the mind in terms of the mind **existing and not existing** when the body is present.

Refuting responses

1. Refuting that it depends by abiding as something already existing
2. Refuting the conducive example for abiding as something already existing
3. Refuting other assertions of the abiding of something already existing
4. Explanation of the refuting a cause maintaining the abiding

Refuting that it depends by abiding as something already existing

1. Refutation by way of examination
2. Refutation by way of consequences

Refutation by way of examination

> **"It is not so. As the cause of the abiding of**
> **that existing, it is the support."**
> **It does not exist as a support.**
> **It is not other than the abider.**
> 64. **If it were other, as the cause of that,**
> **what would be the point of the entity?**

It could be argued, "The above reasoning **is not** established because the body, **as the cause of the abiding of an existing** mind, **is the support** of the mind."

This body **does not exist as a support** of the abiding of an already existing mind because, however it is examined it is not correct, even if the abiding of the mind is one with or distinct from the mind itself. If the abiding of the mind were one with the abider mind, then it follows that the body could not create the abiding of the mind because the abiding of the mind would **not be other than the abider** mind itself and therefore would be created from the cause of the mind. Even **if** the abiding of the mind **were other** than the abider mind, **what would be the point of the entity** of the mind abiding? None, because the body would be **the cause of the** abiding of the mind, which would be other than the mind itself.

Refutation by way of consequences

1. Presenting the consequence
2. Refutation of responses

Presenting the consequence

> **It follows that it would not be subject to disintegration.**

It follows that the mind would **not be subject to disintegration** because its support, the body, constantly keeps it abiding without disintegrating.

Refutation of responses

> **"We assert that is from the cause of its disintegration."**
> 65. **This also induces a similar consequence.**

It could be argued, "**We assert** that the body does keep the mind from disintegrating, but when **that** mind meets the **cause of its disintegration, from that** it will disintegrate.[213] Therefore there is no fault."

This assertion that the disintegration of mind is created by a subsequent cause **also induces a similar consequence**: the disintegration of the mind would be one with or distinct from the mind itself. If the disintegration of the mind is one with the mind, there would be no need for it to be created by a subsequent cause. If it were distinct from the mind, that cause of disintegration would not destroy the mind because the disintegration would function as a substance separate from the mind.

What can the cause of abiding do?
"It remains until it meets the cause of its disintegration."
66. **There is no harm to disintegration**
as the nature of entities;
what can the cause of abiding do?

Furthermore, **what can the cause of** the **abiding** of mind **do** to keep the mind from not being destroyed? Nothing, because if the mind does not meet a cause for its own disintegration, it will not disintegrate even without the presence of the cause for its abiding. If it does meet a cause for its own disintegration, even if the cause for its abiding is present, it cannot prevent the mind from disintegrating.

It could be argued, "**Until it meets the cause of its disintegration**, the body maintains the abiding, without it disintegrating."

What can the cause of the **abiding** of the mind—that is, the body—possibly **do** to the mind? It has no point, because **there is no** valid cognition that can **harm** the fact that the **disintegration** of mind exists **as the nature of entities.**

Refuting the conducive example for abiding as something already existing

"It is like the support for water and so on." This is similar.
67. **If entities are disintegrating moment by moment,**
and there are causes of creating continuity,
it is a support. If not, it is not correct.

It could be argued, "It is the support for the abiding of something existing. For example, **it is like** a pot being **the support for** the abiding of **water and so on,** which is already existing. Similarly, body too is a support for the already existing mind."

"And so on" includes "qualities" and "universals," whose support for their own abiding as something already existing is substantiality.

It is not correct to state that a pot is a support for the abiding and nondisintegration of water and so on, because **this** assertion **is** also subject to **similar** damage by reasoning exposed in the lines from "It does not exist as a support" up to "what would be the point of the entity?" (2.63–64).

So how is it that pot and water are designated support and that which is supported? Pots and so on are not supports of water and so on by way of maintaining their abiding and preventing their disintegration. **If entities** of water and so on **are** subject to **disintegration moment by moment** and pots and so on **are causes of creating continuity**, in the sense of maintaining the status, of the entity of water and so on, then **it is a support** of water and so on. However, **if** it is **not** that kind of support, **it is not correct** to call it a support.

> 68. **If by pouring it out, it is ended,**
> **they are supports.**
> **But the non-moving universal, qualities, and activities—**
> **what need do they have of a support?**

If the water and so on in pots and so on is **ended by pouring it out**, such containers **are the supports** of water, **but what need do the** [permanent] **universal, qualities, and activities have of a support?**[214] They do **not** possess the activity of **moving** to other places.

Refuting other assertions of the abiding of something already existing

> 69. **Because there are no such supports,**
> **this also dispels the abiding of inherence,**
> **the cause of the possessors of inherence,**
> **classification, and so on.**

This reasoning, which refutes a support maintaining the existence of an already existing supported phenomena, **also dispels** assertions of **the** supported **abiding** without disintegration by way **of** supports such as **inherence,**[215] where support and supported are not distinct entities, the self, and so on as **the cause of the possessors of inherence**, the **classification** of "cowness" of a cow, **and so on.**[216] "And so on" refers to the mind abiding in the elements, the color white abiding in the cloth, and so on. This is **because** this reasoning teaches that **there are no such supports.**

Explanation of refuting a cause maintaining the abiding

> 70. **If by another an entity disintegrates,**
> **what could a cause of its abiding do?**
> **Even if disintegrating without another,**
> **the causes of it abiding would have no power.**

If an entity disintegrates by another cause of disintegration, **what could a cause of its abiding** without disintegrating **do** to prevent disintegration? Nothing, because even though its support exists, it disintegrates by its cause of disintegration. **Even if** that entity **disintegrates** by way of its own nature, **without another** cause of disintegration, **the causes of it abiding** without disintegration **would have no power** to prevent it from disintegrating, because that entity disintegrates by its own nature.

> 71. **All that possesses support possesses an abiding,**
> **and all that is created possesses supports.**
> **Therefore all entities at times**
> **would never disintegrate.**

Furthermore, it would follow that **all entities at times would never disintegrate,** because **all that possesses support**, which maintain abiding without disintegration, **possesses an abiding** without disintegration, **and all that is created**—that is, entities—**possesses supports** that maintain an abiding without disintegration.

> 72. **If naturally disintegrating,**
> **what other cause for the abiding would there be?**
> **If not naturally disintegrating,**
> **what other cause for the abiding would there be?**

Furthermore, all entities are either **naturally disintegrating** or not. **If** it is the former, **what other** support **causing the abiding** of an entity **would there be?** None, because it would be an entity that is naturally disintegrating. If it were the latter, what need **would there be for another** support **causing the abiding** of an entity? None, because it would follow that it is an entity that is **not naturally disintegrating**, and it would abide without disintegration.

Refuting by other reasons that mind and body are cause and effect

1. Reasoning refuting other causes
2. The counter pervasion is established within the incongruent example
3. Refutation of those who say the reason is not established
4. Summary of the proof of arising from its own cause

Reasoning refuting other causes

> 73. **Without the development and weakening of the body**
> **but by the factors that cause activities of the mind**
> **do wisdom and so forth develop and weaken.**

Wisdom, compassion, **and so forth** do not arise from the material cause of the body; it is **by the factors that cause the activities of** development and weakening within **the mind**, **without** relying directly upon **the development and weakening of the body**, that the mind **develops or weakens.**

The counter pervasion is established within the incongruent example

> 74. **This is not found in those that depend,**
> **such as the light of a lamp and so on.**

It could be argued there is no pervasion to the above reasoning. We reply that **this** concomitance with the development and weakening within the mind with no development and weakening within the material cause **is not found in** cases of **the light of a lamp and so on, which depend** upon external material causes. That is a case of development and weakening concomitant with the development and weakening of the material cause, which have no connection with the development and weakening within the mind.

Refutation of those who say the reason is not established

> **The particular changes from this,**
> **without affecting the mind, will not happen.**

It could be argued, "The root reasoning is not established because discernment and so forth becomes clear or unclear in dependence upon the flourishing and decline of the body."

These particular changes to discernment and so forth that arise **from this** flourishing and decline of the body is not a case of the flourishing and decline of the body having a direct effect upon the discernment. This is because **it will not happen** and affect discernment **without** the flourishing and decline of the body **affecting the mind**—that is, the sense consciousnesses. Therefore the body affects discernment indirectly.

It could be further argued, "Desire and anger arise from the flourishing and decline of the body. Therefore your reasoning is not established."

> 75. **At times, desire and so on,**
> **increased by flourishing and so on,**
> **are produced from pleasure or pain,**
> **coming from the proximity of the inner phenomena**
> **of elements being in balance and so on.**

Desire and so on—that is, anger—which are in turn **increased by the flourishing and so on**—that is, decline—of the body **at times** of amassing improper mental engagement are not created directly from this flourishing and decline of the body. They **are produced** in turn **from** the sense consciousnesses in the nature of **pleasure or pain**, which are created by the flourishing and decline of the body.[217]

That pleasure and pain are produced as factors of the bodily consciousness **from** the sense faculty of the body and **the proximity of the inner phenomena**, the different physical sensations, **of** the **elements being in balance and so on**—that is, out of balance—which arise from the flourishing and decline of the body.

> 76. **This explains mental deterioration and so on**
> **from fever and so on.**
> **From the features of inner phenomena,**
> **the cognition brings about changes.**

This teaching that desire and so forth are not directly produced from the body **explains** that **the deterioration in the mind**, confusion, **and so on** following on **from fever**, alcohol, **and so on**, are not directly produced **from** alcohol and so on. This is because alcohol and so on create **the features** of the physical sensations **of inner phenomena**, and **the** sense **cognition** produced from those **brings about changes** to the mental cognition, from which the above experiences are formed.

> 77. **For example, in some minds,**
> **from hearing a tiger and seeing blood,**
> **confusion and so on will arise.**

The above have an effect indirectly, but they are not material causes. **For example**, to **some** of a timid **mind**, when **hearing** the shout, "There is **a tiger!**" or see-

ing the **blood** of someone stabbed, **confusion**, fear, **and so on arise** indirectly, but these events are not the material causes of those responses.

Summary of the proof of arising from its own cause

> 78. **Therefore it definitely follows on**
> **from the mental engagement.**
> **Without that, mind would not arise.**
> **Therefore it depends upon mind.**

Because the body is not the direct cause of the mental cognition, mind **depends upon** a previous **mind**, because **without that** previous **mind**, it **would not arise. Therefore it definitely follows on from the** habitual **mental engagement** of previous minds.

Refuting that mind is in the nature of the body

1. Refutation by way of the absurd consequence of body and mind being one
2. Establishing by autonomous reasoning the prior existence of wrong perception and desire
3. Refuting merely not seeing as establishing no past and future life

Refutation by way of the absurd consequence of body and mind being one

> 79. **In dependence upon mind,**
> **mental engagement in learning and so on,**
> **in time, will become manifest in those minds.**
> **Similarly, because of there being no distinction,**
> **those qualities would be in the body.**

Having refuted that the mind is a produced result of the body, it is now refuted that the mind is a quality or a power of the body. **In minds** of **mental engagement in learning**, crafts, **and so on, in time** those qualities of learning and so on **become manifest**, because of that **dependence upon** previous **minds. Similarly,** it would follow that **in the body** too **those qualities would become** manifest **because** the body is **not distinct** from the mind in which those qualities have become manifest.

Establishing by autonomous reasoning the prior existence of wrong perception and desire

80. **By having attachment to self,**
without being led by others,
with desire to gain happiness and abandon suffering,
they have taken such a low status.

81. **The wrong perception of suffering**
and tightly bound desire
are the causes for birth.
Without those there is no birth.

Ordinary beings, **by having attachment to self**, will have had the prior **desire to gain happiness and to abandon suffering**, because, **without being** helplessly **led by others** such as Īśvara, **they have taken such a low status.** This pervades because **the wrong perception of** holding **suffering** to be happiness and the **desire that is tightly bound** to birth **are the causes for birth** into future existences. Those who are **without those** two **do not take birth** into future existence.

Refuting merely not seeing as establishing no past and future life

82. **"Going and coming is not seen."**
Because the senses are not clear, it is not seen.
For example, if the eyesight is not clear,
a trace of smoke will not be seen.

It could be argued, "Sentient beings have no past and future lives because **going** to a future life **and coming** from a past life **is not seen.**"

If this is being presented not as something unseen by all beings but as something unseen by you, then we reply that merely not being seen by the Lokāyata cannot prove that there is no going to a future life and coming from a past life for sentient beings, **because the sense** faculties of the Lokāyata **are not clear.** In that case, the rebirth of sentient beings **is not seen**, but that is not something not seen because of it not existing. **For example, if the eyesight is not clear,** there may be **a trace of smoke**, but it **will not be seen.**

It could be argued, "A sentient being that takes birth cannot enter without obstruction into a place of birth, because a sentient being has a body."

83. **Although they possess a body, it is subtle.**
Therefore some are unobstructed to some,
like water and quicksilver in gold.
Not being seen does not mean not existing.

Some sentient beings are able to enter **some** bodies **without obstruction** because **although they possess a body, it is subtle** and transparent, and because of that, they enter wombs and so on without obstruction, **like water** in a newly made, unfired clay pot **and quicksilver in** softened **gold**.

It could be argued, "It is also not correct to talk of entering a womb, because that is not seen."

Because it is **not seen** by the Lokāyata **does not mean** that entering the womb does **not exist**, because if the sense faculties of the Lokāyata are not clear, then entering the womb would not be seen, as explained above.

Refuting by examination that body can create mind

1. A single substantial entity possessing parts cannot be a cause for mind
2. A body of many parts cannot be a cause for mind (2.103)

A single substantial entity possessing parts cannot be a cause for mind

1. Refuting a single substantial entity possessing parts
2. Refuting the response that there are absurd consequences
3. Refutation in other areas (2.91)

Refuting a single substantial entity possessing parts

84. **If the hand, or some other part,**
is moved, all would move.
Contradictory actions cannot exist in one.
As another, it would be distinct.

85. **If one is covered, all would be covered,**
or, if not covered, it would be seen.
If one is transformed by paint,
it is understood there would be
transformation or not transformation.

86. **Therefore a collection does not exist as one.**

If the body is the material cause of the mind, is that body a coarse and single substantial entity or a body composed of particles? If it is the former, then **if you were to move the hand or some other part, then all** other parts of the body **would move** because they are substantially one with the hand or some other part. This pervades because the **contradictory actions** of moving and not moving **cannot exist within one** partless substantial entity.

It may be argued, "If the hand is moved, one part of the body is moved, but the possessor of the parts does not move."

Then it would follow that the possessor of the parts **would be** a substantial entity **distinct** from the parts, because when the part is moved, the possessor would be **another**—that is, it would not move.

Furthermore, **if one** part, such as the head, **is covered** by a cloth, then **all** other parts of the body **would be covered. Or, if** one part is **not covered, it would be seen** that all other parts would also not be covered, because those parts are of a partless and single substantial entity with the head.

Furthermore, **if one** part, such as the face, **is transformed by paint, it can be understood** that all other parts would be similarly **transformed.** Alternatively, if one part is not transformed, other parts would **not be transformed**, because those parts are of a partless and single substantial entity with the face.

Therefore this shows that the body, **a collection** of many particles, because of those very particles, does **not exist as one** substantial entity, because it possesses many parts that move and don't move.

Refuting the response that there are absurd consequences

1. Presenting the consequence
2. Uprooting the consequence

Presenting the consequence

> **"If many, like the previous,**
> **they would be no different and subtle**
> **and would not be comprehended."**

The Vaiśeṣika might argue, "**If** the body, pots, and so on were not possessors of parts in the form of single substantial entities and existed instead as **many** particles, it would follow that sense consciousnesses **would not comprehend** them and that they would have no obstructive abilities. This is because **they would be no different** from—they would be as one with—the former individual particles [from which they are produced], which themselves are beyond the range of the sense consciousnesses and possess no obstructive abilities. Subsequently, they would still be those former **subtle** particles, and **like** their **previous** coarse and unformed state."[218]

Uprooting the consequence

1. The reason of no difference is not established
2. If the reason of no difference were established, there would be similar faults elsewhere

The reason of no difference is not established

> 87. **It is not that they are not different.**
> **Possessing the features,**
> **they are objects of the senses,**
> **and so are not particles.**

The body and so forth are particles, but **it is not** established **that they are not different** from the former particles that are beyond the range of the senses, because those former particles came into contact with other particles to produce the present body and so forth. Therefore they are something other. The body and so forth that **possess the features** of particles are particles in reality but **are not** designated as **particles because**, by presenting their aspects to sense consciousnesses, **they are the objects of** those **sense** consciousnesses.

This point is made in the autocommentary to *Treasure of Reasoning*, where it says that a direct mental consciousness is a valid cognition but is unable to induce certainty on its own and therefore does not gain the designation *valid cognition*. It goes on to say, "The objects of sense consciousnesses, for example, are subtle particles, but those particles do not appear to those consciousnesses and therefore are not designated as being their objects."[219]

These days, most commentators assert the intent of this verse to be that subtle particles are not the objects of sense consciousnesses. This shows that they have not considered the tenets of the Sautrāntika as explained by the Seven Treatises (of Dharmakīrti). The Sautrāntika school states that subtle particles with no directional parts, and instants of consciousness that contain no former and succeeding parts of time, exist as realities and that the other-knowing direct perception and self-knowing direct perception that apprehend them are unmistaken consciousnesses. Coarseness and all continuums are provisional realities, and the conceptual cognition that apprehends them is mistaken consciousness.

Many particles do not make a single substantial entity of coarse form. Therefore, in reality, there can be no coarse form separate from the particles. The sense consciousness does not apprehend these individual particles, but many particles coming into contact with each other is apprehended by the sense consciousness because that is the aspect presented to the sense consciousness.

Those who state that particles are not apprehended by the sense consciousness are thinking of individual particles that have not come into contact with other particles. This is the unmistaken thinking of the *Compendium of Valid Cognition* and the *Treatise on Valid Cognition*.

Therefore, in this [Sautrāntika] tradition, a sense consciousness apprehends external phenomena via a three-part causal sequence: (1) the cause of bestowing the aspect onto the sense consciousness, (2) the aspect bestowed by that cause, and (3) the object of an ascertaining consciousness induced by the bestowing. The first is the particular particles that have come into contact with each other. The second is the coarse aspect that appears at the time of the sense consciousness. The third is the aspect appearing as one to a subsequent conceptual cognition, projected as an external phenomenon and engaged by way of exclusion. The first is external phenomena. The second is not coarse form because it is the entity of the sense consciousness. The third is a conceptual projection of coarse form.

That which bestows the aspect is in the form of particles, but because the coarse form aspect appears to the sense consciousness, the Vijñaptika[220] point out an internal contradiction in the Sautrāntika tenets, asking, "How do these particles create such a coarse form appearance?"[221] This challenge is built on the above sequence.

In the commentary of Jamyang Gekpo[222] it says:

> Apart from subtle particles, the assertion of intrinsically existing matter is not found in those who hold the tenets of Buddhism. However, there are those Tibetan logicians who presume themselves scholars in the tenets of the Seven Treatises but who have not had even the inclination to explain the tenets of those texts. With one voice, never having discussed it, they nominally refute a possessor of parts existing as something other than its parts. They say that the subtle particles cannot be apprehended by the sense consciousness and that they have no obstructive capabilities.

> However, a coarse form constructed from those particles, which is a separate entity from those particles, does exist as an intrinsically existing phenomenon. This coarse form has obstructive capabilities and is apprehended by the sense consciousness. However, it is not cognized through the weight of the subtle particles but through the truly existing weight of the coarse form constructed by those particles.
>
> Therefore they accept form as the possessor of parts and of this extra weight, as asserted by the Vaiśeṣika. The blessing of great compassion that ensures I do not have the burden of such ignorance is a kindness granted to me by the buddhas and bodhisattvas of the three times.[223]

Those who assume to be scholars these days should think about this. However, it is important not to confuse the aspect of coarse form for actual coarse form.

> **By this, having no obstructive abilities**
> **and so on is also dispelled.**

By this teaching that these two reasonings[224] are not established, the consequence that the body and so on **has no obstructive abilities and so on is also dispelled**, because the body and so on is produced from the previous coming together of particles into a possessor of features that is capable of obstructing.

If the reason of no difference were established, there would be similar faults elsewhere

> 88. **Quicksilver mixed with gold,**
> **or stones with color, how would they appear?**
> **Sense faculties and so on, individually with no ability,**
> **how could they be perceivers?**

With regard to **quicksilver mixed with gold** and so on, **or stones** streaked **with color, how would they appear** to the sense consciousness? They would not appear because they would just be many atoms and not single substances possessing parts.[225]

How could the coming together of the sense faculty, mental engagement, and so on **be** the producer of a sense consciousness as a **perceiver**? They could not because it would be no different from the previous **sense faculty and so on**, which has **no ability** to create a sense consciousness **individually**. You accept the reason for both arguments.

> 89. **If from combination, here,**
> **the consequence is similar.**
> **"Gold and quicksilver possess a combination,**
> **and therefore will appear."**
> **The basis is not seen. How will it be perceived?**
> 90. **It would be contradictory for taste and form to have combination.**

It could be argued, "From the sense faculties and so on coming together, there is a combination,[226] and **from this combination** the sense consciousness is produced."

With this assertion that by the sense faculties and so on coming together, a combination is produced, **here, the consequence** that the sense faculties and so on have no ability to produce a combination **can be similarly** presented because they are no different from the preceding sense faculty and so on, which has no ability to create.

It could be argued, "The mixing of **gold and quicksilver** has no substantial entity of being a possessor of parts, but it does **possess a combination** of different particles coming into contact with each other, **and therefore** it **will appear**."

How can a sense consciousness **perceive** a combination that is a mix of gold and quicksilver? It follows that it cannot because the particles of gold and quicksilver that are **the basis** for the combination are **not seen**. Furthermore, a combination is a quality, and if you assert that a quality cannot have another quality, then **it would be contradictory for** sweet beer **to have the combination** of **taste and form** because sweet beer is a quality.

> **If asserted it is from labeling,**
> **there would be distinct cognition.**
> **How can a row be "long"?**

It could be **asserted**, "The beer does not have taste and form in reality, but because the beer together with actual taste and form are gathered together in the particles that are drunk, the existence of taste and form in the beer **is labeled**, and we engage in those designations accordingly."

In that case, it follows that the form and taste of sweet beer would become an aspect of **cognition distinct** from the actual form and taste, and that cognition would not be of the actual form and taste but from the label "form and taste."

If **a row** of a hundred birds[227] **is** designated as **"long," how** could that term engage? It could not, because it is a number and therefore lacks the characteristic of being long and is not inherent to a single phenomenon.

Refutation in other areas

1. Refuting that number and so on are distinct in substantiality
2. Refuting arguments on being non-distinct

Refuting that number and so on are distinct in substantiality

1. Presenting reasons for them not being distinct
2. Refuting reasons for them being distinct
3. Refuting other arguments put forward against their not being distinct

Presenting reasons for them not being distinct

91. **The natures of number, combinations, functions, and so on,**
do not appear to cognition as separate from
the entity possessing those,
as well as the expressions.

The natures of pot **number, combinations, functions**, generality, divisions, being other or not other than a pot, **and so on**[228] are in reality not separate from **the entity** of the substantial pot **possessing** number and so on, **as well as the** names **expressing** number and so on, because in reality their existing **as separate does not appear to** an unmistaken **cognition.**

Refuting reasons for them being distinct

It can be argued, "The number and so on of pots exist as substantial entities separate from the pots because the object-possessing verbal expression and conceptual cognition engage in them in a manner separate from a pot."

92. **Verbal expression and consciousness**
label by conceptual cognition following
separate entities possessing the objects.
For example, qualities and so forth,
and destruction and the uncreated.

The number and so on of pots as separate in reality from the pots is not established by the reason that the verbal expression and consciousness as object-possessors, which engage in number and so on, are separate from the verbal expression and consciousness that engage in the pot itself.

This is because the object-possessing **verbal expression and consciousness** that engage in number and so on **label by** way of a **conceptual cognition that follows separate entities**—that is, isolated from the pot—and **possess the objects** of number and so on as objects. **For example**, the number and so on of **qualities**, functions, **and so forth** do not exist as separate from these entities, but the object-possessing verbal expression and conceptual cognition engage them separately. Also, number and so on with regard to **destruction and the uncreated** do not exist as separate from these phenomena, but their verbal expression and cognition do engage separately.

Refuting other arguments put forward against their not being distinct

> 93. **You assert that these are by way of labeling.**
> **By the reason that you assert that,**
> **why do you not apply the reason to all entities?**
> 94. **"Not everything is by way of labeling.**
> **It is primarily those of distinct features."**
> **How could that be?**

You assert, "With regard to **these** qualities, the expression of number does not engage by way of actual name but **by way of labeling.**"

By the reason that you assert that verbal expression and cognition of number engage the qualities by way of labeling, **why do you not apply the reason to** the number of **all entities?** You should, because all entities and the number of their qualities are similar in being not separate in reality.

It could be argued, "It is **not** that verbal expressions of number engage with **everything** such as pots **by way of labeling.** If they did, it would not be possible for verbal expressions of number to engage in actuality, and if that is not possible, engaging by labeling would also be impossible. Therefore, in those entities that have distinct **features** of number and so on, verbal expressions of number engage **primarily**—that is, in actuality. To those that do not, they engage by way of labeling."

How could it be that verbal expressions of number engage by way of actual name in those that possess distinct features of number? This cannot be, because those names that enable the unmistaken comprehension of the numbers and so on are the actual names of those numbers and so on.

Refuting arguments on being non-distinct

1. Refuting the argument that distinct expressions would render distinction meaningless
2. Refuting the argument that the sixth case would be impossible

Refuting the argument that distinct expressions would render distinction meaningless

"There would be no meaningful distinction
from that which is not distinct."
95. **Though possessing no reason for being distinct,**
combination, numbers, and so forth
of white and so forth are not synonyms.

It could be argued, "Then verbal expressions of the pot and verbal expressions of the numbers of the pot **would have no meaningful distinction**—they would be synonyms—because they are various names engaging **with non-distinct** phenomena to be expressed."

Then it follows that the expressions of **combination, numbers, and so forth,** concerning the quality of being **white and so forth,** are synonyms, because these expressions **possess no reason for being distinct** entities from the numbers and so on existing upon the quality white. You must accept the reasoning. If you agree, then because they **are not synonyms**, the argument is refuted.

"Even those are intrinsically separate entities."
96. **Quality would not be different**
from the substantial entity.

It could be argued, "**Even that** quality of being white and so on has the number and so on of **intrinsically separate entities.**"

It follows that **quality would not be different from the substantial entity** because the cause of being endowed with function, with quality and with inherence,[229] is the substance itself, and those characteristics of substance depend upon the self-isolate of quality.

Though not intrinsically separate entities,
when divided by way of isolates,
they are distinct, like the expressions
"not a function" and "not a substance."

Therefore, **although** the expressed phenomena, the verbal expressions of pot, and the verbal expressions of numbers of pot **are not intrinsically separate entities**, they are not separate, synonymous object-possessors. This is because these expressed phenomena **are divided by way of** having distinct **isolates**. It is **like the** objects of the **expressions** "This quality is **not a function**" and "This quality is **not a substance**," which **are distinct** isolates but not synonyms.[230]

Refuting the argument that the sixth case would be impossible

1. Expressing properties and property-possessor
2. Expressing class and collection

Expressing properties and property-possessor

It can be argued, "It follows that it would not be possible to express number and so forth by way of the sixth [genitive] case, as in 'a number of pots,' because in reality they are not separate from the pots."

97. **Those expressions that express entities,**
communicated as being distinct
from those that possess number and so on,
differentiate other properties.

That which is **communicated as being distinct** from a pot, by way of **expressions that express entities**—that is, properties, such as **number** of pots, combinations, **and so on—differentiates**, or cuts out and eliminates, **other properties** of the pot except for number and so on, because they are expressions that express properties and that engage with the number and so on of pots.

98. **Wishing to know just that,**
all others are not implied.
For example, sometimes a combination of fingers
is expressed as distinct.

Therefore to a listener who **wishes to know just that** number of pots—having eliminated all other properties of the pot—the expression of a number of pots that **does not imply all other** properties of the pot as the phenomena to be expressed expresses itself in a way that the number of pots is distinct from pots, but that alone does not establish that the number of pots is in reality distinct from pots. An expression expressing the number of pots as an isolate distinct from pots is sufficient to say that these two are distinct. **For example**, a combination of fingers is not separate from fingers in reality, but **sometimes "a combination of fingers" is expressed as distinct.**

> 99. **One is expressed, but all are implied.**
> **"Fingers combined" is known**
> **as an expression of a property-possessor.**
> **In that way, convention is set up.**

Furthermore, the expression "pot" and the expression "a number of pots," as a property, are both **expressing the one** pot, **but** "pot" **is known as an expression of a property-possessor** because it is just the expression of "pot," **implying all** features of pots as the phenomena expressed. Therefore, **in that way**, an expression of the property-possessor **is set up as a convention.** For example, if you say, **"fingers combined,"** it implies all features of fingers as the phenomena expressed.

Expressing class and collection

> 100. **With features of the potentials,**
> **such as form and so on, excluded,**
> **those that are not causes**
> **of similar results are precluded,**
> **and in this the expression "pot" engages.**

So what is the difference between expressing class and expressing a collection? The sound "pot" is an expression that expresses a collection in dependence upon the eight substantial-entity particles. These particles, as the constructor of the pot, have a shared potential and individual potentials. Of these two, **the features of the** individual **potentials, such as form and so on**, which create the cognition of form, for example, are **excluded** by this expression as being the phenomenon expressed. By this exclusion, entities such as trees **that are not**

causes of similar—that is, shared—**results** of form and so on, such as the ability to hold water, are also **precluded, and in this the expression "pot" engages.**

> 101. **Therefore an expression like "pot is form"**[231]
> **is not a single basis.**
> **Therefore this is the difference between**
> **expressions of collection and expressions of class.**

Therefore an expression like "pot is form" is not a single—that is, a common—**basis** of collection-possessor and collection. This is because the expression "pot" eliminates form of the pot as the phenomenon expressed.

An expression that expresses class can have a common basis with an expression of class-possessor because that which expresses class does not eliminate the class-possessor as its phenomenon expressed, as in "an *aśoka* is a tree." An expression that expresses class can have a basis with that expressing a class-possessor, whereas an expression that expresses collection cannot share a basis with the expressing of collection-possessor. **Therefore expressions** that express **collection and expressions** that express **class** are not differentiated by depending upon the same existent and eliminating or not eliminating another feature as the phenomenon expressed. They are differentiated by depending upon individual existents, in which a class-possessor is not eliminated as the phenomenon expressed and collection-possessor is eliminated as the phenomenon expressed. **This is the difference.**

It could be argued, "If pot and the form of pot are not distinct in reality, then the designation 'the form of the pot,' in which form and pot are expressed as being distinct, serves no purpose."

> 102. **With the universal rendering it into parts,**
> **"form of the pot" and so on reveal the specific features.**
> **This point is expressed with others also.**

The form and so on of the pot is **rendered into parts**—that is, features—by the collection **universal.** The expressions **"form of the pot,"** "smell of the pot," **and so on** are not without purpose because they **reveal the specific features** of the potential of form, smell, and so on, from among the many forms within a pot, to develop the visual and other consciousnesses of these features.

This point, whereby the expression "form of the pot" reveals a feature such as the potential that is the form of the pot, **is expressed with others also;** "the smell of sandalwood," for example. This is because it is able to illustrate the smell of sandalwood distinct from other smells.

A body of many parts cannot be a cause for mind

1. The collection of parts is not a cause
2. The individual parts are not a cause

The collection of parts is not a cause

It could be argued, "The many parts of the body are the direct cause of the mind."

> 103. **If all are the cause,**
> **then even if one part is missing,**
> **it will not arise.**

Either all the parts as a collection or individually are the cause. If it is the former, **then** it follows that **even if one part**, such as an ear, **is missing**, cognition **will not arise** because **all** the parts of the body as a collection **are the cause**.

The individual parts are not a cause

1. Presenting the damaging consequence
2. Refuting that the above faults are not there
3. Refuting that the same fault occurs on our side (2.112)

Presenting the damaging consequence

> **If the individual were capable,**
> **many would arise simultaneously.**

In the case where the individual parts are asserted to be the cause, then within a person who possesses a body, **many** cognitions **would arise simultaneously**, and their continuums would be substantial entities, because **the individual** parts of the body **would be capable** of generating individual cognitions.

Refuting that the above faults are not there

1. A single breath is not the cause of cognition
2. Many breaths are not the cause of cognition

A single breath is not the cause of cognition

> 104. **Being similar to the many,**
> **breath does not determine.**
> **Even if one, many would be manifest**
> **because the causes are constantly present.**

It can be argued, "Even if there were many parts, they would not create many cognitions because breath is one, and from that are created the individual cognitions."

Using the reason that **breath** is one **does not determine** that it will create individual cognitions because the breath **is similar to the many**, as in the body and its particles.

Even if you state that this reason is not established because the body and breath are permanent and **one** and therefore will create cognition successively, it would still follow that within a single person possessing a body, **many** cognitions of substantial entities **would be manifest** and created at the same time **because the causes** of these many cognitions—a permanent body and breath—**are constantly present** with unhindered potential.

> 105. **Even if not a cause of many,**
> **there would be no succession**
> **because there would be no difference.**
> **Because many phenomena are apprehended in a single breath,**
> **that is not determined.**

Even if it is argued that the permanent, single body and breath are **not causes** that create **many** cognitions of substantial entities at the same time but create them successively, it would follow that a permanent body and breath **would not** create many cognitions **in succession because**, being permanent, **there would be no difference** from the previous state where it did not create many cognitions.

Furthermore, even if it were accepted that breath is one, it would have to be that within a person possessing a body, a single cognition **cannot be determined** from that breath ascertained as being one, **because in a single** exhaling **breath**, for example, there **are** cognitions **apprehending many** consecutive **phenomena.**

106. "The many are apprehended by a single cognition."
They would be simultaneous
because there is no contradiction.
There would be no sequence
because there would be no difference.

It could be argued that there is no pervasion because **the many** sequential phenomena **are apprehended by a single** partless **cognition.** In that case, it would follow **that** at the time of the preceding phenomena, that cognition **would** apprehend all the consecutive phenomena **simultaneously, because it would not be contradictory** for the cognition to apprehend all the consecutive phenomena simultaneously at the time of apprehending the preceding phenomena.

If you say that this reason is not established, it would follow that this cognition **would not** also apprehend successive phenomena in **sequence, because** later also **there would be no difference** from the time of not apprehending many phenomena.

Many breaths are not the cause of cognition

1. Refuting that cognition is caused by breaths arising in succession
2. Refuting that cognition is caused by breaths arising simultaneously

Refuting that cognition is caused by breaths arising in succession

107. "Many instances of breath in succession,
not of similar type, can be understood to be
the cause of such a mind."

It could be argued, "The **many instances of breath arising in succession,** produced from a permanent body, which is **not a similar-type** entity to the breath, **can be understood to be the cause of such a mind**—that is, successive conceptual minds."

108. Without a cause for possessing sequence,
how can they be in succession?
"The preceding similar-type instance is the cause."
Then the first would not arise
109. because there would be no such cause.

How can these breaths **be** produced **in succession**? They cannot, because there is **no cause for** a production **possessing** a previous **sequence.**

If you reply that the reason is not established because **the preceding similar-type instance is the cause, then** it would follow that **the first** breath in the life of a being possessed of a body **would not arise, because there would be no such** similar-type **cause** of that first breath. If you reply that the reason is not established, then it follows that there must be a previous life.

> **Having places of distinct sources,**
> **breath is ascertained as being many.**
> **Therefore cognitions would arise simultaneously.**

Even if there were preceding similar-type instances, it follows that **breath is ascertained as being many** because it **has** the nature of arising from many **places** that are **distinct sources.** If you agree, **then** in one person many substantial-entity **cognitions** would be produced simultaneously because many breaths **would arise simultaneously.**

Refuting that cognition is caused by breaths arising simultaneously

> 110. **"Even though many, those at one time**
> **are the cause of one mind."**
> **When the breath is weak and so on,**
> **if just one is incomplete, it would not arise.**

It could be argued, "Even though there are many breaths, they do not produce individual cognitions, because **even though many,** the breaths **at one time are the cause of one** conceptual **mind.** Therefore many cognitions do not arise simultaneously."

It would follow that at times **when the breath is weak**[232] **and so on, if even just one** part of these breaths **is incomplete,** the conceptual mind **would not arise** because all parts of these breaths intact are the direct cause of the conceptual mind.

> 111. **"What if, however they are, they are the causes?"**
> **Then the consciousness too would vary.**
> **If the distinctions in this**

> **are not from the distinctions in that,**
> **this is not a result of that.**

As a response, "**What if** the parts, **however they are, are the causes** of the mind?"

Then it follows that from the varying strengths of the breath, **the consciousness too would** be of **varying** strengths, because whether the breath is strong or weak, it is a material cause of consciousness. This pervades because **if the distinctions** of strength and weakness **are not** on account of **the distinct** strengths and weaknesses in a cause, **this is not a result of that** cause.

Refuting that the same fault occurs on our side

It could be argued, "You are similar in asserting that many conceptual consciousnesses can occur in one person."

> 112. **Because the potential is ascertained,**
> **one is the cause of one.**
> **With that consciousness attracted to something else,**
> **there is no ability, and separate forms are not apprehended.**

One preceding conceptual consciousness **is the cause of one** succeeding conceptual consciousness, whereas many consciousnesses of similar type are not produced at the same time, **because the potential is ascertained** as creating succeeding similar type consciousnesses. The reasoning is sound because if **that** conceptual **consciousness** becomes **attracted to something else**, such as a pleasant sound, at that time **there is no ability** to apprehend anything else, such as form. In this way, even if **separate forms** and so forth are close by, it is evident that they **are not apprehended.**

> 113. **"From the body, cognitions are simultaneously produced,**
> **and subsequently from similar types."**
> **By what would the ability of the body be reversed?**

In response it could be argued, "In the beginning, in the womb and elsewhere, **cognitions are simultaneously produced from the body, and subsequently** each succeeding cognition is produced **from** its preceding **similar-type** cognition. So is this not similar to your assertion?"

By what would the ability of the body to create cognition **be reversed** at a later time? It follows that it could not be reversed, because the body even at a later time is no different from, and is one with, the body that created the cognitions previously.

Negating arguments that it is erroneous

1. The argument
2. The response

The argument

114. **"If the body is gone, it is without support,**
and only the mind will remain."

"**If** at death **the body is gone**, it follows that **only the mind will remain** as a discrete entity, because **it** remains **not supported** by the body."

The response

1. The two causes of subsequent sense sources
2. Refuting the proof that there is no connecting to a future state
3. Presenting the proof that connecting to a future state exists

The two causes of subsequent sense sources

For the cause of that to gain the engagement
115. **if the cause of the continuum of mind to be located**
does not become the branch cause, [that would be so].[233]
The five sense sources of this life
are causes that create the other body.

The consequence that after the death of a sentient being possessed of a body, mind remains on its own is not valid. This is because **for the cause of that** body of the next life **to gain the engagement** of creating the body of the next life that follows on from the body at the time of death, **if** the mind at the time of death, as **the cause of the continuum of mind to be located** in the body of the next life, **does not become the branch cause**—that is, its coordinating cause—then after death the mind would remain on its own, but the mind at the time of death does become the coordinating cause of the body of the future life.

"So what is the material cause of the body of the next life?" The body of the future life has a material cause because **the five sense sources** at the point of death **of this life are** the material **causes that create the other body**, the body of the next life.[234]

Most scholars maintain that "if it does not become the branch," mind would exist on its own, as with the taking of birth from the desire realm into the formless realm. If it did become the branch—that is, a coordinating cause—the above argument could not be accepted, as with the taking of birth from the desire realm into the desire realm. Thus they explain the argument by dividing up the response. This is not correct, because the assertion that in the two types of meditative absorption[235] the continuity of mind is cut and that in the formless realms there is no form at all are assertions of the Vaibhāṣika but not of the Sautrāntika. For the Vaibhāṣika, the meaning of "immediately preceding cause" is that there is no intervention by any other similar-type consciousness and not that there is no intervention by another phenomenon. The Sautrāntika assert it to be the direct cause. The Abhidharma commentaries state that there is much argument on the meaning of form existing or not existing in the formless realms for the Vaibhāṣika and the Sautrāntika.

Also, explaining the argument by dividing up the response in this way does not fit with the wording of the text because it has no connection with the line that follows, "The five sense sources of this life." Also, "If it were definitively not stated that similar would not arise from that immediately preceding . . ." is not a subdivided answer, and it is similar here.[236]

The five sense sources as causes of the form present in a sentient being of the formless realm refers to the subtle form that acts as a basis of mind, in the form of imprints planted by these five sense sources and not to the actual five sense sources. Otherwise it would not be possible to avoid the consequence of there being an intermediate state for birth in the formless realm. This is the thinking of Prajñākaragupta and those who follow him when he explains that the imprints are the cause. This, as it is written, is not seen elsewhere in Tibet.

Refuting the proof that there is no connecting to a future state

116. Using not being observed to refute
the branch element of that,
as well as the cause itself,
does not determine, as was well explained.
Sense faculties and so on are with remainder.

It could be argued, "The mind and body at the point of death are not the causes and conditions for the future mind and body because that is not seen."

The reason of **not being observed, used to refute** that **the branch element**, or causal condition, **of that** future body is the mind, **and** that **the** material **cause** is the body **itself** at the point of death, is **not** a perfect reason for **determining** the premise, because that **was well explained** before.

In response it might be argued, "Not observing might not refute this assertion, but using the reason of them being sense faculties, mind, and so on does refute this assertion."

It makes no sense to use **sense faculties and so on** to refute the assertion, because that would be reasoning **with remainder**[237] possessing doubt regarding the pervasion.

Presenting the proof that connecting to a future state exists

> 117. **The potential of preceding sense faculties**
> **can be seen with their similar types.**
> **Because we can see the change, it is established**
> **that others will be produced.**

With the sense faculties at the point of death, if all other conditions are met and there is no obstruction, **it is established that other** future sense faculties **will be produced**, because they are sense faculties. For example, we **can see the potential of preceding sense faculties** of this life to create **similar-type** sense faculties. **We can see** how subsequent sense faculties **change** to become clear or disturbed from previous sense faculties that are clear or disturbed.

> 118. **"Those are created from the body."**
> **Then the consequence follows, as previously.**
> **If from the mind,**
> **another body would be produced from that.**

It could be argued, "**Those** sense faculties of this life are not produced from previous sense faculties but **are created from a** permanent and unitary **body**."

Then the consequence follows, as stated in a **previous** line, "The causes are constantly present" (2.104), that in a single being possessed of a body, many similar-type sense faculties would be simultaneously produced. This is because the permanent body, as the direct cause of many similar-type sense faculties, is constantly present.

If it is argued that the five sense faculties of this life are produced **from the mind,** then it follows that the five sense faculties of **another body**—that is, the body of a future life—**would be produced from that** very mind, because the reasoning is similar to the sense faculties of this life being produced from the mind.

Conclusion: Establishing by refutation

> 119. **Therefore the last minds**
> **having no ongoing connection**
> **because they lack the causes is not proof.**
> **Such are reasonings with remainder.**

Therefore the reasoning that states that **the last minds**, at the point of death, of ordinary people and arhats **lack the causes** of mind, which are breath or the body, **because** the material causes of the mind are breath and the body, **is not proof** that these last minds **have no ongoing connection** to future lives, because breath and the body are not the material causes of the mind.

That reasoning does not prove that there is no connecting to a future life. Therefore **such** proofs, which use as a reason the mind at the point of death, are not perfect reasonings that establish that the cognition of the above subjects will not connect to a future life, because they **are** asserted to be **reasonings with remainder**, which possibly exist in the incongruent class.

37. Training Can Be Developed Limitlessly

Refuting the argument that even though repeated training is possible, it does not go beyond its own nature

1. Presenting the argument by way of example
2. Refuting examples presented by others
3. Examples to establish our own position

Presenting the argument by way of example

> 120. **Although from training,**[238]
> **change in features will occur,**
> **like jumping and heating water,**
> **it does not go beyond its nature.**

The argument runs, "Even though it is possible that **from** repeated **training** in compassion, some **change in features will occur, it does not go beyond its** previous **nature** to result in possessing the characteristics of operating under its own power. **For example**, training in **jumping and heating water** will produce changes, but they cannot be increased limitlessly."

Refuting examples presented by others

1. In the examples, there is no possibility of an increase without limit
2. In the phenomenon, there is the possibility of limitless increase
3. Refuting the argument that the example and the phenomenon are similar
4. Refuting the argument of absurd consequence regarding the phenomenon

In the examples, there is no possibility of an increase without limit

After accomplishment, if again
121. there is reliance upon effort,
or the support is not stable,
the features do not increase.
Its nature is unlike that.
122. The ability to affect them
does not have the power
to produce subsequent features,
and the basis does not remain forever.
123. Though features increase, they do not have that nature.

Jumping and water temperature, **unlike the nature** of **that** compassion, do not increase limitlessly, because although repeated effort will cause some increase in their features, they do not have the nature of increase under their own power. The reasoning is correct because the efforts that have **the ability to affect that** jumping **do not have the power to produce** a limitless increase in the **subsequent features.** Also, **the basis** of the water's hotness is water, and that **does not remain forever.** This pervades because if **after** initial training is **accomplished, there is again reliance upon** subsequent **effort, or the support is not stable, the features** of the phenomena to be trained will necessarily **not increase** limitlessly.

In the phenomenon, there is the possibility of limitless increase

Once accomplished, subsequently
there is no dependence on effort,
and that will characterize other efforts.
124. Compassion and so on produced from training in the mind
will operate naturally on their own,
like fire with wood
and quicksilver with gold and so on.

If the conditions for repeated training are not lacking, then training in **compassion and so on** means that the subsequent features **will operate naturally on their own,** because they are qualities **produced from training in the mind** without having to depend upon physical effort. **For example,** when **fire** burns wood, as long as there are no opposing circumstances, it engages the **wood** under its own power, without depending upon effort. Also, when **gold** is purified by **quicksilver**, there is a one-time effort, and then it purifies under its own power and does not rely upon subsequent effort. This pervades because, when training has been **accomplished once**, for that result to occur **subsequently, there is no dependence upon effort; that** previous effort **will characterize other efforts.** This teaches the lack of similarity with practice in jumping.

> 125. **Qualities produced from that**
> **are produced as the entity itself.**
> **Therefore that effort affects all subsequent.**
> 126. **Because they increase**
> **from the seeds of previous similar type,**
> **if there is training in a mind of compassion and so on,**
> **where do they remain?**

Therefore, as these examples of phenomena operating naturally under their own power illustrate, **if there is** repeated **training in a mind of compassion and so on**, and no lack of the conditions for that practice, **where do they remain** limited? They do not, **because they** are qualities of mind that **increase from the seeds of previous similar types.** This pervades because those **qualities** that are **produced from that** training **are produced as the entity** of mind **itself. Therefore** the previous **effort** necessarily **affects all subsequent** features. This teaches the lack of similarity with the hotness of water.

Refuting the argument that the example and the phenomenon are similar

It might be argued, "If compassion can be developed limitlessly, then jumping also can be developed limitlessly."

> 127. **Unlike that, jumping is not from jumping.**
> **Because its cause, the strength of the body**
> **and the power of effort, is definite,**
> **jumping is an entity that is definite.**

Jumping is an entity with a **definite** limit **because its cause**, which is **the strength of the body and the power of effort, is** of a **definite** limit. This pervades because, **unlike that** increase of compassion from its previous similar-type causes, subsequent **jumping will not** increase **from** the preceding **jumping**, with the preceding and succeeding jumping each dependent upon the physical effort.

It could be argued, "But in the beginning, when untrained, it is possible to jump in the same way as later, when trained, because the effort and the bodily strength are the same."

> 128. **That person not jumping in the beginning as later**
> **is because of unconducive circumstances in the body.**
> **Through effort, unconducive circumstances are gradually removed,**
> **constrained by the strength of the body.**

A person who trains in jumping **cannot jump in the beginning,** when untrained, **as** they can do **later,** when trained, **because** in the beginning, when untrained, **unconducive circumstances in the body**, such as the presence of the phlegm humor, make the body heavy. Later, **through effort**, these **unconducive circumstances are gradually removed.** However, that person training in jumping will not be able to jump limitless distances, because the jumping is **constrained by the strength of the body.**

Refuting the argument of absurd consequence regarding the phenomenon

It could be argued, "If compassion is developed from one's own consciousness, then as all beings have their own consciousness, compassion will develop limitlessly."

> 129. **Compassion arises from its own seed.**
> **If its seed, as the cause, is not damaged**
> **by unconducive circumstances, it becomes**
> **that entity within the mind.**

An ordinary being does not develop compassion limitlessly. **Compassion arises from its own seed, and if there is no damage** caused **by unconducive circumstances**, such as anger, to it becoming the result of this previous seed, **as the cause, it becomes that entity** of compassion **within the mind.** However, unconducive circumstances such as anger exist within an ordinary being.

> 130. **In this way, previous training and**
> **previous minds of the phenomena of compassion,**

> **nonattachment, and so on will be the root**
> **of the manifestation of others.**

If there are no opposing conditions and all conducive circumstances are in place, this is the reason for compassion to develop limitlessly. **In this way, the previous training and previous minds of the phenomena of compassion, nonattachment, and so on will be the root of the manifestation of other** subsequent qualities.

Examples to establish our own position

> 131. **Training develops into the entity of compassion,**
> **as with absence of desire, desire, and revulsion.**

It is argued, "If there are no examples to illustrate how compassion and so on cannot be developed limitlessly, where are the examples to illustrate that it can?"

Training in compassion **develops into the entity of compassion** that resolves to protect beings from suffering. There are examples that illustrate this: **absence of desire, desire, and revulsion**—that is, a meditation on ugly aspects—all of which operate under their own power.[239]

38. From "Compassion" Comes "Teacher"

How "Teacher" arises from that compassion

1. How compassion leads to "Teacher"
2. Training in the focal objects and their aspects
3. The training accomplished in the focal objects and their aspects is the Teacher
4. As a consequence, the aspiration and application become a cause

How compassion leads to "Teacher"

"If it is said, 'the accomplisher is compassion,' how does it become an accomplisher?"

> 132. **The Compassionate One, in order to destroy suffering,**
> **applied himself to methods.**
> **That arising from the method and the cause**
> **are hidden and difficult to explain.**

Although generally it is mistaken to say that just the presence of a cause will ensure the result, there are instances where the mere presence of the cause will cause the result to arise automatically. Therefore, if there is a compassion operating under its own power, "Teacher" and the remaining two[240] will automatically arise, and thus it becomes an accomplisher. Therefore **the Compassionate One, in order to destroy the sufferings** of others, **applied himself to methods**—that is, the paths—corresponding to the pacification of his own suffering because he has resolved to teach without error to others the methods for the pacification of their suffering. This pervades because **that arising from the method**—that is, the pacification of suffering—**and the cause**, the method itself, **are hidden** and not directly perceived, **and** are **difficult to explain** without error to others.

Training in the focal objects and their aspects

1. Analyzing the cause and the nature of that to be abandoned
2. Analyzing the antidote in order to destroy the cause
3. The antidote that destroys, as established by analysis

Analyzing the cause and the nature of that to be abandoned

133. **Analyzing through scripture and reasoning,**
by way of the features of suffering,
he contemplated the cause of suffering
and its nature as impermanent and so on,
134. **because if the cause remained as it was,**
he would not see the reversal of the result.

As suffering is established through causes, the Compassionate One **analyzed** its causes **through scripture and reasoning. By way of the features of suffering** that arise from time to time, **he contemplated** the existence of **the cause of suffering**, the abandonment of which means that the resultant suffering will be destroyed, and he contemplated the **nature** of that cause **as impermanent and so on**—that is, its other characteristics. This he does because he desired to end the resultant suffering. This pervades **because if the cause** of suffering **remained as it was, he would not see the reversal of the resultant** suffering.

Analyzing the antidote in order to destroy the cause

In order to destroy the cause,
he contemplated the opposing force.
135. **Understanding the nature of the cause,**
he ascertained the opposing force to that.

The Compassionate One **contemplated** the antidote that is **the opposing force** to that cause of that suffering **because** he desired **to destroy the cause** of suffering. Contemplating this way, the Compassionate One **ascertained the opposing force to that** cause of suffering **because he has understood the nature of**

that cause, in the same way that by identifying the illness, the medicine can be identified.

The antidote that destroys, as established by analysis

Holding to self and mine,
attachment with composite entities
as its sphere of activity is the cause.
136. **Seeing no-self, the damager of that,**
is the contradiction.

What is that cause and its antidote? By the process of **holding to self and mine,** the **attachment**—that is, the grasping—that **has** the **composite entities** of the five aggregates **as its sphere of activity is the** main **cause** of suffering, because it is autonomously the creator of suffering. The wisdom of **seeing no-self** is the antidote that **damages that** cause of suffering, **because** on a single object it has a **contradictory** object of focus and way of apprehending to the holding to self, the cause of suffering.

The training accomplished in the focal objects and their aspects is the Teacher

From much training
in many aspects over a long time,
137. **qualities and faults of that**
become very clear.

From much training, uninterrupted, **over a long time in** the **many aspects** of the method—that is, the path—for the pacification of suffering, which is the seeing of no-self, comes the result of "Teacher." This is because, with regard to the above, seeing the cause and the resultant saṃsāra, which are objects to be abandoned, and by seeing no-self as the antidote, all **qualities and faults** gradually **become very clear.**

Therefore because his mind is clear,
he has abandoned the imprints of the cause.
138. **The Great Sage, who works for others,**
is superior to the rhinoceros-like and so on.

All the faults and qualities of saṃsāra and nirvāṇa are clear, and therefore the Bhagavan Buddha is one who **has abandoned the** mentally afflicted **imprints of the cause** of suffering that render the features of the body, speech, and mind unserviceable, **because his mind** has arrived at the ultimate **clarity. Therefore the Great Sage**, the Buddha, **who works for others** under his own power, **is superior to the rhinoceros-like** pratyekabuddha **and so on**—that is, the śrāvaka—because he is the one who has abandoned the mental afflictions as well as their imprints and who knows all the faults and qualities of saṃsāra and nirvāṇa.

> **By that cause, trained in the methods,**
> **he is asserted to be the Teacher.**
> 139. **Because of appearing first, before the accomplishment,**
> **these two are explained as the cause.**

The one who has **trained in the methods is asserted to be the Teacher** expressed in the homage of the *Compendium of Valid Cognition* because teaching the path to others is **the cause** of becoming "Teacher."

As a consequence, the aspiration and application become a cause

The aspiration is "resolving to work for the benefit of others," and the application is becoming the "Teacher" trained in the methods. **These two are explained as** being **the cause** of the "Sugata" and the "Protector" in the *Compendium of Valid Cognition* homage, **because** in that homage they **appear first, before** the Sugata and Protector who **accomplish** the welfare of self and others.

39. From "Teacher" Comes "Sugata" and "Protector"

How "Sugata" arises from "Teacher"

1. How the perfect abandonment is the Sugata
2. Refuting the argument that there is no perfect abandonment

How the perfect abandonment is the Sugata

1. Brief explanation
2. Extensive explanation

Brief explanation

Abandonment of the causes,
with three qualities, is sugata itself.
With no basis for suffering, it is "good,"
140. **arising from seeing no-self or from engaging.**

In the Sanskrit term *sugata*, *su* means "good"[241] and so on, while *gata* can be glossed as "abandonment." According to that interpretation, the abandonment that is the **abandonment of the causes** of suffering, together with their imprints, that arises from long-term training in the knowledge of no-self **is *sugata* itself** because it is the abandonment endowed **with three qualities.**

Extensive explanation

1. Well abandoned
2. Abandoned never to return
3. Completely abandoned

Well abandoned

The abandonment possessed by the Buddha **is a good** abandonment because it is an abandonment that is **no basis for** afflicted **suffering.** This establishes it as being superior to that of the outsiders, because **this** abandonment **arises from** directly **seeing no-self or from engaging** in the methods of directly seeing no-self.[242]

Abandoned never to return

Birth and faults, continually arising,
it is explained, will return.
141. **Having abandoned the seeds of the view of self,**
he will not return.
It is true and distinct by nature.

The abandonment possessed by the Buddha is an abandonment from which **he will not return** because it is an abandonment which **has abandoned the seeds of the view of self.** This establishes him as superior to the Lesser Vehicle practitioner, because the truth of suffering that is **birth and faults** such as desire and so on **that continually arise** are abandoned once by the Lesser Vehicle practitioner, but **it is explained** that they **will return.**

What are the causes of that abandonment? **That** wisdom of seeing no-self **is** the cause of the nonreturning abandonment because its objects and aspects are **true**—that is, they are not faulty—it has a **distinct**, contradictory, mode of apprehension from the apprehending of self, and the **nature** of mind has become the entity of that wisdom.

Completely abandoned

With bad tendencies of body, speech, and mind
142. **although no mental afflictions, free from sickness,**
they remain unclear in explaining the paths.
But this is complete abandonment because of training.

The abandonment possessed by the Buddha is a **complete abandonment, because** from the long-time **training** in the many methods with their numerous aspects, it is an abandonment that has eradicated the imprints of mental afflictions. This is superior to that of the śrāvaka and pratyekabuddha arhats because—although they have **no mental afflictions**, which are the causes of suffering, and are **free from** the **sickness** of suffering, which is the result—**they remain** with minds that are **unclear** with regard to **explaining the paths** of the three vehicles.

Moreover, they have **bad tendencies of bodily** activity because, when going for alms, they jump like monkeys. They have bad tendencies of **speech**, because they refer to some as "outcastes." They have bad tendencies of **mind**, because sometimes they are not in meditation and so have times when their minds are in an indeterminate state.[243]

Refuting the argument that there is no perfect abandonment

1. The argument
2. The response

The argument

> **Some say, because he speaks and so on,**
> 143. **he is not one in whom faults are at an end.**
> **There is doubt with regard to the counter pervasion,**
> **and thus this is mistaken.**

Some followers of Jaimini **say**, "The Buddha is **not one in whom faults are at an end because he speaks**, is a person, **and so on.**"[244]

The response

1. Establishing that this is reasoning with remainder
2. Refutation by examining the thesis

Establishing that this is reasoning with remainder

Speaking and so on as a reason **is mistaken** with regards to establishing the Buddha as one in whom faults are not at an end **because there is doubt with regard to the counter pervasion.**

Refutation by examining the thesis

> **You say, because they are permanent,**
> **there is no method, or the method is not known,**
> 144. **his faults are not ended.**
> **When examined, there are causes,**

and by training in the antidotes they cease.
145. **By knowing the nature of those causes,**
it is established that he knows them also.

If you assert that **his faults are not ended**, is **your** proof that the faults **are permanent**, that **there is no method** to abandon the faults, or that there is a **method**, but it **is not known** by him. **When** these are **examined**, all three reasons are not established, because **there are causes** of the faults **and by training in the antidotes** to the causes, **those** causes **cease. By knowing the nature of those causes, it is established that he knows** the antidotes **also.**

How "Protector" arises from "Sugata"

The Protector speaks the path he has seen.
Because of no result, he does not speak untruths.
146. **Because he is possessed of compassion,**
all efforts are undertaken for the welfare of others.

The Bhagavan Buddha is **the Protector** spoken of in the homage of *Compendium of Valid Cognition* because by **speaking** without error of **the path he has seen** and experienced, he protects his disciples from suffering.

How is it without error? The Bhagavan Buddha **does not speak untruths**—that is, an erroneous path—**because** to speak as such would have **no result**, no purpose. Perhaps he spoke erroneously because he has no compassion? The Bhagavan Buddha did not speak without compassion **because he is possessed of** great **compassion.** This is because **all** his physical, verbal, and mental **efforts** have been **undertaken** and perfected over countless eons **for the welfare of others.**

Therefore there is accomplishment

Therefore he is valid.

Therefore there is the accomplishment of the Bhagavan Buddha as a **valid** being because it has been proven by reason that great compassion accomplishes that, and from that, "Teacher," "Sugata," and "Protector" will autonomously arise.

The Four Truths

40. The Four Truths that Establish "Protector"

Refuting that there is no endeavor and establishing that endeavor

1. Establishing "Protector" by entity-based reasoning
2. From the above, "Sugata" is established (2.280)
3. From the above, "Teacher" is established (2.281)
4. From the above, "Compassion" is established (2.282)
5. Therefore endeavor is established (2.282)

Establishing "Protector" by entity-based reasoning

1. Teaching the four truths establishes the Protector
2. Determining the four truths to be taught

Teaching the four truths establishes the Protector

> **Other than that, he is the Protector**
> **because he taught the four truths.**

Other than "Protector" being established by his teaching the truth of the path, or alternatively, other than the mere establishment by way of the four establishing factors presented in forward order, the establishment can be emphasized by an explanation of the reverse order.

The Bhagavan Buddha is **the Protector because** to those who seek freedom, **he taught** without error **the four truths**—namely, the suffering that is to be known, the origins of suffering that are to be abandoned, the cessation of suffering that is be achieved, and the path that is be relied upon.

That "he taught without error" is established by the fact the four truths as taught by this Teacher are established by entity-based reasoning. This should be applied to all instances below.

Determining the four truths to be taught

1. Explaining the truth of suffering by illustration and characteristics
2. Explaining the origin of suffering by determining suffering and its cause (2.179)
3. Explaining the truth of cessation by determining the cessation of suffering (2.190)
4. Explaining the truth of the path by determining the antidote to the view of self (2.205)

Explaining the truth of suffering by illustration and characteristics

1. The illustration of that which "possesses saṃsāra"
2. Establishing the characteristics: impermanence and so on (2.176)

The illustration of that which "possesses saṃsāra"

1. Teaching that which "possesses saṃsāra"
2. Establishing by reasoning that saṃsāra exists
3. The absurd consequences of the assertion that saṃsāra does not exist (2.167)

Teaching that which "possesses saṃsāra"

147. Suffering is the aggregates possessed of saṃsāra.

The appropriated **aggregates that possess** the uninterrupted **saṃsāra** of mental afflictions, karma, and their ripening are the truth of suffering because, directly or indirectly, by way of the three types of suffering, they are the composite entity of **suffering.**

Establishing by reasoning that saṃsāra exists

1. Establishing by the reason of manifestation through habituation
2. Establishing by the reason of the material cause being of similar type (2.164)

Establishing by the reason of manifestation through habituation

1. Presenting the reason
2. Refuting arguments

Presenting the reason

Those who hold nihilistic views say, "It is not correct to speak of being possessed of saṃsāra because past and future lives do not exist."

> **From habituation, it can be seen**
> **that desire and so on manifest.**

For a person at the moment of birth, habituation with desire and so on must have preceded them because they are born with desire and so on clearly manifest in their mind. This pervades because **it can be seen** in this life **that from** previous **habituation** with desire and so on, **desire and so on** clearly **manifest** later.

Refuting arguments

1. Refuting that desire and so on are without causes
2. Refuting that they are produced from unconducive causes
3. Establishing conducive causes (2.163)

Refuting that desire and so on are without causes

> **They are not arbitrary. Being without cause**
> **contradicts their being produced.**

If desire and so on were not produced from habituation, either they would have no cause or they would have some other cause. It is not the former, because desire and so on **are not arbitrary** and without cause because, on occasion, it can be seen that they are produced. This pervades because if they were **without cause**, that would **contradict their being produced** on occasion.

Refuting that they are produced from unconducive causes

1. Refuting that desire and so forth are born from ill health
2. Refuting that desire and so forth are born from the elements

Refuting that desire and so forth are born from ill health

1. Because there is no counter pervasion, they are not the results
2. Because they do not follow, they are not the results
3. The absurd consequences of the results (2.156)
4. Refuting the argument that our assertions are similar (2.157)

Because there is no counter pervasion, they are not the results

> **148. Because of error, they are not**
> **qualities of wind and so on.**
> **"Being mixed entities, there is no fault."**
> **Why do we not see other than that?**

It could be argued, "Desire and so on are not without cause, but they are not produced from habituation because the humors of wind, bile, and phlegm clearly produce confusion, anger, and desire, respectively."

Confusion and so forth **are not qualities** that are the results **of wind and so on**—that is, bile and phlegm—**because** there is an **error** with regard to the counter pervasion to each of those three. This is because we can see instances of a predominance of phlegm and no bile and yet great anger.

It could be argued, "In such instances, **the entity** of bile **is mixed** with phlegm, and **therefore there is no fault** of anger not coming from bile."

In that case, **why do we not see**, within the person possessed of that predominance of phlegm, phenomena of bile **other than that** of anger, such as yellow skin, foul smell, and so on? It follows that we should see these because bile, which is their cause, has an unhindered capability.

> **149. Because all would have similar desire,**
> **they are not phenomena of all.**
> **"There is no fault, as with forms."**
> **150. If the variants of karma are not empowering,**
> **even for that, the argument is comparable.**

It might be argued, "Wind, bile, and phlegm each have the ability to create all three poisons."

Confusion and so on **are not phenomena** that are the result **of all**—that is, wind and so on. If they were, there would be the fault that it would follow that

all people who were alike in having similar levels of phlegm **would have similar** levels of **desire** because they have similar levels of phlegm.

The response could be, "**There is no fault** because the four elements as causes are similar but the results that are the **forms** of sentient beings are not similar. In the same way, phlegm and so on are similar as causes, but the resultant desire and so on are not similar."

If the variants of good and bad **karma are not** the **empowering** causes for the forms of living beings, and they are created instead from the four elements, then **even for such** a production of form from the four elements, it would follow that living beings would be similar in their forms because they are alike in the causes. **This is a comparable argument** to the above.

Because they do not follow, they are not the results

1. Presenting the reason
2. Establishing the three procedures of the reasoning
3. Refuting arguments against the above

Presenting the reason

> **Though there are variations in the faults,**
> **there are no such corresponding variations.**
> **Therefore it does not become invalid.**
> 151. **Changes in all would bring about change.**
> **Therefore production is not from all.**

Confusion and so on do not result from the material causes of wind and so on because **there** may **be variations in** the strength and weakness of **the faults**[245]—that is, wind and so on—**but there are no such corresponding variations** in the confusion and so on.

Establishing the three procedures of the reasoning

It might be argued, "The reasoning is not established because we can see that when bile increases, the body is tormented and anger increases."

The reason **does not become invalid** by this alone. If it did, then all—that is, wind, phlegm, and bile—would be the material cause of anger because **changes in all** three **would** cause torment in the body and therefore **bring about** the **change** of an increase in anger. If you accept that, **then** it follows that the

production of anger **is not from all** three faults—that is, wind and so on—because all three are equal with regard to anger.

> **If the cause is increased,**
> **the result should not decline,**
> 152. **as with heat and so on.**
> **Changes in desire are created from**
> **sufferings and happiness.**

There is pervasion to the main reason above, because **if the** material **cause** of desire and so on, which is phlegm and so on, **is increased**, then **the result**, such as desire, which possesses that material cause, **should not decline. For example**, if bile increases, then the illness of **heat**, which is its result, should not decline **and so on.**

It could be argued, "The main reason the above is not established is because desire arises from the three humors in balance and anger arises from the three not in balance."

The **changes in desire** and so on brought about by the balance and imbalance of these three humors are not directly produced from the three illnesses but **are created from** the **sufferings and happiness**[246] brought about by the balance and imbalance of these three.

Refuting arguments against the above

1. Arguing against the above, asking what the cause is
2. Refuting the two causes given in response

Arguing against the above, asking what the cause is

> **"By the suffering of not being in balance,**
> **desire will not be produced."**
> 153. **Then tell us what creates it!**
> **"From balance, semen increases,**
> **and from that comes desire."**

It could be argued in response, "Generally, phlegm is the cause of desire. However, **by the suffering** caused by the three humors **not being in balance**, that desire is negated, and although phlegm is present, **desire will not be produced.**"

In that case, when the three are in balance, **tell us what creates** desire!

Refuting the two causes given in response

1. Semen is not the cause of desire
2. Form and so on are not the cause of desire

Semen is not the cause of desire

In response, "**Semen**[247] **increases from** the three humors being in **balance, and from that comes desire.**"

> **When not in balance, we see those possessed of desire.**
> **In others, when in balance, there is no desire.**
> 154. **In others, though exhausted and blood falls,**
> **because there is no certainty of semen**
> **with regard to a woman,**
> **they would not develop strong desire.**

Desire is not the direct result of semen when the three humors are in balance because even **when** the three are **not in balance, we** can **see those possessed of desire. In others,** such as those devoid of attachment, even though their humors are **in balance,** we can see **there is no** production of **desire.** Also, **in others** possessed of desire, even **though** their semen is **exhausted and blood falls,** we can see desire. Furthermore, it follows that such persons possessed of desire **would not develop strong desire** toward a beautiful woman **because there can be no certainty of** any increase of **semen with regard to** that **woman** alone.

Form and so on are not the cause of desire

> **"Form and so on are elements."**
> 155. **They are not, because there is no certainty for all.**
> **It would not arise where there is no ascertaining,**
> **but would in those not holding it as a worthy quality.**

It is argued, "**The form,** behavior, **and so on** of a woman, **are elements**—that is, cooperative causes for generating desire by way of semen increase—and therefore it is not contradictory to say that strong desire will be created toward that woman alone."

The beautiful form of a woman **is not** the direct cause of desire, **because for all** those who have turned away from this woman, **there is no certainty** that they will generate desire. If beautiful form is the direct cause of desire, it would follow that desire **would never arise** toward ugly form, **where there is no ascertaining** of a beautiful form; also **in those who do not hold** beauty to be a **worthy quality, it** would follow that desire **would be** generated because beauty is a direct cause of desire.

> **If holding to be a worthy quality**
> 156. **is an element, then everyone**
> **would regard it as a worthy quality,**
> **because there is no difference in the cause.**

If you argue that **holding** beauty **to be a worthy quality is an element** generating desire, **then everyone** possessing semen who sees a beautiful form **would regard** beauty **as a worthy quality**. This is **because, in** being **the** direct **cause** of holding beauty as a worthy quality, **there is no difference** between the beautiful form and the possession of semen. You accept the reason.

The absurd consequences of the results

> **At the times you assert someone possessed of desire,**
> **they would not be possessed of anger.**
> 157. **Because these two are of dissimilar natures,**
> **at this time, it can be ascertained**
> **that it cannot be seen.**

If phlegm caused only desire, then **at the times** of **someone** possessed of phlegm, such a person **would not be possessed of anger** because **you assert** that at such a time they would **possessed of desire**. This pervades **because** desire and anger **are of dissimilar natures**—that is, they are contradictory. You cannot agree with the reason because when there is phlegm, **it is ascertained that it cannot be seen** that there is unequivocally no production of anger.

Refuting the argument that our assertions are similar

It might be argued, "Aren't the faults of saying that desire and so on are created from wind and so on found in your tradition also?"

> **Here, desire and so forth**
> **operate in dependence upon similar type**

158. **and upon the varieties of imprints.**
It does not follow that these faults are here.

It does not follow that these faults can be ascribed to the Buddhist tradition **here** because in such a tradition **desire and so forth operate in dependence upon similar type**—that is, the view of the transitory collection[248]—**and the varieties of imprints** formed from previous habituation with desire.

Refuting that desire and so forth are born from the elements

1. Refuting that they are created anew and did not exist previously
2. Refuting the maintenance of something already existing

Refuting that they are created anew and did not exist previously

The argument is, "Desire and so on are created from the elements because desire is created mostly from earth and water, anger mostly from fire and air, and confusion mostly from water and air."

The above refutes the phenomena of the elements.

The above reasoning that refutes desire and so on being created from wind and so on also **refutes** that desire and so on are **the phenomena**—that is, the results—**of the elements**, because wind, bile, and phlegm are the entities of air, fire, and water, respectively. This is according to Śākyabuddhi.

Refuting the maintenance of something already existing

1. Refuting that they are created by a previous type
2. Refuting the claim that the assertion is contradictory
3. Refuting the claim of an absurd consequence

Refuting that they are created by previous type

Being a support was also refuted.

Desire and so on also do not depend upon the elements because the already existing desire and so on depending upon the elements as a **support was also refuted** by the reasoning found in the lines, "It does not exist as a support for existing and not existing" (2.63).

Refuting the claim that the assertion is contradictory

It could be argued, "Generally, if support and supported are refuted, would it not be contradictory to claim that element evolutes[249] abide in dependence upon the elements?"

> 159. **White and so on do not depend**
> **upon earth and so on.**

Element evolutes such as **white and so on do not depend upon earth and so on** in the manner of something already existing being maintained, because such a support maintaining an existence is impossible.

"Then what does it mean to say that the element evolutes depend upon the elements?"

> **The expression "dependence" means cause**
> 160. **or, alternatively, abiding inseparably from its support.**
> **Other than that, it is not correct to be a support.**

The meaning of **the expression** that form **depends** upon those elements is not that there is the maintaining of something already existing; **it means** that if previously existing elements were **the cause** of form, **or alternatively**, if the form **is inseparable**—that is, indistinguishable—**from** those elements as **its support** and exist simultaneously, in that it *abides* with no difference, then the form depends upon the elements. **Other than** being cause and result, or having no difference, **it is not correct** to say that form depends upon the **support** of elements.

> **"As with the potential for drunkenness,**
> **likewise, there is separation."**
> 161. **The potential is not intrinsically separate.**
> **The entity would also be destroyed.**
> **If the support remains complete,**
> **supported will not be destroyed.**

It could be argued, "**Just as** there is a dependence in which there is separation, as with alcohol, for example, where **the potential** of alcohol **to induce drunkenness and so on** can be eliminated without eliminating the alcohol, **likewise**, elements and element evolutes have a dependency in which **there is separation**."

The potential to induce drunkenness is not ultimately dependent upon the alcohol because it **is not intrinsically separate** from the phenomenon of alcohol. This is because if the potential for drunkenness within alcohol is destroyed, **the entity** of alcohol **would also be destroyed**, and **if the support** of alcohol **remains complete, the supported** potential **will not be destroyed.**[250]

> **"Is this not similar?"**
> 162. **By perceiving them as of distinct appearance,**
> **the elements and the mind are distinct.**

"Like alcohol and its alcoholic potential, **isn't it similar** that the elements and mind are of one entity?"

The elements and the mind are not inseparable because they **are** substantially **distinct**. This is because an unmistaken consciousness possessed of their **distinct appearances perceives them as** being substantially distinct.

Refuting the claim of an absurd consequence

> **For as long as the body changes,**
> 163. **entities of mind would be similar,**
> **as with form and so on.**
> **How could the conceptual mind be**
> **under the force of its object?**

If the elements or the body are the support that maintains the abiding of the mind, then it follows that **for as long as the body changes** under various circumstances, then totally **similar entities**—that is, aspects—**of** the conceptual **mind would be** produced, because the body is the support that maintains the mind, and that mind is consciousness. For example, as long as the body undergoes no change, its **form and so on**, which depend on that body, are **similarly** produced.

It might be argued that there is no pervasion because "Although they share similar supports, the conceptual mind takes on different aspects by the force of its apprehended object."

How could the conceptual mind be under the force of its apprehended **object?** It could not, because it engages merely by its own volition.

Establishing conducive causes

> **Therefore, from some, some will be created.**
> **Without depending upon the body,**
> **some consciousnesses become causes for**
> 164. **awakening the imprints of some.**

Therefore, from some previous instants of desire and so on, **some** subsequent instants of desire and so on **will be created**, because **without depending upon the body, some** previous **consciousnesses become causes for awakening the imprints of some** subsequent moments of consciousnesses.

Establishing by the reason of the material cause being of similar type

1. Because it is consciousness, a conducive-type material cause is established
2. Refuting the argument of the Sāṃkhya that establishes an already existing result

Because it is consciousness, a conducive-type material cause is established

> **Because that which is not consciousness**
> **is not the material cause of consciousness,**
> **it is established also.**

Any instance of awareness that has just been produced will have an instance of awareness that precedes it because it itself is awareness.[251] This pervades **because** the next lines state, "**that which is not consciousness is not the material cause of consciousness**," and by this, past life **is established**. The word "**also**" that follows has been glossed as an inclusive term meaning that if consciousness were created from a permanent body and so on, it would follow that all former and subsequent moments of consciousness would be created simultaneously. Therefore the above is "established" by this consequence "also." However, it actually means that it is not only established by the reasoning of becoming manifest through training but by this reasoning also.

Refuting the argument of the Sāṃkhya that establishes an already existing result

165. **If that is asserted because all entities**
possess the potential for consciousness,
then a hundred elephants could exist
on the tip of a blade of grass and so on,
remaining unseen in the past.

166. **Who apart from the cattle-like Sāṃkhya**
could make such an embarrassing claim?
If you took the causes apart a hundred times,
those entities should appear, but such entities
167. **do not appear at such past times.**
By what means do they exist?

The Sāṃkhya assert, "**All entities**, such as grass and so on, **possess consciousness** in the entity of **potential.** Therefore we can **assert** that a consciousness that has just been produced will have a consciousness preceding it."

Who apart from the cattle-like Sāṃkhya could make such an embarrassing claim that a hundred elephants and consciousness **could exist on the tip of a blade of grass and so on**—that is, within the elements—**unseen in the past?** No one could, because such a claim is damaged by the reasoning of nonapprehension of that which should appear. How? **By what means** can a hundred elephants and consciousness **exist** in **causes** such as grass and the elements? They cannot; **if you took** them **apart a hundred times, those entities** of a hundred elephants and consciousness **should appear** if they were there, **but such entities do not appear at such past times.**

The absurd consequences of the assertion that saṃsāra does not exist

1. The consequence that there would be no certainty of coming into existence with desire and so on
2. The consequence that there would be no certainty of desire and so on being produced on occasion (2.175)

The consequence that there would be no certainty of coming into existence with desire and so on

1. Presenting the consequence
2. Refuting that there is no pervasion

Presenting the consequence

> **Arising from that not previously existing,**
> **there is the consequence of**
> **no certainty of desire and so on.**

The consequence arises that for an ordinary being as soon as they are born, there would be **no certainty** that they would possess **desire and so on** because that being, as well as the desire, **would be newly arisen**[252] **from having no previously existing** similar type.

Refuting that there is no pervasion

1. Refuting uncertainty by way of the cause
2. Refuting uncertainty by way of example

Refuting uncertainty by way of the cause

1. The absurd consequence of desire arising from the entity of the elements
2. The consequence that if there were differences in the elements, an absence of desire would be possible
3. Refuting other responses that attempt to establish there will be no absence of desire

The absurd consequence of desire arising from the entity of the elements

> 168. **"Not being beyond the nature of the elements,**
> **all are endowed with desire and so on."**
> **Then all would have similar desire.**

It could be argued, "**All** living beings **are endowed with desire and so on** because they **do not** exist **beyond the nature of the elements**, which are the direct cause of desire."

In that case, **it would follow that all** living beings would have **similar** amounts of **desire** because the elements, as the direct cause of that desire, exist undifferentiated.

The consequence that if there were differences in the elements, an absence of desire would be possible

> **"It is from the differences in the strengths of the elements."**
> 169. **Though there are no such differences**
> **in living beings from the elements,**
> **the support of such differences,**
> **whatever there are, will increase and decline.**
> **Likewise, desire will cease to exist.**

In response it might be argued, "The reason is not established, because **from the differences in the strengths** of **various elements**, beings are born with different strengths of desire and so on."

In that case, **living beings** that are created **from these elements** would possess differences—such as being a mere living being, a large living being, and a very large living being—because differences in the strengths of desire are created from corresponding differences in the strengths of the elements.[253] **Though there are no such differences,** it follows that **whatever** elements ordinary beings have in their continuum, they **will increase and decline**, and because of that reason, finally, the continuum of those elements will come to an end. **Likewise,** that **desire** previously existing within those living beings **will cease to exist** in certain subsequent differences within those beings, because the elements are **the support for the differences** in increase and decline of desire in their continuum.

Refuting other responses that attempt to establish there will be no absence of desire

1. Refuting that there will be no absence of desire, by way of the cause
2. Refuting that there will be no absence of desire, by way of example

Refuting that there will be no absence of desire, by way of the cause

> 170. **"Though desire and so on are distinct,**
> **the causes, being of similar nature,**
> **will not be negated, and so this is not the case."**

Being causes of similar entities,
all would have similar desire.

A response to the above might be, "There is **distinct** increase and decline in **desire and so on** because of the increase and decline in the elements. **However, it is not the case** that an ordinary being will be free from desire, because the **causes** of desire and so on, **being of similar nature, will not be negated.**"

Then it would follow that **all** beings **would have similar** levels of **desire** and so on **because** as mere elements, there are no differences in **the causes** creating **similar entities** of desire and so on.

171. **Within the cognition "cow,"**
arising from the similar nature,
and alternatively, here too, within earth and so on,
there are no levels of difference in beings.

This pervades because, within **the** subject **cognition** apprehending **"cow," arising from the similar nature** of cow as the cause, there are no distinct thoughts of "cow," "large cow," and "very large cow." **Alternatively, here too**, when the Cārvāka[254] asserts that beings are born **within earth and so on, there are no levels of difference in beings**, such as being, superior being, and so on.

Refuting that there will be no absence of desire, by way of example

172. **"Though there are different levels of heat,**
there will never be fire without heat.
It is similar here."
It is refuted that fire is separate from heat.

It could be argued, "The sensation of **heat** from fire **has different levels** of intensity, **but there will never be fire without heat. Similarly, here**, an increase and decline in the elements bring the increase and decline of desire and so on, but it is not possible for desire to disappear completely. Therefore the pervasion expressed in the line 'will cease to exist' is not certain."

There is no fault because my reasoning contains the difference of increase and decline being a separate entity. Therefore that cannot be applied to fire and heat because **it is refuted** by valid cognition **that fire is a separate** entity **from heat.**

173. **That which is a quality and is other**
possesses the various features
and will cease to exist in some changes of that,
as with white and so on.

Therefore it is possible for the continuum of desire and so on to be cut within the elements, because desire and so on increase and decline from the increase and decline in the elements by way of being separate entities from the elements. This pervades because **that which is a quality and is other** than the quality-possessor **possesses the various features** coming from the increase and decline within the quality possessor **and will cease to exist in some** subsequent **changes of that** quality possessor. For example, the qualities of **white and so on**, which are separate entities from the elements, will cease to exist in certain subsequent changes of the elements.

Refuting uncertainty by way of example

It could be argued, "Form and so on are newly produced from the elements and yet certainly exist within the elements. Likewise, desire and so on are the same. Therefore there is no certainty to the above consequence (2.167) of being newly produced."

174. **Unlike form and so on, there is no certainty,**
as they are inseparable from the elements.
"Isn't that the same?"
That is not so. Desire and so on
would be created intrinsically together.

There is no certainty that desire and so on exist within the elements **like form and so on,** because form and so on **are** indistinguishably **inseparable from the elements** whereas desire and so on can be separated from the elements.

As a response, "**Isn't that** inseparability of form with the elements **the same** for desire and so on?"

That is not so. If it were, it would follow that the elements and **desire and so on would** in every aspect **be created intrinsically together** because they would be indistinguishable phenomena. There would be such a fault.

175. **Because of being an object of thought,**
there is no certainty even with objects.

It might be argued, "Isn't it the case that desire and so on depends upon the condition of external objects. Therefore it arises, but on some occasions it does not arise?"

There is no certainty that **even** external **objects** are responsible for the occasional arising of desire and so on, **because** even when there are no external objects, one's own **thought** will create **an object**, and desire will be produced.

The consequence that there would be no certainty of desire and so on being produced on occasion

> **Lacking a similar-status cause,**
> **there would be no certainty of desire and so on.**
> 176. **Alternatively, because the cause is close by,**
> **all such cognitions would be produced at all times.**

It would follow that in some people **there would be no certainty** that **desire and so on** would arise because desire and so on would be without cause. This is so because they would **lack a similar-status cause**—that is, a similar-type cause.

Alternatively, if you assert that the elements are the direct cause, then it would follow that **all such cognitions** involving desire and so on **would be produced at all times** in all living beings, **because the** direct **cause** of that in all beings—that is, the elements—**is** constantly **close by**. You have to accept the reasoning.

Establishing the characteristics: impermanence and so on

1. Impermanent
2. Suffering
3. Not self
4. Empty

Impermanent

> **Because they are occasionally observed,**
> **they are impermanent.**
> 177. **Because they are the support of faults**
> **and under the control of the cause,**
> **they are suffering.**

These appropriated aggregates, which are an illustration of the truth of suffering, **are impermanent because they are occasionally observed** as arising.

Suffering

The appropriated aggregates **are suffering because they are the support of faults** such as clinging to self and belonging to self, as well as the support of birth, old age, sickness, and death. Moreover, they are suffering because they have become **under the control of** grasping, which is **the cause.**

Not self

> **They are not the self and also not governed by the self,**
> **which is not the cause and not the ruler.**
> **How could something permanent create?**
> 178. **Therefore many could not be produced**
> **from one, at distinct times.**

The appropriated aggregates are **not the self** because they are of characteristics not conducive to a self. This is because they are under the control of many types of impermanence.

Empty

The appropriated aggregates are **also not** "mine" and **governed by the self,** because the self **is not the ruler** of the aggregates. This is because the self is **not the cause** of the aggregates, as that self is permanent. This pervades because **how could something permanent create** a result? **Therefore many** results **at distinct times**—that is, in sequence—**could not be produced from a single** permanent self because that which is permanent does not create results.

> **If other causes are assembled,**
> **a result is not produced,**
> 179. **other causes can be inferred.**
> **That does not exist with such permanent phenomena.**

Furthermore, permanent phenomena, such as the self, cannot possibly be the cause of suffering and so on, because even if the other causes of suffering are assembled, a reversal of suffering brought about by the absence of **such permanent phenomena,** such as the self, **does not exist.** This pervades because **if other**

causes of certain results **are assembled**, and **a result is not produced,** because of the absence of something, **other causes**, separate from that assembly, **can be inferred.** There is no other possibility.

41. The Origin of Suffering

Explaining the origin of suffering by determining suffering and its cause

1. Establishing that suffering has a cause
2. Refuting conceptions of other causes
3. Teaching that craving is the main cause

Here, the *Ornament* commentaries [of Prajñākaragupta and Yamāri] and those who follow them divide each of the remaining three truths into four sections. Devendrabuddhi says that by explaining the cause aspect of the truth of the origin of suffering, the cessation aspect of the truth of cessation, and the path aspect of the truth of the path, the remaining three aspects of each of the three truths are established.[255] Of these two ways of explanation, the latter is followed here.

Establishing that suffering has a cause

1. Establishing the cause by its periodic occurrence
2. Refuting the reasoning that there is no cause

Establishing the cause by its periodic occurrence

Because it is occasional,
suffering is established as having a cause.
180. **Without cause, it would not depend upon other**
and be permanently in existence or not exist at all.

Because it occasionally occurs as birth, **suffering is established as having a cause.** This pervades because if it were without cause, it would either **be permanently in existence or not exist at all** and be pervaded by having no occasional occurrence. This is because if something were **without cause,** it **would not depend upon other** conditions.

Refuting the reasoning that there is no cause

> **"Just as the sharpness of thorns and so on**
> **have no cause,**
> 181. **similarly this has no cause."**
> **Thus some have said.**

Some—that is, those who propound the entity itself as a cause—**say that just as the sharpness of thorns and so on have no cause, similarly this** suffering arises with **no cause.**

> **Whenever, by a particular existent,**
> **there is production**
> **or, by change, there is change,**
> 182. **that is said to be the cause of that.**
> **That also exists with those.**

This is incorrect. The sharpness of thorns and so on and the truth of suffering **also exist with** causes, because the concomitance and nonconcomitance of a preceding existent lies within **them.** This pervades because **whenever** there is **a particular** preceding **existent** in dependence on which a subsequent existent **is produced, or** wherever a preceding existent **changes**—that is, is reversed—and **there is** a subsequent **change** by reversal, such a preceding existent with its subsequent concomitance and nonconcomitance **is said to be the cause of that** subsequent existent.[256]

It might be argued, "But then it follows that the tangibility that creates the objective condition for a visual consciousness[257] becomes a cause for that consciousness because it has a concomitance and nonconcomitance with the subsequent entity of a visual consciousness."

> **Because tangibility is a cause for the form,**
> **it becomes a reason for seeing.**

The **tangibility** that is a cause of the objective condition for a visual consciousness **becomes a reason for seeing**—that is, an indirect cause for the visual consciousness—**because it is a cause for the form** that becomes an objective condition for a visual consciousness.

Refuting conceptions of other causes

> 183. **Permanence is refuted,**
> **and from Īśvara and so on it is impossible,**
> **because they have no ability.**

Thus suffering is established as having causes. Moreover, it is not produced from unconducive causes because **it cannot possibly be** produced **from Īśvara**, a permanent universal, **and so on** because generally **permanence is refuted** as being a cause. This is **because they have no ability** to create a result.

Teaching that craving is the main cause

1. Teaching that craving is the main condition
2. Establishing that by scripture
3. The reason for only explaining craving

Teaching that craving is the main condition

> **Desire for existence is the cause.**
> 184. **The types of objects humans hold**
> **are created by the thought to possess them.**

Suffering is not without cause and does not have permanent causes. Therefore the craving, which goes by the name of the afflicted origin of suffering, and which is the **desire for** body and possessions categorized as samsaric **existence, is the cause** of suffering. Why? With sentient beings, as illustrated by **human beings**, whatever **types of objects** they **hold** to, or take, no matter how small, all **are created by the thought**—that is, the craving—that wishes **to possess them.**[258]

It might be argued, "If desire for existence is the cause of suffering, then this contradicts the sūtra that says, 'What is the ārya truth of the origin of suffering? Craving is that which will bring about existence, possessed of a joyful desire, and an evident joy for this and that. In that way, there is the craving of desire, craving for existence, and craving born of fear,' thereby listing the three cravings as the cause of suffering."

> **That is craving for existence.**
> **Because beings desire to gain happiness**
> 185. **and to leave behind suffering,**
> **these are asserted as craving of desire**
> **and craving born of fear.**

There is no contradiction. **That** verse **is** describing **craving for existence. Because beings desire to gain happiness** and desire **to leave behind suffering,** they engage in the craving that takes and discards. **These are asserted as craving of desire and craving born of fear,** respectively. Thus there is a difference between the general and the specific.

This is Devendrabuddhi's explanation. Śākyabuddhi says that striving for the desire realm is craving of desire, craving for the two higher realms is craving for existence, and that the desire to leave behind suffering is craving born of fear. However, this is mixing in Abhidharma tenets and is not the intention of this work.

> **From the cause of holding to a self,**
> **not happiness is regarded as happiness,**
> 186. **and all is engaged.**
> **Therefore craving is the support for existence.**

Therefore, for an ordinary being, these three **cravings** are the **supports for** birth in **existence,** saṃsāra. This is because **from** the craving **of holding to a self,** as **the cause,** afflicted happiness, which is **not happiness, is regarded as happiness, and** with the craving for happiness, ordinary beings **engage** with and become attached to **all** kinds of good and bad things.

Establishing that by scripture

1. Actual
2. Refuting arguments

Actual

> **Those without desire will not see birth.**
> **Thus the masters have said.**

The masters have said that **those without desire will not see birth** and that therefore desire is the cause of birth. The master Vasubandhu said, "Why? Because those persons without desire will not see birth. Therefore birth has its cause, which is desire."[259]

Refuting arguments

187. **"Because desire is not seen in those without bodies,**
desire arises from the body also."
Because the reason is accepted, we agree.
That was a refutation of the material cause.

The Cārvāka school might respond, "In that case it follows that **desire arises from the body also because**, similarly, **desire is not seen in those without bodies.**"

We agree that a previous body is the mere cause of subsequent desire **because it is accepted to be the reason**—that is, the coordinating cause—for subsequent desire.

They continue, "Then this contradicts your previous refutation of the body as a cause for desire."

It was not refuted that the previous body was a mere cause of subsequent desire because **that** refutation **was** just **a refutation of** the body as **the material cause** of subsequent desire.

188. **If they follow this reasoning,**
they damage their own assertions.

If they follow this reasoning that declares those without desire will not see birth and therefore desire is the cause of birth, then **they**, the Cārvāka, **damage their own assertions** that there are no past and future lives, because while previously saying that there are no past and future lives, subsequently they declare that a previous body and previous desire are the causes of subsequent desire and a subsequent body.

"Because desire is seen in birth,
it occurs together with birth."
189. **Because it is created from a similar status**
preceding existence is established.

It could be further argued, "Desire is not the cause of the body because **it occurs together with birth**—that is, a body. This is **because desire is seen in birth**, in a body, but not seen before."

In that case, it follows that the body is not the cause of desire because it occurs together with desire. If you agree, as desire is not without a cause and is not created by a cause that is other, such as the body, it can be established that it is created from a similar-type cause. Therefore it follows that for the first moment of desire of this life, a similar type **is established** as existing **preceding** that moment, **because it is created from a similar status**, a similar-type cause.

The reason for only explaining craving

It could be asked, "If craving is the only cause of suffering, this contradicts the quote 'Know that it arises from not knowing, karma, and craving,'[260] which mentions three causes of birth."

> **Not knowing is the cause of existence**
> **but is not mentioned. Craving is taught**
> **because it precipitates the continuity and is immediate.**
> 190. **Karma also is not, because although it exists,**
> **there is no certainty of existence.**

Not knowing—that is, ignorance—**is the cause of** future-birth **existence, but** here it **is not mentioned** because there is no certainty that it will precipitate a future existence. The reason that [the eighth link] **craving is taught** here as being the cause is that **it precipitates the continuity** of the aggregates into a future existence; in other words, it impels [the ninth link] appropriation of those aggregates **and is** the **immediately** preceding cause of birth.

Karma also is not suitable to be presented here as the cause **because although it exists**, if it lacks the moisture of craving, **there** can **be no certainty of** the **existence** of birth.

Therefore these verses establish that, generally, suffering has causes, and having refuted unconducive causes, they establish conducive causes. These causes are ignorance, craving, and karma, of which two carry no certainty of creating suffering in the immediate next birth. Therefore, in this context, craving, as the main accomplishing karma, is established to be the cause of suffering.

42. The Cessation of Suffering

Explaining the truth of cessation by determining the cessation of suffering

1. Establishing freedom from suffering
2. Discarding arguments about those obtaining liberation
3. Discarding arguments about the ways to obtain freedom
4. Refuting that the self obtains freedom from captivity

Establishing freedom from suffering

> **That is not eternal,**
> **because obstruction and so on**
> **of that cause is possible.**

That craving, as the main cause of suffering, **is not eternal** because it has ignorance as its cause. This pervades **because obstruction of that cause** of ignorance and for its conditions to be incomplete, **and so on, is possible.**

Discarding arguments about those obtaining liberation

> 191. **"Because of saṃsāra there is no liberation."**
> **Not so, because we agree**
> **and do not accept the reason.**

Thinking of a substantially existing self, some declare, "It follows that living beings **will not attain liberation** from saṃsāra **because** they are the possessors **of saṃsāra**, just as fire will never be free of heat."

This consequence **does not** harm the Buddhists because they can give, without contradiction, the answer of **agreeing** to the reasoning **and not accepting the reason.** This is because there is no such self.

So how are saṃsāra and freedom presented? *Saṃsāra* means engaging solely with these aggregates of suffering together with their cause. *Liberation* is the nonarising of the aggregates because the causes have been abandoned.

It could be argued, "It follows that a person does not make efforts to abandon the causes in order to attain liberation because there is no self that circles in saṃsāra and no self that gains liberation."

As long as attachment to the self is not destroyed
and they are tormented by suffering,
192. **for that long is there the superimposition of suffering**
and no abiding within the nature.
Though there is no one liberated,
to destroy wrong superimposition, effort is made.

On ultimate terms, the above is accepted, and on conventionally designated terms, the reasoning is not established. In terms of conventional designation, such a person does make efforts to abandon the causes in order to attain liberation because for **as long as attachment to the self is not destroyed and** for as long as **those** aggregates, which possess that attachment to self, **are tormented by suffering,** then **for that long** will **there be the superimposition of** a self that is **suffering, and** there will be **no abiding within the nature** of happiness. Therefore in conventionally designated terms the self circles in saṃsāra, and **although** in reality **there is no** self that **is liberated, to destroy** the **wrong superimposition** of self and belonging to self, the aggregates **make effort,** and so it is conventionally designated that the self makes effort.

The essential point is this. Except for the Buddhist Sāṃmitīya[261] school, our three tenet holders who accept true existence[262] assert that self, person, sentient being, and being have no substantial existence, and therefore, in reality, its bondage and liberation cannot be asserted. However, the aggregates do have a substantial existence, and so their bondage and liberation is asserted in reality. In conventionally designated terms, the self engages in bondage and liberation because a self that suffers is superimposed onto the suffering aggregates, and with regard to the aggregates gaining liberation from suffering, there is the superimposition of a self gaining liberation from suffering.

For the Sāṃmitīya and the non-Buddhists, the self does have substantial existence, and therefore its bondage and liberation is asserted as a reality. Dividing aggregates and self into substantial and nonsubstantial existences, presenting on a conventionally designated level the actions of the aggregates and their experience of ripening as the actions of self and the experience of self, is necessary in many contexts.

Discarding arguments about the ways to obtain freedom

1. Refuting the argument that those free of desire do not abide in saṃsāra
2. Refuting the argument that there is no rebirth on the first path of the āryas

Refuting the argument that those free of desire do not abide in saṃsāra

1. The two causes of abiding for those free of desire
2. Refuting arguments on the meaning of those causes
3. Refuting arguments on the meaning of abiding

The two causes of abiding for those free of desire

193. **Abiding free of desire**
is by compassion or by karma.
They wish not to reverse casting karma.

Those who are **free of desire** possess, for the time being, causes to **abide** in saṃsāra, of which there are two. The Great Vehicle ārya being abides in saṃsāra **by compassion,** and the Lower Vehicle arhat abides in saṃsāra **by** the force of **karma** because, for the time being, **they wish not to reverse** the aggregates of this life **cast** by previous **karma.** This is expressed in the *Collection of Verses:*[263]

I have no liking for death
and no fondness for life.
Like the elephant of Indra,
I bide my time.

Refuting arguments on the meaning of those causes

1. Refuting arguments on the meaning of karma
2. Refuting arguments on the meaning of compassion

Refuting arguments on the meaning of karma

It could be argued, "If those who are freed from desire abide in saṃsāra by the force of karma, then their karma will connect them to other births also."

> **Karma transcending the cravings of saṃsāra**
> 194. **has no power to cast another**
> **because the coordinating causes have ceased.**

The **karma** in the continuum of those free of desire who have **transcended the cravings of saṃsāra has no power to cast another** existence **because the coordinating causes** of wrong views and craving **have ceased.**

Refuting arguments on the meaning of compassion

It could be argued, "Those freed from desire have a view of 'sentient beings' because they have compassion."

> **In those who know suffering, adversity is not there,**
> **and by engaging in previous formative factors,**
> 195. **the compassion produced is a phenomenon and entity**
> **not connected to sentient beings.**

The compassion produced in the continuums of **those who know** directly the impermanence, suffering, emptiness, and no-self of the truth of **suffering is not** a view of self that has a **connection with sentient beings** because the **adverse** circumstances of anger and so forth are **not there**, and such compassion is **a phenomenon** that is an **entity** of mind that **engages in** the integrated and **previous formative factors** of the conducive circumstances of compassion.

It could be further argued, "Those who are freed from desire become those with desire because they have compassion."

> **Desire comes from superimposing another nature**
> **onto phenomena not of that nature.**
> 196. **From merely knowing the continuums**
> **of suffering, compassion is created.**

The compassion of those freed from desire is not desire because such **compassion** is without superimposition of any erroneous aspects onto the object and **is created from merely knowing the continuums of suffering** of others. This pervades because **desire comes from superimposing** permanence and so on **onto** the **phenomena** of aggregates, which are **not of** the **nature** of permanence, happiness, self, and belonging to self and which are **other** than the **nature** of those phenomena.

It might also be argued, "When harm is done to those who are objects of their compassion, those who are freed from desire will get angry, because they have compassion."

> **Ignorance is the root of faults**
> **and apprehends "sentient beings."**
> 197. **This does not exist and there is no anger**
> **arising from the cause of the fault.**
> **Therefore compassion is asserted as having no fault.**

Those freed from desire have **no anger arising from the cause of the fault,** which is harm being done to objects of their compassion, because **ignorance is the root of faults,** such as anger, **and apprehends "sentient beings,"** but **this does not exist. Therefore** the **compassion** of those free from desire **is asserted as having no fault** of anger because it does not arise from the cause that is ignorance.

Refuting arguments on the meaning of abiding

1. Refuting arguments on abiding by the force of karma
2. Refuting arguments on abiding by the force of compassion

Refuting arguments on abiding by the force of karma

It could be argued, "If those free of desire possess a body cast by karma, then they are not free of saṃsāra."

> **They are not unfree. The forming has finished,**
> **and there is no connection to another existence.**
> 198. **If the power of formative karma is not finished,**
> **those who abide are without fault.**

Abiding by the force of karma in those free of desire **is not** one that is **unfree** of saṃsāra, because the power of **the** previous karma **forming** the aggregates of this life **has finished.** The body will end, **and** because there is no craving, **there will be no connection to another** future **existence. Those** who are free of desire, **abiding** in saṃsāra, even **if the power of formative karma is not finished,** they are not captive in saṃsāra because they possess **no faults** of saṃsāra.

Refuting arguments on abiding by the force of compassion

It might be asked, "Why do those who are free of desire not stay a long time to work for sentient beings with their compassion?"

Because their compassion is inferior,
there are no great efforts to remain.
199. **Those possessing great compassion**
remain for the sake of others.

Those such as the śrāvaka and the pratyekabuddha **do not make great efforts to remain** a long time for the sake of sentient beings **because their compassion is inferior. Those** Great Vehicle āryas **remain** for all time **for the sake of other** sentient beings because **they possess the great compassion**, which is the cause to remain uninterruptedly for the sake of others.

Refuting the argument that there is no rebirth on the first path of the āryas

"Lacking the view of the transitory collection,
there will be no saṃsāra on the first path."
200. **They have not abandoned the innate view.**
If abandoned, how would there be a future existence?

It will be argued, "If the view of the transitory collection is the cause of samsaric existence, then **on the** path of seeing, which is the **first path** of the āryas, **there will be no saṃsāra because it lacks the view of the transitory collection."**

It is not the case that a stream enterer does not take birth into a future existence because of there being no view of the transitory collection. This is because, although they have left behind the imputed view of the transitory collection, **they have not abandoned the innate view. If** they had **abandoned** it, **how would there be a future existence?** There would not be because they would have abandoned the innate view.

It is asked, "Why have they not left behind the innate view of the transitory collection?"

Wishing "May I be happy; may I not suffer,"
201. **the thought of "I" is an innate view**
regarding sentient beings.

They have not abandoned the innate view because **they have the wish "May I be happy; may I not suffer."** This pervades because **the thought of "I"** at that time **is an innate view regarding sentient beings.**

Not seeing "I," there is no attachment to self,
202. **and with no craving for a self,**
there would be no wishing for
and no pursuit of happiness.

Moreover, it would follow that a stream enterer would not deliberately pursue happiness by wishing for it, because they would have abandoned the innate view of the transitory collection. This pervades because **not seeing "I," there is no attachment** at all **to self, and with no craving for a self, there would be no wishing for and no pursuit of happiness.**

Refuting that the self obtains freedom from captivity

1. Refuting that it is accomplished by the permanent self
2. Refuting that it is accomplished by the inexpressible self

Refuting that it is accomplished by the permanent self

It could be argued, "Sentient beings have a self that is the captive and the liberator because it is the self that is captured by the suffering of saṃsāra and the self that becomes free from that. For example, it is Devadatta[264] that is bound by chains and Devadatta that is freed from them."

The very cause that creates suffering is being bound.
How is that possible with permanence?
203. **The very cause that does not create suffering is freedom.**
How is that possible with permanence?
That not expressed as being impermanent
is not a cause of anything.

How is bondage **possible with a permanent** self? It is not possible because that self is not a cause of suffering. This pervades because **being bound** by suffering

is the very cause that creates suffering. Furthermore, **how is** freedom from suffering **possible with** a **permanent** self? It is not possible because that self is not a cause that will reverse suffering. That pervades because **freedom** from suffering **is the very cause that does not create**—that is, it reverses—**suffering.**

Why is the permanent self not the cause of the above two situations? **That** self **is not a cause of anything,** such as suffering, because it is **not expressed as being impermanent.**

Refuting that it is accomplished by the inexpressible self

The Buddhist Pudgalavādins say, "Captivity and freedom is not possible with a permanent self, but they are possible with a self that is inexpressible as either permanent or impermanent."

204. **That which is inexpressible**
also does not exist in any way as captive or free.
That whose nature is not disintegration,
the scholars have said to be permanent.
205. **Therefore abandon this embarrassing view**
and admit that it is permanent.

A self **that is inexpressible** as permanent or impermanent **also does not exist in any way as** that which is **captive or free,** because it is not a cause for the creating or the reversing of suffering. Such a self is permanent because it is not disintegrating. That pervades because any existence **whose nature is not disintegration, the scholars have said to be permanent.** The Pudgalavādins declare that the self is an entity that is neither permanent nor impermanent. **Therefore abandon this embarrassing view and admit that** this self **is permanent** because such a self is not impermanent.

43. The Truth of the Path

Explaining the truth of the path by determining the antidote to the view of self

1. The understanding of no-self is the antidote
2. Establishing that no-self is the antidote

The understanding of no-self is the antidote

1. Training in no-self brings about transformation
2. Refuting that transformation is gained only to be destroyed by the defilements
3. Refuting the proof that there is no transformation (2.215)

Training in no-self brings about transformation

> **From training in that path, as explained,**
> **comes transformation.**

The path of seeing no-self, **as** already **explained** in the section on the "Teacher" (2.281), is the path of the antidote to saṃsāra, because **from training in that path**, when the meditation is completed, the continuum of the mind that meditates, which is the support for the faults, is completely changed and takes on a **transformation** that is in the nature of understanding no-self.

Refuting that transformation is gained only to be destroyed by the defilements

1. The defilements have no power to destroy

2. Extensive explanation of the proof that the defilements have no power to destroy
3. Refuting arguments on the proof of contradicting modes of apprehension

The defilements have no power to destroy

> 206. **"Although there is transformation,**
> **like the path, the faults will arise."**
> **Not so, because they have no power.**

It could be argued, "**Although** it is possible for the mind possessed of faults to **transform** once into one of no faults, **the faults** of apprehending self and that belonging to self within the mind **will** again **arise**, just **like the path** arising in the mind possessed of faults."

In the mind that has been transformed by training in the path, the faults **will not** arise again **because** the faults **have no power** to arise again.

Extensive explanation of the proof that the defilements have no power to destroy

1. The defilements and the antidotes have contradicting modes of apprehension, and the antidote engages with reality
2. Because of the difference between the nature and the incidental, their power was not there previously
3. Even if they had power, the antidotes can arise without much effort
4. With three features, the antidotes cannot be reversed even with effort

The defilements and the antidotes have contradicting modes of apprehension, and the antidote engages with reality

> **The phenomenon of a consciousness apprehending an object**
> **apprehends in the way that it exists.**
> 207. **The nature of that existence**
> **is also the creator of this.**
> **This is the nature, and by conditions**
> **it deviates from this.**
> 208. **Reversing that depends upon conditions,**
> **like the unstable cognition of a snake.**

Why do they have no power? In this mind that has been transformed by meditation on the path, the faults of apprehending self and so on have no power to arise again. This is because, generally, in the Sautrāntika system, **the phenomenon**, or condition, **of an** unmistaken **consciousness apprehending an object** is that it **apprehends** an aspect corresponding to **the way that** object **exists.** Moreover, **the nature of that existence** that is the reality of the object **is also the creator of this** consciousness. **That nature** of such an unmistaken, object-possessing consciousness apprehending an object **exists** within the mind that has been transformed. **By** the incidental[265] **conditions** of the apprehending of a self, the mind **deviates from this** reality of the object, and **to reverse that** means **depending upon** the **condition** of a valid cognition that possesses the ability to harm the above. For example, **the cognition of** a rope as **a snake** is **unstable** in the sense that it is brought on by superficial conditions and can be removed.

Because of the difference between the nature and the incidental, their power was not there previously

> **The nature of mind is luminous,**
> **and the defilements are incidental.**
> 209. **They have no power previously or subsequently.**

The defilements **have no power** to **subsequently** harm a mind whose continuum, by training on the path, has become the very entity of that understanding of no-self. This is because even **previously**, when no-self was not understood, **they** had no power to harm the mind by way of its nature. The reason stands, because **the nature of mind is luminous**[266] **and the defilements are incidental.**

This verse teaches that previously, at the time of the mind being naturally pure (even though no-self had not been understood), the defilements had no power to harm the mind by way of its nature, and therefore later, at a time when the mind is free of the incidental defilements, they have no power to affect the mind incidentally. The explanation of "previously" as referring to "as soon as no-self was seen" does not bring out the meaning of the two lines beginning "The nature of mind is luminous."

Even if they had power, the antidotes can arise without much effort

> **Even if the power were there,**
> **they have no power to remain**

long within the entity,
210. **because it possesses the essential power to create**
that which adversely affects them,
like fire on wet earth.

Even if the power to create faults **were there**, the defilements **have no power to remain long within the entity** of the transformed continuum of mind, **because it possesses the essential power to create** the knowing of no-self, **which adversely affects** the defilements. **For example, fire** does not stay long **on wet earth**. This verse teaches that on the paths of training the abandonment attained by the worldly path can degenerate, but it is quickly restored.

With three features, the antidotes cannot be reversed even with effort

With no harm, the truth, and being in the nature,
wrong cognition may make effort,
211. **but it will not be reversed because the cognition**
holds firmly in that direction.

Because all harmful thoughts are pacified and its characteristic is one of happiness, it is a mind of **no harm**. Because it is a consciousness apprehending impermanence and so on, it abides in **the truth**, and because its training is complete, it is **in the nature** of comprehending no-self. In such a mind, **wrong cognition may make effort** to create faults, **but** that mind **will not be reversed because the cognition** itself **holds firmly in the direction of**—that is, is in the sphere of—**that** path of understanding no-self.

Refuting arguments on the proof of contradicting modes of apprehension

1. Merely a distinct mode of apprehension does not make for an antidote
2. Partial suppression does not make for an antidote
3. Therefore total uprooting is the antidote

Merely a distinct mode of apprehension does not make for an antidote

It might be argued, "If seeing no-self is an antidote to apprehending a self because it has an object and is in an aspect that is contradictory to apprehending a self, then desire and anger have contradicting objects and aspects and so they must be antidotes to each other."

Because they come from the same cause
and are entities that are causes and effects,
212. **desire and anger may be distinct,**
but they do not adversely affect each other.

Desire and anger are distinct modes of apprehension, but they **do not adversely affect each other because they come from the same cause**—apprehending a self—**and** they are also **entities that are causes and effects** of each other.

Partial suppression does not make for an antidote

It could be argued, "Are not love and so on mentioned as the antidote to anger and ugliness meditation as the antidote to desire and so on? Why is it that only the understanding of no-self is explained as being the antidote?"

Because love and so on do not contradict ignorance,
they do not completely destroy the great faults.
213. **All faults possess ignorance as their root,**
and that is the view of the transitory collection.

Love and so on that is focused upon sentient beings **does not completely destroy**—that is, uproot—**the great faults** because they **do not** possess modes of apprehension that **contradict ignorance** and therefore do not adversely affect it. This pervades because **all faults possess ignorance as their root**. The former reasoning stands because, furthermore, ignorance as the root of all faults **is the view of the transitory collection**, and the above do not possess modes of apprehension that contradict it.

Some from the Buddhist Vaibhāṣika school and others might say, "The view of the transitory collection is a wrong conception, but ignorance is merely the negation of knowing,[267] and therefore these two are not the same."

Because it is unconducive to knowing
and because it is a mental factor that apprehends,
214. **it focuses wrongly and is said to be ignorance.**
Any other is incorrect.
Those that contradict are explained here.

The assertion that ignorance is just the negation of knowing and is **other** than the view of the transitory collection **is not correct**, because focusing on the same object as the knowing that is wisdom, ignorance possesses an aspect that is wrongly engaged.[268] Moreover, focusing on the same object as the knowing that is wisdom, ignorance **focuses wrongly** in terms of its aspect. This is **because it is unconducive to** the **knowing** that is perfect knowledge[269] and is something to be negated. Generally, a mental factor has five features concomitant with a primary consciousness. Ignorance **is a mental factor** and therefore is a cognition **that apprehends** an object. The aspect taken by knowing and the aspect taken by ignorance upon that object are contradictory, and thus ignorance does not take an aspect of truth. Therefore **it is said to be ignorance**, having an entity of superimposing wrongly onto its apprehended object. The *Lamp of the Moon Sūtra*[270] states, "What is the absence of ignorance? It is the absence of superimposition upon phenomena exactly as they exist."

It might be argued, "This contradicts the statement that ignorance is concomitant with the view of the transitory collection because something cannot be concomitant with itself."

Those sūtras that state that these two are concomitant, presented by others as proof that ignorance and the view of the transitory collection are **contradictory**, do not establish that these two are contradictory, because ignorance takes aspects and the view of the transitory collection is one such aspect. Therefore **here it is explained** that they are concomitant.

Therefore total uprooting is the antidote

Because the view of emptiness
is contradictory to that,
215. **it is in complete contradiction**
to that nature and all faults.

So what antidote will completely destroy the faults? The path of **the view** that is the **emptiness** of self upon the aggregates **is in complete contradiction to that nature**—that is, the view of self—**and all** the **faults** of desire and so on that arise from it. Therefore that is the antidote, **because** the view of self has a mode of apprehension directly **contradicting that**, and the path of the view that is emptiness engages with the reality of the object.

Refuting the proof that there is no transformation

"They will not end. They are the nature of living beings,
like form and so on." This is not so. It is not established.
216. **Applied in the direction of the antidote,**
it is seen that these faults are reversed.

Some will argue, "No matter how much one trains in the antidotes, the faults **will not end** because **they are in the nature of living beings, just as form** is in the nature of that which possesses form, heat is in the nature of fire, **and so on.**"

It is not the case that the faults will not end because they are in the nature of the mind, because **it is not established** that they are in the nature of mind. This is because when the continuum of the mind is **applied in the direction of the antidote**—that is, the understanding of no-self—**it is** manifestly **seen that these faults are reversed.**

It could be further argued, "Gold and so on can be melted by fire, but when the fire is not present, the gold becomes solid again. Likewise, the faults can be eliminated at one time, but when the antidote is not there, they return."

Faults that have ceased
are not again produced, unlike solidity,
217. **because being the very entity of that,**
it is never absent.
As with ashes, there is no certainty.

In the continuum of mind in which the **faults have ceased** because of training in no-self, **unlike** gold gaining **solidity**, the faults **are not again produced** by the absence of the antidote, **because by** the continuum of mind **becoming the very entity of that** understanding-of-emptiness antidote, the antidote **is never absent.** Moreover, **as ashes** do not become wood again when fire is not present, **there is no certainty** that when the antidote is not present, the defilement will return.

44. The Antidote to the View of Self

Establishing that no-self is the antidote

1. Understanding no-self is the antidote to the view of self
2. Understanding no-self is the antidote to craving (2.258)
3. Other than that, there is no antidote to karma and body (2.273)

Understanding no-self is the antidote to the view of self

1. The view of self is the root of saṃsāra
2. Reasons why the view of self is the root of saṃsāra
3. Advice to uproot the view of self (2.256)

The view of self is the root of saṃsāra

Why is understanding no-self the antidote to saṃsāra? The root of saṃsāra is the view of self, and understanding no-self has a mode of apprehension that directly contradicts that.

> **Whoever sees the self**
> **constantly clings to it as "I."**
> 218. **With clinging comes craving for pleasure.**
> **With craving, faults are obscured and seen as qualities.**
> **Therefore there is complete craving,**
> **and belonging to me is taken as its accomplisher.**
> 219. **As long as there is manifest attachment to self,**
> **such a person will circle in saṃsāra.**

Why is the view of self the root of saṃsāra? The view of self is established as the root of saṃsāra because **whoever sees** the aggregates as **the self constantly clings to** and is attached to **that** self **as "I,"** and for **as long as there is manifest attachment to that self, such a person will circle in saṃsāra.** This is because **from that clinging** to self is born the **craving for pleasure,** and **from that craving,** the **faults** of belonging to that self **are obscured and seen** instead **as qualities. Therefore,** through the **complete craving** for that which "belongs to me," the apprehending of that **belonging to me** becomes strong, because it **is taken as the accomplisher** of the pleasure of self.

Reasons why the view of self is the root of saṃsāra

1. Teaching that the view of self is the root of faults
2. With the view of self, there is no freedom from attachment
3. Without freedom from attachment, there is circling in saṃsāra (2.254)

Teaching that the view of self is the root of faults

> **If there is self, there is identification of "others."**
> **From self and others, there is apprehending and aversion.**
> 220. **From the connection with them, all faults will arise.**

The view of self is the root of all faults, because **if** a person has the apprehension of **self, there is** the **identification of others** as "other." **From** the perspective of there being **self, there is apprehending**—that is, attachment—**and from** the perspective of there being **others, there is aversion. From the connection with them, all faults**—that is, anger, desire, envy, and miserliness—**will arise.**

With the view of self, there is no freedom from attachment[271]

1. The view of self creates both kinds of attachment
2. There is no other way to eliminate these two kinds of attachment

The view of self creates both kinds of attachment

> **Definitely attached to self, there is no freedom**
> **from attachment to that belonging to self.**
> 221. **There is no cause for the absence of attachment**
> **to that self without faults.**

For those apprehending a self who wish to be free from the attachment for that which belongs to that self, **there is no freedom from attachment to that belonging to self** because they are **definitely** possessed of the **attachment to self.** This reasoning stands because those apprehending a self do **not have the cause for the absence of attachment to that self** because they hold the self to possess the quality of being **without faults.**

There is no other way to eliminate these two kinds of attachment

1. There is no other way to abandon attachment to self
2. There is no other way to abandon attachment to that belonging to self

There is no other way to abandon attachment to self

1. Knowing that it possesses a fault has no power to uproot the conceived object
2. Knowing that it possesses a fault has no power to reverse the direct cause
3. The assertion regarding that possessed of faults is contradictory

Knowing that it possesses a fault has no power to uproot the conceived object

> **"Cannot attachment be seen as a fault?"**
> **What would be the benefit?**
> **"It will be abandoned."**
> 222. **Without uprooting the object of that,**
> **there is no power to abandon that.**

It might be argued, "Even though the self is regarded as having no fault, **cannot attachment** to that self **be seen as a fault?"**

We reply, "**What would be the benefit** of such a view?"

They reply, "**That** attachment to the self **will be abandoned.**"

That person who sees attachment to the self as being at fault **has no power to abandon that** attachment because **the** conceived **object of that** attachment to self, which is the self possessed of merit, **is not uprooted,** as it is seen as something of merit.

> **The abandonment of desire and aversion**
> **following on from qualities and faults and so on**

223. **is by not seeing those in the objects**
and not by any external approach.

This pervades because that attachment to self arises from seeing the self as having merit. Moreover, **desire** for an object **following on from** seeing its **qualities, aversion** for an object **following on from** seeing its **faults**, and likewise, envy, miserliness, **and so on, are abandoned by not seeing those** faults and qualities **in the objects and are not** abandoned **by any external approach**, like extracting a thorn.

Knowing that it possesses a fault has no power to reverse the direct cause

One is not attached by seeing attachment as having merit
but by seeing the phenomenon as having merit.
224. **With the cause complete,**
how will the result be reversed?

For those apprehending a self who see attachment to self as a fault, **how will the resultant** attachment to self **be reversed**? It cannot be, because they apprehend the self as being of merit, which is **the complete cause** of that attachment to self. Apprehending the self to be of merit is the cause of attachment to self because **one does not become attached** to self **by seeing** that **attachment** to self **as having merit. By seeing the phenomenon** self **as having merit** one becomes attached to self.

The assertion regarding that possessed of faults is contradictory

What faults do you see with attachment?
"It is the basis for suffering." That may be so,
225. **but there will be no freedom from attachment**
because it is seen as belonging to self,
like self, for example.

We could ask, "**What faults do you see with attachment** to self?"

The reply might be, "**It is the basis for suffering** and therefore should be eradicated."

That may be so, but this will not bring about **freedom from attachment because** although it is a basis for suffering, from one side **it is seen as belonging**

to self. For example, self is the basis of suffering, but because it is the cause for the cognition that apprehends a self, it will not bring about freedom from attachment.

> **"If it were not there,**
> **self would not be the cause of suffering."**
> **That also would be like that.**
> 226. **In that case, both would have no faults,**
> **and there would be no freedom from attachment to both.**

It could be argued, "It is not proven that self is a fault because **if** attachment to self and that belonging to self **were not there**, in the sense of accompanying it, the **self** alone **would not be the cause of suffering.**"

If that were so, **that** attachment to self and so on **would also be** free of faults, **like that** self, because without the accompaniment of the self, they alone would not be the causes of suffering. **In that case, there would be no freedom from attachment to both** self and attachment to self because **both would have no faults.**

There is no other way to abandon attachment to that belonging to self

1. It cannot be abandoned by meditation on particulars of suffering, such as the sense faculties
2. It cannot be abandoned by understanding that self and the sense faculties are separate (2.247)
3. It cannot be abandoned by turning away from suffering (2.249)
4. Refuting the assertion that the instruction to meditate on suffering is contradictory (2.252)

It cannot be abandoned by meditation on particulars of suffering, such as the sense faculties

1. The assertion
2. The refutation

The assertion

> **"Like a hand or leg seized by a snake,**
> **meditating on suffering will abandon them."**

"When **a hand or leg** is **seized by a snake**, meditating on the limb as the cause of suffering will negate attachment [to that belonging to self].[272] **Likewise,** although apprehending a self exists, **meditating on** attachment to self and that belonging to self as being the cause of **suffering will abandon them**. Therefore there is no pervasion with the line, 'Definitely attached to self'" (2.220).

The refutation

1. Refuting the example
2. Refuting the meaning

Refuting the example

> 227. **By destroying the cognition of belonging to self,**
> **it will be eradicated. With the reverse, it will not.**

Solely meditating on your limb bitten by a snake as being suffering does not abandon attachment. **By destroying the cognition of belonging to self, it will be eradicated.** However, while **the reverse** is present—that is, the cognition of belonging to self—**it will not** be eradicated.

Refuting the meaning

1. If there is apprehension of that belonging to self, there is no eradication
2. If there is eradication of that belonging to self, the self has no characteristics (2.234)
3. If there is apprehension of a self, that belonging to self will be created (2.235)
4. Efforts to meditate on suffering are meaningless (2.238)
5. If self has no faults, there are no objects of attachment to become free from (2.241)
6. Knowing that it has faults cannot abandon attachment (2.243)
7. There is no damage to the cause, and it will not be abandoned (2.246)

If there is apprehension of that belonging to self, there is no eradication

1. If there is apprehension of that belonging to self, there is no freedom from attachment
2. Refuting the proof of the destruction of apprehension of belonging to self

If there is apprehension of that belonging to self, there is no freedom from attachment

> **The sense faculties and so on**
> **are regarded as the support of that which is made use of.**
> 228. **How will there be freedom from attachment to that?**
> **By what will the cognition of self be reversed?**
> **Toward hair and so on cut from the body,**
> **the mind of giving them up will arise.**
> 229. **Toward others, a mind of attachment can arise.**
> **This everyone can know directly.**

For the person apprehending self who knows that the apprehending of that belonging to self is faulty, **how will they free** themselves **from attachment?** They cannot be free, because **by what will the cognition** holding that belonging to **self be reversed?** It will not be reversed, because that which belongs to self, such as **the sense faculties, are the support of that which is made use of** and thus are **regarded** as a cause beneficial to oneself. This pervades because **hair,** nails, **and so on cut from the body** are not held as causes benefitting oneself, and **the mind of giving them up will arise. Toward others,** such as hair still on the body held as causes benefitting oneself, **a mind of attachment can arise. This everyone can know directly.**

Refuting the proof of the destruction of apprehension of belonging to self

1. Refuting that it can be destroyed by meditating on suffering
2. Refuting that it can be destroyed because it creates suffering

Refuting that it can be destroyed by meditating on suffering

It could be argued, "By meditating on attachment to self and so on as suffering, the cognition of belonging to self can be eliminated. Therefore the reason expressed by the line 'By what will the cognition of self be reversed' (2.228) is not established."

> **The cognition of belonging to self**
> **comes from the connection of inherence and so on.**
> 230. **That connection will remain as it was.**
> **It may be seen, but this will not eliminate it.**

Even though inherence and so on does not exist,
that which affects is found in all.

That attachment to self and so on **may be seen** as suffering, **but** it follows that **this will not eliminate** the cognition of belonging to self, because **the cognition of belonging to self** within that attachment **comes from the connection of inherence and so on** with the self. **That connection** may be regarded as suffering, but it **will remain as it was** previously. You must accept the reasoning. This is a refutation of the Vaiśeṣika school.

The Sāṃkhya understood that that which is apprehended as belonging to self and the person that apprehends are one, and in that regard the cognition of belonging to self is produced. Although they are understood as one, they are asserted as being formed by inherence. That is not correct. It follows that there can be no production of the cognition of belonging to self toward form belonging to self because the connection of its **inherence** with the self **and so on**—that is, being regarded as one—**does not exist. Even though** it does not exist, you cannot make that assertion because **that** seen as **affecting** self **is found in all** external phenomena belonging to self.

Refuting that it can be destroyed because it creates suffering

231. **"Because it creates suffering, like the fingers,**
a cognition of belonging to self will not develop."
They are not solely suffering.

It will be argued, "A person who has gained liberation **will not develop a cognition of belonging to self** with regard to the sense faculties and so on, and will abandon it, **because** they see the sense faculties and so on as **creating suffering, like the fingers** of one who has been bitten by a snake. Therefore the reason indicated by the line 'By what will the cognition of self be reversed' (2.228) does not stand."

These sense faculties and so on **are not** to be seen as **solely** creators of **suffering** because it can be seen that they are the causes of temporary happiness also.

"Mostly it is like noxious food, for example."
232. **Attached to superior pleasures,**
they abandon attachment to that contrary.

Craving for superior pleasure,
they abandon lesser pleasures.

The response might be, "The sense faculties and so on are **mostly** seen as sole creators of suffering and are abandoned, in the same way that **noxious food** is mostly regarded as creating suffering and abandoned, **for example.**"

Both the example and what it illustrates are faulty. When those who have these thoughts of accepting and abandoning come across **superior** food, **they are attached to its pleasure and** therefore **have no attachment to** noxious food, which is **contrary with that.** Their **craving for superior pleasure** means that **they abandon lesser pleasures.**

233. **With no such thoughts, and attached to self,**
they will partake as they find it.
Not finding a woman,
they engage in lustful acts with animals.

With no such thoughts of accepting and abandoning, **because of their attachment to self, they will partake** of noxious food and so on **exactly as they find it**, because they have no thoughts of accepting and abandoning and are attached to the mere pleasure of food. For example, those filled with desire, **if they do not find a woman, will engage in lustful acts with animals.**

If there is eradication of that belonging to self, the self has no characteristics

234. **The self that is asserted,**[273]
how can it be disintegrating?
Reversed from being the support
of experience, designation, and qualities,
235. **how can it be asserted and conceived?**
This is not the nature of that conceived.

It follows that the self while in saṃsāra must be **disintegrating** because, from previously possessing that belonging to self, it will progress to a complete absence of that belonging to self. You cannot agree with this reasoning because **how can the self that is asserted** as existing within those traditions **be disintegrating?** It cannot. When that self is liberated, **how can it be** the self that is **asserted and conceived** by those who apprehend such a self? It cannot, because you assert that it is **reversed from being the support of** all **experience, designation, and qualities**, such as wisdom. This pervades because **this is not the nature of that** self **conceived** by those who apprehend such a self, in which experience and so on has been reversed.

If there is apprehension of a self, that belonging to self will be created

1. Proof
2. Refutation of an argument against this proof

Proof

> **In every way, apprehending a self**
> **provides the support for attachment to self.**
> 236. **That remains as the circumstance for the seed**
> **of the conception of that belonging to self.**

A person apprehending a self who has no attachment to that belonging to self will develop an attachment to that belonging to self because they possess the apprehension of a self. This pervades because **in every way, apprehending a self provides the support for attachment to self,** and **that** attachment to self **remains as the** complete **circumstance for the seed of the conception of that belonging to self.**

> **Though there will be effort,**
> **one is possessed of engaging**
> **in reliance upon its qualities,**
> 237. **creating obstacles to freedom from the attachment,**
> **and obscuring the faults of that.**

Therefore a person who meditates upon that belonging to self as suffering, in order to free themself from the attachment to that belonging to self, **though they may make effort** in meditating upon that belonging to self as suffering, the attachment to self **creates an obstacle to becoming free from the attachment** to that belonging to self **and obscures the faults of that** belonging to self, rendering them unseen. This is because **in reliance upon** seeing **the qualities** of the self, regardless of circumstance, one **is possessed of** the seed of **engaging** with attachment to self.

Refutation of an argument against this proof

If free from attachment to self also,
there would be no freedom from attachment.
238. **How would that eradicate self?**
Meditation upon suffering would be in vain.

It might be argued, "If you have attachment to self, you will not be separate from attachment to that belonging to self, but that person who is free from attachment would be **free from attachment to self also**, and the reasoning of their being attached to self would not stand."

Even if such a person **free from attachment** did meditate upon that belonging to self as suffering and was thereby free from attachment to that, by that alone **there would be no** eradication of that belonging to self, because that would be similar to the reasoning that even if there were freedom from attachment to self, **how would that eradicate self?** It would not. If you agree, the person who **meditates upon** that belonging to self as **suffering would be** meditating **in vain**, because even though they might be free from attachment to that belonging to self, they would not eradicate that belonging to self.

Efforts to meditate on suffering are meaningless

1. Presenting the consequence
2. Refuting arguments against it

Presenting the consequence

Meditating on suffering,
they become aware of suffering itself.
239. **Though such has previously been experienced,**
there was no freedom from attachment.

It follows that it would be meaningless for the person who strives for freedom to meditate on that belonging to self as suffering in order to become free from attachment to that belonging to self, because although they **meditate on** that belonging to self as being **suffering, they** only **become** directly **aware of suffering itself**, and by that alone they will not become free from attachment to suffering. This is because **although such** instances of that belonging to self **have previously been experienced** as suffering, they did **not** lead to **freedom from attachment.**

Refuting arguments against it

It could be argued, "Seeing that belonging to self as suffering will eliminate attachment because it can be seen that by regarding certain things as having faults, attachment is eradicated."

> **By that being faulty,**
> **the mind will be reversed for that time,**
> 240. **but that will not become an absence of attachment toward it,**
> **like those with desire having attachment to other women.**
> **If there are attributes to accept and to reject,**
> **whatever attachment arises from one,**
> 241. **when a variety of conditions are created,**
> **becomes the seed of attachment to all.**

For a person apprehending a self, **by** seeing **that** belonging to self as **being faulty, the mind** of attachment to it **will be reversed for that time** it is seen as faulty, **but that will not become a** permanent **absence of attachment toward it** because attachment to other objects will still exist. This pervades because generally, with certain objects **there are attributes to accept and to reject,** and **whatever attachment arises from one** attribute, **when a variety of conditions are created, becomes the seed of attachment to all** objects previously rejected. **For example, those with desire** might see faults in one woman and will reverse any manifest attachment to her, but because they **have attachment to other women**, that becomes a cause, and attachment is created even to that previous woman.

If self has no faults, there are no objects of attachment to become free from

1. Presenting the consequence
2. Refuting arguments against the above

Presenting the consequence

> **To what will they become free of attachment?**
> **The object-possessing attachment is without fault.**
> **The accomplisher also is without fault.**
> 242. **If living beings are just these,**
> **from what is there freedom of attachment?**

To what faulty phenomena of saṃsāra **will** that person **become free of attachment?** It follows that there are none because the self has no faults. Moreover, **attachment**, which is **the object-possessing** cognition of the self, **has no faults**, and those belonging to self, which **accomplish,**[274] **are also without fault.** Therefore these three are not objects of attachment to become free from. This pervades because **living beings are just these** three phenomena of saṃsāra. The consequence has to be accepted, because if the self is without fault, the other two can be logically ascertained to be without fault.

Refuting arguments against the above

> **If that also is with faults,**
> **that is also the same for the self.**
> 243. **Toward that there is no absence of attachment to its faults.**
> **From what is there freedom of attachment?**

It might be argued, "The reason 'attachment as the object-possessing consciousness of the self has no faults,' is not established, because attachment to **that** self is the basis of suffering, and therefore it **is also with faults.**" The word "also" includes it being without fault as the aspect of being the object-possessor of the self.[275]

It follows that the self must have faults, because being a basis of suffering **is also the same for the self.** If you agree, for the person who strives for freedom, because of the mere reason of being possessed of faults, **from what** belonging to self **is there freedom of attachment?** There is no such freedom because **toward that** faulty self also **there is no absence of attachment to the faults of that** self.

Knowing that it has faults cannot abandon attachment

> **Attachment arising from seeing qualities**
> **is eradicated by seeing faults.**
> 244. **That is not the case with sense faculties and so on**
> **because children and so on also experience,**
> **and it even exists in those with faulty faculties.**
> **There is none toward those of others,**
> **even though they possess qualities.**
> 245. **To those of the past and so on,**
> **there is no attachment**
> **to that belonging to self.**

If **attachment arises from seeing** that which belongs to self as having **qualities**, that needs to be **eradicated by seeing** that belonging to self as having **faults.** However, **it is not the case** that attachment to the **sense faculties and so on** as those that belong to self is created solely from seeing belonging to self as having qualities, **because children**, cattle, **and so on**, who do not know how to separate qualities from faults, **also experience** this attachment, **and** attachment **even exists in those with faulty** sense **faculties. There is no** attachment **to** the sense faculties and so on **of others, even though** those sense faculties do **possess qualities.** Moreover, examples of **that belonging to self**, such as **the past**, hair separated from the body, **and so on**, may be seen as having qualities, but **there is no attachment to** them.

It might be argued, "The cause of the attachment to self is the cognition of that belonging to self, and that arises from seeing it as having qualities. Therefore meditating on it as suffering will abandon it."

> **Therefore the cause of the cognition of that belonging to self**
> **is also not from seeing the qualities.**
> 246. **Seeing them as not being qualities**
> **will not abandon that.**

Therefore the cause of the creation of the **cognition of that belonging to self is also not** solely **from seeing the qualities** of that belonging to self because children and others have this cognition. A person **will not abandon that** cognition of that belonging to self toward the sense faculties and so on by **seeing them** as faults and **not as qualities**, because the cognition of that belonging to self also does not arise from seeing it as having qualities.

There is no damage to the cause, and it will not be abandoned

> **Furthermore, by attachment, which superimposes**
> **nonexistent qualities, it is also seen.**
> 247. **Therefore, with a practice that does not damage the cause,**
> **how can it damage that?**

Furthermore, how can the practice of meditating on that belonging to self as suffering **damage** the attachment to **that** belonging to self? It **does not damage that** because it does not damage attachment to self, which is **the cause** of attachment to that belonging to self. This pervades, because attachment **is also seen** for that belonging to self **by** way of **attachment** to the self, **which superimposes nonexistent qualities** on that belonging to self.

Attachment to that belonging to self cannot be abandoned by understanding that self and the sense faculties are separate

The Sāṃkhya say, "Attachment is not produced from seeing the qualities, but when the innate nature that is the object of attachment and the person are held to be as one, then attachment will arise for that object.[276] When these two are seen as being distinct, freedom from attachment will arise."

> **Because they strive to obtain others more superior**
> **and they have the cognition of creation and destruction,**
> 248. **these living beings know the self**
> **as distinct from the sense faculties and so on.**

In that case, it follows that all ordinary **beings** are free from attachment to the sense faculties and so on because they **know the self is distinct from the sense faculties and so on.** This is because **they** do not wish for the self to become something other and instead **strive to obtain other, more superior** sense faculties and so on of that self. Moreover, although they regard the self as permanent, **they have the cognition** that knows the sense faculties and so on as being subject to **creation and destruction.**

> **Therefore attachment is not seeing them as one.**
> **From attachment to self, there follows a natural attachment**
> 249. **toward the apprehending internal factors.**

Therefore attachment is not created by **seeing** the object and the person **as one**, because attachment arises even when knowing that object and person as distinct. So what is the cause of attachment to that belonging to self? **Attachment to self** is the cause of attachment to that belonging to self because **from** its mere existence, **there follows a natural attachment** created **toward** the sense faculties and so on which belong to self, and which are **the apprehending internal factors** that create the consciousness.

Attachment to that belonging to self cannot be abandoned by turning away from suffering

1. Turning the mind away is not freedom from attachment
2. Refuting the consequence that there is no freedom from attachment

Turning the mind away is not freedom from attachment

It could be argued, "Seeing the sense faculties and so on as suffering, the mind will turn away from them, and there will be an absence of attachment."

Renunciation by those because of the suffering
is aversion but is not an absence of attachment,
250. **because even at that time there is attachment**
and at other times they will search for it.

Renunciation by those who possess the apprehension of a self, brought on **because of the suffering** seen in certain objects, is concomitant with **aversion but is not an absence of attachment, because even at that time there is attachment.** This is because, **at other times**, away from the suffering, the **search for** pleasure goes on.

With that aversion having the cause of suffering,
it will last as long as that.
251. **If reversed, they will again return to their nature.**

Therefore **that aversion** possessed of the characteristics of turning the mind away **will last as long as that** suffering because it **has the cause of**—that is, is the result of—that **suffering. If** that suffering is **reversed**, those persons **will again return to their nature** of attachment.

Refuting the consequence that there is no freedom from attachment

Because they have abandoned
that to be acquired and that to be rejected,
they maintain an equanimity toward all,
252. **remaining similarly toward sandalwood and an axe,**
and are said to be those with an absence of attachment.

It might be thought that freedom from attachment is not possible. People who **maintain an equanimity** and equilibrium, without desire and non-desire, **toward all** phenomena, whether attractive or not, **are said to be those with an absence of attachment, because they have abandoned** apprehending objects as phenomena **to be acquired or rejected.**

What level of equanimity constitutes an absence of attachment? A person who **remains similarly**, without attachment and anger, when reverently anointed by someone with **sandalwood** on one side and being angrily hacked at by someone else with **an axe** on the other side is said to be without attachment because they illustrate the abandonment of holding to the acts of acquiring and rejecting.

Refuting the assertion that the instruction to meditate on suffering is contradictory

It might be argued, "If meditating on the sense faculties and so on as being suffering and turning the mind away from that suffering is not an absence of attachment, that contradicts the sūtras, which state that suffering is to be meditated upon."

> **With the formative suffering in mind,**
> **it was said that suffering is to be meditated upon.**
> 253. **Moreover, ours is created from conditions.**
> **It is the basis for the view of no-self.**
> **By the view of emptiness, liberation is gained.**
> **The remaining meditations are for this purpose.**

The Buddha did not have the suffering of suffering in mind when he **said that suffering is to be meditated upon**; he had **the formative,** all-pervading **suffering in mind. Moreover, our** all-pervading suffering **is** simply the afflicted aggregates that are **created from** craving, which is the main **condition** explained in the origin of suffering and does not refer solely to the suffering of suffering.

Previous scholars who have explained this point by saying that all-pervading suffering "is created from the conditions" of momentary entities under the control of causality and is therefore suffering, have not considered the philosophical tenet presented here, because the Sautrāntika school also asserts nonafflicted composite entities to be under the control of causality.[277]

One does not attain liberation by meditating on all-pervading suffering alone because **it is** just **the basis for the view** that understands that there is **no** separately existing entity of a **self. By the view** that understands **emptiness** of this separately existing entity of a self, **liberation is gained. The remaining meditations**, such as those on impermanence, suffering, and so on, **are** performed **with the purpose of** developing **that** view of understanding emptiness.

> 254. **Therefore, it was taught,**
> **from impermanence, suffering,**
> **and from suffering, no-self.**

Therefore the Buddha also **taught** that **from** understanding **impermanence**, one understands **suffering**, and **from** understanding **suffering** comes the understanding of **no-self**:

> Monks, is form permanent or impermanent? Venerable ones, it is impermanent. That which is impermanent, is it happiness or suffering? Venerable ones, it is suffering. Regarding those that possess the aspects of impermanence and suffering, the thought arises, "This is I," "This is mine," "This is the self." Is such a view right?[278] Venerable ones, it is not.[279]

Without freedom from attachment, there is circling in saṃsāra

1. Possessed of three factors, there will be those who circle in saṃsāra
2. The absurd consequences of these three factors not being present

Possessed of three factors, there will be those who circle in saṃsāra

> **Not without attachment, possessing craving,**
> **relying upon all manner of exertions,**
> 255. **not free from mental affliction and karma,**
> **they are known as circlers in saṃsāra.**

Those apprehending a self, who know that that belonging to self is suffering, **are known as circlers in saṃsāra,** and they will not find freedom because they are **not free from mental affliction and karma.** This is because they are **not without attachment** to self, they **possess craving**[280] for that belonging to self, and in order to obtain that, **they rely upon all manner of** karma-gathering **exertions.**

The absurd consequences of these three factors not being present

It might be argued, "When liberation is gained, there is no attachment to that belonging to self, and therefore the reason 'not without attachment' does not stand."

> **If that belonging to self is not asserted,**
> **there will be no engager of that.**
> 256. **Possessing the characteristics of doing and partaking,**
> **self at that time will also not exist.**

Then it follows that at the time of liberation, **there will be no engager of that** belonging to self because **that belonging to self is not asserted**—that is, it has been eradicated. If you agree, then **at that time** of liberation, the **self** of that belonging to self, which you assert, **will also not exist** because there will be no activity and no partaking. You must accept the pervasion because you assert that it is the self that **possesses the characteristics of doing and partaking.**

Advice to uproot the view of self

> **Therefore those wishing liberation**
> **should uproot the view of the transitory collection**
> 257. **that arises from its seed of similar type**
> **and is a result that has no beginning.**

The person who **wishes for liberation**, by means of meditating upon no-self, **should uproot the view of the transitory collection that arises from its seed of** previous **similar type and is a result that has no beginning.** This is because, as has been explained, by striving for liberation without understanding no-self, just meditating upon suffering and so on, it is not possible to find freedom from saṃsāra.

45. The Antidote to Craving

Understanding no-self is the antidote to craving

1. Refuting proof that ritual is the antidote
2. Presenting the proof that ritual is not the antidote
3. Teaching that the perfect view is the antidote

Refuting proof that ritual is the antidote

1. Refuting that the ritual of initiation is the antidote
2. Refuting that the ritual of mantra is the antidote
3. Refuting that the five-fire reliance is the antidote

Refuting that the ritual of initiation is the antidote

It could be argued, "Even if the view of the transitory collection is not uprooted, you will be liberated by receiving the initiation bestowed by Īśvara, because that is explained in the doctrine of Īśvara."

Though it is said merely by doctrine
that you will be free,
258. **those who do not see the reason**
for such a phenomenon in the doctrine
are not impressed.

Though it is said merely by the **doctrine** of Īśvara **that you will be free** by way of the ritual of initiation, **those** with knowledge **are not impressed,** because they **see no reason** for **the doctrine** of Īśvara, however it is taught, to have **such a phenomenon** as its topic.

Refuting that the ritual of mantra is the antidote

The argument is, "If you are consecrated with the mantra spoken of in the doctrine of Īśvara, you will be liberated, because such consecration can cause a seed not to produce its sprout."

> **The ritual establishing a seed and so on**
> **has no power not to produce a person.**
> 259. **It would follow that anointing**
> **with sesame oil, burning, and so on**
> **would also liberate them.**

The ritual whereby it is seen and **established** that **a seed** is consecrated with a mantra and the sprout is not produced does **not** establish that mantra **has the power to not produce** the future birth of **a person.** If it did establish such a thing, **it would follow that anointing** someone **with sesame oil**, then **burning** and cooking them **and so on should also liberate them** from future births, because if you do that to a seed, it does not produce a sprout. Such a fault would ensue.

Refuting that the five-fire reliance[281] *is the antidote*

The argument is, "By relying upon the five fires, you will be free from future births because, by doing so, a person's body becomes lighter than before. This is because their nonvirtuous activities have come to an end."

> **Being previously heavier and later lighter**
> **does not destroy nonvirtuous activities.**
> 260. **The heaviness of this has gone**
> **but not the heaviness of nonvirtuous activities,**
> **which have no physical body.**

A person who relies upon the five fires **does not destroy their nonvirtuous activities** because their body that was **previously heavier later** became **lighter.** It is the water and earth element that makes up **the heaviness of this** body that **has gone** and **not the heaviness of nonvirtuous activities,** because nonvirtuous activities **have no physical body.**

Presenting the proof that ritual is not the antidote

1. The ritual does not weaken the cause of birth
2. Refuting the proof that it does weaken the cause of birth

3. Establishing that there is no weakening of the cause of birth
4. Refuting that the self too is necessary as a cause of birth

The ritual does not weaken the cause of birth

> **By the force of wrong cognition,**
> **the craving from that, and volition,**
> 261. **beings take birth in inferior locations.**
> **Therefore, if severed, that will not occur.**
> **Just from that it will occur.**
> **Therefore they are capable of causing birth.**
> 262. **Because volition and so forth themselves are karma,**
> **the causes for birth have not weakened.**

The **wrong cognition** that holds suffering to be happiness, **the craving** that arises **from that, and** the **volition**[282] that is concomitant with these two, **if** they are **severed**—that is, abandoned—future birth **will not occur** because it is **by the force of** these that living **beings take birth in inferior locations** such as the womb. Therefore wrong cognition, craving, and volition are the causes **capable of causing birth** in a future existence because **just from that** combination a future birth **will** definitely **occur.**

It could be argued, "Previous karma too is a cause for future birth. Therefore 'just from that it will occur' is not correct."

Previous karma is not separate from the volition that is concomitant with wrong cognition and craving **because** such **volition and so forth themselves are** the **karma** that is the cause of future birth. Therefore those apprehending a self and who are bestowed the initiation of Īśvara will be born into a future existence because **the causes for** such a **birth**—which are wrong cognition, craving, and volition—**have not weakened.**

Refuting the proof that it does weaken the cause of birth

1. Refuting the notion that the cause of birth is something other
2. Refuting that this cause of birth is eradicated

Refuting the notion that the cause of birth is something other

> **"The basis of going and perceiving is the faculties,**
> **which arise from the unseen.**

Because the unseen is destroyed,
263. **there will be no going.**
Therefore this is formative activity, not volition."

The argument: "Those who gain the initiation of Īśvara **will not go** to another birth **because the unseen** karma **is destroyed.** This pervades because **the basis of going** from one place to another **and of perceiving** form, sound, and so on **is the faculties,**[283] and **those** faculties **arise from the unseen** karmas that possess the characteristics of Dharma and non-Dharma. **Therefore**, karma, which **is** the **formative activity**[284] creating engagement in the ten virtuous acts and the ten nonvirtuous acts, is a quality of the self, whereas the **volition** that you assert **is not** karma. Therefore it is not established that 'the causes for birth have not been eradicated.'"

Following on from existence or nonexistence,
the power of cognition can be seen
in the creation of the faculties.
264. **It is not by something other.**
With those existing, why should they not go?

The power of the mind of wrong **cognition**, craving, and volition **can be seen in the creation of the faculties** and so on. They are **not** created **by something other**—that is, the formative activity that is a quality of self. This is because these faculties causally **follow on** or not **from the existence or nonexistence** of wrong cognition, craving, and volition and do not follow on from something other—that is, the formative activity that is a quality of self. Therefore **why should those** apprehending self who have gained the initiation of Īśvara **not go** on to the place of birth endowed with the faculties and so on? They will do so because **those** causes for birth—wrong cognition, craving, and volition—**exist** and have not been eradicated.

Refuting that this cause of birth is eradicated

"They are without power."
Immediately upon receiving initiation and so on,
265. **apprehending, engaging, distraction,**
and ceasing by the power of volition
would no longer exist.

It could be argued, "**If** the initiation of Īśvara renders wrong cognition, craving, and volition to be **without power**, there will be no birth into a future existence."

In that case, it follows that for the person who has gained the initiation of Īśvara, **immediately upon receiving the initiation and so on**, those faculties of the eye and so forth **apprehending** objects, **engaging** objects, being **distracted**—that is, disturbed—**and ceasing** being disturbed, all **by the power of** the two kinds of **volition, would no longer exist** because, immediately upon receiving the initiation, wrong cognition, craving, and volition are rendered powerless.

> **"At that time, because of no mind, it would not occur."**
> 266. **If the defilements of cognition are incapable of connecting,**
> **even when alive they would be incapable.**

It could be argued, "However, **at that** initiation given at the **time** of death, the propelling of another birth **would not occur because** there would be **no** propelling of a subsequent **mind**."

The defilements of wrong **cognition** and craving at the point of death **will** connect the person to a subsequent mind of wrong cognition and craving because the causes for such a **connecting** are complete. **If** you say the reason is not established because the initiation has rendered **those** previous wrong cognitions and craving **incapable** of creating subsequent wrong cognition and craving, then it would follow that the initiation would render previous wrong cognition and craving **incapable** of creating subsequent wrong cognition **even when** the person is **alive**.

Establishing that there is no weakening of the cause of birth

> **When its antidote and its own side strengthen,**
> **there is weakening and strengthening.**
> 267. **The continuum of the faults possessing the seed**
> **is not reversed through initiation.**

It follows that **the continuum of the faults** of wrong cognition and craving **is not reversed through initiation** because this continuum is something that **possesses the** apprehending of a self as its **seed**, from which it arises, and the initiation does not affect this. Therefore the continuum of the faults of wrong cognition and craving has a preceding cause that is the apprehension of a self, because **when** the **antidote** to understanding no-self **strengthens**, this continuum **will weaken**, **and** when the **side** of the preceding apprehension of a self **strengthens**, that continuum **will strengthen.**

Refuting that the self too is necessary as a cause of birth

1. Reasoning to damage the permanent self
2. Refuting posited consequences of that

Reasoning to damage the permanent self

It could be argued, "It is not correct to posit wrong cognition, craving, and volition solely as the causes of saṃsāra because the permanent self is also a cause of saṃsāra."

Because in permanence there is no dependency,
268. successive production, as well as producing and not producing,
being of a similar nature, would be contradictory.
The cause and result would be one.
If they were distinct from those,
269. the doer would not exist as the experiencer.
Furthermore, the ability is not established.

Because a **permanent** self **does not depend** upon conditions, it **would be contradictory** for it to **successively produce** results. It **also** could not produce results later because the time of **producing** a result **and** the time of **not producing** a result **are of a similar nature.** Moreover, the doer that is **the cause and** the experiencer that is the **result would be one** and the same because the permanent self is both.

It might be argued, "The reason does not stand because **those** experiencers **are distinct from those** doers of actions."

Then it would follow that the self as **the doer** of actions **would not exist as the experiencer** of ripened actions because it is something other than the experiencer of ripened actions. **Furthermore**, this self is permanent, and therefore it **is not established** that it has **the ability** to produce a result.

Refuting posited consequences of that

It might be argued, "It would follow that that which is experienced, done, seen, and so on by one will be remembered, experienced, and recognized, and so on by another because there is no one thing that experiences and remembers."

This consequence of being remembered,
partaken of, and so on by another does no harm
270. **because there is no such remembering.**
Therefore, memory arises from experience.

Is this consequence posed in terms of a person or a phenomenon? If it is the former, the consequence would be, "It follows that something experienced by one person will be **remembered, partaken of, and so on by another** because the person who experiences and the person who remembers are not the same." **This consequence does not harm** Dharmakīrti **because** he would correctly respond by saying that there is no certainty to the pervasion of that consequence. This is because **there is no such** experiencing and so forth of [up to **remembering** and partaking].[285] If it were the latter, the consequence would be, "It follows that something experienced by one mental aggregate will be remembered and so on by another aggregate because there is no one phenomenon that experiences and remembers." This consequence does not harm Dharmakīrti because from the experiencing by a previous aggregate a subsequent memory arises. **Therefore** Dharmakīrti would respond by saying that he agrees with the consequence. This is because, by the reason of an aggregate experiencing giving rise to an aggregate remembering, **memory arises from experience**. It is not the case that a person experiencing gives rise to a person remembering.

It is important to understand the point being made here. Those propounding realist tenets assert that experiencing, remembering, and so on are phenomena that withstand analysis. Those that assert a substantially existing person say that a person experiencing and a person remembering and so on are phenomena that can withstand analysis. Those realist tenet holders from the Kashmiri Vaibhāṣika upward assert that applying these phenomena to a person is mere designation, and that which withstands analysis must refer to the aggregates. This is because that which is experienced by the visual consciousness apprehending blue is remembered by a subsequent memory, and karma collected by volition is experienced by a subsequent aggregate of feeling.

Therefore experiencing and remembering is not applied to a person, and thus that which is experienced by one person is not remembered and so on by another. However, the remembering performed by an aggregate is other than the experiencing performed by an aggregate because they are cause and effect.

For the Prāsaṅgika Madhyamaka, in terms of designation it is correct to apply experiencing and remembering to both person and aggregate. However, remembering is not other than experiencing because it is asserted that cause and effect are not other. These points are essential for the philosophical system of Pramāṇa and Madhyamaka combined,[286] and so the wise should remember them.

Teaching that the perfect view is the antidote

1. The antidote that destroys craving
2. With no craving there is no future birth

The antidote that destroys craving

> **From the four truths come solidity, pleasure,**
> **self and mine, and so on,**
> 271. **which are the sixteen faulty aspects.**
> **From such superimposition comes craving.**
> **Possessing an insight in contradiction to those,**
> 272. **the perfect view of meditating well**
> **destroys craving and that which follows it.**

The perfect view of meditating well upon the sixteen aspects such as impermanence **destroys** all **craving and that which follows it**, such as miserliness, envy, and so on, because with regard to those four truths as the objects of focus, it **possesses an insight** and a meditation upon the actual aspects, such as impermanence, **in** direct **contradiction to those** of the sixteen aspects such as permanence. This pervades because **from the four truths**, as the objects focused on, **come the sixteen faulty aspects**. These are **solidity**—that is, permanence—**pleasure,** and **self and mine** with regard to the truth of suffering; not being a cause **and so on** with regard to the truth of the origin of suffering; not being cessation and so on with regard to the truth of cessation of suffering; and not being the path and so on with regard to the truth of the path. These aspects are **superimposed** by ignorance, and **from that** ignorance **comes craving**, which craves the acquiring and rejecting of pleasure and suffering.

With no craving there is no future birth

> **Because one is not there,**
> **even remaining with a body and karma,**
> 273. **there is no possibility of birth by the three causes,**
> **like a sprout without the seed.**

For a person who has abandoned the craving that arises from the apprehension of a self, **there is no possibility of** taking **birth by the three causes**—that is, karma, mental affliction, and a body—**even** though they **remain with a body and karma.** This is **because one** of the main causes—that is, mental affliction—**is not there. For example, without the seed, the sprout** will not grow.

On this point, passages in this work dealing with the truth of the path to cessation establish that the path of understanding no-self is the antidote to saṃsāra. However, the cause of the suffering of saṃsāra is ignorance, as categorized by the view of the transitory collection, and the condition of craving. Therefore there are passages that establish the antidotes to these also. The first group of passages, on the understanding of no-self, is taught by the verse beginning "From training in that path, as explained" (2.205), which teaches that the ability to abandon saṃsāra lies in understanding no-self. That is established (1) by consciousness engaging in the object in the way it exists and (2) possessing a mode of apprehension contradictory to the view of self, and (3) by the view of self being the root of self. These three are expressed by the verses beginning (1) "The phenomenon of a consciousness apprehending an object" (2.206), (2) "Because the view of emptiness is contradictory to that" (2.214), and (3) "Whoever sees the self" (2.217).

Other paths—such as knowing attachment to self to be faulty, meditating on the sense faculties as suffering, knowing the sense faculties and self to be separate, and withdrawing the mind from suffering—cannot abandon the view of self because their mode of apprehension does not contradict the view of self. Therefore they are not suitable as antidotes to saṃsāra. These are expressed by the verses beginning "Cannot attachment be seen as a fault?" (2.221). The summary of these points is found in the single verse beginning "Therefore those wishing for liberation" (2.256).

The second group of passages can be found in the sections on "Teacher" and on the origin of suffering, where craving is established as being the condition that will definitely bring about suffering, and consequently, if craving is not abandoned, the suffering of saṃsāra is not eradicated. Those rituals found in doctrine do not damage the cause, which is apprehension of a self, and therefore cannot eradicate the result, craving. This is expressed by the verse beginning "Though it is said merely by doctrine" (2.257).

The path of understanding no-self will abandon the cause, apprehension of a self, and consequently will eradicate the result, which is craving, and all that follows it. This is expressed by the verses beginning "From the four truths" (2.270).

The summary of that is the single verse beginning "Because one is not there" (2.272). The teaching that apart from the antidote to mental affliction, there is no antidote to body and karma is expressed by the verses beginning "Karma and body will not be abandoned" (2.273).

Tibetan commentaries have not paid attention to this process of establishing our Buddhist system of the path to liberation, primarily keeping to the main topics and then refuting, according to the context, the system of liberation posited by non-Buddhists. They create the outlines (1) Gaining liberation by meditating on no-self, (2) Refuting arguments against that, (3) Establishing the understanding of emptiness as the path, and (4) The antidote that does not eradicate apprehension of self is not the path. The fourth is divided into three: (1) The absence of attachment to belonging to self is not the antidote, (2) The mere rituals described in doctrine are not the antidotes, and (3) Methods to put an end to karma and the body are not the antidotes.

Others divide the topic into: (1) Establishing our system of the path to liberation and (2) Refuting the non-Buddhist systems of the path to liberation. The latter is divided into a series of headings: absence of attachment to belonging to self is not the antidote; meditating on the sense faculties as suffering is not the antidote; realizing that sense faculties and self are distinct is not the antidote; withdrawing the mind from suffering is not the antidote; the ritual described in doctrine is not the antidote; and methods to put an end to karma and the body are not the antidotes. Therefore they engage the topics and strive to establish this text as a work of forceful argument without distinguishing the two types of antidote, and without demarcating the individual refutations of the non-Buddhist systems within these two types. By the power of the blessings and teachings of Sakya Paṇḍita, I do not carry the burden of confusion with regard to the logical points of this work.

Other than that, there is no antidote to karma and body

1. No need and no ability to abandon karma and body
2. Refuting that there is an antidote that ends karma
3. Refuting that this contradicts the cessation of karma
4. Refuting that karma and mental affliction are causally similar

No need and no ability to abandon karma and body

It might be argued, "Just as the antidote that eradicates mental afflictions is the path, the antidote that eradicates karma and body is also the path, because karma, body, and mental afflictions are the very causes of birth."

Karma and body will not be abandoned
because there are no antidotes and no ability.
274. **If craving is present, they will again arise.**
Even though working to eradicate two of them,
the fatigue suffered to eradicate karma is pointless.

Those who strive for liberation **will not abandon karma and body** alone **because there are no antidotes** that abandon these two alone, **and** without eradicating craving there is **no ability** to abandon these two. The reason stands because **if craving is present**, karma and body **will again arise.**

It could be argued, "Isn't it right to work to abandon karma and body?"

Even though those who strive for liberation **work to eradicate two of them**—that is, craving and karma—**the fatigue suffered** in order **to eradicate karma** on its own **is pointless** because it is by eradicating craving that karma will not arise again.

Refuting that there is an antidote that ends karma

It could be argued, "The reason 'because there are no antidotes' does not stand because ascetic practices will destroy the power of previous karmas."

275. **Because a variety of results can be seen,**
it can be inferred that karmas have distinct potentials.
Therefore a single hardship of asceticism
will not bring them to an end.
276. **Results produced by some types will lessen,**
but the unrelated will not.

It can be inferred that defiled **karmas have distinct potentials** to create many different results **because** the creation of **a variety of** very different **results can be seen. Therefore** the functioning entity that is **a single hardship**[287]—that is, suffering—**of ascetic** practices **will not bring an end** to all karmas. This is because **results** that relate to that **produced by some types** of ascetic practices, such as hunger, **will lessen, but** those karmic results that produce suffering **unrelated** to these practices **will not** lessen at all.

"By the power of the ascetic practices,
potentials are gathered together and ended."
277. **They are either abandoned by some aspect of the hardship**

or all are abandoned without hardship,
because you assert ascetic practices are other than the hardship.
"They are the hardship."
278. **Because this is the result of karma,**
there is no power to gather together.

It will be argued, "**By the power of the ascetic practices**, all karmic **potentials are gathered together** as one **and ended** either by the experience of a single suffering or a single ascetic practice."

In that case it follows that all karmas **are either abandoned by some aspect of the hardship**—that is, the suffering—of ascetic practice, such as plucking out body hairs, **or** they are **all abandoned without** reliance upon the **hardship**, the suffering. This is **because you assert** that by the power of the ascetic practices, all karmic potentials are gathered together as one and are ended by the experience of a single suffering or a single ascetic practice, and that these **ascetic practices are** something **other than the hardship**, or suffering.

If you say that this reason does not stand because the ascetic practices **are the hardship**, the suffering, itself, then in that case, such an ascetic practice **will have no power to gather** all karmas **together** and end them **because this is the result of** bad **karma.**

Refuting that this contradicts the cessation of karma

It could be argued, "If you assert that understanding no-self results in the cessation of karma, how can there be no antidote to karma?"

Because it destroys the fault of the tendency to produce,
it will put an end to the faults.
279. **It has power with respect to the karma created by that.**
How will those already created be weakened?

The path of knowing no-self is the method to **put an end to the faults** of craving **because it destroys** the seed of later craving, which is **the fault of the tendency to produce** craving in the future, and which arises from a previous craving. Therefore the path of knowing no-self **has** the **power** to destroy **the karma created by that** later craving. However, **how will** the fruits of karmas that have **already** been **created be weakened?** They will not, because the karma created by craving will definitely produce its results.[288]

Refuting that karma and mental affliction are causally similar

It could be argued, "Karma comes from mental affliction. Therefore, if there is mental affliction, there will be no liberation. Similarly, mental affliction arises from karma. Therefore, if there is karma, there can likewise be no liberation."

> **From karma faults will not arise.**
> **With faults, it will be created; from the opposite, not.**
> 280. **Not possessing wrong concepts,**
> **even from happiness, desire will not be produced.**

From karma that has abandoned mental affliction, **the faults** of mental affliction **will not arise** because such karma has no mental affliction. This pervades, because **with** the **faults** of mental affliction, karma **will be created**, but **from the opposite**—that is, without these faults—karma and mental affliction will **not** be produced.

It might be argued, "The reasoning is not sound because from good and bad karma come happiness and suffering, and from those come desire and anger."

For the person who has abandoned the view of self, **desire**, anger, and so forth **will not be produced, even from happiness** and suffering, because they **do not possess wrong concepts** of apprehending I and mine.

Establishing by Way of the Reverse Sequence

46. From "Protector" to "Compassion"

From the above, "Sugata" is established

> **From "Protector" is established**
> **wisdom that knows reality, is stable,**
> **and knows the features of all.**
> 281. **Because the Sugata has the aspect of knowing,**
> **he is superior to outsiders, practitioners,**
> **and those beyond practice.**

With the **Protector** who teaches the four truths without error as a reason, it can **be established** that such a teacher is endowed with a **wisdom** possessing three special features, namely a wisdom **that knows reality** as it is, a wisdom that **is stable** because it cannot be reversed, **and** a wisdom that **knows the features of all** phenomena, as many as there are. This is because the Protector who teaches the four truths without error is the result created from this wisdom possessed of these three features.

It could be asked, "But doesn't this contradict the previous explanation of Sugata, which was explained in terms of abandonment?"[289]

Because **the "Sugata" has these** three **aspects of knowing** and, depending on the context, can refer to a knowing possessed of these three aspects, it is acceptable to explain it as "gone to happiness."[290] Therefore the Buddha **is superior to** those **outsiders** devoid of attachment, to stream enterers and other **practitioners, and** to **those beyond practice**, such as the śrāvaka and pratyekabuddha arhats. The reasons, respectively, are that he possesses the wisdom that knows reality, is stable, and is irreversible.

From the above, "Teacher" is established

Engaged in knowing the needs of others, he is the Teacher,
282. **from which is established compassion.**
Having fulfilled his purposes,
he did not neglect deeds for others.

It is established that the resultant name of "**Teacher**" applied to **engaging in** the methods of **knowing the needs of others** and practicing them preceded the Buddha, because the Buddha is endowed with the wisdom possessed of these three features.

From the above, "Compassion" is established

From that practice in the extensive methods of working for others, it **is established** that the Buddha is one possessed of **compassion** for others. Although he **had fulfilled his** own **purposes** with perfect abandonment and understanding, **he did not neglect** the **deeds** of teaching the Dharma **for** the sake of **others.**

Therefore endeavor is established

With great compassion, he is good.
With wisdom, he spoke the truth,
accompanied by its accomplisher.
283. **Moreover, to teach this way,**
he had application.
Therefore he is a valid being.

It is established **therefore that** the Bhagavan Buddha, by endeavoring in its means, **is a valid being** for those who seek liberation; he is endowed **with great compassion**, meaning that **he is good**—that is, beneficial—and **with** great **wisdom he spoke the truth, accompanied by its accomplisher. Moreover, to teach** in **this way, he** pursued great **application**, that is, perseverance.

The purpose of praising by way of being valid

1. The purpose of establishing validity
2. Establishing valid inferential cognition

The purpose of establishing validity

"What is the purpose of praising the Bhagavan Buddha by way of being a valid person possessing limitless good qualities?"

> **Praising the Teacher by such phenomena**
> **is to know that the validity**
> 284. **is established from his very teaching.**

There is a purpose of offering **praise to the Teacher by** way of the **phenomena of such** excellent qualities, such as "becoming a valid person," because it **is to know that the** presentation of **validity** can be **established from** the **very teachings** of the Bhagavan Buddha. It is not that Dignāga invented it.

Establishing valid inferential cognition

"The Buddha can be established as being valid by way of the direct valid cognition of the scriptures. What is the need of inferential valid cognition?"

> **Because he did not negate inference,**
> **syllogisms of this are seen in many ways,**
> 285. **such as, that with the nature of the slightest production**
> **is wholly subject to cessation.**

The Teacher accepted that inferential cognition is valid **because he did not negate inference** as valid cognition, whereas knowing from words and so on were negated as being valid cognition. Not only did he not negate it, we can see that **in many ways** he taught **syllogisms of this** inference, **such as whatever has a nature of the slightest production is wholly subject to cessation**—that is, destruction—smoke is known from fire, and so forth.

> **A reason with the characteristic of indispensability**
> **is the basis of inference.**
> **Because it shows the thesis pervading the reasoning,**
> **this is clearly taught.**

This pervades because **a reason** whose **characteristic** is that it has an **indispensable** relationship with the predicate of the thesis **is the basis of inference. This** indispensable relationship **is clearly taught** by the above syllogisms **because** they **show** that the predicate of **the thesis**, such as impermanence, **pervades the reasoning**, such as "being created."

The conclusion taught by way of the title of the chapter

> **This has been the second chapter on establishing valid cognition, from the *Commentary on Valid Cognition*.**

This has been an explanation of **the chapter on valid cognition**, or **second** chapter, **from** *Light of Samantabhadra: An Explanation of the Extensive Treatise That Is a* ***Commentary on Valid Cognition*.**

Notes

1. "Base reality" here (*dngos po'i gnas thshul*) does not necessarily refer to an ultimate or hidden reality or phenomenon but to the working reality of our existence. It is a starting point for the path or the foundation upon which practice is built.
2. The various Buddhist tenet systems have different explanations of the process and the causes of consciousness knowing its object. Here I am mainly following the tenets of the Sautrāntika system as presented in this work.
3. Skt. *sāmānya*; Tib. *spyi*. Dharmakīrti refutes the kinds of universal posited by non-Buddhist schools such as the Sāṃkhya but accepts a nonsubstantial type of universal posited by Buddhist epistemology, as will be described in chapter 1 of his work.
4. In Buddhism *permanence* refers to existence that does not function under the laws of cause and effect, such as conceived entities that are the result of conceptual negation. Space is permanent because it is the mere negation of obstructing form. Destruction is the negation of an existent phenomenon by way of its total disintegration.
5. Here the term *pramāṇa* is used to mean "studies in logic and epistemology." Elsewhere it refers to the more literal meaning of "valid cognition, speech, or person."
6. *Compendium on Reality* (*Tattvasaṃgraha*), Toh 4266.
7. *Wheel of Reasons* (*Hetucakraḍamaru*), Toh 4209, translated with Dharmāloka.
8. See Gö Lotsāwa 1976, 70. Van der Kuijp (1983, 29ff.) devotes a whole chapter to the activities of this remarkable translator.
9. The terms in bold make up the essential parts of Dignāga's homage, which is used as the basis for the explanation in Dharmakīrti's second chapter.
10. See Tāranātha 1970, 184.
11. This is a homage to Dharmakīrti using the Hindu myth of creation as a metaphor.
12. Sakya Paṇḍita.
13. This is in the colophon of Nāgārjuna's *Fundamental Wisdom*.
14. Śrāvakas, pratyekabuddhas, and bodhisattvas.
15. This and the following citation both come from the treatise *Uttaratantra* by Maitreya.
16. *Ascertainment of Valid Cognition* (*Pramāṇaviniścaya*), 152a1. This citation has been translated in accordance with the commentaries on *Ascertainment of Valid Cognition* by Gyaltsab Darma Rinchen (*Bstan bcos tshad ma rnam nges ṭīk chen dgongs pa rab gsal*) and Rongtön Śākya Gyaltsen (*Rnam nges rnam bshad rtog ge'i snang ba*).
17. The fault of being like a vessel that is either leaky, dirty, or overturned.

18. The word translated as "although" (*'ng, api*) is somewhat problematic. The syntactical placement of it in the Tibetan suggests that it means "also" or "even." Also, it is difficult to see how it could imply that this work will be of benefit to others. I asked Sanskrit scholar David Reigle about this, who said that this grammatical particle, as used here, expresses contrast with the next line, meaning that the Tibetan should read *bsam pa med na'ng* rather than *bsam pa'ng med*, and is best translated as "although."
19. Sakya Paṇḍita, *Treasure of Reasoning*, 2a1.
20. "Inference for Oneself" is the second chapter of Dignāga's work, not the first. The first three chapters of *Compendium of Valid Cognition* are (1) Direct Valid Perception, (2) Inference for Oneself, and (3) Inference for Others. The chapters of *Commentary on Valid Cognition* are (1) Inference for Oneself, (2) Establishment of Valid Cognition, (3) Direct Valid Perception, and (4) Inference for Others. This difference in chapter ordering is dealt with below.
21. In this work and elsewhere Dignāga's *Compendium of Valid Cognition* is often referred to as the *Valid Cognition Sūtra*, or sometimes as just the *Sūtra*, as evidenced in the following paragraph.
22. Dharmakīrti's autocommentary only covers the first chapter.
23. The phrase "separating of what is meaningful from what is without meaning" appears in the opening lines of Dignāga's *Compendium of Valid Cognition*.
24. Śākyabuddhi (660–720), in his *Explanation of the Commentary on Valid Cognition*.
25. The grammatical and conceptual device of positing by way of preclusion (*rnam bcod*) is employed here with the single term *kho na* and has been rendered above as "totally," "alone," and "only." There are two types of this device: preclusion of nonexistence or preclusion of existence elsewhere, as employed above. This is somewhat similar to placing the word "only" in different parts of a sentence giving rise to a change of meaning. This discussion is found in Śākyabuddhi, *Explanation*, 5b–6a.
26. Devendrabuddhi (630–90) was a disciple of Dharmakīrti.
27. Devendrabuddhi, *Word Explanation of the Commentary on Valid Cognition* (*Pramāṇavārttikapañjikā*), 71a2.
28. The reason is that the separating out of inference for oneself depends upon inference, and the pervasion is that this reason is pervaded by having to be explained before inference for oneself.
29. Dharmakīrti, *Ascertainment of Valid Cognition*, 259a.
30. Devendrabuddhi, *Word Explanation*. This whole citation is a little different in the Degé edition, 122a4.
31. Because both these works teach direct perception as their first chapters.
32. Prajñākaragupta, *Pramāṇavārttikālaṃkāra*, Toh 4221.
33. In the Sautrāntika philosophy, which is the tenet of the first chapter at least, intrinsic existence (*rang mtshan, svalakṣaṇa*) is accepted.
34. Yamāri (eleventh century). In his *Commentary on Ornament to the Commentary on Valid Cognition*.
35. Ravigupta (tenth century). In his *Explanation of the Commentary on Valid Cognition*.
36. Words in quotation marks are from the autocommentary.
37. Dharmakīrti and Dignāga assert the "three criteria," as will be explained.
38. As stated above, the *Sūtra* is Dignāga's *Compendium of Valid Cognition*. These lines open the second chapter.

39. The term *subject under analysis* is literally "the subject about which something is desired to be known." The term *section* (*phyogs, pakṣa*) refers to the subject (*chos can*) of the syllogism, but *subject* is not used because it does not refer to *all* properties of the subject but only to a "section" or part. As Gorampa mentions, there are arguments about the use and necessity of this term rather than *subject* dealt with in the autocommentary. In many monastic textbooks, this is a topic of debate in its own right (*phyogs sgra*).
40. Śaṃkarānanda (tenth century) in his *Pramāṇavārttikaṭīkā*, which comments only on the first chapter up to verse 128.
41. An *indispensable cause* (*ldog byed kyi rgyu*) is one whose nonexistence determines the nonexistence of the result. Fire is an indispensable cause of smoke, and therefore fire can be inferred from smoke, but certain features of fire—such as a flame and its color—cannot.
42. The term "possessing the result" (*'bras bu can*), which is used a lot in this work, simply means "cause." "Possessing the cause" (*rgyu can*) likewise means "result."
43. Although the term used is *piśāca* (*sha za*), which can be a particular kind of supernatural being, the meaning here is just an invisible being.
44. *Shing sha pa*. The Tibetan is said to be a corruption of the Sanskrit *śiṃśapā*, the Indian rosewood tree (*Dalbergia sissoo*).
45. The taste of jaggery is coexistent with, and one nature with, the form of jaggery, and in that aspect it has the ability to create future particulars of that form.
46. *Phyogs chos can gyi gtan tsigs*, a reason that is established as a property of the subject.
47. The Mīmāṃsaka assert that a large body, bright sense powers, and mind indicate the presence of desire.
48. There are non-Buddhists who say that enlightened beings do not speak because speaking is a product of desire and desire is eradicated in enlightened beings.
49. The verses from *Ascertainment of Valid Cognition* listed in this passage also occur in *Commentary on Valid Cognition*. The former is written in prose and verse, indicated here with folio references for their location in the Dergé edition, while the latter is solely in verse, indicated here with chapter and verse. Stcherbatsky (1930, 37) states over half of the verses from *Ascertainment* are from *Commentary* and that the former is an abridgment of the latter. I cannot locate 1.34 in *Ascertainment*.
50. Conflicting remainder reasoning, genuine remainder reasoning, and exclusive uncertain reasoning are divisions of reasoning with remainder and are described in most monastic textbooks on types of reasoning.
51. I cannot locate this line in *Compendium of Valid Cognition*. That text is written in verse, but this line is prose.
52. Īśvarasena (*Dbang phyug sde*), a student of Dignāga and teacher of Dharmakīrti whose misinterpretation of Dignāga's position was recognized by Dharmakīrti.
53. See verse 1.19 and Dignāga's *Wheel of Reasons* (*Hetucakraḍamaru*), where he formulates a nine-point wheel diagramming the possible types of reasoning. See Jinpa 2020, chapter 22, for a presentation of this wheel.
54. Both citations are found in Śākyabuddhi's *Explanation*, 32a7, where he quotes Dignāga.
55. Again, this refers to Dignāga's nine-point wheel of reason schema. A nonexistent subject of the proposition results in the reason not being established as a property of that

subject, but that doesn't mean an incongruent example has to exist in the counter pervasion.

56. This citation is found in Dharmakīrti's *Autocommentary on the Commentary of Valid Cognition*, 351a3, where he cites Dignāga.
57. In other words, "Sound is impermanent because it can be heard" and "Sound is permanent because it can be heard" would both be valid reasonings.
58. This citation is found in Vinītadeva's commentary (*Hetubinduṭīkā*, Toh 4234, 176a4) to Dharmakīrti's *Drops of Proof.*
59. Permanence and impermanence existing together within the subject sound.
60. A physical sensation (*reg bya*) is one of the five sensory objects and is experienced by bodily consciousness. It can be rough, gentle, and so on or neutral. The Vaiśeṣika assert that a neutral sensation is not found upon the visible elements of fire, water, and earth.
61. This entire citation is found in Śākyabuddhi's *Explanation* (34b1) but not in any works by Dignāga. Gorampa (and Gyaltsab) seems to have taken it directly from here.
62. *'Ang*. However, the root text of the Tibetan translation and Gyaltsab have *'am*, "alternatively" (Sanskrit *vā*).
63. *Khyab pa.* In strict logical terms this phrase means that the predicate or phenomenon to be established is found wherever the reason is and only where the reason is. The reason is pervaded by the predicate. In simpler terms it means "This follows," or "This is necessarily so." However, as this is a logic-based work, it is translated as "This pervades."
64. The question is, "Impermanence, the phenomenon to be established, is of one nature with 'product.' Therefore how can 'product' be used separately as a reason?" This point is made in the autocommentary.
65. The whole following section on exclusion of others, through verse 185, is a response to this question: If being a product and being impermanent are indivisible, how can being a product be proof of impermanence?
66. To have distinct isolates (*ldog pa tha dad*) means to be conceptually distinct. The same object can support multiple conceptual identities, like in the example here of sound, impermanent, and being a product. It is called an *isolate* because it distinguishes by way of excluding all that is other than itself.
67. An *object-possessor* is usually a cognition that possesses an object. As all cognitions possess objects that they cognize, it could just be translated as "subject." However, the term also refers to the verbal expression of a particular phenomenon. Therefore the thought "pot" and the expression "pot" both have the intrinsically existing entity of pot as their object. Moreover, *subject* often refers to the subject of a three-part logical assertion consisting of subject, predicate, and reason.
68. *Glo bur ba'i rjes dpag.* Inference that does not go through the normal process of ascertaining the three criteria. This could be, for example, because of former habituation with the subject.
69. *Rnam grangs.* Here *synonyms* is used to refer to separate verbal expressions or concepts for a single phenomenon. Therefore "sound" and "that which can be heard" (its definition) are synonyms, but "sound is impermanent" and "sound is a product" are not.
70. The term *bring about* used a few times in this topic literally means "to assist" (*phan pa*, *pakāra*). It is often used in a causal sense, meaning that the cause "assists" in bringing

about the result. The pot, as the possessor of features of the pot, has the "potential" to assist in bringing about those features.

71. *Zhen yul.* The object determined, conceived, or focused on by way of exclusion within conceptual cognition.
72. *Log pa* and *ldog pa.* Both are used to translate the Sanskrit *vyāvṛtti.*
73. The assertion that a universal (*spyi*) or class (*rigs*) is substantially different from the particulars.
74. A juniper tree possessing the generic title of *tree*, for example.
75. In *Compendium of Valid Cognition* 5.4.
76. *Grong drug, ṣaṇṇagari*, an ancient Indian district of six villages.
77. "Wives" is plural and "woman" is singular. There could be nothing within "woman" that the plural form "wives" could be applied to because the plural form would be caused by plural phenomena alone. The row of houses is part of the six villages, but "six villages" is plural, caused by plural phenomena, whereas a row is singular.
78. Dharmakīrti, *Autocommentary on the Commentary on Valid Cognition*, 282a4.
79. The remaining quotes in the paragraph are from the excerpt of the autocommentary just above.
80. Sakya Paṇḍita, *Treasure of Reasoning*, 6a4.
81. Sakya Paṇḍita, *Treasure of Reasoning*, 6a5.
82. Sakya Paṇḍita, *Treasure of Reasoning*, 6a3.
83. Sakya Paṇḍita, *Treasure of Reasoning*, 6a4.
84. *Kun rdzobs pa.* This is the term used to describe truths other than ultimate truths in this philosophical system. Therefore sometimes it is translated as "conventional truth" in common with higher tenets. However, here it is a truth because it is true in the perspective of that conceptual cognition but not in reality, and it is "concealing" because of the reasons given in the text.
85. *Bzung rnam.* Any cognition or consciousness will have a subjective aspect (*'dzin rnam*) and an objective aspect. The former is the apprehending aspect of cognition, which is synonymous with self-knowing cognition, and the latter is the apprehended aspect. Both of these are real, intrinsically existent, or ultimate phenomena in this school of thinking because both are consciousness and therefore function in reality. But from the perspective of that form which appears to a conceptual mind, such a form does not exist as it appears and has no ultimate reality.
86. Dharmakīrti, *Autocommentary on the Commentary on Valid Cognition*, 292b5.
87. Sakya Paṇḍita, *Treasure of Reasoning*, 8b4.
88. This explains the difference between a universal (*spyi*) and a common basis (*gzhi mthun*). A universal unites all of the same class by way of cognition and verbal expression of, for example, "trees," thereby eliminating non-trees. The cognition and verbal expression that isolates a single type of tree from all other trees nevertheless has a common basis with tree. Every other type of tree named and conceived is an expansion of this common basis.
89. Dharmakīrti, *Autocommentary on the Commentary on Valid Cognition*, 284b4.
90. This verse indicates the difference between designation (*tha snyad, vyavahāra/vyapadeśa*) and convention (*brda, saṃketa*). See glossary.
91. "Resorting to falsity" means that the conceptual cognition that takes a class, exclusion, or other universal as its object is mistaken with regard to the object that appears

because it is a mere mental construct of the reality. However, this does not invalidate that cognition as performing useful functions such as analysis.

92. The basic question here is, when we see a cow and then think or say "This is a cow," what is the cause of that identification? Is there some pervading universal that produces that recognition? The thought "This is a cow" in the recognition of a creature that has the characteristics of a cow is the application of a convention and a universal and is accepted by Dharmakīrti, but his understanding of the nature of this universal differs from non-Buddhist schools, as described previously.
93. *Phan 'dogs*. Also translated as "to bring about."
94. Śākyabuddhi, *Explanation of the Commentary on Valid Cognition*, 78a7.
95. Verses 111 and 112 are commented on out of sequence.
96. *Mi ldan rnam gcod* and *gzhan ldan rnam gcod*. These are the two types of preclusion discussed above; see note 25.
97. Although verses 119–21 are complex, they do explain Dharmakīrti's understanding of how conceptual identification operates without the need for an all-pervading universal that exists as an entity of affirmation and not of exclusion. The process begins with the direct perception of particulars of trees that naturally cause the separating out of trees from non-trees in conceptualization. The convention "These are trees" is applied or engaged, and later, during verbal and conceptual designation, when no trees are present, *trees* are expressed by way of exclusion.
98. Dharmakīrti, *Autocommentary on the Commentary on Valid Cognition*, 295b7.
99. Dharmakīrti, *Autocommentary on the Commentary on Valid Cognition*, 296a3.
100. Śākyabuddhi, *Explanation of the Commentary on Valid Cognition*, 143a.
101. In the above commentary on verses 127–28, the term "reality" is a translation of *dngos po*, which is elsewhere translated as "entity." The Sautrāntika are realists, and in positing the reality of ultimate truths such as intrinsically existing phenomena, they establish in contrast the non-reality of conceived phenomena such as isolates. Therefore, in this section, "reality" is preferred.
102. Śākyabuddhi, *Explanation of Commentary on Valid Cognition*, 153a4.
103. *Dkar zal*. Primarily white with black patches.
104. Sakya Paṇḍita, *Treasure of Reasoning*, 6a4.
105. The Sanskrit *badara* means the jujube. The Tibetan *rgya shug* also has this meaning but can also mean the juniper tree. *Kuṇḍa* is Sanskrit for a pot, bowl, basin, and so on, as is the Tibetan *'khar gzhong*, although it often refers to a metal basin. The Sanskrit suggests a bowl of jujube fruit, but the Tibetan translation could be taken to refer to a growing juniper tree or bush in a large container. Such a sight is not uncommon in India. Also, references to the material cause and water suggests that Tibetan commentators have taken this interpretation.
106. *Nyer len*. This term occurs in Śākyabuddhi's commentary at this point. It is usually taken in philosophical works to mean a substantial or material cause, but here it seems to be more akin to its meaning as "appropriated," as in "the appropriation of the aggregates" (*nyen len gyi phung po*).
107. That which is illustrated (Tib. *gsal bya*) is done so by that which illustrates (*gsal byed*), such as light illuminating form. The particulars illustrate the universal because they are evident manifestations or instances of the universal that remains hidden. The Tibetan term (*gsal ba*) translated elsewhere as "particulars" is translated in this section

variously as "that which illustrates" and "that which is illustrated." However, in terms of its relation to the Buddhist presentation of a universal, it is rendered as "particulars." In Sāṃkhya philosophy the particulars illustrate the universal, and so here they are "that which illustrate."

108. Tib. *'du byed*, Skt. *saṃskāra*.
109. *Be lu ka*. Gyaltsab has *dpe lu ka*. According to Negi 1993, 3298, he was called Pailuka and was a disciple of Kaṇāda.
110. Cited in Dharmakīrti, *Autocommentary on the Commentary on Valid Cognition*, 306b6.
111. *Ser skya*. An important Sāṃkhya philosopher.
112. The Jaina philosophical school, also called the Naked Ones, are called "immodest" here because they have no shame about their nakedness.
113. *Spyi gtso*. Used interchangeably by Gorampa with *universal* (*spyi*).
114. *'Dun*. But the root text and Kunga Wangchuk both have *mdun*, "in front."
115. Sakya Paṇḍita, *Treasure of Reasoning*, 6a3.
116. The above long section on exclusion, universals, and so on was a necessary digression from the main topic of reasoning by nature. The reason for the digression began from verse 40.
117. It is important to note that *existence* (*yod pa*), as used here and in the following verses on this topic, means "entities" (*dngos po*), which is synonymous with impermanence, product, and so on. Usually *existence* includes permanent existents. Gorampa explains this at the end of this section, after verse 193.
118. Often the terms *bsgrub bya* and *bsgrub bya'i chos* have been translated as "thesis" and "predicate," but in this section it may be preferable to render them more literally as "that to be established" and "phenomenon to be established" because the aspect of establishing is the focus of this argument.
119. The reason here would be, "The universal exists as an entity because it has the ability to function." However, the root verse also expresses the point in a more general way, that existence itself cannot be the predicate to be established in a reason because that existence would have already been established in the subject of the reason. However, if the existence of that subject is yet to be established, then it cannot be the subject of the reason.
120. These two pieces of text, which are also found here in *Commentary on Valid Cognition* (1.186 and 1.193), occur in Dharmakīrti's *Ascertainment of Valid Cognition* at 177b2 and 178a7, and no other verses appear between these two.
121. This topic is revisited in a section beginning from verse 1.269.
122. In the Sautrāntika system, disintegration (*'jig pa*), as the nature of all that is created, is a functioning phenomenon and of one nature with being produced, impermanent, and so on. The state of being destroyed (*zhig pa*), when that entity is no longer existing, is a non-entity, without causes and therefore permanent.
123. As indicated by this heading, there are two types of negation reasoning, or reasoning by way of nonapprehending. They are usually known as *nonapprehension by way of nonappearance* and *nonapprehension of that which should appear*. See glossary.
124. Dharmakīrti, *Autocommentary on the Commentary on Valid Cognition*, 318b6.
125. Devendrabuddhi, *Word Explanation of the Commentary on Valid Cognition*, 162a5.
126. Devendrabuddhi, *Word Explanation of the Commentary on Valid Cognition*, 162a7.

127. Śākyabuddhi, *Explanation of the Commentary on Valid Cognition*, 230a6.
128. Kamalaśīla, *Commentary on the Compendium on Reality*, 18b2.
129. Kamalaśīla, *Commentary on the Compendium on Reality*, 111a6.
130. Kamalaśīla, *Commentary on the Compendium on Reality*, 24a2.
131. A direct perception *apprehends* every aspect of its appearing object, but it does not *ascertain* all of them, such as impermanence, unless that aspect generates a conceptual valid cognition. Therefore, if it is not ascertained, there can be no valid cognition of its existence or nonexistence.
132. I cannot find the source of this citation.
133. *Sgra don. Sgra* is the verbal expression, and *don* is the actual entity. This two-word phrase, which occurs regularly, can mean "verbal expression *and* entity" or "the entity *of* the verbal expression." Both meanings are used. The former is used in the definition of a conceptual cognition where the universals of the verbal expression of the actual entity are mixed or appear as mixed. That meaning could be applicable here because that is what is "superimposed by conceptualization arising from past imprints." However, the latter rendering is clearly used by other commentators when glossing this verse. The verbal expression will have a referent and that referent is of three types.
134. The conceptualization or verbal expression *universal* has no actual object that it engages, but the object of that conceptualization is a representation of a universal appearing to the cognition, and that mental construct does exist.
135. The topic of fallacious reasoning comprises the remainder of Dharmakīrti's first chapter, including the extensive refutation of the Vedas that begins in verse 224 below.
136. *U yug rigs pa'i sen ge*, a thirteenth-century master who composed a commentary on the whole of *Commentary on Valid Cognition* after hearing an exposition of it from his teacher Sakya Paṇḍita.
137. See pages 52ff.
138. "Reversing" (*log pa*) refers to the above reasoning by nonapprehension, where reasoning by same nature and reasoning by result are used negatively to refute. The two types of valid cognition are direct perception and inference.
139. These two lines are included in the root text of some editions, but they do not appear in the Miyasaka edition used here for numbering the verses. They are found in Dharmakīrti's *Autocommentary*, 322a3.
140. Therefore, *rab tu nges pa yis* becomes *rab tu nges pas bstan pa yis*.
141. *Skye bu phul byung*. This may well refer to an ārya being, but the relevant term (*'phags pa*) is not used.
142. *Gti mug.*
143. The Vedas are asserted as being authorless (*apauruṣeya*) or of divine authorship. They are revealed texts, pure, and cannot be mistaken. The meanings of the Vedas, which are often obscure, are brought out by later Vedānta philosophers, such as the Mīmāṃsaka.
144. The term *don* (*artha*) can mean the actual phenomenon or reality as opposed to a mental construct of that reality, or it can mean "meaning." The actual pot is the *don* of the expression "pot," although the actual pot is also the referent or meaning of that expression.
145. When an elephant washes itself, it first covers itself in water to remove the dust and then rolls in the dust to dry itself.
146. *Gsal ba byed.* This term can also be translated as "illustrate" or "make manifest," in the

sense that particulars are manifestations or illustrations of the all-pervading prime universal asserted by the Sāṃkhya. However, "illuminate" is used here because of the following example of the sun.

147. Gyaltsab Jé points out that here it is being taught that words and speech from the perspective of expressing objects are without reality but that in themselves they are phenomena. If the expression *pot* from its perspective of expressing a bulbous container had reality, such a bulbous container would appear to the mind of someone unfamiliar with the word *pot* when they heard it.
148. The time it takes for the eyes to blink is considered to be the length of time needed for a recognized sound to become a letter.
149. These names come from Dharmakīrti's autocommentary. The figures are authors of Vedic mantras.
150. An illustration of a statement of belief (*yid dpyod*) that is not based on ascertaining reasoning: "There was water in the old well as used by our ancestors, so there must be some now."
151. *Dbyig gi snying po.* This is the golden womb from which all creation is said to have sprung. It is also an epithet of Brahma, the creator of the Vedas.
152. *Gzhon nu 'byung ba can*, a poem by Kālidāsa. This text describes the life of goddess Parvatī and her marriage to Śiva.
153. *Phyis kyang*. Literally "later also," in the sense of being similar to the previous verse. However, other editions of the root text have *cis kyang* ("by all means") here, which is used to qualify the evident dependence stated in the preceding line.
154. The actions of the tongue create individual sounds or parts of syllables that become syllables when amalgamated. It is a case of the cause being labeled as the effect.
155. This section is similar to the section running from verses 1.193–97. In Tibetan, "destruction" (*'zhig pa*) is the past tense of "disintegrating" (*'jig pa*). Although in Tibetan these two words are the present and past of the same verb, that does not work well in English with either the verb *to disintegrate* or *to destroy*. Therefore *disintegration*, as used here, means "disintegrating" or "in the state or process of being destroyed." *Destruction* is a one-off state and a total absence of reality. In that sense, it is a concept with no functional reality and is therefore permanent. However, the root text uses *'jig pa* throughout, and sometimes Gorampa glosses it as *'zhig pa*.
156. "Existence" (*yod pa*) here refers primarily to entities or functioning phenomena (*dngos po*).
157. In other words, it may be true that being uncreated by persons does not always pervade that which is possessed of the truth, as the examples of firelight and moonlight above illustrate. However, speech created by humans is always seen to exist in the possessing of untruths.
158. Sometimes, entire verses of the Vedas are called mantras.
159. There is a play on words here in both Sanskrit and Tibetan. *Veda* and the Tibetan *rig byed* mean "knowledge," and here in the verse "not knowing" is *rig byed min* and *na veda*. Therefore it reads something like "Not knowing the knowledge."
160. The Sanskrit for "goddess" here, rendered in Tibetan as the generic *lha mo*, is *uvarśī*, who is a particular celestial nymph. The stick is one that is vigorously turned to create friction needed to ignite the fire. But I cannot find any reference for the Vedic interpretation of these two terms.

161. Saying that linguistic convention engages by desire or wish means that the object of a linguistic convention is determined by conception and exclusion and not by a phenomenon naturally and intrinsically existing from the side of the object.
162. The root text is *G.yem ma mu cor gyis rgyal lo, Jayed dhārṣṭyena bandhakīm.* This is glossed by Gorampa and Gyaltsab Jé as "a lustful woman foolishly claiming victory over her master." The story, fictional or otherwise, is described in the autocommentary and in Śākyabuddhi's commentary. However, it seems that there is some difference in the Sanskrit and Tibetan versions. Essentially, an unchaste woman is caught with another man by her husband, who confronts her. She retaliates by trying to prove her innocence, claiming that the blind old wood-seller from the village tried to seduce her but she refused. The difficulty seems to be the understanding of the word *rgyal ba / jayet*. The Sanskrit uses this term to mean "surpass," therefore rendering the analogy to mean that the claims of the Vedānta scholars surpass in absurdity even that of an unchaste woman. The Tibetan scholars render this term to mean "victory," the woman foolishly believing she has succeeded in convincing her husband. I am indebted to the Sanskrit scholar David Reigle for this information.
163. Inferential and direct valid cognitions.
164. This verse refers back to nonapprehension reasoning where merely not apprehending a phenomenon is not sufficient to determine whether it exists.
165. This verse is the first two lines of the homage in Dignāga's *Compendium of Valid Cognition.* It is not in this root text or in Gorampa's commentary, but it has been inserted here because, as mentioned in the introduction, the following chapter uses its sequence of Buddha's qualities to establish the Buddha as a valid authority.
166. This phrase features in both commentaries but primarily in Devendrabuddhi's when he says, "The Ācārya having presented inference, which is the basis for the explanation of the treatise of the characteristics of valid cognition...." This is explained at the beginning of Gorampa's first chapter. "Ācārya" refers to Dignāga and *Valid Cognition Sūtra* to his *Compendium of Valid Cognition*, in which the first chapter is on direct perception (*pratyakṣa*).
167. This phrase is found in the opening lines of Dharmakīrti's *Ascertainment of Valid Cognition* and also in his autocommentary to the first chapter of *Commentary on Valid Cognition.* See Gorampa's introductory remarks on pages 42ff.
168. Prajñākaragupta and Yamāri.
169. See Gorampa's introductory section, pages 42ff.
170. Times when there is no perception: sleep, fainting, the state of nonperception in the higher formless realm, meditative equipoise on cessation, and meditative equipoise on nonperception.
171. *Kun rdzob pa'i blo.* This conceptual cognition (*rtog pa*) is in contrast to direct sense perception.
172. The Buddhist Vaibhāṣika school says that it is the sense faculties that sense the material objects of the senses—that is, the eyes see, the ears hear, and so on.
173. Interrupted in the sense of being an indirect result, separated from its cause by time and other factors. An uninterrupted result is one in which the valid cognition continuously engages its comprehended object.
174. *Kun tu tha snyad kyi tshad ma*, valid cognitions whose engaged or conceived objects

are wholly designated by way of terminology, verbal expression, and conceptualization.

175. *Nges pa blo'i tha snyad.* This is one division of a twofold division of *designation* (*tha snyad*). The other is *expression as a designation* (*brjod pa sgra'i tha snyad*). See glossary.
176. *Don ldog*, the essential character or definition of the phenomenon.
177. Sakya Paṇḍita, *Treasure of Reasoning*, 16a5.
178. Gorampa and other commentators take this line (2.5c) as a complete sentence in itself and gloss the following lines (2.5d and 2.6ab) to be the assertion of an opponent.
179. "The former" refers to the definition of valid cognition in verse 5, "Validity is a nondeceptive consciousness." The line "revealing unknown phenomena" is a quote from Dignāga in verse 6, and the query is asking if Dharmakīrti's definition does not contradict Dignāga's. Also, this aspect of the definition gives rise to valid cognition being qualified as a "new" cognition, as found in the Sautrāntika definition of valid cognition posited by some schools in Tibet.
180. Dharmakīrti's "Validity is a nondeceptive consciousness" in verse 5 and Dignāga's "revealing unknown phenomena" in verse 6.
181. In Hinduism Īśvara (*dbang phyug*) is often an epithet of the god Śiva, but in some schools it is regarded as the creator of the universe.
182. *Sdod cing 'jug pa, sthitva pravṛtti.* Could be rendered as "stay and go," in the sense of remaining unused and then being engaged. The examples of an axe and the rest are found in Śākyabuddhi's commentary, as is much of this section.
183. Vasubandhu, *Treasury of Abhidharma*, 4.1.
184. Īśvara is an uncreated permanent entity and therefore could not be a creator.
185. In a logical argument, the reason must be the property of the subject of that thesis. A particular man-made shape is not found to be the shape of the environment in its totality, and so the reason "The environment and so on was created by a supreme being because it is a man-made shape" does not stand.
186. Smoke, the result of fire, may be white in color, but it does not follow that any white substance indicates fire.
187. This means that when presented with the reasoning "Sound is impermanent because it is a product; as with a pot for example," you reply by saying that the reason is not valid because a pot is not sound.
188. The term "flawed refutation" (*ltag chod*) as used here refers to faulty refutations given by opponents in debate. Dignāga mentions twenty-four such refutations. These are enumerated and explained by Sakya Paṇḍita in his *Treasure of Reasoning* root text and autocommentary, in the eleventh chapter, "Inference for Others." (The first two of these are mentioned in Gorampa's following sentence.) They are called "similarities" because the opponent tries to refute the reasoning by positing faulty comparisons or similarities. For example, if I say, "A tomato is a fruit because it possesses the general characteristics of a fruit, like an apple, for example," that might provoke the rejoinder that this is not good reasoning because tomato and apple are distinct phenomena and therefore the fruit characteristics of an apple are not found in a tomato. But this is false refutation because the original reasoning is relying upon a generality and not on a specific.

    The "faulty refutation, similar effect" (*'bras mtshungs ltag chod*) mentioned here is the seventh in the list; "effect" here is more like a quality or feature than a result in the strict sense of the word.

189. *'Dod rgyal ba'i ming*, the arbitrary naming of something without recourse to etymology, reason, and so on.
190. Dignāga, *Compendium of Valid Cognition*, 12a4.
191. Sakya Paṇḍita, *Autocommentary to Treasure of Reasoning*, 392.
192. This verse is cited in many works such as those of Nāgārjuna and in a commentary to the *Guhyasamāja Tantra*, but its source is not clear. Moreover, the list varies occasionally. Some have nine meanings while others have ten.
193. *Blo bde*. Hayes divides this: "intellect and happiness."
194. We say that trees "die" but this is mere expression and for Buddhists does not mean that the trees possess life in the sense of having consciousness. Also, in Tibetan when a flame is extinguished, it "dies."
195. Some schools state that sound is a "quality of space."
196. Aulūkya are followers of Ulūka, alias Kaṇāda, founder of the non-Buddhist Vaiśeṣika school of Indian philosophy.
197. This verse is not found in any of the Sanskrit editions I looked at. Miyasaka has numbered it as 20[b].
198. This example does not work when taken out of Sanskrit. It does not really work in Tibetan either. The Sanskrit word *jagat* (*'gro ba*) means "cow" and, literally, "move." The Sanskrit *karin* (*lag ldan*) means "elephant" and, literally, "possessing limbs" in Tibetan but "possessing a trunk" in Sanskrit.
199. A common name for an ordinary person.
200. A cause has the power or capacity to produce a result, and therefore removing that cause negates any possibility of a result, but as Īśvara is permanent, removing him has no bearing on the result.
201. *Rnam bcad* (preclusion) and *yongs gcod* (affirmation).
202. (1) A valid cognition that knows all hidden existence does not exist, (2) there is no cause that accomplishes such a state, and (3) endeavor in such a cause does not exist.
203. These three are explained in the commentary to verse 280 of this chapter.
204. *Sgrub byed*. This term can mean "establisher" or "proof" in the sense of a reason establishing a thesis and also "accomplisher" in the sense of being a cause producing a result. Here, either meaning is possible, but scholars have suggested that compassion is described in the text as the first *sgrub byed* and therefore is a creating force, or accomplisher.
205. Verse cited in Prajñākaragupta's *Ornament to the Commentary on Valid Cognition*, 46a3. The essential meaning is that as I cannot know, for example, how many atoms there are in the universe, I just leave the question alone.
206. *'Phen byed kyi las*, a type of karma that is capable of "throwing" the consciousness into a particular type of rebirth, thereby creating the mental and physical aggregates of a future life.
207. Sakya Paṇḍita, *Treasure of Reasoning*, 17b4.
208. *Gzhan rig*. Knowing can be divided into self-apprehending, or self-knowing (*rang rig*), and other-apprehending (*gzhan rig*).
209. *Ldog byed kyi rgyu*. Indispensable in the sense that if the cause is negated, the result must also be negated.

210. *Nyer len gyi rgyu*. Sometimes translated as "substantial cause."
211. The logic here is that there are "incurable illnesses" as determined by the criteria above—end of life and no medicine as yet discovered—but if it was only down to the pathology of the disease itself, there would be no incurable illnesses because every disease is potentially curable by medicine and treatment.
212. *Ba men / ba min, gavaya*. Said to be the crossbreed of the wild Indian ox and the domestic cow.
213. When the Lokāyata materialists use the term "disintegration" they are referring to the destruction of the mind that occurs when the body, its cause, is destroyed. This is dissimilar to the Buddhist use of the term, which refers to disintegration as being an innate quality of all produced phenomena.
214. Qualities, actions, and universals are three of the six categories of existence (*tshig don, padārtha*) posited by the Vaiśeṣika: substance (*dravya*), quality (*guṇa*), action (*karman*), universal (*sāmānya*), particularity (*viśeṣa*), and inherence (*samavāya*).
215. *'Phrod pa 'du ba, samavāya*. Inherence is one of the six categories of existence posited by the Vaiśeṣika. According to Monier-Williams, "Perpetual co-inherence, constant and intimate union, inseparable concomitance; the sixth *padārtha* or category of the Vaiśeṣika, expressing relation which exists between a substance and its qualities, between a whole and its parts, *e.g., between cloth and the yarn composing it*, between a genus and its individuals."
216. See the commentary on verse 1.60 above.
217. This refers to the belief that your desire increases or decreases in conjunction with your weight.
218. It is generally recognized that the Vaiśeṣika were atomists believing that all entities are ultimately reducible to indivisible particles (*paramāṇu*). They also accept the six categories of existence, the first of which is substantiality. Tibetan commentators on non-Buddhist tenets say that this substance is self-sustaining, independent, and acts as the support for other qualities. Therefore, although they are atomists, they would still assert the above consequence.
219. Sakya Paṇḍita, *Autocommentary to Treasure of Reasoning*, 259, line 6.
220. *Rnam rig pa*, the Mind Only school.
221. This question is posed in *Commentary on Valid Cognition* 3.321c (130b6).
222. 'Jam dbyangs sgegs po, a student of the Tibetan master Chomden Rikpai Raldri (1227–1305).
223. I am unable to source this passage.
224. The Vaiśeṣika assertions that "sense consciousnesses would not comprehend them" and "they would have no obstructive abilities."
225. The argument from our side here is that parts and possessors of parts are separate and different, but the possessors are not substantially separate or substantially one.
226. *Ldan pa, saṃyoga*, one of the twenty-four types of "quality," which is the second of the six categories of existence asserted by the Vaiśeṣika and other schools. Can also be described as "accompaniments" and "conjunctions."
227. *Bya rgya*, possibly a corruption of *bya brgya* (hundred birds), as found in Gyaltsab and Kunga Wangchuk.
228. These are also types of "qualities" asserted by the Vaiśeṣika. See note 214.
229. *'Phrod 'du, samavāya*. See note 215 above.

230. Although "distinct," and "separate" are generally similar in meaning, here phenomena such as isolates are distinct (*tha snyad*) from each other but not intrinsically separate (*don gzhan*). Therefore they are said to be "different" (*khyad par*).

231. The commentary seems to read the root text as "pot, form, and so on" (*bum pa gzugs sogs*). All editions of the root text I have seen have "pot is form" (*bum pa gzugs so, rūpam ghaṭa*), as does Kunga Wangchuk's *Annotations*, who follows Gorampa almost verbatim. Therefore it is likely that that *sogs* ("and so on") is a misprint of the final grammatical particle *so.*

The point being made in this passage is that the expression *pot* expresses a collection but does not express the collection-possessors of form, subtle particles, and so on because they are excluded by this expression. Therefore here *pot* expresses a collection. The expression "an oak is a tree" is an expression of class and does not exclude the class-possessor *oak*. Therefore Gyaltsab says that the expression *pot* in relation to the form and so on of a pot expresses collection but in relation to a gold pot and so on, it expresses class.

232. *Rgyu ba zhan pa*, as per the canonical version of the root text. The versions of Gorampa's commentary all have "when the breath is flowing" (*rgyu bzhin pa*), but this seems to be a printing error, and *zhan pa* occurs a few sentences later.

233. Gyaltsab might be among the "most scholars" that Gorampa criticizes below, because Gyaltsab reads Dharmakīrti's reply to the consequence of the mind remaining on its own as referring to a sentient being about to take rebirth in the formless realm. But Gorampa does not, as can be seen from his gloss.

234. Here "material cause" (*nyer len*) of the body does not refer to the substantial cause of sperm and egg that derives from the parents but to the sense sources (*skye mched, āyatana*).

235. That of cessation (*'gog pa'i snyoms 'jug*) and that of no identification (*'du shes med pa'i snyoms 'jug*).

236. Here Gorampa is citing a line from verse 392 of Dharmakīrti's third chapter to illustrate his point. This verse is from the section in chapter 3 asserting that external phenomena do not exist. The line is a response to those who assert that there must be a third cause, other than the sense faculty and the immediately preceding mental continuum, for the coming into being of a sense consciousness, and it can be inferred that this third cause must be the existence of phenomena external to the mind. The line states that if it were not explicitly stated that the sense consciousness arises from a similar and immediately preceding cause then such an argument would have weight, but it is stated. This is compared to the argument put forward here by "other scholars" who leaved out the hypothetical "if" in verse 115 and divide the answer up into two parts. Gorampa instead glosses the line to read "if it did not become the branch cause, mind would exist on its own, but it does," and uses the line from the third chapter to back up his argument.

237. Reasoning with "remainder" is the root text technical term for uncertain reasoning, as explained in chapter 6 above.

238. The word translated as "training" here is *goms* (*abhyāsatā*), which is often translated as "familiarization" or "habituation" and is related to the Tibetan word translated as "meditation" (*sgom*). It could also be translated as "practice" in the sense of "practice makes perfect." Later, in the section on the four truths, it is translated as "habituation."

239. The important phrase here and above is "operating under their own power" whereby the cause for continuation and development is within the phenomenon itself, as with fire burning wood, without any need for extra effort from elsewhere. The examples given here all do that. Desire, for example, even though it cannot develop limitlessly, once generated, runs under its power.
240. Sugata and Protector.
241. More precisely, "good" when used as an adjective and "well" when used adverbially.
242. Gyaltsab says that these two causes refer to the abandonment gained when newly reaching the path of seeing, where emptiness is seen directly for the first time, and to the subsequent abandonments of the path of meditation.
243. *Lung ma bstan*. Neither virtuous nor unvirtuous.
244. For the Mīmāṃsaka speech from a person arises from desire, and therefore such a person has not abandoned all faults. For them, the pure and true speech is that of the Vedas, which were not authored by a person.
245. *Skyon, doṣa*. The Sanskrit term is often used to describe the three humors. When out of balance, they become bodily faults.
246. This refers to the feelings of pain and well-being, which can precipitate anger and desire.
247. *Khu ba*. The Sanskrit *mada* can also mean passion, intoxication, and so on, but the reference to "blood falling" seems to indicate that "semen" is the better translation.
248. *Jig tshogs*, the five aggregates, wrongly viewed as self and belonging to self. Sometimes translated as "identity view."
249. *'Byung 'gyur*, the forms that are created from the four basic elements.
250. There are variations in the root text of this verse. In some the third line reads "With the support destroyed (*chad pa*), the abiding of the supported is destroyed." Others read, "With the support complete (*tshang ba*), the abiding of the supported is destroyed," which cannot be right. Others read, "With the support of the alcohol (*chang*), the abiding of the supported is destroyed," which also cannot be correct. This commentary and Gyaltsab have followed the Indian commentaries and the Sanskrit root text, which read the fourth line as "will not be destroyed" (*avikale*). For the third line, Gorampa reads, "If the support remains complete."
251. *Rig pa*, often translated as "knowing."
252. The commentary has "would not be newly arisen," but this seems to be a misprint, as indicated by Kunga Wangchuk 2015, 91b2.
253. The examples of the three types of living beings are taken from the Indian commentaries. If the same elements that produce the bodies of living beings also produced their desire, then those of great desire would have large bodies and those of minimal desire would have small bodies. But "there are no such differences."
254. Another name for the Lokāyata materialist school.
255. Each of the four truths has four attributes. The four of suffering are listed in full. Only the first and most important attributes of the other three truths are listed.
256. *Rjes su 'gro ldog*. If the cause is present, there will be the concomitance of a subsequent result, and if the cause is negated, there will be the concomitance of no subsequent result.
257. "Tangibility" refers to the assembling of particles to create a form visible to the eye.
258. *Sred pa, tṛṣṇā*. Although often synonymous with desire (*'dod chags*), here it refers to

the craving that is the eighth of the twelve links, and is the cause of appropriation, the ninth link, as glossed by this sentence. Also, "objects" here refers to body, possessions, and place.

259. This citation is found in Devendrabuddhi's *Word Explanation* (80b3), but I cannot locate it in Vasubandhu's works.
260. Nāgārjuna, *Friendly Letter*, 92b3.
261. *Mang pos bkur ba*. The Sāṃmitīya, a Buddhist school whose tenets were in line with the Vaibhāṣika school, expounded a person that was beyond description, a view known as *pudgalavāda*. The Sāṃmitīya are sometimes conflated with, or said to be a subschool of, another Pudgalavādin school, the Vātsīputrīya.
262. Vaibhāṣika, Sautrāntika, and Cittamātra.
263. *Udānavarga*. This verse is cited in Devendrabuddhi's *Word Explanation* (83b3), but I cannot locate it elsewhere. Devendrabuddhi has "musk deer" instead of "elephant."
264. Devadatta is often the name used for a fictional ordinary being in an example. Devadatta was the name of the Buddha's cousin, someone who had doubts about the Buddha's enlightenment, so there may be a connection.
265. *Glo bur, āgantu*: something added, incidental, adventitious, accidental—that is, a sudden or temporary change that does not affect the actual nature of the situation.
266. *'Od gsal, prabhāsvara*, often translated as "clear light."
267. "Ignorance," *ma rig pa*, is literally "not knowing."
268. *Dmigs pa* is the object focused upon or apprehended, and *rnam pa* is the aspect the consciousness takes of that object.
269. Here "knowledge" is *shes rab*, "wisdom" is *ye shes*, and "knowing" is *rig pa*.
270. This sūtra is cited in Devendrabuddhi's Indian commentary and is another name for the *King of Samādhis* (*Samādhirājasūtra*).
271. Here, "attachment" is *chags pa*. While *'dod chags* (desire) and *chags pa* are sometimes synonymous, *attachment* is taken to refer to something one already possesses, or perceives oneself to possess, such as a "self," while *desire* refers to longing for something we do not possess. *Chags pa* translates more than one Sanskrit term, but a common one is *snih*, which also means "sticky" or "glutinous," hence the sense of attachment.
272. Neither the root text nor the commentary state that it is the attachment to that belonging to self that is abandoned, but that is clear from the headings. Therefore, the non-Buddhist meditates on the body, or sense faculties, as being the cause of suffering and thereby eliminates attachment to them. In this way, through austere practices of nonattachment, they reduce attachment to the desire realm and eventually take rebirth in the form and formless realms.
273. The Tibetan term for "assert" here and elsewhere is *'dod pa*. However, it can also mean "to desire." The Sanskrit here is *vallabha*, which does mean "to want," "to love," etc. Gorampa and other Tibetan commentators have glossed this verse with *'dod pa* meaning "to assert," and consequently the root-verse translation reflects this.
274. The sense faculties "accomplish" the happiness of the self.
275. In other words, the mere object-possessor of the self is without faults, but as attachment to the self, it is with fault.
276. The two fundamental phenomena of the Sāṃkhya school are the *innate nature* (*rang bzhin, prakṛti*), also known as the universal, primordial matter, first principle, and so on, and the *person* (*skye bu, puruṣa*), also identified as the self and consciousness. The

dualistic relationship between these two is fundamental in the Sāṃkhya pursuit of liberation. Gyaltsab says that although the *prakṛti* is hidden and not manifest, knowing the separation of self and the sense faculties, together with their pleasures, is to know the separation of self from its innate nature.

277. Being under the control of cause and effect is not necessarily a characteristic of suffering because the nonafflicted phenomena not classified as saṃsāra are also subject to cause and effect.
278. Text has *rig*, but Devendrabuddhi has *rigs*, which I have followed here. Moreover, Gyaltsab has *rung*, "appropriate."
279. This sūtra citation is found in the Indian commentaries, but I cannot find any correspondence in the Tibetan Kangyur.
280. *Sred pa*, but the text has *srid pa* (samsaric existence). These two are very close in spelling and have been confused before. Versions of the root text have either. Gyaltsab goes with *srid pa*, but Kunga Wangchuk in his commentary, which follows Gorampa closely, has *sred pa*, which seems the more likely in Gorampa's gloss.
281. An austerity ritual where the meditator is positioned with fires in front, behind, and on either side along with the sun above.
282. *Sems pa, cetanā.*
283. *Byed pa, kāraṇa*, which is glossed as "sense faculties" (*dbang po*).
284. *'Du byed, saṃskāra.*
285. Kunga Wangchuk says that because the person has no substantial existence, there is no "other" person remembering what "another" person has experienced. Gyaltsab says that this consequence refers to a permanent self.
286. *Dbu tshad.* Pramāṇa and Madhyamaka combined are known as the lion with two necks, to illustrate the importance of reasoning, inference, and valid cognition in the pursuit of the ultimate truth.
287. *Nyon mongs, kleśa.* Usually refers to the mental afflictions such as anger and desire, but this term in Tibetan and Sanskrit also means distress, pain, suffering, and so on, especially that of the physical kind.
288. Gyaltsab points out that the last line of this verse is not asserting that karmas destined to be experienced cannot be nullified, because by way of the four powers and so forth, their ripening can be stopped.
289. In the forward reasoning, Sugata was explained in terms of possessing three types of abandonment. See verse 2.139.
290. *Bde bar gshegs pa.* Previously (2.139), the etymology of "well abandoned" was used.

Glossary

appearing object (*snang yul, pratibhāsaviṣaya*). The object that appears to a sense perception or a conceptual cognition. A consciousness takes on the aspect (*shes rnam*) of the object that appears to it in much the same way as a mirror takes on the form of a reflection. Therefore music appears to the audial consciousness, and the memory of that music is a mental construct appearing to a conceptual cognition.

belonging to self (*bdag gi ba, ātmīya*). Could be translated as "mine," but this term is often paired with "self" (*bdag*), and "that belonging to self" maintains a consistency.

class (*rigs, jāti*). A classification of phenomena of similar characteristics; as used in this text, it is synonymous with universal.

cognition (*blo, buddhi*). Many of the Tibetan terms for types of cognition, perception, consciousness, and so on are not always used with technical consistency. *Cognition* as used here is primarily a conceptual consciousness.

conceived object (*zhen yul*). This is the object conceived or determined by a conceptual cognition, in the sense that it is not determined by an external reality—as in the case of sense consciousnesses—but by the conceptualizing itself. Because of that, there are no conceived objects apprehended by sense consciousnesses. It also means that a conceived object does not necessarily have to exist, as in the case of the self being apprehended wrongly. When a conceived object exists, it is synonymous with the referent or engaged object of that conceptual cognition, but it is not the appearing object.

concomitant pervasion (*rjes khyab, anvayavyāpti*). One of the two pervasions necessary (the other is counter pervasion) to be ascertained when establishing the same-nature or causal relationship between the reason and the predicate, in which the reason is definitively ascertained as existing solely in the congruent class.

congruent class (*mthun phyogs, sapakṣa*). In reasoning it refers to the class of phenomena that is not empty of the predicate of the thesis. For example, impermanence in the reasoning used to establish that sound is impermanent.

congruent example (*mthun dpe, udāharaṇa*). An example given while presenting the reason in order to aid understanding, in which the pervasion between reason and predicate is also found in the example. "Sound is impermanent because it is a product, like a pot, for example."

convention (*brda, saṃketa*). The essential meaning of this term is "that which creates understanding." In other words, it is something that communicates. Here it is primarily linguistic convention that is being referred to. It is a *convention* because there is a shared understanding about what is being communicated. Certain hand gestures communicate certain messages to those they are directed at. Therefore the person will make a gesture knowing that it will communicate. Language is a convention insofar as among those who share the same language and similar vocabulary, words communicate by convention. Therefore the Tibetan term also carries the meaning of sign, signal, indicator, and so on.

A convention is first created with the actual phenomenon present. When teaching her child, a mother points to a cow and says "cow." Its purpose is that later, when the cow is not present, it can still be expressed by designations in the form of the verbal expression "cow" and the conceptual construct "cow." This is the meaning of the pithy saying found in related texts: "At the time of the convention, the object. At the time of the designation, the name." Also, "By convention, the designations of words are formed," and, "Words have no meanings inherently but come from convention." However, it is not the case that conventions and designations exclude each other.

coordinating cause (*lhan cig byed rkyen, sahakāripratyaya*). A cause that in the process of creating its result does not transform into the object itself, in contrast to the material cause, which does. Craving, for example, is a coordinating cause at death for the body of the future existence, and sunlight and moisture are coordinating causes for the seed to become a sprout.

counter pervasion (*ldog khyab, vyatirekavyāpti*). One of the three criteria, in which the incongruent class is ascertained as not existing within the reason that establishes the thesis. For example, in the reasoning "Phenomena do not truly exist because they are of dependent origination," the incongruent class of truly existing is ascertained as not existing within anything of dependent origination.

designation (*tha snyad, vyavahāra/vyapadeśa*). The Tibetan for this term carries a few related but distinct meanings. However, the main meaning in this text is of a linguistic term enabled by verbal expression and conceptualization. Therefore it is of two types: ascertainment as a cognitive designation (*nges pa blo'i tha snyad*) and verbal expression as a vocal designation (*brjod pa sgra'i tha snyad*). A single phenomenon can be divided into parts, properties, and features by way of conceptualization and by way of names, even though those parts are indivisible in terms of being part of an intrinsically existing phenomenon. This is the process of exclusion resulting in isolates, as extensively explained in the text. This detailed dividing and classification of phenomena gives rise to another meaning of this term, which is "terminology" or, in some cases, "jargon." As this term is used for identifying the proliferation of aspects of various phenomena, it has come to be associated with non-ultimate designations accepted in the world and thus carries the meaning of **convention**, in the sense that these designations are generally accepted and agreed upon. Such phenomena are "conventionally true" (*tha snyad bden pa*), a term used by the higher philosophical schools in Buddhism for all phenomena ascertained by non-ultimate cognition. These phenomena are cognized by valid cognitions known as wholly designated valid cognitions. Ascertainment as a cognitive designation and verbal expression as a vocal designation can both produce wholly designated valid cognitions.

dharma (*chos*). Comes from the Sanskrit *dharaṇa*, meaning "hold." Something that holds its own entity is a dharma. Therefore anything that exists is a dharma. In this usage the term is left in its Sanskrit. When used to mean the property of a property possessor, it is translated as such. These usages are found in this work. That which holds us from falling into suffering is also a dharma. This usage is often capitalized and is a synonym for religion.

direct contradiction (*dngos 'gal*). Two phenomena whose individual existences naturally negate the other. Light and darkness, for example.

direct valid perception (*mngon sum, pratyakṣa*). A direct perception or cognition that does not utilize conceptual constructs in the apprehending of its object and that correctly apprehends its engaged object. The most common examples are the sensory consciousnesses facilitated by the sense powers.

directly affecting (*phan byed*). A term describing the essential function of a phenomenon as a cause. The cause directly affects the result, and the result comes about from the existence of its directly affecting cause. Smoke is the result of fire because it necessarily follows from the directly affecting existence of fire.

disintegration and destruction. In Tibetan, *destruction* (*zhig pa*, *vinaṣṭa*) is the past tense of *disintegration* (*'jig pa*, *nāśa/vināśa*). In Tibetan, these two words are two parts of the same verb, but that does not work well in English with either the verb *to disintegrate* or the verb *to destroy*. Therefore *disintegration*, as used here, means disintegrating or being subject to destruction. All entities are momentarily disintegrating and in the process of being destroyed. Therefore it is said that entities are in the nature of disintegration. *Destruction* is a mental construct formed when an entity ceases to exist. When a pot is destroyed, the broken shards are entities formed from this act and possess an intrinsic reality. Its state of destruction is an absence of intrinsic reality. In that sense it is conceived with functionality in reality and is therefore permanent, according to the Sautrāntika school. However, the root text uses *'jig pa* throughout, and sometimes Gorampa glosses it as *zhig pa*.

distinct (*tha dad*, *bheda*). Generally distinct by way of characteristics, isolate, and exclusion but not necessarily distinct by way of being a separate entity.

element evolute (*'byung gyur*). Elements are individual particles classified as earth, water, fire, and air. When combined to create visible form they become evolutes.

engage by affirmation (*sgrub 'jug*). A cognition that engages its object through the power of the object itself and not by conceptual exclusion. Nonconceptual consciousnesses, such as the sense consciousnesses, do not conceptually isolate objects that appear to them.

engaged object (*'jug yul*, *pravṛttiviṣaya*). This is the object that a direct valid perception, such as a visual consciousness, beholds as an appearing external phenomenon and the object that a valid conceptual cognition engages with but to which that object does not directly appear. For example, when thinking about chocolate, chocolate is the engaged object, but the appearing object is not actually chocolate, because you can't eat it.

engaging by exclusion (*sel 'jug*). See **exclusion**.

entity (*dngos po*, *vastu/bhāva*). The two main characteristics of *dngos po* are its ability to function and its reality. In the Sautrāntika system it is an ultimate truth and ultimately real. Often this term has been translated as "phenomenon," but here "entity" is preferred to reflect these two features.

"Phenomenon" is used as a translation of *chos* (*dharma*) and sometimes of *don* (*artha*).

exclusion (*gzhan sel, apoha*). Fundamental tenet proposed by Dignāga and Dharmakīrti to explain how verbal expressions and conceptual cognitions engage with the phenomena they express or engage with. "Exclusion" refers to the excluding of phenomena in order to isolate a class or universal for the purposes of identification, examining, and so on. In such a process, many phenomena of the same class can be homogenized as one, and one phenomenon can be divided into many isolates for the above purposes. The universals and isolates created by exclusion are not the intrinsically existing phenomena themselves but are conceptually created.

fallacious reasoning (*gtan tshigs ltar snang ba, hetvābhāsa*). Flawed reasoning in which an ascertainment of the three criteria is incomplete.

hidden phenomena (*lkog gyur, parokṣa*). Phenomena not accessible to the senses of ordinary beings. Even though fire may be hidden and is cognized by the logic of smoke, fire is not a hidden phenomenon because by its nature it is accessible to the visual consciousness. Therefore hidden phenomena must first be detected by logic. There are very hidden phenomena and slightly hidden phenomena, requiring different types of reasons.

homogenous result (*'bras bu gcig pa*). The word *result* refers to the fact that certain groups of phenomena are produced with certain similarities to form a class. A homogenous group of trees or cows are resultant phenomena directly perceived by the visual consciousness, after which a conceptual cognition holds them as belonging to a homogenous class.

incongruent class (*mi mthun phyogs, vipakṣa nāstitā*). As used in reasoning it refers to a class of phenomena that is empty of the predicate of the thesis. For example, permanence in the reasoning used to establish that sound is impermanent constitutes an incongruent class.

incongruent example (*chos mi mthun pa'i dpe / mi mthun dpe*). An example presented within a reason to illustrate the counter pervasion. For example, in the reasoning that sound is impermanent because it is a product, stating, "Whatever is permanent is not pervaded by being a product, as with unconditioned space."

indispensable relationship (*med na mi 'byung 'brel, avinābhāva / nāntarīyaka*). A relationship between the reason and the predicate that is one of cause and effect, or one of the same nature. It is indispensable because if one part is not there, the other will not arise. The relationship between fire and smoke is that if there had been no fire, there would be no smoke, and so there cannot be smoke without a previous existence of fire.

inference (*rjes dpag, anumāna*). When used with cognition, it refers to a valid knowing of a hitherto hidden phenomenon induced by perfect reasoning.

inference for oneself (*rang don rjes dpag, svārthānumāna*). Inference concerning hidden phenomena induced by reasoning, with the purpose of generating conviction within oneself. It is also the title of the first chapter of this work. The fourth chapter is "Inference for Others" (*gzhan don rjes dpag, parārthānumāna*) and deals with presenting reasons in order to convince others.

innate nature (*rang bzhin, svabhāva/prakṛti*). Also known as the universal, universal principle, primordial matter, first principle, and so on. A prime tenet of the non-Buddhist Sāṃkhya school, it pervades all things but is hidden. According to the Sāṃkhya, the innate nature or universal principle is solely a cause, whereas its evident manifestations in the form of the phenomena of the world are results as well as being particulars of that universal.

intrinsically existing phenomenon (*rang mtshan, svalakṣaṇa*). A phenomenon whose existence is established by way of its own intrinsic features and characteristics. In the Sautrāntika school of thought as followed here, this refers to phenomena or entities directly accessed by way of the senses, such as form, sound, and so on. These phenomena are "real," and such schools are known as realists (*dngos po smra ba*). Conceptually constructed phenomena, such as universals, are not intrinsically existent.

isolate (*ldog pa, vyāvṛtti*). The conceptual isolation of a feature or phenomenon from other similar or dissimilar phenomena for the purposes of examination, communication, and so on. In the reasoning that sound is impermanent because of being a product, "impermanence" and "product" are not separate entities from sound but are isolated out for the sake of establishing something about sound that is hidden from the senses, thereby giving rise to the expression "one nature, different isolates." In the Sautrāntika school, whose assertions underpin this text, all intrinsically existent phenomena such as sound are the support of many isolates. Therefore verbal expressions and conceptualizations engage by way of isolation. In that sense, isolate and exclusion are mostly synonymous.

isolate of its own meaning (*don ldog*). Refers to the essential characteristics or definition of the phenomenon.

Jaimini (*rgyal dpog pa*). Founder of the Mīmāṃsā school.

Jain (*gcer bu pa*). A non-Buddhist school that began in India around the same time as Buddhism and, like Buddhism, does not assert a creator god. Adherents are sometimes called the Nirgrantha.

Lokāyata (*rgyang 'phen pa*). Ancient Indian materialist school, sometimes called the Cārvāka, that asserted that the world arose from inanimate matter, without purpose and design. They also claimed that mind arises from the body and ceases when the body ceases. Consequently, they denied rebirth, and they denied the fruits of karma beyond the present lifetime.

material cause (*nyer len, upādānahetu*). This is a cause whose very entity transforms into the result it is creating. Clay is a material cause of a pot, for example. Dharmakīrti devotes many verses to proving that the body, or any physical part of it, is not a material cause of mind. Often translated elsewhere as "substantial cause."

Mīmāṃsā (*rgyal dpyod, dpyod pa ba*). The school of followers of Jaimini, frequent opponents of Buddhist philosophers in India. The Mīmāṃsaka took the words of the Vedas as the supreme source of valid knowledge.

nonaffirming negation (*med dgag, prasajyapratiṣedha*). A negation that does not imply any other existence. *No-self* is a nonaffirming negation.

nonapprehension by way of nonappearance (*mi snang ba ma dmigs*). Reasoning by way of nonapprehension in which the existence or nonexistence of something cannot be definitively established because its appearance is not feasible in that particular situation to that particular person. If something is naturally hidden to someone, that person cannot ascertain its existence or nonexistence. Generally, nonappearance does not prove nonexistence, but neither does it deny nonexistence.

nonapprehension of that which should appear (*snang rung ma dmigs*). Reasoning by way of nonapprehension in which a nonexistence is established by the fact that if it did exist, it would appear, but it does not. His Holiness the Dalai Lama uses this type of reasoning to establish that Mount Meru does not exist. In the cosmology based around Mount Meru, nighttime is created by the sun traveling behind Meru, which blocks out its light and creates a shadow that we call night. Meru then must be coarse form, and coarse form, especially something so large, is accessible to the visual consciousness. It should appear, but observation from space does not detect it. Therefore it does not exist. Generally, nonappearance does not prove nonexistence, but under certain conditions it does.

Nyāya (*rigs pa can pa*). The orthodox philosophy of ancient India, whose primary concerns were epistemology—asserting four means of valid knowledge as contrasted to the two asserted by Buddhists—and reasoning, especially the mechanics of the syllogistic form that came to dominate philosophical disputation in India. Nyāya followers are called Naiyāyika.

other-knowing (*don rig, arthasaṃvitti/arthasaṃvedana*). A cognition, juxtaposed with a self-knowing cognition, that apprehends an object other than itself. The five sense consciousnesses, by knowing form and so on, are other-knowing consciousnesses, whereas the aspect of a sense consciousness that is aware of itself is a self-knowing consciousness.

particulars (*gsal ba, vyakti*, and *bye brag, bheda*). A *particular* is a phenomenon that belongs to a class, which means that *class* and *universal* are, for the most part, synonyms. In this work Dharmakīrti and Gorampa mostly use *gsal ba* (*vyakti*) rather than *bye brag* (*bheda*). The two are largely synonymous. The former can mean something that is evident, clear, illuminated, manifest, and so on. This usage relates to the Sāṃkhya assertion of a universal principle or innate nature, which is hidden and not evident, whereas instances of this universal are resultant phenomena that illustrate and manifest this principle. The same can be applied to the Buddhist understanding of particulars, which are illustrations of their class or universal. The phenomena that make up "tree particulars" are individual trees that belong to the class or universal "tree."

phenomenon expressed (*brjod bya, abhiṣya*). The referent of a verbal expression. According to Dharmakīrti, the phenomenon expressed by a verbal expression (*brjod byed*) is a universal in the aspect of an exclusion appearing to a conceptual cognition.

phenomenon to be established. See **predicate of the thesis**.

potential (*nus pa, śakti*). Often used here to indicate a support or basis for the existence of features, even if those features are not substantially different from that basis. The pot has the potential to produce the impermanence of the pot, for example.

preclusion (*rnam bcod, vyavaccheda*). The grammatical and conceptual device of positing that something exists by way of precluding something else. There are two types of this device: (1) preclusion of the possibility of something not being there—for example, sound is only impermanent—and (2) preclusion of something existing elsewhere—for example, only sound is audible. This preclusion is often employed by the term *kho na*, which can be translated as "totally," "alone," "only," and so on.

predicate of the thesis (*bsgrub bya'i chos, sādhyadharma*). The phenomenon to be established by the reason. In the thesis "sound is impermanent," the predicate is impermanence.

presence in doubt / inaccessible phenomena (*skal/bskal don, viprakṛṣṭatva/viprakṛṣṭārtha*). This refers to phenomena that are not necessarily beyond the range of the senses but because of the limitations of the observer, their presence is in doubt. The common example used is ghosts.

property (*chos, dharma*). Used with property-possessor to indicate a feature of a particular entity that in reality is inseparable from that entity but can be separated out conceptually to form a separate isolate, like fire and its heat, for example.

property of the subject (*phyogs chos, pakṣadharma*). One of the three criteria, in which the reason is validly established as being within the subject of the thesis. In the reason "Sound is impermanent because it is a product," being a product has to be validly established as existing within sound.

property-possessor (*chos can, dharmin*). That which possesses a property intrinsically inseparable from itself but conceptually isolated.

quality (*yon tan, guṇa*). Used mainly to refer to the excellent characteristics of something or someone, but sometimes used as a synonym for feature.

reason (*rtags, liṅga*). The sign or evidence used to establish the thesis; smoke, for example, establishing the presence of fire. Within the three criteria the reason must be validly established as existing within the subject—it is actually smoke you are seeing and not a cloud or fog, and it is established that the reason exists exclusively in the congruent class, as smoke exists exclusively with fire, and that the incongruent class is never found within that reason—that which is not fire is not found in a causal relationship with smoke. Put simply, the predicate pervades the reason.

reasoning based on an entity (*dngos stobs rigs pa*). The establishment of a thesis by a reason, where the entity of the predicate and reason are used to establish an existence that is only slightly hidden, as opposed to reasoning by way of trust and by way of renown.

reasoning by nature (*rang bzhin gyi rtags, svabhāvaliṅga/svabhāvāṅga*). One of the three types of reason, in which the thesis is established by way of the reason having an indispensable relationship with the predicate of the thesis by way of enjoying a same-nature relationship.

reasoning by nonapprehension (*ma dmigs pa'i rtags, anupalabdhihetu*). Type of reason that negates by way of nonapprehension and in which the predicate is a negation. It is of two types: (1) nonapprehension of that which should appear and (2) nonapprehension by way of nonappearance. These are discussed in the text from 1.198 onward, under the heading Negation Reasoning.

reasoning by result (*bras rtags, kāryāṅga*). One of the three types of reason, in which the thesis is established by way of the reason being the result of the predicate of the thesis. For example, "There is fire on that hill because there is smoke on the hill."

relationship (*'brel ba, saṃbandha*). Mainly refers to the relationship between the reason posited to establish the thesis and the predicate of that thesis. For example, in the reasoning "There is fire over there because there is smoke," it is the relationship between fire and smoke that establishes the existence of fire.

same-nature relationship (*bdag gcig 'brel*). A relationship and essential part of reasoning by nature, in which the reason is established as being pervaded by the predicate of the thesis. The state of impermanence, for example, pervades the state of being a product. There is not always mutual pervasion, because in the valid reasoning, music is impermanent because it is produced by human effort but impermanence is not pervaded by being produced by human effort, as in the case of natural sounds.

Sāṃkhya (*grangs can pa*). Orthodox philosophy of ancient India founded by Kapila. The Sāṃkhya assert an innate nature or universal principle that serves as a primordial strata birthing all material forms, which are its instances or particulars, while remaining itself unchanging and eternal. This is contrasted with the person (*puruṣa*) or self (*ātman*), which is consciousness.

self-knowing consciousness (*rang rig, svasaṃvitti/svasaṃvedana*). A direct perception and experience of the apprehending process of consciousness by an aspect of the consciousness itself. Therefore the object of a self-knowing consciousness is not of a separate entity to the consciousness, and a self-knowing consciousness is therefore nondual. According to those schools, such as the Svātantrika, that accept such a consciousness, it is the luminous and clarity aspect of consciousness. Proof of its existence is provided with our function of memory. I can remember seeing someone yesterday because, alongside the person, the visual consciousness of that person was also directly experienced, and that experience appeared to the self-knowing consciousness or apprehending aspect (*'dzin rnam*).

sense faculties (*dbang po, indriya*). The five form and substance-based faculties, such as the eye sense faculty, that allow for the sense consciousnesses to meet their objects.

separate entity (*don gzhan, arthāntara*). Radically and factually separate. In the

Sautrāntika system, substantial entities (*rdzas*) are separate entities from each other and therefore substantially separate.

single nature (*rang bzhin gcig pa*). The assertion made by the Sāṃkhya school that all phenomena, though temporally distinct, are of a single nature referred to as the universal principle or innate nature. A sprout is the result of many causes—such as seed, water, and so on—but these are all of a single nature. That is how the many give rise to a single result.

subject (*chos can, dharmin*). The subject of the thesis to be established. The same term can also be translated as property-possessor in other contexts.

substantial existence (*rdzas yod, dravyasat*). Something that is able to sustain itself without reliance. A phenomenon that can be held by a cognition without the need to rely upon the cognition of another phenomenon. The objects of the five senses, for example.

superimposition (*sgro 'dogs pa, adhyāropa*). Engaging by exclusion negates superimposition of other phenomena by a conceptual cognition, even if that superimposition refers to a valid existence. This is because exclusion by verbal expression and conceptualization negates all that is not the phenomenon engaged. For example, the conceptual cognition that engages impermanence excludes the superimposition of being a product and so on.

The Vaiśeṣika and Sāṃkhya non-Buddhist schools assert that the actual referent of a convention is a substantially existing universal, whereas Dharmakīrti argues that it is a universal in the aspect of an exclusion appearing to a conceptual cognition.

thesis (*bsgrub bya, sādhya*). That which is to be established by the reason existing within the subject of the thesis and by the reason being pervaded by predicate of the thesis. For example, "Sound is impermanent," in which sound is the subject and impermanence is the predicate.

three criteria (*tshul gsum, trairūpya*). The three cognitive processes that must be determined and validated upon a line of reasoning in order to induce a valid inferential cognition of the thesis. These three validate the reason as a property of the subject, and its possession of both concomitant and counter pervasion.

uncertain reasoning (*ma nges pa'i gtan tshigs, anaikāntikahetu*). Reasoning in which the reason is only unseen, or partially seen, within the incongruent class and not ascertained as nonexistent, or in which there is doubt about the pervasion because the reason is found in both the congruent and incongruent classes. For example, "All these apples are ripe because this apple, which is of a similar shape and color, is ripe," or, "Sound is impermanent because it exists."

undeceiving (*mi bslu ba, avisaṃvāda*). This is the essential and innermost meaning of *valid* and *valid cognition*. A valid person, valid speech, or valid cognition will not let you down. The term in Tibetan is often used to describe the qualities of a good friend. It is also translated as "incontrovertible" and "infallible."

universal (*spyi, sāmānya*). A phenomenon that is concomitant with its particulars or instances. Accepted by both Buddhists and non-Buddhist schools but with considerable difference of meaning. Much of the first chapter is devoted to explaining this difference. In Buddhist thinking, a universal can be intrinsically existing phenomena such as pots, although here it mainly refers to that which appears to a conceptual cognition and possesses its own particulars.

universal principle (*spyi gtso bo, prakṛti*). See **innate nature**.

Vaiśeṣika (*bye brag pa*). Orthodox Indian philosophy founded by Ulūka, alias Kaṇāda Kāśyapa, author of *Vaiśeṣikasūtra*. The Vaiśeṣika, like the Buddhist Vaibhāṣika, saw the elements as composed of indivisible atom-like particles, but unlike their Buddhist counterparts, they insisted that these are permanent. They classified all that exists in six categories—substance, quality, activity, universal, particularity, and inherence—and their understanding of universals and particulars was especially influential in Indian logic.

Vaiyākaraṇa (*brda sprod pa*). The Grammarians, who insist that the foundations of knowledge are found in the treatises on Sanskrit grammar.

valid cognition (*tshad ma, pramāṇa*). The essential meaning of the "validity" expressed in this term is undeceiving. While the term is primarily applied to cognition as seal of valid knowledge, it can also be applied to people and speech. Therefore the second chapter sets out to prove that the Buddha is a valid person by proving that his teachings are valid speech, in the sense that they are not deceptive and are reliable. Buddhist epistemology only accepts two kinds of valid cognition: inferential and direct. The first chapter explains how perfect reasoning is the tool for producing inferential cognition. The third chapter deals with direct perception.

I have never felt that "valid cognition" is the perfect translation of the Tibetan and Sanskrit terms. Cognition can be reliable and authoritative, but "valid" does not seem to sit easily with "cognition." However, it is the prevalent translation, and I cannot think of anything better. The Sanskrit suggests "authority" or "standard," in the sense that the Vedas are seen as authorities and are therefore the standard by which everything else is judged. The Tibetan also carries the meaning of "measure," beyond which nothing carries authority. The Sanskrit also means the means or instrument to securing valid cognition, as in the assertion that the Vedas are an instrument of valid cognition. The Tibetan term is also used for the whole field of logic and epistemology.

Vātsīputrīya (*gnas ma bu ba*). Buddhist school from the eighteen śrāvaka schools that asserts no-self in common with other śrāvaka schools but nevertheless asserts a self that is inexpressible in being one with or separate from the aggregates and so on.

verbal expression (*brjod byed, abhidhāna*). The verbal expression "tree," for example, creates or arises from a conceptual cognition in which non-tree is excluded, to leave a resultant class (*rigs*) or tree universal.

verbal expression and phenomenon expressed (*sgra don, śabdārtha*). A verbal expression such as "chocolate" causes an understanding of the phenomenon by way of linguistic convention. The phenomenon of chocolate indicated by that expression is the apprehended object of a conceptual cognition, in which the verbal expression and the actual phenomenon are seemingly blended to become a universal.

wholly designated valid cognition (*kun tu tha snyad kyi tshad ma*). Valid cognitions whose engaged or conceived objects are designated by way of terminology, verbal expression, conceptualization, and so on and used as basis to create ultimate cognition focused on ultimate reality. Without validly ascertaining isolates existing upon phenomena, it is not possible to reason into hidden aspects of that phenomenon, such as its ultimate truth. Therefore this kind of cognition is sometimes known as a conventional or non-ultimate cognition. See **designation**.

Bibliography

Works Cited by the Author

Kangyur

A Collection of Verses from the Buddhist Canon. Udānavarga. Ched du brjod pa'i tshoms. Toh 326, mdo sde *sa.*

King of Samādhis Sūtra. Samādhirājasūtra. Ting nge 'dzin gyi rgyal po'i mdo. Toh 127, mdo sde *da.*

Mañjuśrī Root Tantra. Mañjuśrīmūlatantra. 'Jam dpal rtsa rgyud. Toh 543, rgyud 'bum *na.*

Tengyur

Devendrabuddhi. *Word Explanation of the Commentary on Valid Cognition. Pramāṇavārttikapañjikā. Tshad ma rnam 'grel gyi dka' 'grel.* Toh 4217, tshad ma *che.*

Dharmakīrti. *Analysis of Relations. Saṃbandhaparīkṣ. 'Brel ba brtag pa.* Toh 4214, tshad ma *ce.*

———. *Ascertainment of Valid Cognition. Pramāṇaviniścaya. Tshad ma rnam nges.* Toh 4211, tshad ma *ce.*

———. *Autocommentary on the Commentary on Valid Cognition. Pramāṇavārttikavṛtti. Tshad ma rnam 'grel gyi 'grel pa.* Toh 4216, tshad ma *ce.*

———. *Commentary on Valid Cognition. Pramāṇavārttika. Tshad ma rnam 'grel.* Toh 4210, tshad ma *ce.*

———. *Drops of Proof. Hetubindu. Gtan tshig thigs pa.* Toh 4213, tshad ma *ce.*

———. *Drops of Reasoning. Nyāyabindu. Rigs pa'i thigs pa*. Toh 4212, tshad ma *ce*.

———. *Establishing the Minds of Others. Saṃtānāntarasiddhi. Rgyud gzhan sgrub pa*. Toh 4219, tshad ma *che*.

———. *Principles of Debate. Vādanyāya. Rtsod pa'i rigs pa*. Toh 4218, tshad ma *che*.

Dignāga. (Attr.) *Entrance to Valid Cognition Reasoning. Tshad ma rigs sgo*. Identified with *Tshad ma rigs pa la 'jug pa* (Trans. from Chinese). Toh 4208, tshad ma *ce*.

———. *Compendium of Valid Cognition. Pramāṇasamuccaya. Tshad ma kun las gtus pa*. Toh 4203, tshad ma *ce*.

———. *Wheel of Reasons. Hetucakraḍamaru. Gtan tshig gi 'khor lo gtan la dbab pa*. Toh 4209, tshad ma *ce*.

Kamalaśīla. *Commentary on the Compendium on Reality. Tattvasaṃgrahapañjikā. De kho na nyid bsdus pa'i dka' 'grel*. Toh 4267, tshad ma *ze*.

Maitreya. *Uttaratantra (Mahāyānottaratantraśāstra/Ratnagotravibhāga). Theg pa chen po rgyud bla ma'i bstan bcos*. Toh 3786, shes phyin *ka*.

Nāgārjuna. *Friendly Letter. Suhṛllekha. Bshes pa'i spring yig*. Toh 4182, spring yig *nge*.

———. *Fundamental Wisdom of the Middle Way. Mūlamadhyamakakārikā. Dbu ma rtsa ba'i tshig le'ur byas pa*. Toh 3824, dbu ma *tsa*.

Prajñākaragupta. *Ornament to the Commentary on Valid Cognition. Pramāṇavārttikālaṃkāra. Tshad ma rnam 'grel gyi rgyan (Rgyan mdzad pa)*. Toh 4221, tshad ma *te*.

Ravigupta. *Explanation of the Commentary on Valid Cognition. Pramāṇavārttikavṛtti. Tshad ma rnam 'grel gyi 'grel pa*. Toh 4224, tshad ma *pé* (chapters 2 and 3 only).

Śākyabuddhi. *Explanation of the Commentary on Valid Cognition. Pramāṇavārttikaṭīkā. Tshad ma rnam 'grel gyi bshad pa*. Toh 4220, tshad ma *je*.

Śaṃkarānanda, the brahman. *Explanation of the Commentary on Valid Cognition. Pramāṇavārttikaṭīkā. Tshad ma rnam 'grel gyi 'grel bshad*. Toh 4223, tshad ma *pe*.

Vasubandhu. *Treasury of Abhidharma. Abhidharmakośa. Chos mngon pa'i mdzod*. Toh 4089, mngon pa *ku*.

Vinītadeva. *Commentary to [Dharmakīrti's] Drops of Proof. Hetubinduṭīkā. Gtan tshig thigs pa rgya cher 'grel pa*. Toh 4234, tshad ma *we*.

Yamāri (Jamāri). *Commentary on Ornament to the Commentary on Valid*

Cognition. Pramāṇavārttikālaṃkāra-ṭīkā. Tshad ma rnam 'grel rgyan gyi 'grel bshad. Toh 4226, tshad ma *phé.*

Tibetan Works

Sakya Paṇḍita Künga Gyaltsen (Sa skya paṇḍita kun dga' rgyal mtshan). *Autocommentary to Treasure of Reasoning. Tshad ma rigs pa'i gter gyi rang 'grel. Collected Works of the Glorious Sakya Tradition*, vol. 16, p. 47. Mi rigs dpe skrun khang, 2004.

———. *Treasure of Reasoning. Tshad ma rigs pa'i gter.* Collected works, vol. 2. Kathmandu: International Sakya Center, 2006.

Gorampa Sönam Sengé (Go rams pa Bsod nams seng ge). *Madhyamaka Overview. Dbu ma'i spyi don / Rgyal ba thams cad kyi thugs kyi dgongs pa zab mo dbu ma'i de kho na nyid spyi'i ngag gis ston pa nges don rab gsal. Collected works*, vol. *ca.* Dehra Dun: Sakya College, 1979.

Uyukpa Rikpai Sengé (U yug pa Rigs pa'i seng ge). *Great Treasury of Reasoning on Commentary on Valid Cognition. Rnam 'grel rigs mdzod chen mo.* Delhi: Patshang Lama Sonam Gyaltsen, 1982.

Works Consulted by the Translator

Bhawuk, Dharm P. S. 2011. *Spirituality and Indian Psychology: Lessons from the Bhagavad-Gita.* Edited by Anthony Marsella. New York: Springer Verlag.

Butön Rinchen Drub (Bu ston rin chen grub). 1999. *The History of Buddhism in India and Tibet.* New Delhi: Sri Satguru Publications.

Cabezón, José, and Geshe Lobsang Dargyay. 2013. *Freedom from Extremes: Gorampa's "Distinguishing the Views" and the Polemics of Emptiness.* Boston: Wisdom Publications.

Chattopadhyaya, D. 1986. *Indian Philosophy: A Popular Introduction.* New Delhi: People's Publishing House.

Dungkar Losang Trinlé (Dung dkar Blo bzang 'phrin las). 2002. *Dung dkar tshig mdzod chen mo.* Beijing: Krung go'i bod rig pa dpe skrun khang.

Gnoli, Raniero. 1960. *The Pramāṇavārttikam of Dharmakīrti.* Rome: Istituto Italiano per il Medio ed Estremo Oriente.

Gö Lotsāwa Shönu Pal ('Gos lo tsā ba Gzhon nu dpal). 1976. *Blue Annals. Deb ther ngon po.* Translated by George Roerich. Delhi: Motilal Banarsidass.

Göhler, Lars. 1995. *Wort und Text bei Kumārila Bhaṭṭa: Studie zur mittelalterlichen indischen Sprachphilosophie und Hermeneutik.* Frankfurt am Main: Peter Lang. (Cited in Wikipedia.)

Gyaltsab Darma Rinchen (Rgyal tshab Dar ma rin chen). 1980. *Bstan bcos tshad ma rnam nges tīk chen dgongs pa rab gsal.* Collected works, vol. *ja*. New Delhi: Ngawang Gelek Demo.

———. 1974. *Rnam 'grel thar lam gsal byed.* Varanasi: Mtho slob dge ldan spyi las khang.

Hayes, Richard P. 2004. *On the Buddha's Authority: A Translation of the Pramāṇasiddhi Chapter of Dharmakīrti*'s *Pramāṇavārttika, verses 1–59.* Unpublished manuscript.

Hayes, Richard P., and Brendan S. Gillon. 2008. "Dharmakīrti on the Role of Causation in Inference as Presented in *Pramāṇavārttika* Svopajñavṛtti 11–38." *Journal of Indian Philosophy* 36.3: 335–404.

Hayes, Richard P., and Brendan S. Gillon. 1991. "Introduction to Dharmakīrti's Theory of Inference as Presented in *Pramāṇavārttika* Svopajñavṛtti 1–10." *Journal of Indian Philosophy* 19: 1–73.

Jackson, David P. 1987. *The Entrance Gate for the Wise: Sa-skya Paṇḍita on Indian and Tibetan Traditions of Pramāṇa and Philosophical Debate.* 2 vols. Vienna: Arbeitskreis fur Tibetische und Buddhistische Studien Universität Wien.

———. 1994. *The Status of Pramāṇa Doctrine According to Sa skya Pandita and Other Tibetan Masters.* London: School of African and Oriental Studies.

Jinpa, Thupten, ed. 2020. *Science and Philosophy in Indian Buddhist Classics, Volume 2: The Mind.* Translated by John Dunne and Dechen Rochard. Somerville, MA: Wisdom Publications.

Kundu, Bratati. 2014. *Nyāya and Vaiśeṣika on Śabda Pramāṇa: A Critical Study.* PhD thesis. Burdwan, West Bengal: Dept. of Philosophy, University of Burdwan.

Kunga Wangchuk (Kun dga' dbang phyug). 2015. *Annotations on Commentary on Valid Cognition. Rgyas pa'i bstan bcos tshad ma rnam 'grel gyi mchan 'grel.* Mysore, India: Tashi Lhunpo Cultural Society.

Miyasaka, Yūsho, ed. 1972. *Pramāṇavarttika-Kārikā. (Sanskrit and Tibetan).* Acta Indologica. Tokyo: Naritasan Shinshoji.

———. 1974. *An Index to the Pramāṇavarttika-Kārikā: Sanskrit to Tibetan.* Acta Indologica. Tokyo: Naritasan Shinshoji.

———. 1977. *An Index to the Pramāṇavarttika-Kārikā: Tibetan to Sanskrit.* Acta Indologica. Tokyo: Naritasan Shinshoji.

Mookerjee, S., and Nagasaki Hojun. 1964. *The Pramāṇavārttikam of*

Dharmakīrti: An English Translation of the First Chapter with Autocommentary and Comments. Patna, India: Nava Nālandā Mahāvira.

Negi, J. S. 1993. *Tibetan-Sanskrit Dictionary*. Sarnath, India: Central Institute of Higher Tibetan Studies.

Norbu Gyatso (Nor bu rgya mtsho). 1991–92, 1996, 2000. *Blo'i tha snyad dang sgra'i tha snyad bshad pa*. Bod kyi shes rig dpyad rtsom phyogs bsgrigs 5. Beijing: Krung go'i bod kyi shes rig dpe skrun khang.

Perrett, Roy. 2007. "Sāṃkhya-Yoga Ethics." In *Indian Ethics: Classical Traditions and Contemporary Challenges, Volume 1*, edited by P. Bilimoria et al., 149–60. Aldershot, UK: Ashgate. (Cited in Wikipedia.)

Rongtön Śākya Gyaltsen (Rong ston Shākya rgyal mtshan). 1999. *Rnam nges rnam bshad rtog ge'i snang ba*. Collected works, vol. *ga*. Kathmandu: Sakya International Center.

Sadukhan, Sanjit K. 1994. *A Short History of Buddhist Logic in Tibet*. Gangtok, Sikkim: Bulletin of Tibetology.

Sharma, C. 1997. *A Critical Survey of Indian Philosophy*. Delhi: Motilal Banarsidass. (Cited in Wikipedia.)

Stcherbatsky, Th. 1930–32. *Buddhist Logic*, 2 vols. Bibliotheca Buddhica 26. Leningrad: Akademii Nauk.

Tāranātha. 1970. *History of Tibetan Buddhism in India*. Delhi: Motilal Banarsidass.

Tillemans, Tom. 2020. "Dharmakīrti." In *Stanford Encyclopedia of Philosophy*, edited by Edward N. Zalta. https://plato.stanford.edu/entries/dharmakiirti/.

van der Kuijp, Leonard W. J. 1983. *Contributions to the Development of Tibetan Buddhist Epistemology from the Eleventh to the Thirteenth Centuries*. Alt- und Neu-Indische Studien 26. Wiesbaden: Franz Steiner Verlag.

Index

A

abandonment, 220–21, 313, 374, 377–80, 420, 427–28, 441, 461, 479n242, 481n289. *See also* renunciation

absurd consequences, 171–72, 177–78, 322–25

aggregates

  appropriation of, 322, 408, 470n106

  memory and, 451

  self and, 401, 410–11, 422, 426, 479n248

  suffering and, 322, 375, 384, 401, 410, 441

  superimposition onto, 413

  and throwing karma, 476n206

  See also self

Akaniṣṭha realm, 36

analysis, 4, 7–9, 22, 51–53, 451, 467n39, 470n91. *See also* reasoning

Analysis of Relations (*Saṃbandhaparīkṣā*), 33

anger, 62, 221–222, 387–88, 479n246, 481n287

appearing object, 65, 116, 117, 121–22, 150–51, 154, 162

āryas, 405, 411, 414–15. *See also* bodhisattvas; superior beings

ascertainment, 99–100, 103–4

  two types of, 82–83

  and verbal expression, 108

  See also knowing; valid cognition (*pramāṇa*)

Ascertainment of Valid Cognition (*Pramāṇaviniścaya*), 20, 33, 37, 38, 43, 45, 46, 53, 195, 202, 215

  commentaries on, 21

  indispensable relationship in, 65–67

ascetic practices, 23, 455–56, 480n272, 481n281

aspiration, 38, 376

attachment, 375, 410, 415, 425–28, 480n271, 480n472

  abandoning, 429–41

  to self, 36

aversion, 426, 427–28, 440

awareness. *See* consciousness

B

base reality, 1–2, 3, 4, 6, 465n1

Beluka, 169–79

Bhavyarāja, 22

birth. *See* past and future lives; rebirth

bodhisattvas, 36, 411, 414

body, 61, 73, 75, 76, 283, 452–53, 479n253

  abandoning, 454–57

  and mind, 6, 17, 24, 321–27, 328–51, 362–65

  See also sense faculties

breath, 322, 331–33, 358–61

Buddha, 23, 33, 36, 45, 317, 461–63

  consciousness of, 219

  enlightenment of, 203

  validity of, 291–92, 297, 299

See also Compassionate One; Protector; Sugata; Teacher
Buddhist cosmology, 10
Buddhist practice. *See* meditation; path; training
Butön Rinchen Drup, 15, 21

C

Cabezón, José, 24
Cārvāka school. *See* Lokāyata school
cause and effect, 10–11, 23, 60, 61, 65, 67, 79, 148–49, 267, 268, 481n277. *See also* karma; products; results
Chan (Zen) school, 19
Chapa Chökyi Sengé, 20, 22
Cittamātra tradition, 15, 34, 35. *See also* Yogācāra
clarity, 105, 376
classes, 167, 174, 355–357, 469n73. *See also* universals
Collection of Verses (*Udānavarga*), 411
Commentary on Valid Cognition (*Pramāṇavārttika*), 15–16, 17, 19, 33, 215, 283
  autocommentary, 42, 81
  commentaries on, 21
  explanation of title, 34–35
  homage in, 31–33, 35–39, 288, 291–92
  "Ornament" (*Alaṃkāra*) commentaries, 44–45, 287, 296, 403
  overview, 41–47
  structure of, 22–24, 287, 466n20
common basis, 124–25, 154–55, 160, 469n88
common knowledge, 247, 274–76, 308
communication. *See* verbal expression
compassion, 23, 320, 322, 368, 369, 370–71, 413, 414, 462
  leading to "Teacher," 373–76
Compassionate One, 313
Compendium of Valid Cognition (*Pramāṇasamuccaya,* Dignāga), 15–16, 23, 33, 69, 151, 210–11, 217, 304, 313
  commentaries on, 21
  homage in, 23, 297, 299, 376, 380
  structure of, 466n20
  See also *Valid Cognition Sūtra*
conceptual cognition, 113–14, 116–18, 123–25, 128–29, 143–44, 146, 148–52, 153, 157–58, 171–74, 210–11, 265, 321, 322, 347–48, 351–57, 361–62, 393, 469–70n91, 470n97, 472n133
  of number, 351–52
  three aspects of, 121–22
  See also conceptualization; consciousness; labeling; valid cognition
conceptualization, 5–6, 8, 98, 102, 230, 253–54
  three types of, 207–8
  See also conceptual cognition
confusion, 242, 283, 295, 342–43, 386–87, 391, 420, 447–50. *See also* ignorance; wrong cognition
consciousness, 5, 138–39, 165–67, 228–29, 394, 418–19
  aural, 240, 242, 264
  conventional, 293
  self-knowing, 294, 469n85
  and syllables, 266–67
  See also conceptual cognition; mind; volition
conventional truth, 116, 469n84
conventions, 108, 125, 131–35, 142–43, 145–47, 148–49, 157–58, 160, 224–26, 263–64, 278–79, 470n92, 474n161. *See also* conventional truth; verbal expression
craving, 405–6, 408, 409, 425–26, 447, 448, 449, 452–54, 479–80n258. *See also* attachment; desire

D

Dalai Lama, First, 22
Dalai Lama, Fourteenth, 10
death, 2, 306, 322, 332–34, 362–63, 449
debate, 11, 13–14, 15, 16, 19, 20, 80, 193, 209, 307, 475n188. *See also* reasoning
defilements, 417–20. *See also* mental afflictions
dependence, 164–65
designation, 104, 116, 125, 161–62, 433–34,

451, 469n90, 475n175
desire, 62, 109, 221, 386, 388–92, 394, 396–400, 406–8, 411–13, 479n253, 480n271
abandonment of, 428–29
See also attachment; craving
desire realm, 363
Destiny Fulfilled, A (Tsongkhapa), 22
destruction, 250–54, 255, 465n4, 471n122, 473n155
Devadatta, 415, 480n264
Devendrabuddhi, 43, 44, 45, 203, 287, 296, 328
Dharmakīrti, 14–16, 33, 451, 465n11
Dharmapāla, 14
Dignāga, 14, 16, 19, 33, 69, 211, 280
direct sense perception (*pratyakṣa*), 5–6, 7, 9, 17, 41, 43, 46, 96, 97, 104–5, 296, 347–48, 470n97, 472n131, 474n271
discernment, 5, 37–38, 341
disintegration, 197–99, 249–55, 338–40, 471n122, 473n155, 477n213
divine creator, 11, 18
doubt, 68, 69, 74, 125, 150, 259, 276, 280, 302, 318
Dreyul Kyetsal Monastery, 24
Drops of Proof (*Hetubindu*), 33
Drops of Reasoning (*Nyāyabindu*), 33
Dzongsar Khenpo Kunga Wangchuk, 21

E

elimination of other, 109–10, 146–48. *See also* exclusion (*apoha, gzhan sel*)
emptiness, 401–2, 441–42. *See also* no-self
engaged object, 65
enlightenment, 3, 13, 23, 36, 376. *See also* liberation
entities, 116–17, 195–96, 198, 338–40, 471n117
disintegration as, 253
See also particulars; sixteen faulty aspects
entity, 54
Entrance to Valid Cognition Reasoning, 72
epistemology in ancient India, 16–19
equanimity, 38, 320, 440–41
equilibrium, 18, 441
Establishing the Minds of Others (*Saṃtānāntarasiddhi*), 33–34
exclusion (*apoha, gzhan sel*), 8–9, 91–93, 96–100, 107–8, 114–15, 124, 144, 157–58, 161–62, 180, 185
refutations concerning, 145–56
three types of, 181
and verbal expression, 187–88
See also elimination of other; isolates
existence, 192–96, 202, 255, 471n117
six categories of, 477n214–15, 477n218, 477n226
See also nonexistence

F

faith, 1, 3–4, 6, 7, 35–36
fallacious reasoning, 215–16, 223, 302–4. *See also under* reasoning
feature-possessor, 108, 109, 127–28
features, 7, 9, 62–63, 76, 101–5, 107
hidden, 10 (*see also* hidden phenomena)
See also isolates (*vyatireka, ldog pa*)
fifth (ablative) case, 330
five kinds of contradiction, 206
formless realm, 363
four mistaken conceptions, 44
four truths, 46, 219, 319, 452, 461, 479n255
establishing protector, 383–402
See also path; suffering
Fundamental Wisdom of the Middle Way (*Mūlamadhyamakakārikā*, Nāgārjuna), 35

G

Garuḍa Tantra, 269
Geluk tradition, 21–22
generality, 62, 68, 217–19, 303–4, 305, 351, 475n188. *See also* isolate; verbal expression
Gnoli, Raniero, 24
goddess, 275, 473–74n160
Gorampa Sönam Sengé, 24–25
Gyaltsab Dharma Rinchen, 22, 473n147

H

hallucination, 4, 5
happiness, 17, 306, 344, 388, 406, 410, 413, 415, 420, 432, 442, 447, 457, 467, 480n274
hidden phenomena, 7, 9–10, 11, 12, 18, 41, 217, 218–19, 271, 272, 274–75, 312, 313, 317, 318, 319, 465n1, 470n107
Hiraṇyagarbha, 232
humors, 386–88, 389, 391, 479n245

I

identification, 137–44, 219, 426, 470n92, 470n97
ignorance, 12–13, 17, 18, 186, 221–22, 349, 408, 409, 413, 421, 452
  in Sāṃkhya school, 18
  See also confusion; wrong cognition
Immodest Ones. *See* Jainism
impermanence, 9–10, 11–12, 66, 75, 77, 79, 83, 91, 93, 96, 97, 100, 153–54, 159, 173, 221, 240, 256, 300–301, 308, 374, 400–401
imprints, 115–16, 207–8, 257–58, 363, 375–76, 377, 378, 391, 394
improper mental engagement, 342–43
indispensable relationship, 52, 54, 65–69, 82, 88, 215, 216, 282, 463
inference. *See* inferential valid cognition
inferential valid cognition, 11, 12–13, 23, 43, 44, 59–62, 80, 96–100, 124, 199, 217, 219, 295, 463–64
  basis of, 51–52
  for oneself, 41, 42, 44–45, 65, 466n28
  for others, 41
inherence, 339, 353, 431–32, 477n215
innate nature, 439, 480–81n276. *See also* prakṛti
intelligent design, 11
intrinsically existent phenomena, 45, 92, 95–96, 114, 117, 121–22, 124–29, 131–32, 143, 153, 171, 181–82, 184–85, 230–31, 265, 469n85
isolates (*vyatireka, ldog pa*), 7–8, 92–93, 107–10, 114–15, 123–26, 157–58, 159–60, 175, 185, 353–54, 468n66, 478n230
  refutations concerning, 145–56
  See also exclusion (*apoha, gzhan sel*); features
Īśvara, refutations concerning, 300–302, 309–10, 311–12, 405, 446–49, 475n184
Īśvarasena, 14, 16, 72, 467n52

J

Jaimini, 17, 270, 273, 277
Jainism, 17, 186, 306, 471n112. *See also* Nirgrantha school
Jamyang Gekpo, 348–49

K

Kamalaśīla, 19, 203
Kaṇāda, 169
Kapila, 175, 471n111
karma, 17, 301, 324–25, 332, 384, 386–87, 408, 413–14, 447–48, 452–53, 476n206
  abandoning, 454–57
  See also cause and effect
Khedrup Gelek Palsang, 22
knowable phenomena, 41, 149–50. *See also* knowing
knowing, 1, 4, 34, 104–5, 118–19, 148–49, 204, 257, 292–94, 296–97, 300, 319, 380, 412–13, 421–22, 439, 453, 462, 463, 476n208, 480n269
  and faith, 3–4
  perfect, 43–44
  three aspects, 461
  ways of, 4–6
  See also ascertainment; direct perception (*pratyakṣa*); inferential cognition; knowable phenomena; omniscience; valid cognition (*pramāṇa*); wisdom
Kumārasambhava, 233

L

labeling, 113, 117–18, 350–53
liberation, 17, 18, 19, 22–23, 318–19, 409–10, 441–42, 455. *See also* enlightenment; path
listeners, 14, 37–38

logic, 9–12
  soteriological quality of, 13–14
  See also analysis; epistemology in ancient India; reasoning
Lokāyata school, 17, 76, 325–27, 328–65, 398, 477n213, 479n254

M
Ma Lotsāwa Gewai Lodrö, 19, 20, 22
Madhyamaka, 15, 21, 25
  and Pramāṇa, 481n286
  See also *Madhyamaka Overview*; Prāsaṅgika Madhyamaka
Madhyamaka Overview (Gorampa), 115, 142, 181, 296
Mangtö Ludrub Gyatso, 21
Mañjuśrī, 37
Mañjuśrī Root Tantra, 33
materialists, 17, 326, 327, 477n213. *See also* Lokāyata school
meditation, 1, 12, 13, 371, 379, 417, 419, 421, 429–30, 434–35, 452, 478n238
memory, 267, 450–51
mental afflictions, 17, 220–21, 376, 378–79, 384, 454, 478n236, 481n287
  abandoning, 457
mental continuum, 60, 98–99, 321, 326, 331, 362, 397, 399, 412, 417, 419–20, 423, 449–50
mental engagement, 162, 342–43, 349
Mīmāṃsā school, 17–18, 61, 62, 223–24, 232, 243, 247, 270, 280, 317, 379–80, 467n47, 472n143, 479n244
mind, 1, 2–3, 4, 9–10, 12, 14, 17, 92, 101, 116, 167, 218–19, 221, 253, 267, 301, 306, 393, 412, 448–49, 454, 467n47, 469n85, 477n213, 478n236
  of Buddha, 11, 203, 375–76
  nature of, 378–79, 419, 423
  refuting material cause of, 323–51, 362–65
  training, 368–71, 417, 418–20, 440–41
  See also conceptual cognition; consciousness; discernment; knowing; mental continuum
mistaken conception. *See* wrong cognition
motivation, 2, 38, 216
Mount Meru, 10, 32

N
Naiyāyika school, 68, 283
Nālandā Monastery, 14, 15, 16
nature
  of compassion, 368
  of destruction/disintegration, 249–51, 255–56, 340, 471n122
  of elements, 323
  of entities/existence, 1, 5, 6–7, 8–9, 12, 18, 54, 93, 95–96, 99, 101–3, 110, 114, 116, 121–25, 143–44, 157, 183–84, 204, 273, 279–80, 307, 311, 338, 340, 412–13, 418–19, 423, 439
  of faults, 380, 390–91, 398
  of mind, 378–79, 419, 423
  of numbers, 351–52
  single, 67, 93, 175–76, 179–88, 265–66
  of validity, 292, 294
  See also innate nature; reasoning; relationships
Ngawang Chödrak, 21
Ngok Lotsāwa Loden Sherab, 20, 22
Ngok tradition, 20
Ngor Ewam Chöden Monastery, 24
Ngorchen Kunga Sangpo, 24
Nirbhartsanā, 232
Nirgrantha school, 17. *See also* Jainism
nirvāṇa. *See* enlightenment
nonapprehension. *See under* reasoning
nonattachment, 371, 480n272
non-Buddhist schools, 7, 17–19, 23, 75–76, 454, 467n48, 480n272
  See also individual schools
nondeceptive consciousness. *See* valid cognition
non-entities, 91, 187–88, 231.
nonexistence, 54–55, 72, 81, 155, 194–95, 204–5, 206, 259, 282–83, 467n41
nonvirtuous activity, 446, 448
no-self, 10, 221, 375, 377, 378, 417–23, 425, 441–42, 450, 456
Nyāya school, 18, 73
Nyāya Sūtra, 18

O

object-possessors, 41, 107, 144, 154, 209, 468n67
obscuring cognition, 115–116, 426, 434
omniscience, 1, 17, 46, 313, 319
Ornament to the Commentary on Valid Cognition. See under *Commentary on Valid Cognition*

P

particulars, 102, 117–19, 121–22, 128–29, 132–35, 137–44, 161, 185, 208–9, 469n73, 470–71n107, 472–73n146
  and universals, 158–60, 164–74, 210–11
  See also entities
past and future lives, 321–65. *See also* rebirth
path, 1, 2–5, 12, 13, 18, 19, 221, 277, 313, 319, 417–23. *See also* training
permanence, refutations of, 75, 119, 127, 164–65, 173, 228–29, 240, 257–58, 405, 450, 465n4
  reasoning refuting, 227–28
potentials, 60, 101–3, 355, 455–56
Prajñākaragupta, 20, 363
prakṛti, 18, 480–81n276. *See also* innate nature; prime universal; substance: primordial
pramāṇa tradition, 21, 22, 452, 465n5
  and Madhyamaka, 481n286
Prāsaṅgika Madhyamaka, 451–52
pratyekabuddhas, 378–79, 414
preclusion, 466n25
prime universal, 175–76, 179–80, 193, 472–73n146
  refuting similarity to exclusion universal, 180–81
  See also prakṛti
Principles of Debate (*Vādanyāya*), 33
"producing sequentially," 183–84
products, 66, 79, 83, 91, 93, 100, 304. *See also* results
Protector, 313–14, 380, 383–84, 461
Pudgalavādins, 416. *See also* Sāṃmitīya school; Vātsīputrīya school

R

Ravigupta, 46, 328
reasoning, 23, 52–53, 467n39, 467n55, 468n63, 475–76n185–188
  ineffective criteria for, 47
  negation, 77–78, 81, 150, 201–6, 471n123
  non-dependence, 192–96
  refutations of flawed, 56–57, 61–62
  three modes of (*trairūpya, tshul gsum*), 11–12, 51–52, 59–62, 65, 66, 69
  three perfect reasons, 53–56
  by way of nature, 59–60, 65, 67, 83, 87–88, 92, 191, 197–200, 314, 472n138
  by way of nonapprehension, 54–57, 62, 66, 68–69, 71–76, 81–82, 201–2, 203–5, 207, 211, 293, 471n123, 472n138
  See also absurd consequences; analysis; fallacious reasoning; refutations
rebirth, 404, 447–50, 452–53, 476n206
  of āryas, 414
  higher, 17, 226, 274, 275, 305, 406
  See also past and future lives
recitation. *See* Vedic mantras
relationships
  concomitant pervasion in, 6, 9, 12, 47, 67, 69, 74, 79–81, 87, 177, 259–60
  counter pervasion in, 71–73, 77–81
  same-nature, 23, 69, 72, 88, 204–5, 281–82
  three types of, 11–12, 51–52, 59–62, 65, 66, 69
  See also cause and effect; indispensable relationship
Rendawa Shönu Lodrö, 21
renunciation, 440. *See also* abandonment
results, 1, 3, 54, 86, 125–126, 142, 148, 153–54, 160–62, 177, 182, 256. *See also* cause and effect; products
reversal. *See* exclusion (*apoha, gzhan sel*)
rituals, 2, 18, 262–64, 445–47, 453, 454, 481n281
Rongtön Śākya Gyaltsen Sheja Kunrik, 21

S

Sakya Paṇḍita, 20, 21, 22, 295, 296
Sakya school, 20, 21, 25

Śākyabuddhi, 43, 57, 143, 154, 203, 287, 328, 391
Śākyaśrī, 20, 22
Sāṃkhya school, 18, 76, 132, 168, 176–78, 183, 186, 192, 306, 395, 439, 470–71n107, 480n276–77
Sāṃmitīya school, 410–11. *See also* Pudgalavādins; Vātsīputrīya school
saṃsāra, 222, 322, 375, 376, 384–85, 409–10, 413–14, 425–26, 437
  antidote to, 417
Samyé Monastery, 19
Sangphu Monastery, 20, 22
Sāṅkṛtyāyana, Rāhula, 24
Śāntarakṣita, 19
Sautrāntika system, 15, 35, 347–49, 363, 465n2, 470n101, 471n122
scripture, 41, 55, 71–73, 128–29, 151, 210–11, 272, 281–83, 325, 327–28, 374, 406–7
  and entities, 282
  possessing three features, 216–18
  reversing, 216
  See also individual scriptures
section, 51–52, 467n39
self, view of, 6, 18, 73, 76, 154, 400–402, 410–11, 415–16, 426–39, 449–50
  antidote to (*See* no-self)
  See also view of transitory collection
Sengé Ribong, 22
sense consciousness, 119, 142, 311–12, 341, 342, 346–51, 478n236
sense faculties, 5, 7, 61, 166–67, 294, 311, 322, 323–25, 329–30, 362–65, 474n172
  and mental cognition, 324–25
  See also body; direct sense perception (*pratyakṣa*)
Seven Treatises (Dharmakīrti), 33–34, 347, 348
shape, 302–3, 305–6
Short History of Buddhist Logic (Sadhukhan), 19
sixteen faulty aspects, 452
sixth (genitive) case, 108, 111–12, 354–55
space, 112, 257–58, 307, 308, 465n4, 476n195
śrāvakas, 378–79, 414
Status of the Pramāṇa Doctrine, The (Jackson), 13
Subhūtiśrīśānti, 19, 22
substance, 109
  primordial, 7, 17
  two types, 308
subtle particles, 307–8, 347, 348–49, 478n231
suffering, 12–13, 18, 19, 23, 219, 313, 322, 374–75, 388, 401, 435, 441–42, 447, 452, 455–56
  abandonment of, 377–80
  basis of (*See* self, view of)
  cessation of, 409–16
  origin of, 403–8
  in Sāṃkhya school, 18
  See also four truths
Sugata, 313, 377–80, 461
superimposition, 96, 98–99, 104, 247, 253, 413, 438–39, 452
  of suffering, 410
superior beings, 219–22. *See also* āryas; bodhisattvas; Buddha

T

Taktsang Lotsāwa Sherab Rinchen, 21
tantra, 269. *See also individual tantras*
Tāranātha, 15
Teacher, 33, 313, 314, 317–19, 373–76, 462, 463
Tengyur, 15, 16, 19
three enlightened forms, 35, 36
three faults, 37–38, 110, 388
three types of disciples, 36, 465n14
training, 320, 321–22, 367–71, 374–376, 377, 378, 380, 417–423, 478n238. *See also* path
Treasure of Reasoning (Sakya Paṇḍita), 20, 38, 81, 115, 117, 162, 187, 296, 324–25
  commentaries on, 21
Treasure of Reason Autocommentary (Sakya Paṇḍita), 304–5, 347
Trisong Detsen, 14
Tsongkhapa, 21, 22, 25

two modes of engagement, 157–58, 185. *See also* direct sense perception (*pratyakṣa*); inferential valid cognition

U

ultimate reality, 117, 121–22, 127–28, 177, 469n85
  and particulars, 208–9
ultimate truth, 7, 21, 470n101, 484n286. *See also* emptiness
universals (*sāmānya, spyi*), 8, 98, 107, 113–19, 121–22, 133–35, 146, 162, 183–84, 192, 207–8, 465n3, 469n73, 469n88, 470–71n107, 470n92
  established by mistaken designation, 123–29
  mantra, 265–66
  and particulars, 138–44, 209–11
  refuting, as entities, 158–62, 163–74
  See also classes; prakṛti; prime universal
Uyuk Rikpa Sengé, 21, 215

V

Vaibhāṣika school, 18, 75–76, 101–2, 107, 110–12, 132, 159–60, 167–68, 169, 293–94, 307–8, 349, 363, 451, 474n172, 476n196, 477n218, 477n224, 477n226
Vaiyākaraṇa school, 86–87, 111
valid cognition (*pramāṇa*), 3–5, 23, 41, 42, 43, 44, 54–55, 69, 81, 128–29, 143–44, 201–2, 203, 216, 218, 220, 272, 281, 292–95, 296, 312–13, 474n173, 475n179–80, 476n202
  ascertaining cause and result, 85–86
  direct, 203
  in Nyāya and Vaiśeṣika schools, 19
  ordinary, 283
  in Sāṃkhya school, 18
  self-arisen, 300–301
  three kinds of, 280
  See also ascertainment; direct sense perception (*pratyakṣa*); exclusion (*apoha, gzhan sel*); inferential valid cognition; nondeceptive consciousness
Valid Cognition Sūtra, 41–42, 287. See also *Compendium of Valid Cognition*
Vāmanadeva, 232
van der Kuijp, Leonard, 20
Vasubandhu, 19
Vātsīputrīya school, 93. *See also* Pudgalavādins; Sāṃmitīya school;
Vedas, refutations concerning, 17–18, 216, 472n143
  comprehending meaning of, 273–83
  creation of, 223–35
  syllables and words of, 237–47
  See also Vedic mantras
Vedic mantras, 261–72. *See also* Vedas
verbal expression, 8, 62, 99–100, 107–10, 111–12, 124, 126–27, 129, 131–35, 137–38, 143, 144, 146–54, 157–59, 170–74, 207–8, 281–82, 303, 305–6, 307–9, 351–57, 472n133, 473n147, 473n157, 479n244
  analysis of, 215–22
  and exclusion, 187–88
  of number, 352–53
  syllables in, 238–47, 266–68
  and universals, 160–62, 163, 209–11
  See also conventions; labeling
view of transitory collection, 221–22, 391, 414–15, 421, 422, 443, 445, 453. *See also* self, view of
Viṣvamitra, 232
volition, 266–68, 393, 447–51

W

wisdom, 224, 283, 318, 341, 375, 378, 422, 434, 461, 462, 480n269. *See also* knowing
wrong cognition, 4, 45, 46–47, 420, 447, 448–50. *See also* confusion; ignorance; obscuring cognition

Y

Yamāri, 20, 46
Yogācāra, 15. *See also* Cittamātra school

About the Authors

Gorampa Sönam Sengé (1429–89) was a monk and one of the premier scholars of the Sakya school of Tibetan Buddhism, and his works, which fill many volumes, are still widely studied within the tradition today. Born in Eastern Tibet, he made his way to central Tibet when he was twenty and studied with and took tantric transmissions from such luminaries as Rongtön Sheja Kunrik, Ngorchen Kunga Sangpo, and Muchen Sempa Chenpo. He went on to lead several monasteries, including Ngor Evam Chöden. Renowned as a skilled teacher, he was an outspoken defender of the tradition of the great Sakya Paṇḍita.

Gavin Kilty studied in Dharamsala, India, from 1970–84, where he spent eight years training in the traditional Geluk monastic curriculum through the medium of class and debate at the Institute of Buddhist Dialectics. He has been a full-time translator for the Institute of Tibetan Classics since 2001 and has translated four of its volumes and is working on a fifth. He has also translated books commissioned by four other organizations, and he has taught many Tibetan language courses in India, Nepal, and elsewhere. Winner of the inaugural Shantarakshita Award for Tibetan translation in 2017, he now has a fellowship grant from Tsadra Foundation to translate a volume from Jamgön Kongtrul's *Treasury of Instructions*. He lives with his wife in the UK and Dharamsala.

KHENPO APPEY FOUNDATION

The Khenpo Appey Foundation (KAF) was established in 2010 to honor Venerable Khenchen Appey Rinpoche (1927–2010), an eminent Tibetan Buddhist scholar, teacher, and practitioner who dedicated his life to the transmission and preservation of the Buddhadharma. The foundation was established by Madam Doreen Goh Poh Joo, a devoted follower and sponsor of Khenchen Appey Rinpoche.

Inspired by Khenchen Appey Rinpoche's vision, the Khenpo Appey Foundation is dedicated to the support and enhancement of Buddhist study and practice through activities such as translation projects and sponsorship of monastic institutions. The foundation's primary aim is to extend the Buddha's wisdom and compassion as widely as possible in order to benefit all beings.

Find out more at www.khenpoappey.org.

The Khenpo Appey Collection of Sakya Classics

The Khenpo Appey Collection of Sakya Classics aspires to fulfill Khenchen Appey Rinpoche's vision of making important and authoritative Sakya works accessible to English-speaking audiences. This series, conceived by the Khenpo Appey Foundation and published by Wisdom Publications, will contain translations of texts central to Tibetan Buddhist study composed by influential Sakya masters such as Rendawa, Rongtön, and Gorampa. Topics will include Pramāṇa, Madhyamaka, and Abhidharma, and the collection will provide a holistic and comprehensive presentation of Buddhist thought and philosophy.

What to Read Next from Wisdom Publications

Freedom from Extremes
Gorampa's "Distinguishing the Views" and the Polemics of Emptiness
José I. Cabezón and Geshe Lobsang Dargyay

"A magnificent translation of a pivotal Tibetan examination of the nature of reality. Essential for comprehending the variety of views on the middle ground."—Jeffrey Hopkins, University of Virginia

Ornament to Beautify the Three Appearances
The Mahāyāna Preliminary Practices of the Sakya Lamdré Tradition
Ngorchen Könchok Lhundrup
Translated by Cyrus Stearns
Foreword by His Holiness the Sakya Trichen

This is the first book of a two-volume set of works written by Ngorchen Könchok Lhundrup (1497–1557) to explain the Lamdré teachings, the most important system of tantric theory and practice in the Sakya tradition of Tibetan Buddhism. (Volume 2 is only available in a restricted box set that includes this first volume and can only be obtained from wisdomexperience.org.)

The Freeing the Heart and Mind Trilogy
His Holiness the Sakya Trichen

This trilogy is "required reading" for any Sakya practitioner, and will also be deeply inspiring for Buddhists of all traditions.

Bodhisattva Path from Ground to Fruition
Commentary on Sakya Paṇḍita's Clarifying the Sage's Intent
His Holiness the 42nd Sakya Trizin

Discover profound teachings on the Buddhist path from His Holiness the 42nd Sakya Trizin Ratna Vajra, one of Tibetan Buddhism's most prominent leaders.

Foundations of Dharmakīrti's Philosophy
John D. Dunne

"A brilliant work!"—Shoryu Katsura, professor of Indian philosophy, Hiroshima University

Taking the Result as the Path
Core Teachings of the Sakya Lamdré Tradition
Translated by Cyrus Stearns

"*Taking the Result as the Path* represents a major breakthrough by bringing these teachings to light with the full blessings of the Sakya masters. This collection will be an invaluable resource for practitioners of the Lamdré system."—*Buddhadharma*

The Sakya School of Tibetan Buddhism
Dhongthog Rinpoche
Translated by Sam van Schaik

Since its 1976 publication in Tibetan, Dhongthog Rinpoche's history of the Sakya school of Tibetan Buddhism has been a key reference for specialists in Tibetan studies. Now English readers can consult it as well through Sam van Schaik's authoritative, fully annotated, and accessible translation.

Scripture, Logic, Language
Essays on Dharmakīrti and His Tibetan Successors
Tom J. F. Tillemans

"A masterpiece that specialists in Dharmakīrtian and Tibetan epistemological studies must read."—*Journal of the Royal Asiatic Society*

Luminous Lives
The Story of the Early Masters of the Lam 'bras Tradition in Tibet
Cyrus Stearns

"A seminal manuscript history of its earliest practitioners and masters, and a detailed description of the Lam 'bras teachings."—*Tricycle*

Song of the Road
The Poetic Travel Journal of Tsarchen Losal Gyatso
Cyrus Stearns

"A rare gem."—Thupten Jinpa, Institute of Tibetan Classics

Freedom through Correct Knowing
On Khedrup Jé's Interpretation of Dharmakirti
Edited by Geshe Tenzin Namdak and Ven. Tenzin Legtsok
Foreword by His Holiness the Dalai Lama

"In accordance with the extensive deeds and esteemed wishes of His Holiness the Dalai Lama, the Sera Jey Translation Department has taken great care to translate this text on valid cognition with the aim of bringing about vast benefit to all both now and in the long term. I congratulate them. The ability to easily induce consciousnesses ascertaining emptiness and all the other points of inner science belonging to sūtra and tantra depends on the path of the science of valid cognition or reasoning. Having read this translation and commentary on Khedrup Jé's *Clearing Mental Darkness*, those who understand the meaning should familiarize their minds with and meditate on it again and again, thereby making meaningful their lives that are endowed with leisure and opportunity."
—The 104th Gaden Tripa Kyabjé Jetsun Lobsang Tenzin Palsangpo

About Wisdom Publications

Wisdom Publications is the leading publisher of classic and contemporary Buddhist books and practical works on mindfulness. To learn more about us or to explore our other books, please visit our website at wisdomexperience.org or contact us at the address below.

Wisdom Publications
132 Perry Street
New York, NY 10014 USA

We are a 501(c)(3) organization, and donations in support of our mission are tax deductible.

Wisdom Publications is affiliated with the Foundation for the Preservation of the Mahayana Tradition (FPMT).